KT-118-167

Contents

Introduction

Perhaps the most obvious feature setting Cape Town apart from other big cities is the land on which it lies: a dramatic coastline of pristine white beaches and icy waters, with the iconic flat-topped Table Mountain overseeing all. Then there's its unique ethnic mix, which sets it apart from the rest of South Africa: only 31 per cent of its people are black Africans (the national average is just under 80 per cent); many Cape Town residents have a mixed heritage, including those from the distinctive Cape Malay community. And while many of the city's residents still live divided lives, those kids born after 1994 are paving the way for a truly integrated society, one that strives to embrace the South African concept of the rainbow nation.

Cultural life flourishes in this vibrant atmosphere, from original theatre productions to film festivals and a thriving urban art scene. Cape Town and the nearby Winelands also take the lead when it comes to gastronomy, with far the best food – and wine, of course – in the country, and some serious destination restaurants.

But while Cape Town may be different from the rest of South Africa, it shares many problems with the wider nation: poverty, the AIDS epidemic, crime (although it is one of the nation's safest cities). At the time of writing, however, the prevailing mood was one of exhilaration. The 2010 FIFA World Cup Football Tournament is coming to town, and with the gigantic new Green Point stadium taking shape, Capetonians can't help but be excited about the people, investment and interest that this event will bring.

Whatever challenges it faces, one thing is constant: this multifaceted city has a habit of making people fall in love with it. For some it could be the view of Camps Bay and the glistening ocean as you crest Kloof Nek that's the draw; for others the sound of the muezzin's call to prayer wafting over Bo Kaap on a misty morning; or the smell of a fresh espresso at the Neighbourgoods Market in gritty Woodstock; or the sensation of sand between the toes while walking with penguins on Boulder's Beach; or simply the taste of aromatic spices as you dig into a midnight samosa from a roadside stall on Long Street.
Lisa Van Aswegen, Editor

Time Out

Cape Town

timeout.com/capetown

Time Out Guides Ltd
Universal House
251 Tottenham Court Road
London W1T 7AB
United Kingdom
Tel: +44 (0)20 7813 3000
Fax: +44 (0)20 7813 6001
Email: guides@timeout.com
www.timeout.com

Published by Time Out Guides Ltd, a wholly owned subsidiary of Time Out Group Ltd.
Time Out and the Time Out logo are trademarks of Time Out Group Ltd.

© **Time Out Group Ltd 2009**
Previous editions 2004, 2007

10 9 8 7 6 5 4 3 2 1

This edition first published in Great Britain in 2009 by Ebury Publishing.
A Random House Group Company
20 Vauxhall Bridge Road, London SW1V 2SA

Random House Australia Pty Ltd 20 Alfred Street, Milsons Point, Sydney, New South Wales 2061, Australia

Random House New Zealand Ltd 18 Poland Road, Glenfield, Auckland 10, New Zealand

Random House South Africa (Pty) Ltd Isle of Houghton, Corner Boundary Road & Carse O'Gowrie, Houghton 2198, South Africa

Random House UK Limited Reg. No. 954009

For further distribution details, see www.timeout.com.

ISBN: 978-1-84670-156-6

A CIP catalogue record for this book is available from the British Library.

Printed and bound by Firmengruppe APPL, aprinta druck, Wemding, Germany.

The Random House Group Limited supports The Forest Stewardship Council (FSC), the leading international forest certification organisation. All our titles that are printed on Greenpeace approved FSC certified paper carry the FSC logo. Our paper procurement policy can be found at http://www.rbooks.co.uk/environment.

Time Out carbon-offsets its flights with Trees for Cities (www.treesforcities.org).

Cape Town in Brief

IN CONTEXT

Despite a troubled past, today Cape Town stands proudly as a city of the new South Africa. We look at the challenges and issues that it faces, from xenophobia to the much-anticipated FIFA 2010 World Cup Football tournament. And we take you on a tour of the Mother City's diverse architectural heritage, with some of its zany downtown sculptures thrown in for good measure.
▶ *For more, see pp13-40.*

SIGHTS

With sights as diverse as Robben Island, where Nelson Mandela was imprisoned for many years, and Kirstenbosch Botanical Gardens, with its abundant range of African flora, Cape Town's attractions cover the natural world and the country's fascinating history in equal measure. Add in wine farms, a string of stunning beaches, and opportunities to see wildlife for a rounded picture of this unique city.
▶ *For more, see pp41-76.*

CONSUME

Cape Town has the best food and drink in the country, from cutting-edge molecular gastronomy, to classic bistro fare and African dishes. Wine bars are becoming increasingly popular and the traditional pub is making a comeback. This section also covers the full gamut of the city's diverse shops and includes over 60 hotel reviews – from hip budget options to lavishly luxurious accommodation.
▶ *For more, see pp77-156.*

ARTS & ENTERTAINMENT

The city is the hub of a cutting-edge art scene, with new galleries – many concentrated in the Woodstock area – showcasing the works of up-and-coming artists and openings packed to the rafters. There's also a vibrant and diverse music scene, pumping nightlife and a lively gay culture. In this section you'll find listings for everything from rock venues to contemporary galleries.
▶ *For more, see pp157-210.*

ESCAPES & EXCURSIONS

No visit to Cape Town is complete without a tour of the Cape Winelands. Discovering wine farms and phenomenal food along the way is one of the greatest pleasures of the Mother City's hinterlands. We also cover the windswept charm of the West Coast, the Whale Route's winding roads, and the spectacular natural beauty of the Garden Route.
▶ *For more, see pp289-300.*

Cape Town in 48 Hrs

Day 1 Mountain, Museums and Marine Animals

8AM Start the day with a trip up **Table Mountain** (*see p48*). Get there early so you can catch the first cable car up. The quick ride will give you a bird's eye view of the City Bowl, which you'll be exploring during the day.

10AM Head down to explore the boutiques of **Kloof Street** (*see p44*), sip a restorative latté and nibble on a gooey *pasteis de nata* at **Vida e Caffè** (*see p109*). Keep walking down for more shops and markets around **Long Street** (*see p43*), or go downtown via **Museum Mile** (*see p51*) and the **Company's Gardens** (*see p51*) for a spot of culture.

1PM Go to **Caveau** (*see p99*) at **Heritage Square** (*see p45*) for a lunch of bistro-style bites and an amazing array of local wines by the glass, or grab a burger at the coolest burger spot in town, **Royale Eatery** (*see p106*).

3PM Head over to the Waterfront and visit the **Two Oceans Aquarium** (*see p58*) for sharks, penguins and other marine life. Feeding time is at 3pm, so be sure to catch the action. Add in time for some serious shopping at the **V&A Waterfront** (*see p56*) – there's everything here from boutiques to chain-store fashion and treats for those back home.

6PM Wind down the day with a sundowner, or three, in glitzy **Camps Bay** (*see p60*). Watch the sun dip into the ocean from a cool spot like **Baraza** (*see p126*).

8PM Opt for dinner at the **Roundhouse** (*see p113*) – Cape Town's oldest hunting lodge has been revamped into a sexy gastronomic destination.

11PM If you still have energy, head back to Long Street for some partying: bars like **Julep** (*see p125*) and the **Waiting Room** (*see p126*) are seriously cool, while **Neighbourhood** (*see p125*) has a laid-back feel and a vast balcony from which to watch the goings-on on the street below.

NAVIGATING THE CITY

Cape Town is ridiculously easy to navigate, thanks to Table Mountain towards the south and the Atlantic Ocean to the north, hemming in the City Bowl. The City Bowl itself is remarkably compact, making it ideal for gentle strolls. If you're walking, Long Street in the city centre will probably be your starting point. As you make your way south towards the mountain, it turns into Kloof Street. To the east are Government Avenue, with its Museum Mile, and Adderley Street. Further east lies the Cape of Good Hope Castle. Parallel to Long Street, to the west, run Loop, Bree and Buitengracht streets, taking you further towards the Atlantic Seaboard, with the V&A Waterfront being its main attraction. Further west lie Camps Bay and Clifton.

On the other side of Table Mountain are the Southern Suburbs, and further

Day 2 Penguins, Beaches, Wining and Dining

9AM Head off to the Southern Suburbs, passing the **Rhodes Memorial** (*see p67*) and the ivy-clad buildings of the **University of Cape Town** (*see p67*) on your way. Start your day's sightseeing with a brisk walk around the lovely **Kirstenbosch National Botanical Gardens** (*see p64*), home to more than 9,000 plant species indigenous to South Africa.

11AM It's onwards to **Kalk Bay** (*see p70*). If the walk has given you an appetite, call in at the **Olympia Café** (*see p121*) for a quick sandwich, or perhaps something sweeter if energy levels need a boost. Spend the rest of the morning rummaging around the antique shops and hip boutiques lining the main road.

1PM Grab a seaside seat at **Harbour House** (*see p120*) for fabulous seafood with a view over the ocean. Alternatively, the more relaxed **Live Bait** (*see p121*) below serves great sushi and calamari, or simply do as the locals do and buy fish and chips from **Kalky's** (*see p120*) to eat sitting on the harbour wall. Then either head back towards Constantia for some wine-tasting at Cape Town's oldest wine estates, or head further south to **Simon's Town** (*see p72*) and enjoy some beach time with the jackass penguins who call the African Penguin Colony at **Boulder's Beach** (*see p72*) home.

7PM Head back to town to indulge in some seriously good food: the best gastronomy is to be found dotted around the central city. Try **Jardine** (*see p102*) for pared down, subtle flavours, **Bizerca Bistro** (*see p96*) for bistro classics with a fresh twist, or **Nova** (*see p106*) for Cape Town's very own molecular gastronomy.

11PM End the evening off with a late-night tipple at stylish **Planet Bar** (*see p125*) at the Mount Nelson. The Nellie, as it's affectionately called, is the grand dame of local hotels, with many a celeb calling it home when in town.

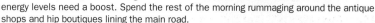

on Simon's Town and Cape Point. Cape Town Tourism offices can hand out free maps and lots of advice. But all you really need to do to get your bearings is to look up at the mountain to see where you are.

SEEING THE SIGHTS

Many smaller sights close on Saturday afternoons and Sundays, so it's best to check that the places you want to visit are open at weekends before setting out.

GOOD DEALS

Winter is a good time to visit, with many accommodation bargains available: visit www.capetownonsale.co.za. The City Sightseeing Bus is a good way to get to various attractions throughout the day, with a hop-on-hop off system and two routes around the peninsula. The first bus leaves from the Aquarium at the V&A Waterfront at 9am, with buses every 20 minutes until 5pm.

Cape Town in Profile

CITY BOWL

Sitting between Table Mountain, Devil's Peak and Lion's Head to the north and the Atlantic Ocean to the south, the City Bowl is the city's hub. Its backbone is **Long Street**, home to numerous shops and bars. Cafés, art galleries and nightclubs co-exist happily in the city centre, while the **Company's Gardens** povides much-needed green space and is surrounded by many of the city's museums. The neighbouring mountains oversee Cape Town in spectacular fashion.

▶ *For more, see pp43-55.*

ATLANTIC SEABOARD

Stretching from the shopper's haven of the **V&A Waterfront** all the way to secluded **Llandudno** – with Cape Town's hottest beaches, such as **Clifton** and **Camps Bay**, in between – the Atlantic Seaboard happily mixes gritty **Sea Point** street life with glitzy Camps Bay partying. This is the place to don your designer shades and watch the sun set over the ocean.

▶ *For more, see pp56-61.*

SOUTHERN SUBURBS

Further south on the Cape Peninsula lie the leafy, affluent suburbs of **Constantia** and **Newlands**, with the spectacular **Kirstenbosch National Botanical Gardens** and the wine farms of **Constantia** the major attractions.

▶ *For more, see pp62-67.*

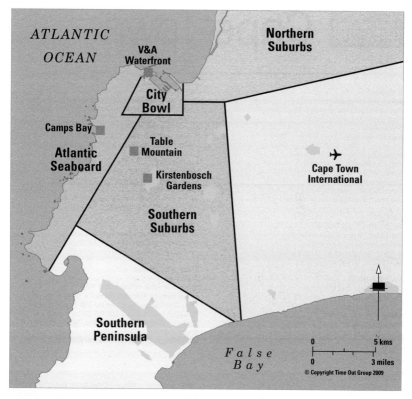

ATLANTIC OCEAN

V&A Waterfront

Northern Suburbs

City Bowl

Camps Bay

Atlantic Seaboard

Table Mountain

Kirstenbosch Gardens

Cape Town International

Southern Suburbs

Southern Peninsula

False Bay

| 0 | | | 5 kms |
| 0 | | | 3 miles |

© Copyright Time Out Group 2009

SOUTHERN PENINSULA

Cape Town's deep south boasts **Cape Point** and the charming seaside villages of **Kalk Bay**, **Simon's Town** and **Hout Bay**. Warmer waters to the west make these beaches ideal for a day of swimming and enjoying local seafood.

▶ *For more, see pp68-74.*

NORTHERN SUBURBS

The views of Table Mountain from **Milnerton** and **Table View** are simply perfect. The beaches at both Table View and **Blouberg Strand** are notoriously windy, making them popular with windsurfers and kite flyers. Further inland lies the 'burb of **Durbanville**, with its wine farms, and beyond are the Winelands towns of **Stellenbosch**, **Paarl** and **Franschhoek**.

▶ *For more, see pp75-76.*

TimeOut Cape Town

Editorial
Editor Lisa van Aswegen
Copy Editors Edoardo Albert, Albert Buhr, Ros Sales
Fact checker Carolyn Meads
Proofreader Marion Moisy
Indexer Jonathan Cox

Managing Director Peter Fiennes
Editorial Director Ruth Jarvis
Series Editor Will Fulford-Jones
Business Manager Dan Allen
Editorial Manager Holly Pick
Assistant Management Accountant Ija Krasnikova

Design
Art Director Scott Moore
Art Editor Pinelope Kourmouzoglou
Senior Designer Henry Elphick
Graphic Designers Kei Ishimaru, Nicola Wilson
Advertising Designer Jodi Sher

Picture Desk
Picture Editor Jael Marschner
Deputy Picture Editor Lynn Chambers
Picture Researcher Gemma Walters
Picture Desk Assistant Marzena Zoladz
Picture Librarian Christina Theisen

Advertising
Commercial Director Mark Phillips
International Advertising Manager Kasimir Berger
International Sales Executive Charlie Sokol
Advertising Sales (Cape Town) New Media Publishing: Aileen Lamb (advertising director); Andrew Baranowski, Sameegha Samaai (advertising sales)

Marketing
Marketing Manager Yvonne Poon
Sales & Marketing Director, North America & Latin America Lisa Levinson
Senior Publishing Brand Manager Luthfa Begum
Art Director Anthony Huggins

Production
Group Production Director Mark Lamond
Production Manager Brendan McKeown
Production Controller Damian Bennett

Time Out Group
Chairman Tony Elliott
Chief Executive Officer David King
Group General Manager/Director Nichola Coulthard
Time Out Communications Ltd MD David Pepper
Time Out International Ltd MD Cathy Runciman
Time Out Magazine Ltd Publisher/MD Mark Elliott
Group IT Director Simon Chappell
Marketing & Circulation Director Catherine Demajo

Contributors
Introduction Lisa van Aswegen. **History** Max du Preez, Mark van Dijk, Annette Klinger. **Cape Town Today** Mark van Dijk (*Africa in the Bowl* Ilze Hugo). **Architecture** Vicki Sleet (*Sculpting the City* Ingrid Sinclair). **Sightseeing** Annette Klinger (*Magic Mountain, Whale of a Time, Secret Beaches* Annette Klinger; *Shark Tactics, Fever Pitch, Urban Terroir* Ilze Hugo). **Hotels** Vicki Sleet. **Restaurants & Cafés** Annette Klinger, additional reviews Vicki Sleet (*French Revolution, Streetwise Snacking, Something Fishy, Wine and Dine* Vicki Sleet; *Well-Bread; Lip-Smacking Local Food*, Annette Klinger). **Pubs & Bars** Bianca Coleman, additional reviews Vicki Sleet (*Boozy Bites* Bianca Coleman). **Shops & Services** Vicki Sleet (*Millionaire's Mile, Jewellery Trail, Spa for the Course* Vicki Sleet; *Love Thy Neighbour* Ilze Hugo). **Calendar** Annette Klinger. **Children** Mark van Dijk (*Running Away to the Circus* Annette Klinger). **Film** Ilze Hugo. **Galleries** Ilze Hugo. **Gay & Lesbian** JP de la Chaumette. **Music** Stefan de Witt (*Indie Rock Revival* Stefan de Witt; *Local Beats* Ingrid Sinclair). **Nightlife** Bianca Coleman. **Sport** Mark van Dijk (*Get Sporty* Annette Klinger). **Theatre & Dance** Ilze Hugo (*Watch This Space* Annette Klinger). **Escapes & Excursions** contributors to *Time Out Cape Town Weekend Breaks*. **Directory** Annette Klinger.

Maps john@jsgraphics.co.uk

Photography Jurie Senekal, except: pages 5 (top right), 39, 40 (bottom) Julian Goldswain Juice Magazine; page 6 Table Mountain Aerial Cableway; page 17 The Bridgeman Art Library; pages 19, 197 Getty Images; page 22 Popperfoto/Getty Images; pages 24, 25 AFP/Getty Images; pages 28/29 Time & Life Pictures/Getty Images; page 72 Corbis; page 101 Heloise Bergman; page 125 Mount Nelson PR; pages 177, 178 Cape Town Pride; pages 157, 182 Hugh Masakela; page 184 Liam Lynch; page 193 Deborah Rossouw; pages 195 AFP/Getty Images; page 203 Garth Stead; pages 226, 228, 230, 242, 243 © CTRU; pages 232, 233, 237 Shaun O'Meara; page 244 Kobus van der Merwe.

The following images were provided by the featured establishments/ artists: pages 77, 78, 79, 80, 83, 84, 85, 87, 89, 92, 93, 113, 114, 116 (bottom), 132, 147, 150, 151, 158, 166, 171, 181, 199, 227, 231, 240, 241.

The editor would like to thank all contributors to previous editions of *Time Out Cape Town for Visitors* and *Time Out Cape Town Weekend Breaks*, whose work forms the basis for parts of this book.

About the Guide

GETTING AROUND

The back of the book contains street maps of Cape Town, as well as overview maps of the city and its surroundings. The maps start on page 267; on them are marked the locations of hotels (❶), restaurants and cafés (❶), and pubs and bars (❶). The majority of businesses listed in this guide are located in the areas we've mapped; the grid-square references in the listings refer to these maps.

THE ESSENTIALS

For practical information, including visas, disabled access, emergency numbers, lost property, useful websites and local transport, please see the Directory. It begins on page 247.

THE LISTINGS

Addresses, phone numbers, websites, transport information, hours and prices are all included in our listings, as are selected other facilities. All were checked and correct at press time. However, business owners can alter their arrangements at any time, and fluctuating economic conditions can cause prices to change rapidly.

The very best venues in the city, the must-sees and must-dos in every category, have been marked with a red star (★). In the Sights chapters, we've also marked venues with free admission with a FREE symbol.

PHONE NUMBERS

The area code for Cape Town is 021 and must be dialled when making a call, even within the Cape Town area.

From outside South Africa, dial your country's international access code (00 from the UK, 011 from the US) or a plus symbol, followed by the South African country code (27), 21 for Cape Town (dropping the initial zero) and the number as listed in the guide. So, to reach the Houses of Parliament, dial +27 21 403 2266. For more on phones, including information on calling abroad from the UK and details of local mobile-phone access, see p254.

FEEDBACK

We welcome feedback on this guide, both on the venues we've included and on any other locations that you'd like to see featured in future editions. Please email us at guides@timeout.com.

Time Out Guides

Founded in 1968, Time Out has grown from humble beginnings into the leading resource for anyone wanting to know what's happening in the world's greatest cities. Alongside our influential weeklies in London, New York and Chicago, we publish more than 20 magazines in cities as varied as Beijing and Beirut; a range of travel books, with the City Guides now joined by the newer Shortlist series; and an information-packed website. The company remains proudly independent, still owned by Tony Elliott four decades after he launched Time Out London.

Written by local experts and illustrated with original photography, our books also retain their independence. No business has been featured because it has advertised, and all restaurants and bars are visited and reviewed anonymously.

ABOUT THE EDITOR

Born and bred in Cape Town, **Lisa van Aswegen** has edited Time Out Cape Town magazines and the Time Out Cape Town guide since 2006 and has contributed to both local and international food and travel publications.

A full list of the book's contributors can be found opposite. However, we've also included details of our writers in selected chapters throughout the guide.

In Context

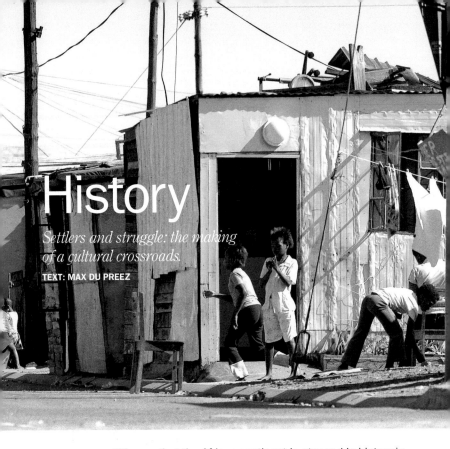

History

*Settlers and struggle: the making
of a cultural crossroads.*

TEXT: MAX DU PREEZ

*Max du Preez is
a prominent editor
and columnist with
a number of books
on local history to
his name.*

To say that the African continent is steeped in history is
a vast understatement. It is, in fact, the seat of human
civilisation. The area around present-day Cape Town was
inhabited by early man long before those first peoples began
to migrate out of Africa to establish themselves in other
continents. Europeans returned to their African roots in
the 16th century, when the Dutch East India Company
established a presence on the Cape, with a refreshment
station for sailors working the Far East route. Within decades
a colony had been established. Other settlers arrived:
Calvinist protestants who would later call themselves
Afrikaners; Muslims from Indonesia and around, who would
come to be known as Cape Malays; indentured servants
from India; slaves from elsewhere in Africa, the British.
European commercial agriculture threatened the way of
life of the Cape's indigenous Khoikhoi people, and many
resorted to life as labourers on settler farms. The basis
for the complicated racial, ethnic and social jigsaw that
still characterises the Cape was formed.

AS OLD AS THE HILLS

South Africa is an ancient land. Its rocks and plains date from the time when Africa was still part of Gondwanaland, a composite continent made up of South America, Africa, Antarctica, India and Australia that existed until more than 100 million years ago. Human beings walked these plains and rocks hundreds of thousands of years ago, when the species developed along the east side of Africa. Some of the oldest fossilised remains of our pre-human ancestors were found in South Africa, in places such as the Cradle of Humankind outside Johannesburg.

The area around present-day Cape Town and along the coastlines to the west and east was inhabited by Homo Sapiens long before other continents were discovered. The human remains excavated in caves at Klasies River Mouth on the southern Cape coast were between 75,000 and 120,000 years old – the oldest examples of Homo Sapiens to date. In 1993, it was proved that the people who occupied the Blombos Cave in the same area, at least 77,000 years ago, had a well-developed culture.

It was around this time that some started to leave Africa, gradually moving through the Middle East, southern Europe and southern and south-east Asia. Climate, culture, diet and genetic isolation meant that those settling in Europe, Asia and the Americas developed different physical features over time. Only 500-odd years ago did those pale-skinned humans return to 'discover' the southern part of the continent of their origin.

REAL PEOPLE

At the time of colonisation, the indigenous people of the area were known collectively as the Khoikhoi ('men among men', or 'real people', as khoi means 'person'). The first Europeans to meet them named them the Hottentots, apparently after a word used in the Khoikhoi welcoming dance. Historians now believe the Khoikhoi derived from aboriginal hunters who lived in northern Botswana, and that they moved down the Atlantic Coast to the western Cape about 2,000 years ago, after they had switched from hunting to herding. At first they only kept fat-tailed sheep, but by the time the Europeans encountered them, they had acquired cattle, most likely from the Bantu-speaking farmers in the eastern Cape.

The Khoikhoi were closely related to a hunter-gatherer people whose ancestors probably never left the subcontinent. The first Dutch settlers called these hunters Bosjesmannen (men of the bush, later Boesmans or Bushmen) and the Khoikhoi called them Sonqua or San. They spoke a variety of languages characterised by the use of clicks or implosive consonants, very similar to the sounds of the Khoikhoi.

While the San lived mainly in caves and overhangs in small, mobile groups with a weak hierarchical system, the Khoikhoi lived in round reed huts in larger settlements. Each clan had a headman, a hereditary position, and the villages of a particular tribe fell under a chief. The chief ruled by the consent of a council of elders. They acted as a court to settle disputes and hear criminal cases. The Khoikhoi had a complex system of customs such as initiation rituals, weddings and funerals, and livestock were central to much of their culture. Biogeneticists recently found that the San and Khoikhoi have genetic threads linking them to the first ever human beings.

EARLY STRUGGLES

In February 1488, the Portuguese seafarer Bartholomeu Dias rounded the Cape and landed at Mossel Bay, east of Cape Town. He was met by the Khoikhoi, and when they tried to defend their precious watering hole, Dias's men killed one of their group with a crossbow. This incident could be regarded as the first act of resistance by the indigenous people of southern Africa against European colonialism, and the beginning of the struggle for land. Others point to an incident 11 years later when Dias's colleague, Vasco Da Gama, planted a cross and a padrao (commemorative pillar) on the Mossel Bay dunes. As they sailed away, they saw the Khoikhoi men defiantly push the cross and the padrao over.

IN CONTEXT

'Within five years, the Dutch East India Company allowed a number of its employees to set up private farms around Cape Town.'

If Dias and Da Gama had travelled a little further along the east coast, they would have come across another group of indigenous people, the amaXhosa. They were part of a large family of farmers, together called the Bantu-speakers, who had migrated in stages from Africa's Great Lakes District to the south around 2,000 years ago.

The early European settlers, and to some extent even the Bantu-speakers, regarded the San hunter-gatherers as primitive beings not worth much more than animals. Many were killed in unequal battles with settlers. Only small groups of San survive today in Namibia and Botswana, but their ancestors left an astonishing legacy in the form of rock paintings and engravings all over southern Africa, the oldest surviving examples being 20,000 years old. The paintings reflect a very complex spiritual relationship with the environment. Thousands of examples have, remarkably, survived across South Africa. Many San were assimilated into Bantu-speaking societies – the clicks in the Xhosa language are a result of this.

CAPE COLONY

After Bartholomeu Dias's 1488 visit, many European ships on their way to the East stopped at the Cape to replenish water and food supplies. Without exception, the seafarers' diaries reflect the astonishment they experienced when Table Mountain, the peaks of the Peninsula and the bay came into view. Dias himself named it Cabo de Boa Esperanca, Cape of Good Hope, although neither he nor Da Gama actually went into Table Bay. Antonio de Saldanha was probably the first European to land there, in 1503. He climbed the mountain and named it 'The Table of the Cape of Good Hope'.

It was not until 1652 that Europeans settled at the Cape. The Dutch East India Company, or VOC, had decided that the mortality rate among sailors of their fleet trading with the East was too high, especially due to scurvy, and ordered Jan Van Riebeeck to establish a halfway refreshment station with vegetable gardens and a hospital at the Cape. On 6 April 1652, Van Riebeeck arrived with three ships in Table Bay. He was met by Autshomato, also called Herrie die Strandloper, a Khoikhoi chief who had spent a year with the English on a trip to the East between 1631 and 1632. Fluent in English, he was enlisted as Van Riebeeck's interpreter. Later he fell out of favour and was jailed at first in Van Riebeeck's fort and then on Robben Island (*see p27*, **The Long Walk to Freedom**), from where he escaped in a leaky boat.

Initially, the VOC had no intention of creating a colony on the Cape. But within five years it allowed a number of its employees to set up private farms around Cape Town. The presence of 'free burghers' increased quickly over the next few decades.

The new colony needed more people, and before the end of the 17th century groups of French Huguenots and German immigrants joined the Dutch settlers at the Cape. Most of them were Calvinist Protestants. The descendants of these settlers would later call themselves the Afrikaners. Most of the Huguenots were given farms in the Franschhoek ('French corner') and Paarl areas and contributed greatly to South Africa's wine-making culture. Almost from the beginning the free burghers were in conflict with the authorities, and distrusted the government. Their sense of vulnerability as frontiers people would inform their behaviour for three centuries.

The development of commercial agriculture soon threatened the Khoikhoi's way of life. As early as 1659, a group of Khoikhoi attacked the settler farms, driving off much of the livestock. Van Riebeeck tried to keep settlers and Khoikhoi apart by planting a

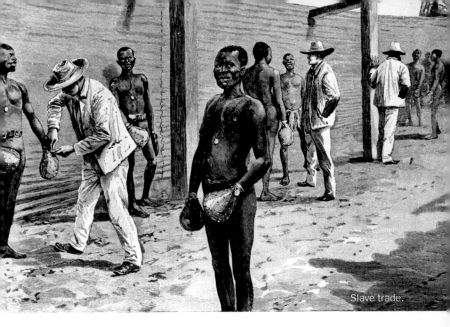
Slave trade.

hedge of bitter-almond on the outskirts of Cape Town. The Khoikhoi society quickly disintegrated under settler pressure. Many resorted to lives as labourers on settler farms, others moved inland, only to be displaced later by settler farmers. Many Khoikhoi died during the smallpox epidemic of 1713.

SLAVE TRADE

The VOC did not want to encourage more European labourers to come to the Cape, because they proved to be troublesome. Still, they did need more workers on the farms, so in 1658, the first ships carrying slaves arrived at the Cape. The slaves came from Dahomey, Angola and Mozambique in Africa and from India, the East Indies and Madagascar. Between the arrival of the first slave ships and the end of the slave trade in 1807, about 60,000 slaves were brought to the Cape.

Slavery changed the basic political and social character of the Cape of Good Hope. By 1795, two-thirds of the burghers around Cape Town and three-quarters of the farmers in the districts of Stellenbosch and Drakenstein owned slaves. The burghers' European tradition dictated that the sanctity of property rights was central to their own freedom. Slave owners included their slaves on inventories of property together with their cattle and sheep. All slaves were black, and this instilled a distorted image of black people in many white minds. Add to this the perpetual fear of slave uprisings on isolated farms and it becomes easier to understand white attitudes in the following centuries, which ultimately resulted in formalised apartheid.

APARTHEID RULES

Apartheid, the ideology of racial separation formally adopted by the National Party government in 1948, theoretically presupposed that pure races existed in South Africa. Yet there had been thousands of 'mixed' marriages during the first century of colonialism on the Cape, the majority between settler men and slave women. Virtually all old Afrikaner families can trace a slave mother somewhere in their past.

A slave woman who married a white man was integrated into white society, together with her children. It was a female slave's easiest way to get her freedom. There were more white men than women in the colony and almost twice as many male slaves as females. On the farms outside Cape Town, the best chance male slaves had to find a wife was among the Khoikhoi. A child between a slave and a Khoikhoi would be born free, but forced to work on the farm for a period. These offspring were later called Baster Hottentotte, and they occupied a very low position on the social ladder. Descendants of white and Khoikhoi relationships outside of marriage and without formal acceptance by the church were called Basters, and they enjoyed much more freedom than the Baster Hottentotte. The Basters later formed the nucleus of the Reheboth Basters of Namibia and the Griqua, mostly of the northern Cape.

Between the two main cultural-economic groups, those being the Christian European group and the Muslim or 'Cape Malay' group, another group existed at the Cape – some were slaves, some were freed slaves, some were Baster Hottentotte, some were the offspring of white and black liaisons but were not claimed by their white fathers. This group was later called the Cape Coloureds.

The VOC had discouraged the use of French and German among the first settlers, with Dutch being the dominant language. But the slaves, the Basters, the Cape Malays and the Baster Hottentotte who worked on the farms and in the kitchens developed a creolised version of Dutch to communicate with their masters and one another. This developed into a fully fledged indigenous language later called Afrikaans – the language white Afrikaner nationalism later claimed as its own property and tribal symbol.

In 1795, Britain conquered the Cape, then returned the colony to the Dutch eight years later – only to reclaim it in 1806. It would remain a British colony for more than a century. Under pressure from British missionaries working in the Cape and humanitarians in Britain, the British government scrapped the regulations limiting the rights of the Khoisan and freed slaves in 1828. In 1834, all slaves were liberated, although they had to serve four years of 'apprenticeship' before they were completely free. By this time, the settler farmers had expanded their operations in the interior and along the coast to what became known as the Eastern Cape, where they started to compete with another indigenous group, the amaXhosa. This conflict had the same root as the conflict with the Khoikhoi: land.

SOCIAL UPHEAVAL

Around 3,000 years ago, black farming peoples who lived in the region of the Great Lakes of Africa developed a common language that was later called Bantu. During the next 1,000 years, many of them migrated south. These farmers kept cattle, sheep and goats and grew sorghum and millet. They had an advanced social culture and mostly lived in large permanent settlements. A thousand years ago one of the main centres of power of the Bantu-speakers of southern Africa was at Mapungubwe Hill on the border between South Africa and Zimbabwe, now best known for the finely crafted gold artefacts that were found there.

The migrators split into four language groups as they moved into South Africa: the Nguni-speakers moved down the east coast, the Venda and Tsonga stayed in the north, and the Sotho-Tswana-speakers migrated down the centre. The Xhosa were the Nguni-speakers who moved all the way down to the Eastern Cape, while those who spoke the Zulu dialect of Nguni settled in present-day KwaZulu-Natal.

At the end of the 18th century, these black farmers (the term 'Bantu' that was used to depict them became a derogatory word during the apartheid years) were living in a number of small chiefdoms. The early years of the 19th century brought a great social upheaval. It was a period of serious suffering, but also nation-building. By the end of it Shaka had forged the Zulu nation from several chiefdoms and Mzilikazi established the Ndebele and Matabele under his leadership. Moshoeshoe, an extraordinary diplomat and statesman for his time, had collected a number of chiefdoms and thousands of refugees – Nguni-speakers as well as Sotho-Setswana-speakers – at his mountain stronghold in Lesotho and formed the Basotho. The Tsonga and Venda remained in

IN CONTEXT

their mountainous territory in the north; Sekwati built up the Pedi; Sobhuza the Swazi. In the Eastern Cape, the Xhosa developed a form of unity with smaller groups such as the Thembu, the Mfengu and the Mpondo.

A small community, the Lemba, whose individuals have great artistic skill, believe that they are descendants of black Jews from the Middle East, and they still live among the Venda. Their claim was recently proved to be correct after extensive DNA testing. Many Lemba still live strictly as Orthodox Jews.

WAR TORN

The trekboers, as the burghers who had moved well away from the Cape were called, waged war against the Xhosa, but while the trekboers had firearms, the Xhosa had greater numbers. When the British Army was deployed against the Xhosa after 1811, the balance of power was tipped. During the brutal war of 1834-35 the Xhosa king, Hintsa, was decapitated. The Eighth Frontier War of 1850-52 was the most savage war against the Xhosa. Some 16,000 Xhosa were killed, and large numbers of settlements burned and cattle captured.

A great tragedy that befell the Xhosa can partly be explained by the trauma of these wars. In 1856, a young woman called Nongqawuse had a vision in which two men who were long dead told her that a great resurrection of her people was about to occur. To ensure that it happened, the people had to kill all their cattle and not plant any more crops. She convinced her uncle, a well-known seer named Mhalakaza, of the authenticity of the vision and he convinced paramount chief Sarili. The killing took place over the next year. By the end of December 1857, tens of thousands, perhaps as many as 50,000, Xhosa had died of starvation. More than 25,000 left for the Cape Colony to seek work.

Preparing for the **Boer War**, 1899.

IN CONTEXT

'The Voortrekkers' migration, which was later known as the Great Trek, would change South Africa fundamentally.'

BRITISH RULE

In 1820, the British settled some 4,000 British subjects, mostly farmers and tradesmen, in the Eastern Cape. The colonial government started promoting the use of English at the expense of Dutch-Afrikaans and elevated the new British settlers into public positions. This caused deep bitterness among the Cape burghers.

Around the middle of the 19th century, developments in South Africa started to move away from the Mother City. But events in the central and northern interior would have a direct and lasting impact on Cape life.

After the 1835 war against the Xhosa, the Afrikaner trekboers in the Eastern Cape started to plan to move north into the interior of South Africa. They were unhappy about Britain's abolition of slavery, felt insecure so close to the frontier with the Xhosa, and needed more land for their cattle. Between 1835 and 1845, 15,000 Afrikaners, accompanied by 5,000 servants, left the colony in convoys of oxwagons and on horseback. They were called Voortrekkers. Their migration, which was later known as the Great Trek, would change South Africa fundamentally and ultimately lead to the formation of a formal nation-state. The Voortrekkers took with them the European convictions and traditions of white dominance and used these in structuring their relations with the black peoples of the interior.

The Voortrekkers staked out farms in what are today the provinces of KwaZulu-Natal, Gauteng, the Free State and Mpumalanga. The black societies in most of these regions were still suffering the after-effects of the great upheavals of the beginning of the century. Some of these areas were therefore not actively occupied at the time of the Voortrekker settlement, but others were and this led to violent clashes with the black tribes.

The Voortrekkers declared the Republic of Natalia in Natal, but Britain annexed it as a colony in 1843. Most of the Voortrekkers trekked further west and declared the South African Republic with Pretoria as its capital in 1843 and the Republic of the Orange Free State with Bloemfontein as its capital in 1854. With the Cape and Natal under British colonial rule, the whole country was now occupied by whites.

From 1860 onwards, another population group was added to South Africa's ethnic diversity. Shiploads of indentured labourers from India were taken to Natal to work in the new sugar plantations. Later, Indian traders came to South Africa under their own initiative, mainly to set up shops in the towns of Natal, the Free State and the Transvaal. In 1893, an Indian lawyer arrived on a legal assignment to Indian traders in Pretoria. He decided to stay on when he suffered racial discrimination by whites and realised that Indians' rights were threatened. His name was Mohandas Gandhi, and he later became one of the most powerful moral influences in the world.

DIAMOND DISCOVERY

Britain's two South African colonies were not regarded as prize possessions back in London, but this changed dramatically when diamonds were discovered near the confluence of the Gariep and Vaal Rivers in 1867 and gold outside Pretoria in 1886. But the Boers of the Free State, as well as the Griqua of Griqualand, claimed ownership of the diamond area and the gold reef fell inside the South African Republic. The diamond fields were extraordinarily rich and attracted fortune-seekers from all over the world. The town of Kimberley developed rapidly amid the abundant diamond pipes. The British declared that the Orange Free State border ran about a mile east of the richest mines, and annexed the area into the Cape Colony, together with the whole of Griqualand West.

In 1889, Cecil John Rhodes, an entrepreneur and ardent believer in British imperialism, acquired the monopoly over the four Kimberley diamond pipes. His company was called De Beers Consolidated Mines. Rhodes later became the prime minister of the Cape Colony. Tens of thousands of black people from all over South Africa rushed to Kimberley in the hope of finding jobs. It was De Beers who first started the practice of employing rural black men and putting them up in closed barracks. Thus a system that lasted in some form to the end of the 20th century was established. Men from the rural areas were employed in the cities and put up in single-sex accommodation, only seeing their families once or twice a year. It was called the migrant labour system.

In 1886, a reef of gold, the richest deposit in the world, was discovered in the South African Republic. Once more there was a rush of fortune-seekers, but again big mining houses stepped in and within a few years eight conglomerates controlled all the mining on what became known as the Witwatersrand. Virtually overnight a city sprang up, named Johannesburg. Black workers from across the subcontinent rushed to the mines and were employed under similar conditions to those at the diamond mines.

SCORCHED EARTH

The discovery of diamonds and gold gave a new urgency to British plans for a confederation of the four political units in South Africa. It put such pressure on the South African Republic that its president, Paul Kruger, declared war with Britain in 1899. The Republic was joined by the Republic of the Orange Free State.

It was the fiercest war ever fought on the African subcontinent. More than 300,000 British soldiers took on the two republics with a total white population of around 300,000 and fewer than 70,000 soldiers. It was an uneven war, but the Boer commandos were highly mobile, sometimes using tactics that would later be called guerrilla warfare. By 1902, most Boer women and children were in diseased concentration camps and the captured men and boys in prisoner-of-war camps in Ceylon (Sri Lanka), St Helena and Burma. These practices did much to destroy the Boers' spirit, as did the British 'scorched earth' policy toward the end of the war, burning farmsteads and crops and killing cattle. In May 1902 the two republics surrendered and signed the Peace of Vereeniging.

The war, which was for a long time called the Anglo-Boer War but is now called the South African War, did not only affect the Boers and the British soldiers. Thousands of black and Coloured South Africans fought on both sides, although most fought with the British. Tens of thousands of blacks, mostly farm workers, were also put in concentration camps and 30,000 died there. Some 110,000 white women and children were put in concentration camps; 27,000 of them died. And 30,000 farms were destroyed. The war created deep bitterness and anti-British sentiment among Afrikaners for generations.

WHITE DOMINATION

In May 1908, delegates from the Cape, Natal and the two former republics met at a National Convention to negotiate the establishment of a united South African state. Only white delegates were invited. Despite the fact that there were four times as many black people as whites in the four regions, black people were only given a very limited franchise in the Cape alone. The South African Act was approved by the British Parliament. On 31 May 1910, the Union of South Africa came into being, with four provinces. Parliament was to be seated in Cape Town. The exclusion of the majority black population from political power in South Africa was now formalised.

Black intellectuals and community leaders protested against the new constitution, but when their protest fell on deaf ears in Cape Town and London, they formed the South African Native National Congress in January 1912. It was the first national body of indigenous people in South Africa and the first co-ordinated movement to resist

IN CONTEXT

IN CONTEXT

WE BUILD A NATION

THEY DIVIDE and SEGREGATE the PEOPLE

Cape Town protest against apartheid, 1952.

white domination. The executive of 11 were all highly educated, five of them having studied in the US or Britain. The movement later changed its name to the African National Congress. The ANC stepped up their protest in 1913, after the Native Land Act was adopted, limiting black land ownership to about eight per cent of the land surface. The figure was increased to 13 per cent in 1936.

Two years after the ANC's birth, white Afrikaners also formed their first national political party, the National Party. In 1918, a secret males-only body, the Afrikaner Broederbond, was formed to further the cause of Afrikaner nationalism in business, education and culture. It became very powerful in later years. In 1938, Afrikaner nationalism experienced a massive upsurge with a national re-enactment of the Great Trek a century earlier. Ten years later the National Party defeated the United Party of General Jan Smuts in the general election. The party ruled South Africa until 1994.

SEPARATE DEVELOPMENT

Racial separation and a denial of black South Africans' political and human rights began in 1652 and continued under British rule until 1948. But the National Party turned these practices and attitudes into a formal ideology they called apartheid, literally meaning 'separateness'. The new government spent considerable energy during its first years in power to write numerous apartheid laws. The population was classified according to race; sex between mixed couples and marriages across the colour bar were criminalised; separate residential areas and public amenities were enforced; separate education was instituted; and the movement of black South Africans was regulated by the carrying of pass books.

The National Party later called their policies 'separate development', protesting that they did not discriminate, but that for the sake of peace and fairness black Africans should exercise their political rights in ten tribal states, or homelands. The theory was that South Africa proper was white man's land where blacks would enjoy limited rights, but that their homelands would eventually become independent, sovereign states where they would enjoy full rights. Some of those Bantustans, like Transkei, Ciskei and Bophuthatswana, did later become 'independent', but South Africa was the only country that recognised them. The man who championed the homelands policy and under whose leadership South Africa left the Commonwealth and became a republic in 1961 was Dr Hendrik Verwoerd, the National Party's third prime minister.

The ANC slowly grew as a movement and organised a successful 'Defiance Campaign' in 1952 to protest against unjust laws. In 1955, delegates from all over the country gathered in Kliptown outside Johannesburg to adopt the Freedom Charter. This document, which was headed 'The people shall govern!', remained the ANC's ideological compass for four decades. But a group of Africanists in the ANC did not like the fact that the Charter acknowledged whites as full citizens with equal rights, and in 1957 they broke away to form the Pan Africanist Congress (PAC) with Robert Sobukwe as their first leader.

In 1960, the PAC organised protests against the pass laws, forming large demonstrations. It was at one of these, in Sharpeville south of Johannesburg, that the police panicked and killed 69 people. Later the same day a crowd of 6,000 from Langa and Nyanga just outside Cape Town marched to the city, led by a young PAC activist, Philip Kgosana. The police opened fire, killing three and injuring 47.

These two events were turning points in South African history. The government banned the ANC and PAC, and both organisations went underground and formed military wings: the ANC formed Umkhonto we Sizwe (Spear of the Nation) and the PAC formed Poqo (Pure). Most of the first Umkhonto we Sizwe leaders, including the young lawyer Nelson Mandela, were arrested in 1963 and jailed on Robben Island. Some ANC leaders went into exile.

It was also during this time that many African colonies gained their independence. In March 1960, Verwoerd declared: 'A psychotic preoccupation with the rights, the liberties and the privileges of non-white peoples is sweeping the world – at the expense

IN CONTEXT

Burning barricades, Mannenberg Township, Cape Town, 1992.

of due consideration of the rights and merits of white people. The fundamental reality being disregarded is that without white civilisation, non-whites may never have known the meaning of idealism or ambition, liberty or opportunity.'

Verwoerd was stabbed to death in his seat in Parliament, Cape Town, in September 1966. A court declared that his killer, a parliamentary messenger named Demitrio Tsafendas, was mentally disturbed.

CAPE CLEARANCES

One of the cruellest aspects of apartheid was that over three million blacks were forcibly removed over four decades because the areas where they lived were declared 'white'. In Cape Town, this was a particularly painful experience.

District Six was a vibrant, colourful suburb situated right next to the Cape Town City Centre at the foot of Devil's Peak. The majority of the residents were Coloured – their ancestors had been living there since the emancipation of the slaves in the 1830s – but whites, blacks, Indians and Chinese also lived in the area. Between 1965 and 1967, it was declared a 'white' area under the Group Areas Act. The same fate befell Coloured residents living in Kalk Bay and Simonstown.

The residents were moved to new Coloured townships miles away on the Cape Flats and Mitchell's Plain behind Strandfontein. District Six was then razed to the ground, saving only the churches and mosques. The new townships were situated far from shops and places of work; parts of them soon developed into slums. Gangsterism and crime increased progressively.

PUTTING UP RESISTANCE

The arrests of ANC leaders in the early 1960s forced the ANC into a period of near dormancy, but internally the resistance simmered. During the early 1970s a charismatic young intellectual, Steve Biko, gained a strong following with his Black Consciousness views. Early 1973 saw a series of strikes and industrial unrest. In June 1976, Soweto schoolchildren protested against the Bantu

Education system and the use of Afrikaans in schools. Some were shot dead by police. Many youngsters left to join the ANC in exile, injecting the movement with new energy. Steve Biko was detained in the Eastern Cape in August 1977. He was first assaulted in the police cells, then thrown naked into a police van for the trip to Pretoria. He died on the way.

That same year a scandal broke over the way funds for the Department of Information were misused, and a year later Prime Minister John Vorster resigned and was replaced by his minister of defence, PW Botha. Botha appointed General Magnus Malan as minister of defence. In response to internal and international opposition to apartheid, they militarised South Africa. Important decision making shifted to the State Security Council, and security forces believed they had a licence to kill anti-apartheid activists. Hundreds of young white men were conscripted into the Defence Force, which was engaged in destabilising operations in neighbour states and a full-scale war in Angola.

But Botha also tried to reform apartheid and instituted a programme of 'power sharing' with Coloured and Indian South Africans getting their own chambers of Parliament. But the exclusion of blacks provoked deep anger and was one of the motivating factors for the birth of a new national resistance movement, the United Democratic Front, which was formed in Cape Town in 1984. The United Democratic Front was ideologically aligned with the ANC, as was the new trade union movement, the Congress of South African Trade Unions (Cosatu).

SPIRAL OF VIOLENCE

The period between 1984 and 1990 was a turbulent one. There were regular violent protests, often put down by overwhelming force. Month after month the streets of Cape Town's townships, even the inner city, reverberated with the stomping feet of marchers

IN CONTEXT

Nelson Mandela leaves jail, 1990.

'In the late afternoon of 11 February 1990, Nelson Mandela walked out of prison after 27 years of incarceration.'

and the crackle of gunfire, while tear gas often lingered in the air. At one stage the police sprayed protestors in the city with purple-dyed water so they could be identified later. The purple stains remained on city walls for days, and then a famous graffito appeared: 'The Purple shall govern!'

On 15 October 1985, a truck travelled through a crowd of protesting youths in Athlone on the Cape Flats. It turned round and drove past them again. This time they hurled stones and bricks at it. Suddenly armed men hidden in empty crates at the back of the truck leapt up and started firing with shotguns. Three youngsters were killed and 20 wounded. The incident, called the Trojan Horse shootings, caused great anger in Cape Town. The period was also marked by strikes and mass action by trade unions that destabilised the economy, already crippled by international sanctions and financial restrictions by international banks.

RECONCILIATION BEGINS

It was in the late 1980s that the government and the ANC came to realise that neither side could win the battle and that a settlement was the only way to stop South Africa from being completely ruined. Nelson Mandela started secret talks with the government from his jail cell, and government agents had several meetings with ANC leaders in exile.

In January 1989, PW Botha suffered a stroke and in August that year FW de Klerk became president. UDF leaders in the Cape called his bluff after his first reconciliatory speech and staged a mass march through the streets of Cape Town, led by Anglican Archbishop Desmond Tutu. It led to a nationwide demonstration of 'People's Power', with marches in most cities and many towns. In October, at the request of Mandela, the first group of political prisoners, all old stalwarts of the ANC like Walter Sisulu, were released from jail after more than 25 years behind bars.

In November 1989, the Berlin Wall fell and the Soviet Union started to disintegrate. This meant the old National Party argument, that the ANC had to be suppressed because they were tools of communist imperialism, fell away. A month later Nelson Mandela and FW de Klerk had their first face-to-face meeting in the president's Cape Town office. The Old South Africa was fast unravelling.

De Klerk opened the 1990 session of Parliament on 2 February with announcements that stunned the world. He unbanned the ANC, PAC and Communist Party; lifted large sections of the emergency regulations; and announced the release of many political prisoners. And, he declared, Nelson Mandela would be released unconditionally within a few days.

De Klerk ended his speech: 'The season of violence is over. The time for reconstruction and reconciliation has begun... I pray that the Almighty Lord will guide and sustain us on our course through uncharted waters.'

BIRTH OF DEMOCRACY

In the late afternoon of 11 February 1990, Nelson Mandela walked out of prison after 27 years of incarceration. South Africans and the world were stunned to witness his lack of bitterness and huge capacity for reconciliation.

By April most senior ANC leaders in exile had returned to South Africa, and on 3 May, the first formal meeting between the government and the ANC took place at the

IN CONTEXT

The Long Walk to Freedom

The story of Robben Island.

Robben Island is rather innocently called Seal Island ('rob' is the Dutch word for seal), but the story of this place is mostly a sad, and often brutal, one.

The island was known for thousands of years to the indigenous San and Khoikhoi people, but it is unlikely that they ever went there before the first European ships arrived in the 15th century. And when they did go to the island, it was more often than not as prisoners. During the 16th and early 17th century many Khoikhoi who displeased the Dutch, English or Portuguese seafarers were left on the island as punishment. But it was also used as a post office during this period, because many of the seafarers were afraid of the Khoikhoi on the mainland and preferred to pick up their post, fresh water and seal or penguin meat here.

In 1610 ten English criminals who had escaped the gallows and been taken to work in the Cape instead, fled from the mainland and lived on the island for more than a year. The 'Newgate Men' as they were called, were eventually taken back to England and hanged.

After Jan van Riebeeck of the Dutch East India Company established a permanent refreshment station at Cape Town, many 'troublesome' Khoikhoi were banished to Robben Island, the first being a man called Autshomato, who spoke English and was used as an interpreter by the Dutch.

When the European settlers clashed with the Xhosa in the Eastern Cape in the early 19th century, rebellious Xhosa leaders and chiefs were regularly imprisoned on the island. Later that century it was also used as a colony for lepers and those suffering from mental illness.

During World War II the South African Navy took control of the island. It built houses and roads and installed heavy cannon to defend Cape Town from possible enemy ships. In 1961 the Prisons Department took over the island and built a new jail. From the early 1960s onwards many political prisoners were sent to the jail, but kept apart from the sentenced criminals.

Among the most famous political prisoners were Nelson Mandela, Walter Sisulu and Govan Mbeki. Robben Island became 'the University' where hundreds of young activists were taught by Mandela and his older friends – and where some prisoners obtained university degrees through correspondence study. In 1986 Mandela was transferred from Robben Island to Pollsmoor prison, but some prisoners remained until 1990.

Robben Island was transformed into a museum after 1994 (*see p57*).

official state residence, Groote Schuur in Cape Town. Senior ANC delegate Thabo Mbeki remarked after the first day that the delegates 'quickly understood that there was nobody there with horns'. After three days the meeting issued the Groote Schuur minute that contained a commitment to negotiations and a review of security legislation and of the armed struggle.

After intense negotiations, which lasted 18 months, the Convention for a Democratic South Africa (Codesa), comprising most of the country's political parties, met on 20 December 1991 at Kempton Park to begin the task of preparing an interim constitution for a democratic South Africa.

The next two years were complicated by politically inspired violence, especially between supporters of the Inkatha Freedom Party and the ANC, and dramatic events such as the assassination of the popular Communist Party leader Chris Hani, a right-wing

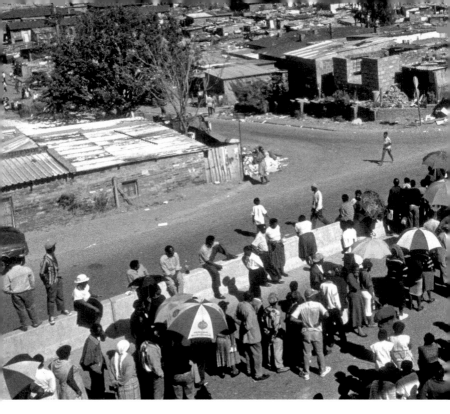

attack on the Codesa building and an abortive invasion of the Bophuthatswana homeland by the Afrikaner Weerstands-beweging. But each time the two main sides, led by Nelson Mandela and FW de Klerk, brought the negotiators back to the table.

In the early hours of 18 November 1993 the parties agreed to the final text of the Interim Constitution, and two months later a parallel government, the Transitional Executive Council, was established.

A POSITIVE FUTURE
On 17 April 1994, millions of South Africans of all races and classes queued together at polling stations for the first election in a united South Africa. The ANC won by a large majority and formed a Government of National Unity with cabinet seats for the National Party and the Inkatha Freedom Party.

On 10 May 1994, Thabo Mbeki and FW de Klerk were sworn in as deputy presidents in Pretoria. Then Nelson Mandela took the oath as the first president of a democratic South Africa. Six fighter planes, which had only a few years earlier dropped bombs on ANC camps in neighbouring states, flew past in a salute. Mandela ended his inauguration speech with the words: 'Let freedom reign. God bless Africa.'

The elected members of Parliament formed a Constitutional Assembly to define a final Constitution. It was adopted on 18 November 1996 and signed into law by President Nelson Mandela on 10 December in Sharpeville.That same year the Truth and Reconciliation Commission, which was part of the negotiated settlement, started to hear evidence that came from victims of past human rights violations. It was chaired by Nobel Peace Laureate Archbishop Desmond Tutu. The Commission also had the power to grant amnesty to the perpetrators, most of them security policemen.

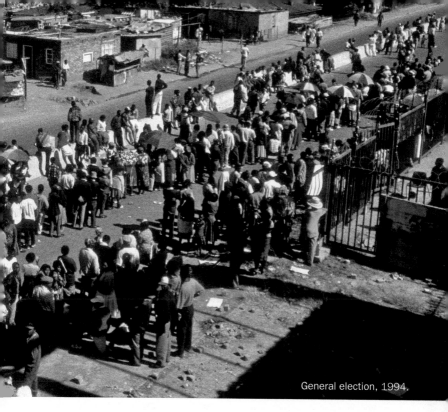

General election, 1994.

In the years that have passed since the first elections of 1994, South Africa has become a stable, progressive democracy with a vibrant economy and a strong leadership role in Africa. District Six was given back to its original owners; large numbers of other displaced communities were given their land back or were compensated for their loss; more than a million new homes were built for the homeless within the first ten years and millions of people had clean water on their doorstep for the first time.

Now in the second decade of democracy, South Africa is not a land without problems. Violent crime remains unacceptably high, and the wave of xenophobic violence against immigrants in 2008 shocked many. The HIV/AIDS figures make for grim reading. The economic disparity between the wealthy minority and the vast majority has only worsened these social problems. As the tough realities of change replace the doe-eyed hopes for a post-apartheid panacea, huge numbers of skilled white professionals are now emigrating.

But despite the complex challenges of crime, HIV/AIDS and the 'brain drain', South Africans can draw on many positives. The country is a continental leader: the African Union was launched in Durban in July 2002, with South Africa's then premier, Thabo Mbeki, serving as its first president; Mbeki was also one of the key figures behind the African economic development programme NEPAD (New Partnership for Africa's Development). He was replaced as president by Jacob Zuma in April 2009. And a much-needed beacon of light is the imminent 2010 FIFA World Cup, which has necessitated long-overdue upgrades of everything from sports stadiums and transport systems to safety and security, bringing with it billions of rands in investment.

Key events

1488 Portuguese explorer Bartholomeu Dias rounds lands at Mossel Bay, where he is met by the indigenous people, Khoikhoi.

1652 Jan Van Riebeeck arrives. Cape Town becomes the Dutch East India Company's mainland base of operations.

1795 British occupation of the Cape Colony begins.

1816-28 Shaka emerges as one of Africa's greatest military leaders, his Zulu army becoming one of the most powerful in southern Africa.

1836-8 Afrikaners (white farmers of mainly Dutch descent) leave the Cape and British rule. These 'Voortrekkers' embark on the Great Trek north.

1867 Fortune-seekers descend after diamonds are discovered in Kimberley. The British seize control of the area in 1871.

1887 Cecil Rhodes's De Beers conglomerate takes over diamond operations in Kimberley.

1899-1902 Thousands of British soldiers and Boer guerrillas are killed in the Boer War, and thousands more women and children die in concentration camps. The war ultimately results in the formation of the British-ruled Union of South Africa in 1904.

1910 Britain grants independence, but the government of the Union of South Africa continues to recognise only the whites' rights.

1912 The South African Native National Congress (later the ANC) is founded.

1948 The National Party begins its domination of South African politics with election victory. Laws turn apartheid practices into official policy: ethnic groups are officially defined, separate institutions are created and intermarriage is outlawed.

1960 ANC President Albert Luthuli is awarded the Nobel Peace Prize. The ruling National Party Government officially leaves the Commonwealth and later becomes the Republic of South Africa. Many are killed during anti-pass law protests in Sharpeville. The ANC is then outlawed; the government declares the first State of Emergency.

1961-2 The ANC abandons non-violent protest and takes up arms against the South African government. Nelson Mandela undergoes training in Algeria, and on his return is arrested and sentenced to five years in prison.

1963-4 The leaders of the ANC's military wing are arrested and tried. Mandela sentenced to life imprisonment.

1976-7 A student revolt in Soweto ignites protests throughout the country, and tensions escalate when black-consciousness activist Steve Biko dies while in police custody.

1984 Cabinet minister Piet Koornhof announces to the world that 'apartheid is dead'.

1985 Township leaders launch a civil disobedience campaign to protest against apartheid (which appears to be still alive), prompting the National Party to establish South Africa's third State of Emergency.

1990 President FW de Klerk announces the end of the ban on the ANC and authorises the release of political prisoners. Mandela released from prison and elected president of the ANC.

1993 Mandela and de Klerk share the Nobel Peace Prize.

1994 South Africa holds first free elections. The ANC wins with over 60 per cent of the vote, and on 10 May Nelson Mandela is inaugurated as President of the Republic of South Africa.

1995 Truth and Reconciliation Commission, chaired by Archbishop Desmond Tutu, is established to expose apartheid crimes.

1999 Thabo Mbeki is elected State President.

2004 South Africa wins the bid to host the 2010 FIFA World Cup.

2006 South Africa named a non-permanent member of the UN Security Council.

2009 Jacob Zuma elected president.

Cape Town Today

A city that dances to its own beat.

TEXT: MARK VAN DIJK

The urban legend goes that it was jazz giant Hugh Masekela… or it could have been *mbaqanga* star Johnny Clegg (it's sometimes hard to keep track of the musicians who dance through town) who ended a show in Cape Town by telling the audience: 'Good night! I'm going back to South Africa now.' Those words perfectly sum up the Mother City's relationship with the rest of the country. Cape Town may be part of South Africa, but things are different here. Starting with the weather. Johannesburg has dry winters and stormy summers; the Cape has wet winters and clear summers. Durban has warm-water beaches and the Agulhas current; Cape Town has cold-water beaches and the icy Benguela Current. While the cities 'up north' make money out of what's under the ground (gold in Jo'burg, diamonds in Kimberley, platinum in Rustenburg), the Fairest Cape enjoys the bounty of the vineyards and orchards above ground. And while the small towns of the Free State and the Karoo maintain a solid conservatism, Cape Town hosts the Mother City Queer Project and Knysna's Pink Loerie Festival.

Mark van Dijk is a writer and editor, and a lifelong resident of Cape Town.

Africa in the Bowl

People from all over the continent call Cape Town home.

'*Merde*!' the guy selling sunglasses at the intersection swears in French, while your waitress serves your latte with a thick Portuguese accent. Just who are these people and what are they doing in Cape Town?

The city is a melting pot for African immigrants: on any street corner you may hear French, Shona or Kinyarwanda. Many of these immigrants are refugees from wars and political unrest. In their own countries they were teachers, accountants and doctors. (A 2003 national survey revealed that nearly a third of refugees and asylum seekers were tertiary students before they came to South Africa.) But in Cape Town they are working as informal car guards and street vendors.

Following South Africa's liberation in 1994, many Africans saw it as the continent's own American Dream – a land of tolerance and bright opportunities. The xenophobic attacks in May 2008 shattered this illusion, leaving more than 50 dead. The violence started in Alexandra township near Johannesburg – residents felt that immigrants where stealing their jobs and resources – and soon spread to Cape Town. But despite this tragedy, many immigrants still call the city home.

Jean-Claude Ngoyi has been here for four years. 'I was running from my country, the Congo, because of the war,' he says. 'I came through Zambia and Zimbabwe, but didn't feel safe there. So I came to South Africa.'

At home Ngoyi taught high-school accounting and economics. Today he washes and parks cars in Hatfield Street in Gardens. 'When I came here I couldn't get a job because of the language – I'm a Frenchman – so the first thing for me was to learn English. What I'm doing now is a job just to get food; bread every day,' he says. 'I wish, God willing, I can get a nice job. But for now I'm a car washer and a car parker.'

He talks about the xenophobic attacks and how the intolerance still continues. 'They call us *kwerekwere* [a pejorative word for foreigner], you know,' he says. Why does he think there are so many foreigners living in Cape Town? 'South Africa is what they call the Rainbow Nation,' he explains. 'It means a country for everybody – all races and cultures. The foreigners here are working for themselves, and they are doing well.'

GATEWAY TO AFRICA

The notion that Cape Town is somehow separate from the rest of South Africa is such a part of the local mindset that, in 1987 and with no small sense of irony, the residents of the seaside suburb of Hout Bay jokingly proclaimed a republic and started printing their own novelty passports.

Cape Town's deep sense of difference – and of uniqueness – goes beyond climate, economy and politics. Demographically, too, there's a telling difference between the Mother City and the rest of South Africa: in the most recent census (2001), black Africans accounted for just 31 per cent of Cape Town's population, compared to a national average of 79.5 per cent. But despite all its differences with the rest of the country, Cape Town still feels like Africa in microcosm. Walking across the City Bowl today – and it'll only take you about half an hour if you don't stop to look around – you'll brush up against an African Union of continental cultures, as well as visitors from around the world. On Green Market Square you'll meet central African and Somali stall holders, many of them refugees, some with papers, some without. Walk up to Long Street – with its mosques next to bars next to bookshops next to boutiques – and you'll pass European and American tourists, and Asian sailors fresh from the docks. And wherever there's parking anywhere in the city you'll find a Nigerian or Congolese parking guard. In between you'll encounter the locals: Afrikaners, Xhosas, Zulus, whites, coloureds, blacks, Christians, Muslims, Jews. A cosmopolitan collection of people that make it hard to believe that Cape Town could ever – let alone as recently as 16 years ago – have been such a racially divided society.

Because of its status as a multi-ethnic, multicultural melting pot – and that innate sense of difference, perhaps – the Western Cape province, and the City of Cape Town especially, has become the fiercest battleground state in contemporary South African politics. Since South Africa's first fully representative democratic elections in 1994, the ruling African National Congress (ANC) has never achieved the dominance in the Cape that it has in the rest of the country.

Local politics tend to feature complicated narratives of divided loyalties, deal-making, inter-party power-sharing deals and narrow majorities. Not that the locals really care. The city's political shenanigans are seldom really felt on the street (with the xenophobic violence of the winter of 2008 being a tragic and sobering exception), and political figures are generally regarded with ho-hum, here-we-go-again abstraction. Capetonians prefer to focus on more important things. Like sport. And music. And relaxing on the beach.

SPORTS TOWN

The newspaper headline posters that adorn the city's lamp-posts are as likely to be about cricket, soccer or rugby union as they are to be about the city's mayoral merry-go-round. South African sport still tends to be divided along ethnic lines, with soccer regarded as a black/coloured sport, cricket as a coloured/white sport, and rugby as a coloured/white sport. But despite Cape Town's sporting enthusiasm, it's not easy being a sports fan here. The Western Cape Stormers have only reached rugby's Super 14 playoffs twice in 12 seasons. Cricket fans are a happier bunch, with the domestic Cape Cobras franchise boasting a well-stocked trophy cabinet, and the traditional Tweede Nuwe Jaar Test match (pitting the South African national team against a touring side) being a highlight of the local calendar. Soccer fans, meanwhile, have two local top-flight sides (Santos and Ajax Cape Town) to cheer for – even though the country's biggest clubs are based in Soweto, and even though the post-apartheid national team has only ever played four games in the Mother City.

It is this that makes the 2010 FIFA World Cup so interesting. When Cape Town got around to deciding where to put its World Cup stadium (opting, eventually, to rebuild the old Green Point Stadium), locals got to worrying about whether the city – and, by extension, South Africa – would actually be ready to host the tournament before the

'Whatever the World Cup brings, at least it has given the city a much-needed new sports venue.'

big kick-off. But when the tickets went on sale in early 2009, with the stadium casting an impressive, sweeping shadow across the city, the collective mood shifted to somewhere between giddy excitement and please-don't-let-us-stuff-this-up nerves.

GRAND DESIGNS

Whatever the World Cup brings, at least it has given the city a much-needed new sports venue in the dramatically remodelled Green Point Stadium. But that has not been the only site of inner-city improvement – across town the skies are dotted with cranes, while the streets hum to the perpetual percussion of construction equipment. The N2 highway leading into the city seems to be in a constant state of expansion and upgrading, as the transport network promises to become bigger, better, and less likely to cause interminable traffic jams. New buildings seem to be going up in every inner-city neighbourhood, with sparkling edifices like the Cape Town International Convention Centre, the Icon building and Wembley Square now casting shadows over the established Edwardian and art deco structures. The result is an eclectic architectural mix that reflects the city's many faces.

Swish new blocks like Mandela Rhodes Place (a luxury hotel/apartment complex) and the Building In the District (in the old District Six) are symptomatic of the city's recent property boom. But with that growth has come the growing gentrification of old inner-city neighbourhoods like the Bo-Kaap, where charming old homes are being converted into expensive new offices. This gentrification is a discomfiting echo of the forced removals of the 1970s, when apartheid laws sent coloured residents out of areas like District Six and into the sandpits of the Cape Flats, on the far side of the Cape Peninsula. Today, at least, when the residents move out of their homes it's to leafier suburbs and with money in their bank accounts.

TROUBLED TIMES

Scratch the surface, though, and beneath the prosperity and the property boom you will still find a city with problems. In a modern-day twist on Van Riebeeck's early trading station, Cape Town has become a 'Gateway to Africa' for drug dealers – with the United Nations' World Drug Report 2008 listing South Africa as one of the world's largest producers of cannabis. On a street level, gangs continue to push drugs into schools, especially around the Cape Flats. The World Drug Report stated that 'there are no indications that South African methamphetamine (known locally at 'tik') is produced for export – manufacture growth appears to be for increasing domestic consumption'.

HIV and AIDS, too, are cutting deep scars. The HIV prevalence rate in the Western Cape rose from 7.8 per cent in 2003 to 15.2 per cent in 2006, and while that is lower than elsewhere in South Africa, 'elsewhere in South Africa' includes the likes of KwaZulu-Natal, where rates were 39.1% in 2006; the national average is 29.1 per cent.

It may sound like a platitude, but the Mother City doesn't let its problems get her down. Politicians come and go (some with alarming regularity). Buildings go up and come down. And people pass through the Cape, as they have been doing for centuries. But its people – whether they call the place Cape Town, Kaapstad, iKapa or Le Cap – seldom let gloomy realities interfere with their enjoyment of the city. Sure, it can be crazy. And undoubtedly, it's different. But, even at its worst, Cape Town is always a charming, beautiful mess. After all, a city that's slowly being nudged into the sea by a flat-topped mountain can't afford to take life too seriously, now can it?

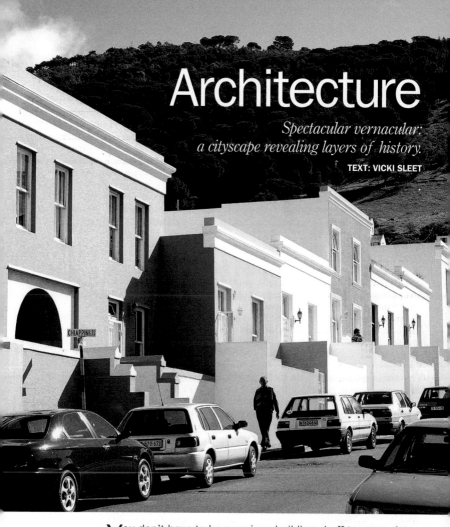

Architecture

Spectacular vernacular:
a cityscape revealing layers of history.

TEXT: VICKI SLEET

Vicki Sleet
is a freelance
lifestyle journalist
specialising in
decor, food and
design.

You don't have to be a serious buildings buff to appreciate the fascinating array of architectural styles that come together to create Cape Town's unique urban landscape. Early Cape Dutch buildings can be found dotted throughout the city, their style based on contemporary Dutch architecture of the time. Later arrivals, the British, brought Victorian architecture with them; rows of Victorian merchant warehouses still line Long Street. And Cape Town's many examples of art deco were an attempt to move away from the British idiom with a new style drawing on the ancient world for inspiration. A leisurely morning's walk can reveal the interesting tale of the city's development from small Dutch settlement to cosmopolitan hub, told through its buildings.

Early days

Cast your mind's eye back to the mid 1600s, when the city was little more than a trading post, set up by the Dutch East India Company (VOC) to provide food and water for their ships en route to Asia and the spice lands, and inhabited by a hotch potch of VOC officials and settlers hoping to make a new life for themselves in this exotic, bountiful land. Over time, as merchants and the more well-off citizens came into their own, the architecture of the settlement began to take on the look and feel of a Dutch town, with typical steep pitched roofs. The architectural style morphed with the arrival of German sculptor Anton Anreith and Parisian architect Louis Thibault, who relished the opportunity to realise their creativity on the many buildings being constructed at the time. They brought new ideas and energy and the result is the **Cape Dutch** vernacular, typified by single-storey thatched and gabled homes, as well as flat-roofed, pedimented double-storey houses of the same period, many with the trademark 'T', 'U' and 'H' interior layout plans.

MUST SEE
● **Koopmans de Wet Huis**, 41 Strand Street, has one of the most beautiful and well-preserved Cape Dutch vernacular façades in the city, thought to be the work of Louis Thibault and much lauded for its symmetry and beautiful interior displays of antique Cape Dutch furniture.
● **Martin Melck House**, 96 Strand Street (now the Gold of Africa Museum, *see p45*), was built in the style of a typical Dutch townhouse and has Cape Town's last surviving *dak kamer* or roof room.
● **Tuynhuys** in the Company Gardens was home to Dutch and English governors of the Cape for over 200 years. Its façade features a semicircular pediment with the Dutch East India Company logo.
● **Rust-en-Vreugd**, Buitenkant Street, was built in 1777 and is characterised by its striking teak veranda and rococo-style upper-storey window by Anton Anreith. It is a typical 18th-century Cape Town upper-class house design – and is also said to be one of the most haunted houses in the city.

IN CONTEXT

Bo-Kaap.

Colourful cottages

The **Bo-Kaap**, officially known as District 2, came into being as local artisans and families of freed slaves established their first homes in an area above – 'bo' – the city. The legacy of the predominantly Muslim population still remains, with the sounds of the muezzin calling the faithful to prayer a feature of the city's everyday soundtrack. Rose and Wale streets are the main thoroughfares here, but wander the steep and narrow roads that branch off them and you'll get a little closer to the heart of the suburb. Snap-happy photographers will relish the eye candy that features at every turn here – the terraces of Cape Dutch meets Edwardian-style cottages, painted in a spectrum of colours.

Bo-Kaap.

MUST SEE
● **Bo-Kaap Museum**, 71 Wale Street, was built in 1768 and is furnished as a typical Muslim home of the 19th century.
● **Auwal Mosque**, 39 Dorp Street. Built in 1804, the first mosque in the Bo-Kaap is still very much in use.

Cool Britannia

British rule came to the Cape in 1814 and, in just a few years, merchants, tradesmen and missionaries were flocking to this imperial outpost to make their fortunes – or convert the locals. As they prospered, so their desire increased to transform the city from a rural Dutch settlement with open sewerage systems and dusty streets to an altogether more sophisticated and 'civilised' town. For the first time modern shops appeared and many Georgian-influenced homes, built in red brick, arose. They stood in direct contrast to the typically whitewashed Cape Dutch buildings. Excellent examples of **Cape Victorian** architecture can be seen throughout the city, especially on **Long Street**, where tradesmen and wholesalers struck business deals in the warehouses that lined the streets. Over the past few years, many of these original

Long Street.

buildings have been restored and their intricate styles enhanced with colourful coats of paint. 'Broekie lace' ironwork is typical of this vernacular and gives Cape Victorian architecture its 'prettied' look.

MUST SEE

● **Long Street** still has its original street-level shop fronts, for premises that are now hip boutiques and restaurants. And remember to look up, too – many of the upstairs balconies feature great examples of Victorian ironwork.

● **Adderley Street** has many beautiful examples of Victorian architecture and was once full of smart shop fronts.

● **Ginja**, 121 Castle Street. The restaurant is housed in a semi-renovated Victorian warehouse, and still has many original features.

● **Origin Coffee**, 28 Hudson Street. In a well-preserved warehouse on the outskirts of the original city, the building has been renovated as a tea and coffee shop and hip hangout.

● **NewSpace Theatre Complex**, 44 Long Street. A recently restored celebration of the Victorian vernacular.

● **Mount Nelson Hotel**, 76 Orange Street, is a beautiful example of Victorian architecture, complete with interiors furnished to reflect this. Built in 1899, it is one of the city's most well-loved grand dames.

Mutual Heights.

Deco darlings

In among the quaint Victoriana architecture and the Cape Dutch buildings so prevalent in the city are a series of buildings that stand out from the crowd. Much of the detailing so typical of the **art deco** era that began to take shape in the early 1900s takes its reference from ancient civilisations, despite the fact that deco emerged as a conscious move away from the styles of the past. Having been bruised in the Anglo-Boer war, South African architects of the period embraced the style that was so atypical of the British vernacular that had previously been so celebrated in this country. Cape Town has numerous examples of art deco architecture. The area of Vredehoek has the largest concentration of such buildings in one suburb in South Africa (visit Wexford, Bellair and Davenport roads for a taste).

MUST SEE

● **Mutual Heights**, 14 Darling Street, is the most prestigious art deco building in Africa, thanks to the fact that it was once the tallest building on the continent, as well as its immense deco detailing. Look out for a façade that incorporates carved figurines and triangular windows and stick your head in the door (it's now a swish apartment block) for a peek at the impressive marble banking hall.

● **African Banking Corporation (ABC) Building**, 130 Adderley Street, occupies an entire city block and is a superb example of art deco architecture. A listed heritage building, it is now occupied by the upmarket Riboville restaurant (complete with private dining in the bank vault).

● **Market House**, Greenmarket Square, is an ornate example from the deco era, complete with detailed figurative and relief work on the exterior.

● **Mullers Optometrists**, corner Parliament and Longmarket streets, is a beautifully preserved building complete with original lead glass windows and chrome inlays in the façade.

Modern talking

Though the various vernaculars of Cape Town architecture give an outstanding sense of the city's history, there's no denying the impact that some of the city's newer buildings have had on the urban landscape.

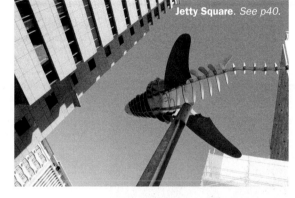
Jetty Square. *See p40.*

MUST SEE

● **Green Point Stadium**, Green Point. With the FIFA 2010 World Cup set to expose the city to thousands of fans and international visitors, architects and engineers have been hard at work to complete this magnificent structure in time. With seating for 68,000 and a number of hi-tech design elements – like the skin that covers the stadium and limits the force of the wind on it – the structure is a major talking point in Cape Town. Designed to mimic the undulating lines of Signal Hill behind it, it has a sculptural beauty.

● **Cape Town Station**, Strand Street, looks set to give the city's train station and transport infrastructure a major overhaul. A brand new concourse and underground track system, plus improved shopping facilities, promise to offer commuters a better travel experience.

● **Cape Town International Convention Centre**, 1 Lower Long Street, is an exercise in clean lines and a contemporary approach to public building design. The CTICC resembles a large ship from the side situated closest to the V&A Waterfront, a reference to its proximity to the city's port.

● **Cape Town Jewish Museum**, 88 Hatfield Street. The modernist structure is clad in Jerusalem stone and acts as a bridge between old and new, joining the city's oldest synagogues and the Albow Centre, housing the Cape Town Holocaust Centre.

Sculpting the City

A weird – and wonderful – variety of sculpture.

Mesmerising artworks are all around you in Cape Town, and no, it's not only Jan van Riebeeck's statue. Here's our guide to the weird and wonderful sculpture you'll see.

The Knot (1981) by Eduardo Villa was commissioned in the 1980s. Perched behind the Civic Centre (12 Hertzog Boulevard), it resembles an over-sized jungle gym. The creator of this orange-painted steel work came to South Africa in 1942 as a prisoner of war.

The sculpture set at **Pier Place** (Heerengracht Avenue) by Egon Tania (2007) is an uncanny depiction of the people that live and work in the city: a man on a bench, another walking while talking on his cell phone, a woman playing with her child and one carrying shopping. Life-sized and incredibly life-like too.

Jetty Square (2005) by Ralph Borland (between Pier Place and Thibault Square) is a feat of

engineering. Borland fashioned 'ghost sharks' swimming three metres above the ground that pivot in the wind like weathervanes. Jetty Square was reclaimed from the ocean during the last century, making these sharks a reminder of what came before.

Mythological Landscape (1992) by John Skotnes in Thibault Square (Hans Strijdom Avenue) is an intricate mishmash of animals and birds. The towering piece was commissioned by the JK Gross Trust in collaboration with the Association for Visual Arts as part of a contest.

Africa (1999) by Brett Murray is St George's Mall's famously idiosyncratic sight: a totem-like sculpture covered in... Could it be Bart Simpson? Erupting from the smooth bronze African limbs and head are stylised heads of the American cartoon anti-hero in bright yellow plastic – it's the ultimate in mixed messages.

The Company's Gardens (entrances in Orange or Adderley streets) hosts older sculptures that recall the Cape's early history. Look out for the 1908 bronze cast of **Cecil John Rhodes** and a stone sculpture of **Jan Smuts**.

South Africa's four Nobel Peace laureates – Albert Luthuli, Desmond Tutu, FW de Klerk and Nelson Mandela – are honoured at the **V&A Waterfront**. The diminutive bronze statues here were created by Claudette Schreuders in 2006.

Sightseeing

St James Beach. *See p72.*

City Bowl

The fascinating heart of Cape Town rewards the foot-soldier.

The best way to unpick the many intricacies of this cosmopolitan quilt of sights, sounds and cultures is to explore it on foot. A good place to start is the oak-lined **Government Avenue**, a bench-studded stretch running past a series of museums and galleries. It's flanked by the **Company's Gardens**, which has grassy patches and shady spots for walk-weary tourists and townies. Once you've had your fill of museums, head to the city centre, amble through the cobbled, open-air **St George's Mall** and **Greenmarket Square**, and stop at one of the many pavement cafés.

The area's backbone – and its shopping hub – is **Long Street**, which has everything from antique stores and second-hand clothing shops to African shops and modern boutiques, interspersed with a good selection of restaurants – ideal for refuelling stops.

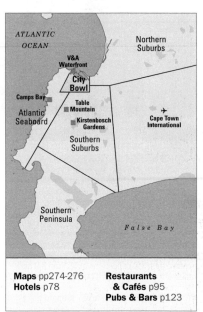

Maps pp274-276
Hotels p78

Restaurants & Cafés p95
Pubs & Bars p123

CITY CENTRE

Nucleus of the urban business district, the city centre is home to an immense diversity of commerce and cultures. Much of the area's economic life is centred on **Long Street**. The name starts making sense, should you decide to meander the length of the one-way 20-block stretch. Dotted with fast-food joints and discount furnishing stores, the bottom, harbour side of the mile isn't exactly thrilling, but things start getting interesting from the Wale Street intersection up towards the mountain, with an eclectic collection of shops, restaurants and hangouts. And when the lights go down the party people come out to play: night owls of all persuasions will find a spot to flaunt their feathers here, be it at an Irish pub, grotty pool bar or svelte cocktail lounge. There are plenty of places to sleep too, from stylish boutique hotels to bustling backpackers' hostels.

Off Long Street, between Shortmarket and Burg streets is **Greenmarket Square** (*see*

p132). This frenetic hub of stalls (open 9am-4pm Mon-Sat), selling predominantly African curios, used to be the spot where farmers sold their fruit and vegetables. Once you've worn out the phrase 'No, thank you, I'm just looking,' it's a good idea to head over to one of the pavement cafés where you can watch the commerce unfold from a distance over a cappuccino – all the while keeping an eye out for those sticky-fingered pickpockets, of course. Overlooking the square is the Gothic **Central Methodist Mission** (*see p44*).

There's retail of a different kind at **St George's Mall**, an open-air strip starting at Thibault Square near the station and ending at St George's Cathedral. It's a lively stretch, usually resounding to the sound of drum beats, and is home to lots of cafés and fast-food outlets. It's good for bling too, and known as the Jewellery Route because of the jewellery shops peppering the road.

Heritage Square (*see p45*), on the other side of Long Street from St George's

Long Street. *See p43.*

SIGHTS

Mall, is a block of restored buildings that is now another of the city centre's hubs, home to restaurants and bars.

At the southern end of Long Street is **Kloof Street**. On any given weekday morning, you'll see a congregation of espresso-wielding yuppies at Vida e Caffè (*see p109*). Emo-kids can maintain their meticulously cultivated coiffs at hipster hair salon Scar (no.43), and vinyl devotees get the chance to expand their LP collections at Hi5 (no.34) and Mabu Vinyl (*see p156*). The city's newest holistic hotspot, Wellness Warehouse (*see p152*), offers the chance to stock up on goji berries and massage oils. At the other end of the health spectrum, there are enough fast-food joints lining Kloof Street to fulfil all deep-fried dietary requirements. Heading south up the hill, the street starts to go upmarket: you'll find everyone from dog-walking mothers to students surveying the lie of the land over steaming lattés.

Castle of Good Hope

Cnr Buitenkant & Darling Streets (021 787 1249/www.castleofgoodhope.co.za). **Open** 9am-4pm daily. *Tours* 11am, noon, 2pm Mon-Sat. *Key ceremony & cannon firing* 10am, noon Mon-Fri. **Admission** R20; R10-R15 reductions; half price for all Sun. **No credit cards.** **Map** p276 H4.

The Castle of Good Hope is South Africa's oldest surviving colonial building. Completed in 1679, the moated, five-pointed fortress was initially built by Commander Zacharius Wagenaer of the Dutch East India Company to ward off possible attacks from the British, and later served as the hub of the Cape's civilian and military activities. It's still the seat of the Cape Town military today, and if you time it right, you can catch the key ceremony,

as performed by the Castle Guard. The military museum showcases several impressive pieces, interspersed with display cases of filled with glassy-eyed mannequins kitted out in their military best. The Anglo Boer War section features a coin-operated model armoured train huffing and puffing past seres of block houses and through hostile British territory.

▶ *The William Fehr collection gives a peek into the opulent 17th century heyday of the Dutch East India Company.*

ＦＲＥＥ Central Methodist Mission

Cnr Longmarket & Burg Streets, Greenmarket Square (021 422 2744). **Open** 9am-3pm Mon-Fri; 10am-2pm Sat. *Services* 1.10pm Tue; 10am Sun. **Admission** free. **Map** p276 H4.

Resembling a location from a Tim Burton movie, this grey Gothic revivalist church with its needle-like spires looks a tad out of place (and a bit too dignified) amid the noisy colour explosion of informal stalls in Greenmarket Square. The contrast of the outside bustle with the quiet calm inside the church is intense, and it's worth a visit to marvel at the impressive architecture of pointed arches and flying buttresses, and to find out more about the erstwhile Methodist Church in Buitenkant Street, which served as a haven for activists during the struggle years, from the leaflets that you can pick up here.

INSIDE TRACK
MOREISH MASSAGE

For a full body massage at a snip of the price you'll pay elsewhere, try the **Long Street Baths** (*see p47*). The price includes a session in their steam room.

Church Street Antiques Market

Church Street. **Open** 9am-4pm Mon-Sat.
No credit cards. Map p276 G3.
This small cobbled stretch is a trove of vintage garb, rare coins, plastic jewellery, twee porcelain doggies and rows of empty perfume bottles. Even more interesting than the wares are the people that frequent the pedestrianised area of Church Street, who range from coffee-sipping arty folk and stealthy antique hounds to fashionistas that would put Sarah Jessica Parker to shame.
▶ *For more on the market, see p132.*

CTICC – Cape Town International Convention Centre

Convention Square, 1 Lower Long Street (021 410 5000/www.cticc.co.za). **Map** p276 H3.
An arresting site on the city's foreshore, this colossal modern building has become an iconic Cape Town landmark in its relatively short lifespan of six years. The centre houses some of the most sophisticated conference facilities in the country. Apart from the state-of-the-art auditoriums, conservatories and spiffy restaurants, it is also synonymous with the hundreds of expos held there every year, including Design Indaba and Cape Town Fashion Week.
▶ *For some events held at the Convention Centre, see pp158-160.*

District Six Museum

25A Buitenkant Street (021 466 7200/www. districtsix.co.za). **Open** 9am-2pm Mon; 9am-4pm Tue-Sat. **Admission** R15; R5 reductions. **Credit** AmEx, DC, MC, V. **Map** p276 H4.
This award-winning community museum lays bare the time in South African history when the ruling government declared District Six a 'whites only' area and over 60,000 of its residents were forcibly taken from their homes and shipped out to the Cape Flats, before their houses were reduced to rubble. The museum includes a memorial hall and a sound archive, and many of the exhibits are interactive, created with the help of former residents; they rely heavily on the medium of storytelling to reconstruct the time of the forced removals and the devastating repercussions it had on the once-vibrant community. A haunting map of District Six painted on the floor of the museum invites evicted residents to indicate with chalk where they once lived.

★ Gold of Africa Museum

96 Strand Street, Martin Melck House (021 405 1540/www.goldofafrica.com). **Open** 9.30am-4.30pm Mon-Sat. **Admission** R25; R15-R20 reductions. *Pangolin Night Tour & Golden Lion Walking Tour* R40; R25 reductions. **Credit** AmEx, DC, MC, V. **Map** p276 H3
Located in the historic mustard-hued Martin Melck House, this museum boasts the largest assortment of African gold objects in the world. Most notable is the 300-odd piece Barbier Mueller collection of 19th- and 20th-century West African artefacts such as the massive gold pangolin and gravity-defying shell-like earrings worn by the Peul women of Mali. Especially interesting is the room dedicated to the history of gold, featuring detailed timelines covering every conceivable gold-related event ranging from the making of Tutankamun's coffin circa 1300 BC to the introductiono of the Kruger Rand in 1900.
▶ *Martin Melck House is a perfect example of Cape Dutch architecture; see p36.*

Grand Parade & City Hall

Cnr Buitenkant & Darling streets. **Map** p276 H4.
The time for the facelift of South Africa's oldest public space has finally arrived. R21 million has been forked out to repave and upgrade the previously run-down Grand Parade, which is set to serve as a fan park for the 2010 FIFA World Cup. Keeping an eye on the proceedings is the sandstone City Hall, with its elaborate Renaissance-style columns and slightly out-of-place Big Ben-proportioned clock tower. The place is a landmark when it comes to South African history: one of the biggest multiracial protests against apartheid culminated here on 14 September 1989, and the following year Nelson Mandela made his first public speech from the City Hall balcony, just hours after his release from prison. Cape Town mayor Helen Zille recently released a proposal for the restoration of the City Hall and its conversion into a cultural and music centre. *Photo p47.*

FREE Groote Kerk

39 Upper Adderley Street (021 422 0569/ www.grootekerk.org.za). **Open** 10am-2pm Mon-Fri. **Services** 10am, 7pm Sun. **Admission** free. **Map** p276 H4.
Originally a Cape Dutch building, the church underwent so much work over the years that the only remnants of the original are the old tower and the ornate pulpit carved by sculptor Anton Anreith. The construction of this, the country's first Dutch Reformed Church and the oldest in South Africa, commenced in 1678; it was finally consecrated in 1704. Interesting highlights include the country's largest organ and the biggest unsupported domed ceiling in the southern hemisphere.

Heritage Square

Cnr Bree and Shortmarket streets. **Map** p276 G3.
Bordered by Buitengracht, Hout, Bree and Shortmarket streets, this block of Dutch and Georgian buildings was probably the closest thing Capetonians had to a mall back in the 18th century – gunsmiths, bakers and cigarette makers all conducted their businesses from here. The historical site was set to make way for a multi-storey car park, but luckily fate was on its side, and in the 1980s it was given a new lease of life, becoming the largest private conservation project ever seen in the city. Miraculously, the country's oldest vine, dating from

CAPE TOWN
BIG 6

ONE DESTINATION
SIX UNFORGETTABLE EXPERIENCES

V&A WATERFRONT

TABLE MOUNTAIN CABLEWAY

ROBBEN ISLAND

DAY TRIP 1

KIRSTENBOSCH

CAPE POINT

CONSTANTIA VINEYARDS

DAY TRIP 2

City Hall. *See p45.*

SIGHTS

1781, made it through all the ructions in one piece, and can still be spotted in the courtyard today.

▶ *Heritage Square holds many restaurants, among them the Caveau Wine Bar & Deli; see p99.*

Koopmans-De Wet House

35 Strand Street (021 481 3935/www.iziko. org.za/koopmans). **Open** 10am-5pm Tue-Thur. **Admission** R10; R5 reductions; free under-16s. **No credit cards. Map** p276 H3.

Set amid the hustle and bustle of Strand Street, this Cape Dutch building designed by the architect Louis Thibault was the first privately owned townhouse to be opened as a public museum – in 1914. Once belonging to the wealthy socialite Marie Koopmans-De Wet, it is furnished to re-create an 18th-century residential home and showcases an exquisite collection of Cape furniture, eastern and Dutch crockery and red quarry tiles imported from Batavia.

▶ *Thibault also designed the Groote Kerk; see p45.*

INSIDE TRACK
RIKKIS

These budget door-to-door taxis don't have meters – the price is fixed. Opt for a 'city direct' or a 'city share' ride: the latter is cheaper but you have to share with other punters. Ring them on one of the free Rikkis phones you'll find at venues across the city (0861 745 547, www.rikkis.co.za).

Long Street Baths

Cnr Long and Orange streets (021 400 3302). **Open** *Pool* 7am-7pm daily. *Turkish Bath* Ladies 9am-6pm Mon, Thur, Sat. Gents 1-7pm Tue; 8am-7pm Wed, Fri; 8am-noon Sun. **Admission** *Turkish baths* R70 adults; R35 per hour. *Pool* R11; R7 children; free pensioners. **No credit cards. Map** p276 G4.

The Long Street Baths have been around for 100 years (they were built in 1908), so don't expect a contemporary candlelit spa experience. The indoor pool attracts a diverse crowd of swimmers. Or, if you prefer something a little less labour intensive, head over to the traditional Turkish baths for a soothing steam without an inflated price tag.

FREE Michaelis Gallery

UCT Hiddingh Campus, 31-37 Orange Street, Gardens (021 480 7111/www.michaelis.uct.ac.za). **Open** 10am-4pm Mon-Fri when exhibitions are showing. **Admission** free.

This cosy gallery on UCT's Hiddingh Campus is part of the Michaelis School of Fine Arts, which has been around since 1925. Apart from serving as an exhibition space for its students (the fourth-year final exhibition is an annual highlight in the art community), it's also seen its fair share of *de jour* local and international artists through the years. Being the only gallery in the country dedicated to video art, it regularly features head-bending conceptual film and multimedia pieces, and has hosted work by the internationally acclaimed Turner Prize-winning artist Steve McQueen.

Magic Mountain

Myths and legends of the iconic Table.

SIGHTS

Ever heard the one about the scruffy seafarer who smoked the devil under the Table? Story goes that during the 18th century, a pipe-puffing pirate called Jan van Hunks was approached on Table Mountain by a stranger wanting to borrow some tobacco. This set Van Hunks off on a boastful tirade about his unequalled smoking abilities, and when the newcomer took him up on his challenge, the two embarked on a puffathon that lasted several days.

Despite Van Hunks transpiring to be the toughest toker, the joke was very much on him when a gust of wind blew off the stranger's hat, revealing a pair of horns. Not one to accept defeat gracefully, the devil proceeded to make them both disappear – quite aptly – in a puff of smoke. Whenever the south-easterly wind howls and covers Cape Town's

flat-topped mountain with a thick cloak of clouds, locals still whisper that the two old cronies are at it again.

The iconic mountain has been the subject of many other myths and legends through the ages and forms an integral backdrop to the city's identity, history and culture. Up until the 16th century the indigenous Khoikhoi people dubbed it Hoerikwaggo, meaning Sea Mountain. When Portuguese seaman António de Saldanha came ashore in 1503, he came up with the ingenious name of Taboa do Cabo, or Table of the Cape, and marked this christening by carving a cross in the rock face, traces of which can still be found on Lion's Head today.

The sandstone colossus is still very much in the spotlight – a string of four floodlights bathe the mountain in a

▶ *This was once the location of one of Jan Van Riebeeck's many vegetable gardens in the Cape.*

FREE Old Town House & Michaelis Collection
Old Town House, Greenmarket Square (021 481 3933/www.iziko.org.za/michaelis).
Open 10am-5pm Mon-Sat. **Admission** free; donation appreciated. **Map** p276 H4.
The first two-storey building ever to grace Cape Town's cityscape, this ornate 1761 Cape Rococo-style construction must have elicited quite a few

oohs and aahs back in the day. Originating as a Burger Watch House and later used as a magistrate's court, police station and town hall, it was declared Cape Town's first art museum in 1914 after a very generous donation of 17th-century Dutch and Flemish art was made by Sir Max Michaelis. The esteemed Michaelis collection features paintings by Dutch Golden Age masters including Rembrandt van Rijn, Jacob Ruisdal and Frans Hals. When you're all arted out but find the thought of braving the bustling Greenmarket Square too much, step into the calm courtyard for a relaxed alfresco lunch.

celestial glow each festive season, and hundreds of thousands of people visit it each year. The mountain's plateau top is three kilometres long, and its highest point, marked by Maclear's Beacon, towers at 1,088 metres, making it visible from as far as 200 kilometres at sea. The summit can be reached through a multitude of beautiful, albeit exhausting, trails, giving you the chance to meet the mountain's furry mascot, the rock rabbit, more commonly known as the dassie – a little creature that is said to be the closest living relative to the elephant – and brush up against some of the 1,470 species of *fynbos* that blanket the mountain.

If you want to stay overnight, take the Hoerikwaggo trail, which incorporates an eco-friendly tented campsite with unbeatable views (*see p83* **Hot Beds**). If you're less inclined to physical exercise, the Table Mountain Cableway (*see p55*), will take you straight to the top – without the sweat.

Flanking Table Mountain to the east is **Devil's Peak**, said to derive its name from Van Hunks's horned companion. It's the site of several historical attractions, including **Rhodes Memorial** (*see p67*), the **University of Cape Town** (*p67*), **Mostert's Mill** (*p67*) and **Groote Schuur Estate** (*p66*). **Lion's Head** and **Signal Hill** (*see p54*) lie towards the west.

The trinity of mountains is said to bear an uncanny resemblance to an armchair – an extremely auspicious shape according to the ancient Chinese philosophy of Feng Shui – making the city of Cape Town the seat of magic moments and good vibes. No wonder Capetonians are such a laid-back bunch.

FREE Palm Tree Mosque

185 Long Street (083 444 4613). **Admission** free, by appointment only. **Map** p276 H3.

When Tuan Guru, the father of the Islamic faith in South Africa, died in 1807, he left his imamship of the Auwal Mosque (*see p55*) to Abdulalim, much to the dismay of two of his congregation members, Frans van Bengalen and Jan van Boughies. The two resigned from the mosque and started a *langgar* (prayer room) in the upper storey of Jan's house in Long Street, which received mosque status in 1825. Legend has it that Jan wasn't exactly the easiest person to get along with, and so, within a year of the mosque's existence, Frans left the country, and the majority of the congregation returned to the Auwal Mosque. A century and a few decades later, the name of Jan van Boughies Mosque was changed to a more succinct one, alluding to the towering palm out front, which is said to have been planted by Jan himself.

★ Pan African Market

76 Long Street (021 426 4478/www.pan african.co.za). **Open** *Summer* 8.30am-5.30pm

Mon-Fri; 8.30am-3.30pm Sat. *Winter* 9am-5pm Mon-Fri; 9am-3pm Sat. **Credit** AmEx, DC, MC, V. **Map** p276 G4.

A grand old Victorian building is the unlikely haven for African artefacts from all over the continent. You can easily get lost here among the three floors of craft-crammed rooms. Among the art, artefacts, antiques and jewellery are fertility figurines and masks. A resident traditional healer will cure you of 'drunkedness and financial troubles' among a host of other ills, and seamstresses can kit you out in custom-made traditional attire on their sewing machines in no time. And when the relentless bartering gets you down, grab a seat on the balcony of the upstairs coffee shop and enjoy the African tunes.

▶ *For more African shopping experiences, try Greenmarket Square; see p132.*

Prestwich Memorial Building & Garden
St Andrew's Square (021 487 2755).

This modern rectangular ossuary houses the remains of more than 2,500 exhumed bodies that were discovered on a building site in Green Point in 2003. The unmarked graves are believed to have been those of slaves, servants and other underprivileged Cape Town inhabitants from the 17th and 18th centuries, and the memorial pays tribute to these forgotten people and the contribution they made to building the city into what it is today. At the time of writing the city was still in search of a permanent curator for the building, but visits can be organised by arrangement.

FREE Rust & Vreugd
78 Buitenkant Street (021 464 3280/www.iziko. org.za/rustvreugd). **Open** 8.30am-4.30pm Tue-Thur. **Admission** free; donation appreciated. **Map** p276 H4.

This tranquil house – seen as the finest surviving example of an 18th-century Cape Dutch farmhouse – is set in what is now a particularly unglamorous industrial length of lower Buitenkant Street. Behind the peach-coloured walls lies a period-style secret garden landscaped according to its original 1798 design, with hedges, walkways and a gazebo. The impressive William Fehr art collection provides a glimpse into life in the early Cape colony.

FREE South African Slave Church Museum
40 Long Street (021 423 6755). **Open** 9am-4pm Mon-Fri; 9am-noon daily during school holidays. **Admission** free. **Map** p276 G4.

Founded by a certain Reverend Vos in 1799, the South African Missionary Society was formed in an effort to convert slaves to Christianity, and this inconspicuous structure in Long Street was built in 1804 as the first official slave church in the country. Today it houses a tiny museum depicting the history of South African missionary work.

> **INSIDE TRACK**
> **TABLE MOUNTAIN**
> **ON THE CHEAP**
>
> Cable car trips to the top of Table Mountain are half-price after 6pm in summer; with the added bonus of catching the sunset for free (*see p55*).

MUSEUM MILE

Running straight as an arrow down the leafy haven of Company's Gardens is the oak-lined pedestrian strip of **Government Avenue**, providing access to Adderley Street, the **National Gallery**, **Houses of Parliament**, the **Iziko Museum** and **Planetarium**, and the **Slave Lodge**.

★ FREE Cape Town Holocaust Centre
88 Hatfield Street, Gardens (021 462 5553/ www.ctholocaust.co.za). **Open** 10am-5pm Mon-Thur, Sun; 10am-1pm Fri. **Admission** free. **Map** p276 G5.

By showing us the faces of some of the six million Jews – as well as gypsies, homosexuals and others – who were murdered during the Holocaust, the Cape Town Holocaust Centre has succeeded in giving an identity to some of those killed. Exhibits consist of text, photos, film, artefacts and re-created environments. They follow the course of the holocaust from the early days of the Nazi Party and its espousal of antisemitism, to the Third Reich and the development of the concentration camp system, and the adoption of the Final Solution. The Centre also focuses on wider issues of racism, with sections on apartheid and the South African experience.

FREE Centre for the Book
62 Queen Victoria Street (021 423 2669/www. centreforthebook.org.za). **Open** 8am-5.30pm Mon-Fri. **Admission** free. **Map** p276 G4.

Just down the road from the Planetarium (*see p54*), stands another eye-catching, domed beauty. This Edwardian building dedicated to all things bookish was created to cultivate a love of reading and writing among young and old, well-read and illiterate. Apart from its involvement with disadvantaged communities, it hosts writing workshops for budding talents. Catch up on the latest offerings from home-grown talents in the central hall, where the newest releases from local publishers are showcased.

★ FREE Company's Gardens
Government Avenue, enter via Adderley Street. **Open** dawn-dusk daily. **Admission** free. **Map** p276 G4.

A symbolic bell silently stands testimony to the slaves who tilled and toiled away in what was once

SIGHTS

The Diamond Works

Complimentary Diamond Cutting Tour.
Jewellery Manufacturing and Individual Designs.
Platinum and Gold Jewellery.
Tanzanite Boutique.
Courtesy Transport Service.

OPERATING HOURS: MON - SUN: 09h00 - 19h00

THE DIAMOND WORKS
www.thediamondworks.co.za

CAPE TOWN CNR. LOWER LONG STREET, FORESHORE, (OPPOSITE THE CTICC)
TEL: +27 (0)21 425 1970 ▪ FAX: +27 (0)21 425 1988 ▪ EMAIL: info@thediamondworks.co.za

FRANSCHHOEK SHOP 1 BIJOUX CENTRE, 58 HUGUENOT STREET, FRANSCHHOEK
TEL: +27 (0)21 876 3318 ▪ FAX: +27 (0)21 876 3319 ▪ EMAIL: info@thediamondworks.co.za

a veggie garden providing sustenance for scurvy-stricken sailors of the Dutch East India Company. The cabbage patches have since made way for grassy lawns and park benches, with a few fish ponds and statues thrown in for good measure. It's an accessible oasis (an estimated 700,000 people a year frequent it), and smack in the middle of a culture cluster including the Iziko South African Museum, Iziko National Gallery and Slave Lodge.

▶ *Buy a pack of peanuts from the vendors and watch the squirrels come out of the oak trees that line the avenue.*

FREE Great Synagogue

88 Hatfield Street, Gardens, entry via Jewish Museum gate (021 465 1405/www.gardens shul.org). **Open** *Tours* 10am-4pm Mon-Thur, Sun. *Services* 7am Mon, Thur; 7.15am Tue, Wed, Fri; 8.30am Sat; 8am Sun. **Admission** free. **Map** p276 G5.

Referred to by its members as the Gardens Shul, Cape Town's oldest practising synagogue was consecrated in 1905, the same year the city appointed its first Jewish mayor, Hyman Liberman. The 1,400-seater Baroque-style structure features stained-glass windows and an interior richly embellished with gold-leafed friezes and mahogany woodwork. When Cape Town's population boomed after World War II, the temple saw many of its members relocating to the 'burbs, but the completion of the Jewish Museum and the Holocaust Centre in 1998 breathed new life into the dwindling congregation.

FREE Houses of Parliament

90 Plein Street (021 403 2266/021 403 2201/ www.parliament.gov.za). **Tours** 10am, noon Mon-Fri. **Admission** free; bring ID/passport. Booking essential at least 1wk in advance. **Map** p276 G4.

Back in 1878 Charles Freeman won the grand sum of £250 prize money for his proposed design of the Houses of Parliament, but things went horribly pear shaped (costs ended up double what the government had bargained for) and Harry Greaves ended up finishing the job in 1885. These buildings have seen their fair share of action through the years, one of the most memorable events being when former prime minister and apartheid devotee, Hendrik Verwoerd, was stabbed to death during a parliamentary session by Dimitri Tsafendas, who later explained that a tapeworm had instructed him to do it. These days, armed with your ID or passport, you can watch a parliamentary sitting unfold from one of the gallery seats, or take a guided tour through the building and find out how this whole democracy thing actually works.

★ Iziko National Gallery

Government Avenue (021 467 4660/www. iziko.org.za/sang). **Open** 10am-5pm Tue-Sun. **Admission** R15; R5 reductions; free under-16s. **No credit cards. Map** p276 G4.

The permanent collection dedicates space to British, Dutch, Flemish and South African art spanning centuries, interspersed with traditional African beadwork and contemporary South African works such as Jane Alexander's hauntingly realistic trio of beasts, *The Butcher Boys.* The temporary exhibitions are the biggest draw, however, featuring both young and established local artists, alongside occasional retrospectives of the likes of Picasso and Marlene Dumas. Recent temporary exhibitions have included work by the 'alternative modernist' Pancho Guedes and an extensive collection of Cecil Skotnes's work.

Iziko Slave Lodge

49 Adderley Street (021 460 8242/www.iziko. org.za/slavelodge). **Open** 10am-5pm Mon-Sat. **Admission** R15; R5 reductions; free under-16s; free public holidays. **Credit** MC, V. **Map** p276 H4.

Completed in 1679, this building at the north-east end of the Company's Gardens was built by the Dutch East India Company to house up to 9,000 slaves, convicts and the mentally ill; it continued to do so until the early 19th century. With no windows apart from tiny slits with bars, and a stream running beneath the Lodge, living conditions were wet, dark and dank. Fork out a few extra bucks for the audio headset and retrace the steps of German salt trader Otto Menzl as he is given the guided tour through the corridors of the slave lodge by a proud VOC official in the 1700s. Through his comments you get a pretty good idea of the squalor these slaves had to live in – the horrible stench, lack of ventilation, no view of the outside world and bedding so wet that slaves preferred to sleep on the floor.

▶ *Around the corner from the Slave Lodge lies a commemorative plaque set into the pavement of Spin Street, marking the spot of the old fir tree under which the slaves were sold.*

Iziko South African Museum

25 Queen Victoria Street (021 481 3800/ www.iziko.org.za/sam). **Open** 10am-5pm daily. **Admission** R15; R5 reductions; free under-15s. **Credit** MC, V. **Map** p276 G4.

This sadly neglected child of the Iziko family recently got a bit of press (albeit bad) when crafty robbers broke into the museum and absconded with a mounted white rhino's horns. Despite its recent brush with fame, there sadly isn't whole lot new happening at this Cape Town icon. If the animal kingdom in all its dusty, taxidermied glory gets your heart racing, though, you won't be disappointed. All creatures great, small and slightly ridiculous get their moment in the sun, whether it's the pesky tsetse fly, the duck-billed platypus or the great blue whale. One definitive SA Museum experience is the perverse pleasure of sitting in the yellow submarine-like sound booth and listening to the yelping whale cries while looking out over their stuffed and skeletised counterparts. Some of the newer expos include the Sunlit Sea World, with its full-sized model of a

SIGHTS

giant squid, and the Shark World section, where you get to examine the business end of a megatooth shark, the world's largest apex predator.

The social history section includes artefacts from prehistory, including stone tools from up to 115,000 years ago, as well as objects from the ancient world, plus furniture, glass, weaponry and much more.

▶ *The natural history section is particularly appealing to children; see p163.*

Planetarium

25 Queen Victoria Street (021 481 3900/www. iziko.org.za/planetarium). **Feature** (phone to check) 2pm Mon-Fri; 1pm, 2.30pm Sat, Sun. **Children's show** 2pm Sat, Sun. **Admission** R20; R10 adults going to a children's show; R6-R8 reductions. **Credit** MC, V. **Map** p276 G4.

The sky is perpetually clear in the domed auditorium of the Iziko Museum's Planetarium. Features vary from live interactive lectures on how to go about spotting the various constellations to prerecorded local and international shows covering topics such as the legitimacy of astrology and celestial clouds, and a range of kids' shows that'll have them begging for their own telescope in no time.

▶ *For more, see p163.*

FREE St George's Cathedral

5 Wale Street (021 424 7360/www.stgeorges cathedral.com). **Open** 8.30am-4.30pm Mon-Fri. **Admission** free; donation appreciated. **Services** 7.15am, 1.15pm Mon-Fri; 8am Sat; 7am, 8am, 10am, 7pm Sun. *Evensong* 7pm Sun Sept-May; 6pm Sun June-Aug. **Map** pp76 G4.

Even if you're not religious, this beautiful Victorian structure inspires a bit of silence and contemplation about the human condition. Its elaborate stained-glass windows depict not only a lily-white Jesus figure, but also a black Christ and a panel dedicated to Mahatma Gandhi. Known as the People's Church, it was central in the fight against apartheid. Its members openly rejected the rules of the government, opening its doors to all races and regularly drawing huge crowds of protesters to listen to Archbishop Desmond Tutu and other speakers. Today the cathedral's ten church bells ring out triumphantly every Sunday morning and evening. If you'd like to see the bellringers in action, pop into one of the regular practice sessions held every Tuesday at 7.30pm.

★ South African Jewish Museum

88 Hatfield Street (021 465 1546/www.sajewish museum.co.za). **Open** 10am-5pm Mon-Thur, Sun; 10am-2pm Fri. **Admission** R50; R15-R35 reductions. **Credit** DC, MC, V. **Map** p276 G5.

Built according to the same proportions as King Solomon's temple, the beautiful Old Synagogue (South Africa's first) was built in 1863, and serves as the entrance to the rest of the Jewish Museum, which was founded by Mendel Kaplan in 2000. It traces the history of South African Jewry from the

INSIDE TRACK
CAPE MALAY COOKING
SAFARIS

Find out what goes into making the perfect Cape Malay curry: Andula's cooking safaris include a walking tour of the Bo-Kaap and a cooking workshop (021 790 2592, www.andulela.com).

first Lithuanian settlers who arrived in the 1800s to the present day. Large amounts of information are made very accessible through interactive displays, films and installations. On the top floor are exquisite Judaic artefacts such as a solid silver replica of the Kimberley Synagogue; you can also discover interesting titbits about the diamond rush and ostrich feather boom and learn more about the South African Jewish community's active involvement during the struggle. A serpentine staircase takes visitors to a re-created Lithuanian *shtetl* (small town). Also worth a look is the room housing Isaac Kaplan's impressive collection of delicate Japanese Netsuke figurines.

TABLE MOUNTAIN

The distinctive flat-topped mountain has several hiking trails snaking through a spectacular array of fauna and flora, making it well worth your while to explore up close. Maps are available from the Information Centre at the V&A Waterfront (*see p255*) and the Kirstenbosch National Botanic Gardens (*see p64*). You need to respect the mountain: during spring and autum, gale force winds can cover it in thick mist, and it's easy to lose your way and become disorientated. Never hike on your own, don't take short cuts and no matter how stable the weather seems before the ascent, always take a waterproof windbreaker, map, compass, torch, spare food and enough water.

Lion's Head & Signal Hill

Follow directions to Signal Hill from top of Kloof Nek Road. **Map** p 274 E3.

Once a lunar cycle, werewolves and romantics get to appreciate the full moon in all its glory from one of the most spectacular vantage points in all of Cape Town. To get in on the action, grab your torch, hoodie and a bunch of friends and start this relatively short trek that'll take anywhere from 40 minutes to an hour and a half from the parking area at Signal Hill. Once at the top you'll be rewarded with sensational views over the City Bowl and Atlantic Seaboard. To the east lies Signal Hill; for a more leisurely experience, pack a picnic and some bubbles and take in the scenery from its lookout point, with car park and picnic area.

★ Table Mountain Aerial Cableway

Lower Cable Station, Tafelberg Road (021 424 8181/www.tablemountain.net). **Open** Weather permitting 8am-7pm mid Sept-Oct; 8am-8pm Nov; 8am-9pm Dec, Jan; 8am-8.30 Feb; 8am-7.30pm Mar; 8am-6.30pm Apr; 8am-6pm May-mid Sept. **Admission** cable car R145 return; R76 reductions; under-4s free; R370 family ticket (2 adults, 2 under-18s). **Credit** AmEx, DC, MC, V.

Watch as Cape Town's landscape slowly gets transformed into a contemporary Liliput from the comfort of a rotating cable car. Opened in 1929, the Cableway has transported over 18 million visitors to the iconic flat summit. Meander along the pathways leading to the various jaw-dropping vantage points for views of Table Bay, Robben Island and Cape Point, and then head to the newly renovated Table Mountain Café for a sophisticated bit of tuck served on biodegradable plates. Birthday boys and girls get to go up for free, provided they bring along their IDs.

▶ *For more, see p48* **Magic Mountain***.*

BO-KAAP

Characterised by its steep cobbled streets and multi-coloured houses, this area used to be known as the Malay Quarters in the apartheid years and is still home to a flourishing Muslim community today.

Auwal Mosque

43 Dorp Street. **Map** p276 G4.

Bo-Kaap.

The Auwal Mosque (South Africa's oldest) was established in 1798 by Iman Abdullah Kadi Salaam. Once an Indonesian prince, he was banished to Robben Island for conspiring with the English against the Dutch. During his incarceration he was said to have written out several copies of the Koran from memory, and upon his release in 1793, he established a *madrasa* (Islamic school) in Dorp Stree. Five years later one of his students, Achmat van Bengalen, gave one of his properties to him, which became the Auwal Mosque. Today the building looks very different to what it did at its inception, with only two of the original walls having remained intact after it collapsed back in the 1930s.

Bo-Kaap Museum

71 Wale Street (021 481 3939/www.iziko. org.za/bokaap). **Open** 10am-5pm Mon-Sat. **Admission** R10; R5 reductions; free under-16s. **No credit cards. Map** p276 G3.

Through the years the Bo-Kaap has been known by many names, ranging from Malay Quarter and Slamse Buurt (Islamic neighbourhood) through to Schotcheskloof and Waalendorp. The area, with its multicoloured houses and steep cobbled streets, was developed in the 1760s by Jan de Waal (hence the name Waalendorp); the museum is the only structure built by him that's remained more or less unchanged through the years. It tells the story of the area's Cape Malays, a culturally rich community descended from East African and South-east Asian slaves and responsible for the introduction of Islam to South Africa.

DE WATERKANT

Built in the 19th century by slaves and convicts, this gay-friendly cobbly quarter has undergone a major overhaul, with renovations of historic Somerset Street. Streets are narrow here and parking is difficult, so the best bet is to take a taxi and then explore on foot. Art galleries and pricey boutiques are interspersed with an array of cafés, restaurants and cocktail bars. *See also pp177-81.*

Noon Gun

Military Road, follow the signs from cnr Bloem Street and Buitengracht. **Map** p274 F3.

Even though they know it's coming, many Capetonians still jump out of their skin six days a week as the noon gun emits its loud boom. Head to signal hill just shy of 11.30am to watch the Cape's oldest tradition (begun in 1806) unfold. A member of the South African Navy loads the two cannons with gunpowder, and then the guns are fired. The guns were initially housed in the castle, firing to aid passing ships check the accuracy of their on-board chronometers. As the city's population grew, the noise grew too much, and so the guns were moved to their current location in 1902.

SIGHTS

Atlantic Seaboard

Swanky real estate, clean beaches and cracking ocean sunsets.

Even though the houses along this sapphire stretch are destined for real-estate moguls and trust-fund kids, there's nothing to stop you dreaming about owning a little seaside pad of your own while you cruise along the shores of the Atlantic. This stretch of beach-dotted seaboard starts at the Cape's consumer capital, the **Victoria & Alfred Waterfront**, then heads west to **Green Point**, home to the giant 2010 World Cup stadium and a smattering of clubs, coffee shops and restaurants.

Blink and you'll miss Green Point's suburban morph into **Sea Point** further south, with its iconic promenade and idiosyncratic collection of both upmarket and seedy spots. Meanwhile, **Clifton**, **Camps Bay** and **Llandudno** are suburbs characterised by pristine beaches and moneyed mansions, making it the preferred stomping ground of the Mother City's wealthy and well-known.

Map p273	Restaurants &
Hotels p85	Cafés p109
	Pubs & Bars p126

V&A WATERFRONT

glorified shopping mall

Dock Road, Foreshore (021 408 7600/ www.waterfront.co.za). **Open** *Shops* 9am-9pm Mon-Sat; 10am-9pm Sun. *Craft Market and Wellness Centre* 9.30am-6pm daily. *Restaurants & bars* open late. **Credit** AmEx, DC, MC, V.

In 1860, Queen Victoria's second son, Alfred, tipped a ceremonial bucket load of stones into the sea,

thus initiating the construction of Cape Town's harbour. If only he and his mother could have foreseen the vast waterside development now bearing their name today…

Armed with a credit card or two, Cape Town's sprawling harbour can provide an impressive dose of retail therapy with its myriad shops, restaurants and other attractions. From the mall that draws in shopaholics with its brand-name heavy boutiques and high-street chain stores, to the kid-luring Two Oceans Aquarium, and touristy beacons like the Clock Tower Precinct and Maritime Museum, the V&A is pretty much a guaranteed stop on most visitors' itineraries – especially given that it's also the departure point for ferries to Robben Island and the museum that bears its name. *Photo p58.*

Clock Tower Precinct

V&A Waterfront (021 405 4500). **Map** p275 H1.
Now a maritime mall-cum-heritage site, the brick-red octagonal clock tower was built in 1882 as the port captain's office, so he could check the

Secret beaches

Dip your toes into these hidden waters.

To avoid squealing kids, whirring jet-skis and wayward Frisbees, head to one of these secluded sandy shores for some undisturbed rest and relaxation.

BETA BEACH
Map p273 A9.
It's easy to miss this sandy patch at the footsteps to a series of private residences in the posh suburb of Bakoven, situated a mere ten minutes' drive from the city centre. Once you find it, though, you'll realise why locals are so secretive about it. The postage-stamp-sized beach is flanked by big boulders, which makes it great for swimming as well as uninterrupted sunbathing. To get there from the city, follow Victoria Road past Camps Bay, then turn right into Beta Road. From there, look out for a small walkway between houses leading to the beach.

OUDEKRAAL
Map p273 A9.
Another well-kept secret, Oudekraal, lies right next door to Beta Beach. It proffers a protected cove at the bottom of a steep set of stairs, which is surrounded by a thicket of milkwood trees. Since this area forms part of the Table Mountain National Park, there's a R10 entrance fee, but it's a negligible amount to pay for the splendour that waits inside. To get there, take the first signposted right turn after passing the Twelve Apostles Hotel on Victoria Road.

SMITSWINKELBAAI
Further out of town, and heading in the direction of Cape Point, keep a lookout for the tiny gravelled parking area by the side of the road between Simon's Town and the Cape of Good Hope Nature Reserve. Once there, dash across the road and commence the 15-minute downward amble along the overgrown footpath until you reach the unspoilt, isolated Smitswinkelbaai. The view of the lush valley is well worth the extra effort involved in getting here and the calm water makes for great snorkelling.

TIETIESBAAI
Naughtily named Tietiesbaai is another far-flung cove offering respite from the masses. Situated in the Cape Columbine Reserve on the West Coast, it boasts carpets of colourful wild flowers in spring and a guaranteed soundtrack of silence thanks to the prohibition of anything that blares, barks, roars and whirrs. Get there from the city by taking the R27 turnoff from the N1 and making a left turn on to the R45 at Vredenburg. Continue straight through until you reach Paternoster, taking a left at the four-way stop and going straight until you see the Tietiesbaai signpost, just under two hours' drive from town.

Beautiful though these secluded beaches are, they're not immune to crime. Always go in a group and never leave your valuables unattended.

SIGHTS

comings and goings of the harbour from the comfort of his mirrored bureau. These days it houses the ruins of the Chavonnes Battery, one of the oldest European structures in the country (dating from 1714 to 1725), which was excavated nearby a couple of years ago. Aside from the history, there's the useful Cape Tourism Office in the small shopping precinct.
▶ *Refuel here with a scrumptious pancake at the popular restaurant Harrie's Pancakes (ground floor, Clock Tower).*

★ Robben Island Museum
Ferries depart from Nelson Mandela Gateway, Clock Tower Precinct, V&A Waterfront (021 413 4220/1/www.robben-island.org.za). **Open** *Museum* 7.30am-7pm daily; closed 1 May. *Ferries* 9am, 11am, 1pm, 3pm daily, weather permitting; book in advance. **Cost** *Ferry & museum* R180;

R90 reductions. **Credit** AmEx, DC, MC, V. **Map** p275 H1.
A symbol both of centuries of cruel oppression and the triumph of hope, Robben Island has become synonymous with the former leader of the free and democratic South Africa, Nelson Rolihlahla Mandela, who spent 18 years in its maximum security prison. For nearly 400 years the island served as a place of banishment – not just for supposed criminals but also for many other unwanted members of society, including lepers and the mentally ill. It was declared a World Heritage Site in 1999. The blinding-white limestone quarry, where political prisoners toiled away doing hard labour in the blazing heat, and Mandela's claustrophobic cell in the prison are but a few of the harrowing reminders of the injustices carried out during the apartheid era, and of the final defeat of the regime. Fascinating and inspirational, Robben Island is a must-visit.

V&A Waterfront. *See p56.*

FREE SA Maritime Museum

Union Castle Building, V&A Waterfront (021 405 2880/www.iziko.org.za/maritime). **Open** 10am-5pm daily. **Admission** Donations appreciated. **No credit cards**. **Map** p274 G1.

This small museum, appropriately located at the V&A Waterfront, displays models of ships that have come and gone from this port city over the last hundred years or so. It boasts the largest collection of model ships in the country as well as some interesting information on the whaling industry, local wrecks and the history of Table Bay. Outside, you can board SAS Somerset and a coal-fired steam tug for a nose around.

★ Two Oceans Aquarium

Dock Road, V&A Waterfront (021 418 3823/ www.aquarium.co.za). **Open** 9.30am-6pm daily. **Admission** R82; R38-R65 children; under-4s free. **Credit** AmEx, DC, MC, V. **Map** p275 H2.

This underwater wonderland offers some of the most bizarre sea life you might ever care to meet – schools of unicorn fish, lumo jellyfish and honeycombed moray eels all get their moment in the spotlight, and, of course, there's also an abundance of cuter creatures to keep the little 'uns happy. Still capitalising on the popularity of the little clownfish from *Finding Nemo*, there's a tubular feature showing about a zillion colourful critters swimming around. However, the I&J Predator Tank is the undisputed pièce de résistance, with its mob of ocean predators, including ragged tooth sharks, blue stingrays and black mussel crackers, all drifting together in seeming harmony – until feeding time, that is.
► *For more, see p162 Children.*

GREEN POINT

As the 2010 World Cup looms, Green Point, home to the city's new football stadium, is abuzz with soccer fever.

Green Point Market

Parking lot, Bowling Green, Green Point (021 439 4805). **Open** 9am-6pm Sun. **Map** p274 F1.

As is the case with all Cape Town flea markets, African objets d'art abound in this buzzing Sunday bazaar just shy of the hammering and cement-pouring at the up-and-coming Green Point Stadium. It's not exactly a hub for necessities, and you'll have to fight your way through a heck of a lot of Fong-Kong clutter before you happen upon a genuinely valuable relic, but it's worth a visit if you're after last-minute kitsch souvenirs.
► *For more, see p133.*

Green Point Stadium Visitor Centre

Vlei Road, Green Point (021 430 0410/ www.greenpointstadiumvc.co.za). **Open** *Visitor centre tours* Mon-Fri 10am, 2pm; Sat 10am, noon.

Stadium tours 5.30pm Mon-Fri; 1.30pm Sat. **Admission** R100. **Credit** MC, V.
If you get yourself kitted out in a hard hat and reflector vest you can take a guided tour of the construction site of this mammoth 70,000-seater stadium. There's a video at the end where you'll be bombarded with head-spinning trivia.
▶ *For more, see p60* **Fever Pitch**.

SEA POINT

This central seaside stretch with its snaking promenade is much loved by stressed-out city types looking for a bit of space as well as dog-walkers, Rollerbladers and strolling old-timers.

Mouille Point Lighthouse
100 Beach Road, Mouille Point (021 449 5172).
Open 9am-12.30pm,1-3.30pm Mon-Fri.
Admission R16; R8-R10 reductions.
No credit cards.

This candy-striped beacon of light dates from 1824 and was declared a national monument almost 40 years ago. In the heyday of the Cape colony shipwrecks were a common sight in Table Bay and the lighthouse still serves its original purpose, as well as being open to the public for an inside peek during weekdays.

Mouille Point Promenade
Beach Road, Mouille Point.
This promenade is about as family-friendly as they come, with its putt-putt course, miniature train and maze all vying for your little ones' attention. There's also a pretty decent supply of scenester cafés along here.

Sea Point Promenade
Beach Road, Sea Point (021 434 3341 for swimming pool). **Open** Winter 8.30am-5pm daily. Summer 7am-7pm daily. **Admission Pool** R13; R5-R7 reductions. **No credit cards**.
Map p272 B3.
Offering sea-sprayed solace to everyone from power-walking gym bunnies to pram-pushing mothers, this strip on the lip of the Atlantic is the ideal spot for a people-watching picnic. Kids and the young at heart are spoiled for choice when it comes to traditional seaside action with lovely merry-go-rounds, swings and slides all calling out to be used. Serious swimmers can perfect their stroke at the open-air Sea Point swimming pool complex, while children can bomb each other from the spring-boarded pool.

SIGHTS

Clifton. *See p60.*

CLIFTON

Four divergent beaches rub shoulders along this breathtaking shore south of Sea Point. Four seasons in one day is pretty much what you can expect from this popular haunt, frequented by everyone from touch rugby-playing jocks to pretty boys topping up their tans.

Coming from the Camps Bay (south) side, you'll find **Fourth Beach,** which is the biggest, most crowded beach of the lot – a place where the likelihood of being struck by a wayward Frisbee is quite high. The calm waters near the boulders on the left-hand side is the ideal swimming spot for kids, should they care to brave the freezing water, that is. **Third Beach**, aka C3, is where the tank-topped and toned gay crowd soak up the sun, while **Second Beach** sees sun-kissed scenesters getting in a bit of topless tanning. Last in the line and popularity is the quieter **First Beach**. Whichever you favour, you'll need to tackle plenty of steps to gain access.

CAMPS BAY

Dubbed the St-Tropez of Cape Town, this classy cove offers an array of swish bars and restaurants, Riviera-style palm trees and yachts bobbing on the water. As you cruise down the Victoria Road stretch, the rows of ritzy drinking holes with their blinged-up, tanned-to-a-tee and beautiful patrons mean that you're unlikely to be winning any best-dressed trophies should you turn up in flip-flops and a weather-beaten sarong. At the northern, and less busy, end of the beach surfers wait for a few killer waves; at the southern end, you can practise your

Fever Pitch

How Cape Town is gearing up for the World Cup in 2010.

Excitement is running high and locals are dusting off their *vuvuzelas* in anticipation of the biggest sporting event in the country's history. The run-up to the arrival of the FIFA World Cup in 2010 has seen Cape Town buzzing with activity. Roads have been revamped, the transport system has been overhauled and the airport has been upgraded, while Green Point Stadium has slowly risen.

Watching the yellow cranes hovering over Green Point like nosy, mechanical giraffes has made it hard for locals to remember a time when all this seemed like an impossible feat. Getting the stadium off the ground was a battle – cost controversies, legal scuffles, complaining home-owners, striking construction workers and public outcries concerning the distance between the stadium and its fan base had to be conquered. But everything eventually fell back on track; and as of summer 2009, the contractors looked set to make the December 2009 deadline.

IN THE BEGINNING

Green Point Common, on which the stadium is being built, has a colourful history dating back to the 18th century. Originally it was much larger, stretching all the way from Signal Hill to the ocean. But since its inception, various sporting pursuits, including 18th-century sailing regattas (there used to be a shallow 'vlei' on the common), horse racing, cycling and golf, have taken place here. Some of the country's earliest rugby and cricket matches were also played here.

SIGHTS

bobbing skills in the tidal pool. The current here is strong and there's no resident lifeguard, so take care if you venture into the water.

LLANDUDNO

On a wind-free day, this small, secluded cove wedged in the valley of the Twelve Apostles mountain range is worth the trek from the car park (which gets filled up quickly). A great hideaway for sundowners and an icy dip, Llandudno offers it all – great surf conditions, a perfect swimming sea (if you can bear the cold, that is), bulbous boulders for kids to scramble over. It's also the ideal spot for daydreamers wishing upon a towering condo of their very own (look back inland from the beach to see first-hand what money and bad taste has brought this way so far). This is the last beach

to see the sun, so it's a great place to enjoy a sunset in the company of friends (bear in mind that alcohol is forbidden here).

SANDY BAY

Naturists let it all hang out at this *au naturel* dune-shielded seaside spot, conveniently out of the way. It'll take you about 20 minutes' walk from Llandudno's parking lot before you see the shimmery sands of this nudist Shangri-La. Since it's so off the beaten track and ice-cream vendors shy away from this nudey neck of the woods, make sure to bring ample refreshments. Its seclusion makes it very popular with gay men over the weekends, but unfortunately has also made it a target for muggings, so don't go wandering around on your lonesome.

FACTS AND FIGURES

The R2.85 billion development will have seats for 68,000 punters and the entire structure will be a dizzying 15 storeys high. To guarantee neighbouring home-owners a good night's sleep, the walls will be covered with noise-reducing cladding, while the glass roof – designed by German architects and built in New York – will bounce noise back into the stadium. Inside, amenities will include four television studios, 250 VIP suites, a medical centre and a police station.

The grass for the pitch was planted on a Stellenbosch farm in December 2008. To be able to withstand heavy traffic and comply with strict FIFA guidelines, it has to be of an exceptionally high standard. Once planted, the surface has to be 28 milimetres high at all times, and mowed by groundskeepers in both a horizontal and vertical direction.

SOCCER MAGIC

To whet fans' appetites a visitors' centre opened its doors to the public in 2007 (*see p58*). Delights include a tour of the construction site, a virtual tour of the stadium and a theatre production outlining the history of the Green Point common.

2010 AND BEYOND

The hope is that the effects of 2010 will linger long. FIFA, the City of Cape Town, the South African government and the Local World Cup Organising Committee are placing a strong emphasis on leaving behind 'legacy benefits'. These will include more green community spaces across the city, with Green Point Common being upgraded to a sports and recreation precinct (an urban park on the common is also on the cards).

The tourism industry is also set for a whopping boost: an estimated 500,000 soccer fans will descend on the country during the event, while the upgrades to the transport system and world-wide press coverage should, it's hoped, benefit the industry for years to come.

GREEN POINT MATCH DATES, 2010

Round 1: Friday 11 June
    Monday 14 June
    Friday 18 June
    Monday 21 June
    Thursday 24 June
Round 2: Tuesday 29 June
Quarter-final: Sunday 3 July
Semi-final: Tuesday 6 July

SOCCER SOUTH AFRICANISMS

Learn these terms and cheer like a local...

Laduma! A cheer often heard when a goal is scored; from isiZulu, meaning 'it thunders'.
Vuvuzela A brightly coloured, plastic, trumpet-like instrument; much loved by local soccer fans.

SIGHTS

Southern Suburbs

Beer, wine and sports loom large in the city's leafy south.

Although the Southern Suburbs aren't exacly as sexy as the City Bowl, they do offer a certain leafy brand of charm. First mention goes to **Newlands**, its biggest draw being the vast, picnic-perfect **Kirstenboch National Botanical Gardens**, which hosts a popular series of sundowner concerts each summer. Those preferring their outdoor excursions slightly more action-packed should head to the **Newlands Rugby Stadium** and **Sahara Park** cricket ground, and since spectatorship is such thirsty work, a pit stop at the neighbouring **SAB Breweries** should definitely be worked into the itinerary. The adjoining suburb of **Rondebosch** is an academic enclave, housing the University of Cape Town, as well as a collection of museums, monuments and mills once belonging to imperialist Cecil John Rhodes. Further south lies the town of **Constantia**, with a series of beautiful wine estates (some of them boasting accompanying award-winning restaurants) in its surrounding region.

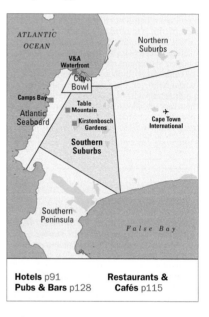

Hotels p91
Pubs & Bars p128

Restaurants &
Cafés p115

CONSTANTIA & AROUND

Towering mountains, old Cape Dutch houses – and, above all, vineyards – characterise Constantia and the area around it.

Buitenverwachting

Klein Constantia Road, Constantia (021 794 5190/www.buitenverwachting.com). **Open** 9am-5pm Mon-Fri; 9am-1pm Sat. **Credit** AmEx, DC, MC, V.

Watch out for kamikaze squirrels as you cruise towards the manor house at the end of the oak-flanked drive, with its views of hilly vineyards. Stroll the bucolic grounds to work up a thirst and head off to the tasting room to sample the award-winning wines: the fruity, easy-drinking Blanc de Noir, and flagship wine, Christine, both being well worth the dent in your pocket. Indulge your stimulated appetite in style at the swanky restaurant, or

grab a bottle of the estate's Brut Cap Classique for a bubbly picnic under the trees. *See also p65* **Urban Terroir**; for the restaurant, *see p115*.

Constantia Uitsig

Spaanschemat River Road, Constantia (021 794 1810/www.constantia-uitsig.com). **Open** *Tastings* 9am-4.30pm Mon-Fri; 10am-4.30pm Sat, Sun, public holidays. *Sales* 9am-5pm Mon-Fri; 10am-5pm Sat, Sun, public holidays. **Cost** *Informal tastings* fewer than 8 free; 8 or more R20 per person. *Formal tastings* available by arrangement. **Credit** AmEx, DC, MC, V.

This golden child of the South African wine industry offers just about everything bar the partridge in the pear tree. Viticulturalist André Rousseau has been behind the success of award-winning wines, while the three estate restaurants, including the award-winning La Colombe, continue to attract enthusiastic patrons. Add to this a four-star hotel with a panoramic vineyard vista and a sophisticated, tranquil spa that gives a whole new meaning to indulgent opulence (the African body-butter massage is a must), and you've just about ticked off all the boxes that make this wine estate top of the pops. *See also p65* **Urban Terroir**; for the restaurant, *see p116*.

★ Groot Constantia

Groot Constantia Road, Constantia (021 794 5128/www.grootconstantia.co.za). **Open** *May-Oct* 9am-5pm daily. *Nov-Apr* 9am-6pm daily. **Admission** *Manor House Museum* R10 adults; R5 reductions. *Informal tastings* R25 (5 wines). *Cellar tours* R30 (includes a tasting). **Credit** AmEx, DC, MC, V.

Founded in 1685 and South Africa's first vineyard, Groot Constantia Estate was the grape-stomping ground of Simon van der Stel, first governor of the Cape, back in the day. Through the years, the estate's wines have tickled the palates of kings and conquerors and had poets and authors waxing lyrical about their ambrosial eminence. The orientation centre, imposing old manor house and the Cloete Cellar wine museum cover the history of winemaking and the estate. Or head straight for the cellar for a guided tour and a chance to taste what all the fuss is about, before heading off to one of the two restaurants to enjoy the vista with a few glasses of *vino. See also p65* **Urban Terroir**.

Klein Constantia

Klein Constantia Road, Constantia (021 794 5188/www.kleinconstantia.com). **Open** 9am-5pm Mon-Fri; 9am-1pm Sat. **Tastings** free for groups of up to 5; R20 pre-booked tastings of 8 or more. **Credit** AmEx, DC, MC, V.

**INSIDE TRACK
ROSE PICKING**

Why buy a bouquet smothered in gaudy cellophane if you can personally select and pick your own roses? **Chart Farm**, a lovely rose farm overlooking the Constantia Valley, gives you the chance to do just that (Klaassens Road, Wynberg Park, Wynberg, 021 761 0434, www.chartfarm.co.za).

The reputation of the Klein Constantia estate's revered Vin de Constance muscadel recently transcended the human realm when a young African goshawk's curiosity got the better of him and he swooped in for a closer peep into the cellar where the precious bottles were being wax-sealed. Apart from the expertise of resident winemaker Adam Mason, the historic estate's top terroir is also said to play a huge part in creating their beguiling range of wine that is served in some of the top restaurants in the world. *See also p65* **Urban Terroir**.

Steenberg Vineyards

Steenberg roads, Tokai (021 713 2211/www.steenberg-vineyards.co.za). **Open** 9am-4.30pm Mon-Fri; 10am-4pm Sat, Sun, public holidays. **Tastings** free; R20 per person for groups of 10 or more. **Credit** AmEx, DC, MC, V.

It's believed that Catharina Ras, the tough-as-nails first owner of Steenberg, originally named her farm Swaaneweide ('the feeding place of the swans') in a bout of nostalgia when she mistook a few splashing spur-winged geese for the swans of her German

SIGHTS

Tokai Forest. *See p64.*

Kirstenbosch National Botanical Gardens

NEWLANDS

★ Kirstenbosch National Botanical Gardens

Rhodes Drive, Newlands (021 799 8783/ www.sanbi.org). **Open** *Summer* 8am-7pm daily. *Winter* 8am-6pm daily. **Admission** R35 adults; R10-R20 reductions; free under-6s. **Credit** AmEx, DC, MC, V.

In 1913 a professor Pearson, then chair of botany at the South African college, set about developing this vast botanical garden into what it is today – one of the country's most popular visitor attractions. Neatly tended lawns tumble down the eastern slopes of Table Mountain, punctuated by flowering gardens, ponds and indigenous trees all knitted together by paved pathways. The grounds have a tangle of walking trails leading visitors to spots like the Bath in the Dell, a wild almond hedge planted by Jan van Riebeeck back in the 1600s, and a lane of gigantic yellowwoods housing a few shy owls. Heading towards the fynbos-covered foot of Table Mountain, you'll find the beginnings of the Skeleton Gorge and Nursery Ravine hiking trails. The weekly Sunday summer sundowner concerts have become a tradition and feature bands like Fokofpolisiekar, Goldfish and Freshly Ground. *See also p183.*

FREE Josephine Mill

Josephine Mill Museum, Boundary Road, Newlands (021 686 4939/www.josephinemill. co.za). **Open** 9am-4pm Mon-Fri. **Admission** free. **Tours** R20 adults; R10 concessions. **Credit** AmEx, DC, MC, V.

In 1818 Johannes Dreyer built a watermill on the banks of the Liesbeeck River. Upon his death, his widow Maria employed a young lad by the name of Jacob Letterstedt (who had immigrated from Sweden to escape bad debt) to run the mill, and ended up marrying him a few years later. More than 20 years younger than Maria (a photo of her scowling face is still up in the museum today), Jacob is said to have fallen in love with the crown princess of Sweden, Josephine, and built a second watermill as a testament of his love for her. The on-site museum houses a few relics from the mill's heyday, and there are guided tours including a peek into the gigantic engine room, where you can see cogs working to produce the stone-ground flour sold in the shop. Incidentally, Letterstedt went on to own the Mariendal Brewery, which still stands across the road at the SAB Breweries.

Newlands Breweries (SAB)

3 Main Road, Newlands (021 658 7255/021 658 7511/www.sablimited.co.za). **Tours** 11am Mon, Tue, Thur, Fri. Booking essential. **Admission** R10, no under-18s.

Be sure to book well in advance for a guided tour where you can see how the guys at SAB transform

---

hometown, Lübeck. Unlucky in love (she married five times and was generally referred to as the Widow Ras) Catharina focused her energy on toiling away on the piece of land that was granted to her by Simon van der Stel. Today winemaker Ruth Penfold carries on the legacy of talented women associated with Steenberg, roping in accolades for her superbly crafted wines. If you're up for more than just a taste and a trundle on the estate, raise the stakes a notch and book into the luxurious Steenberg Hotel, where you can drink a toast to the original *femme extraordinaire* in the hotel's popular restaurant, Catharina's (*see p115*). *See also p65* **Urban Terroir**.

Tokai Forest

Tokai Road (021 712 7471). **Open** *Picnic area* 8am-6pm (last admission 5pm) daily. **Admission** R5 per person; R5 vehicles; R20 cyclists; R30 horse-riding day pass.

This huge pine forest, popular with braai-tong wielding, mushroom-picking families, is snaked with well-marked hiking routes. The hardest route is the two-and-a-half-hour trek to Elephant's Eye Cave, which offers breathtaking views of the surrounding area. The arboretum houses more than 247 tree species from across the globe, first introduced in 1885 by Cape Colony forest conservationist Joseph Lister. Despite the trees alien vegetation status, the arboretum was declared a National Heritage Site, and the trees thus escaped destruction by the Parks Board.

SIGHTS

Urban Terroir

Winning wineries wait within the city limits.

Keen on a taste of Cape wine, but pressed for time? Don't despair, there are two dedicated wine routes within greater Cape Town – both with a terroir best suited for white wines, but capable of producing some reds that are worth writing home about too.

The **Constantia Wine Route** is the busiest, with five farms (*see p62*) and the oldest vineyards in the country. It was at one of them that Cape Governor Simon van der Stel planted the vines that produced Vin de Constance, a sweet, fortified wine so coveted by European aristocracy that Jane Austen wrote about it and Napoleon chose it to accompany him into exile. In the 1980s winemakers at Klein Constantia began reproducing it – you can visit the tasting room for a sip. Meanwhile, those interested in the history of the South African wine industry can visit the manor house at Groot Constantia and the orientation centre that explores the history of the farm. And vineyards are home to some of the country's top restaurants too, like Constantia Uitsig's French-inspired La Colombe.

The **Durbanville Wine Route** is for those seeking something more off the beaten track. There are nine farms (*see p75*), ranging from historic estates to swanky, modern wineries and cosy boutique estates where you will most likely meet the winemaker in the tasting room. Sauvignon blanc is king here, with most of the wineries touting it as their signature wine. Recently the route also started winning awards for its Merlots. There's good food here too: Nitida's stylish Cassia restaurant is popular, while children love Nitida Café's jumping castle and sweet-laden food-art station.

Each route offers award-winning wines as well as its own unique charms; so flip a coin if you must, choose a direction and get tasting.

humble hops and malted barley into the golden elixir responsible for turning civilised gentlemen at the neighbouring Newlands rugby stadium into foul-mouthed *naartjie*-wielding ruffians. Once you've worked up a sufficient appetite, head down to the Letterstedt Pub and taste all that fermentation and filtration come to fruition. Those interested in the history of South Africa's beer industry can check out relics from SAB's heyday in the museum, such as the old-school Lion Beer locomotive that was used to offload barley at the Mariendal Brewery.

Newlands Rugby Stadium

11 Boundary Road, Newlands (021 659 4600/ www.wprugby.com). **Tours** *Gateway to Newlands (021 686 2151/www.newlandstours.co.za).* **Times** Mon-Fri; phone or see website for details. **Tickets** R58 adults; R36-R40 reductions. **No credit cards.** Sorry folks, no guitars, drums or vuvuzelas allowed in this stadium. At 119 years, it is the second-oldest rugby stadium in the world. Enthusiasts and stalkers alike can retrace their heroes' steps through the players' entrance, locker rooms and surgery and ultimately follow the light at end of the tunnel to the chalky field where all the bone-crunching action goes down. *See also p196.*

Sahara Park Newlands

Cricket Ground, 146 Camp Ground Road, Newlands (www.capecobras.co.za). **Tours** *Gateway to Newlands (021 686 2152/ www.newlandstours.co.za).* **Times** Mon-Fri; phone or check website for details. **Tickets** R44 adults; R28-R30 reductions. **No credit cards.** Home to the Cape Cobras, this emerald cricket ground is less than a drop-kick away from the rugby stadium, and since being a cricket spectator is such thirsty work, it's also conveniently located up next to the South African Breweries. With Table Mountain keeping an ever-watchful eye on the scores, this is definitely one of the country's more scenic stadiums, so it should come as no surprise that it was chosen to host the opening ceremony of the 2003 Cricket World Cup. During the guided tours fans can get a thrilling behind-the-scenes glimpse of the president's suite, the hoity-toity South Club, the scoreboard control room and the third umpire's booth. *See also p196.*

FREE South African Rugby Museum

Sports Science Institute, Boundary Road, Newlands (021 686 2151/www.newlands tours.co.za). **Open** 8am-4.30pm Mon-Thur; 8am-4pm Fri. **Admission** free. **Tours** (incl tour of Newlands Rugby Stadium) R52 adults; R33-R35 reductions. **No credit cards.** The revered rugby ball has come a far way from its inflated sheep's bladder days, and – should you be the type of person who is interested in this sort of thing – there's a whole section in the museum documenting the ball's evolution and manufacturing process. Among the other exhibits are rugby props and paraphernalia ranging from the country's first rugby caps to a replica of the

1995 World Cup trophy and the magic rugby boot that made it all possible. Old timers can enjoy a blast from the past with the push of a button as radio commentators from the '50s, '60s and '70s talk (shout, actually) them through legendary tries and kicks, and kids from the TV generation can sit down on the old Newlands rugby benches and watch an omnibus of memorable rugby reruns.

Sports Science Institute of South Africa

Boundary Road, Newlands (021 659 5600/ www.ssisa.com). **Tours** *Gateway to Newlands (021 686 2151/www.newlandstours.co.za).* **Times** Mon-Fri; phone or check website for details. **Tours** R25 adults; R12-R17 reductions. **No credit cards**.

There's nothing sissy about some of the buffed-up individuals strolling through the high-tech halls of SSISA. This place is all about applying science to turn you from zero to well-toned hero. The on-site specialists range from biokineticists and physiotherapists to nutritionists and psychologists; all lend a hand in your optimal sporting development, whether you're a boep-bearing omie looking to lose a few, or a Springbok rugby player with a sprained ankle. But don't take our word for it; head on over and ask to be taken on a tour of the facilities and check them out for yourself. *See also p200.*

OBSERVATORY

A slightly rough-around-the-edges district that's popular with students, artists and bohemians.

Transplant Museum

Block E, Groote Schuur Hospital, Old Main Building, Hospital Road, Observatory (021 404 1967/www.capegateway.gov.za/gsh). **Tours** 9am, 11am, 1pm, 3pm, 5pm daily. **Admission** R100 adults (R200 for foreign visitors); R35 reductions. **Credit** MC, V.

Rhodes Memorial.

Get to know more about Dr Christiaan Barnard and the day he made history when he transplanted the world's first human heart in 1967. The attention to detail in this slick museum is astounding – from the carbon copy of Denise Darvall's (the first heart donor's) bedroom, to reams of correspondence, including a reluctant congratulatory letter from Barnard's American counterpart, Dr Norman Shumway. There are also quirky artefacts such as the bumper sticker exclaiming 'Drivers beware: Barnard is waiting'. Step through the painstakingly re-created operating theatres where eerily realistic wax sculptures of Dr Barnard and his team are displayed, shown giving first heart recipient Louis Washkansky a new lease of life, complete with a soundtrack of clinking scalpels.

RONDEBOSCH

Home to the University of Cape Town, this suburb is also the location of the historic Groote Schuur Estate, where Cecil Rhodes once lived.

Groote Schuur Estate

Klipper Road, Rondebosch (083 414 7961). **Tours** by appointment. **Admission** R75 (including tea and refreshments). **No credit cards**.

The former Cape Town residence of the state president, the gabled Groote Schuur ('Big Barn') was originally built in 1667 to serve as the VOC's granary before it was bought by Cecil John Rhodes in 1893 and converted into a grand mansion and

---

INSIDE TRACK
THUNDER CITY

Fancy starring in your own private version of *Top Gun*? **Thunder City** boasts the largest civilian-owned collection of ex-military jets in the world, including the world's last four English Electric Lightings. You can be one of only a handful of people on the planet to see the curvature of the earth from 15,240 metres (50,000 feet). But be warned, the experience comes with a hefty price tag (Site 10, Tower Road, Cape Town International Airport, 021 934 8007, www.thundercity.com).

office by his chum Herbert Baker. Along with the building, Rhodes bought several other properties on Table Mountain's eastern slopes during the late 19th century, including the summer house of Rudyard Kipling, the Woolsack, and Mostert's Mill (*see p67*). On the slopes above the UCT campus you can still see the ruins of the lion enclosure known as the Groote Schuur Zoo, which replaced the original cage-like structure commissioned by Rhodes in 1897. Rhodes died in 1910 and bequeathed his estate to the nation; an elaborate neoclassical shrine was erected in his memory two years later (*see right*).

Irma Stern Museum

Cecil Road, Rosebank (021 685 5686/www. irmastern.co.za). **Open** 10am-5pm Tue-Sat. **Admission** R10 adults; R5 reductions. **No credit cards.**

Hidden behind a rather unattractive wall in Cecil Road in Rosebank, an adjoining suburb to Rondebosch, lies the house where one of South Africa's most revered artists lived, painted, and entertained for close to four decades. In comparison with the rest of the museum, the cramped front lobby feels a bit soulless, but as soon as you step into the colourful main house, you get a sense of the intriguing, eccentric character Stern must have been. The collection of artefacts from her travels through Africa and Europe includes a Congolese Buli stool that often features prominently in her paintings, as well as a mob of scary-looking masks from around the world. The red-carpeted sitting room, with ornate, handcrafted furniture, features a green accent wall studded with portraits. She hosted many a dinner party in the dining room, which now houses her collection of religious paintings and sculptures – she had a fondness for biblical themes. The most personal touch in the museum, however, is the re-creation of Stern's studio, complete with easel, muddied tubes of paint and colour-caked easel.

Mostert's Mill

Rhodes Avenue, Mowbray (021 762 5127/ www.capeofgoodhope.org/mmill). **Open** 10am-2.30pm Sat, when milling is in progress. Book well in advance. **Admission** R5; R10 family day ticket. **No credit cards.**

A convenient landmark for out-of-city folk looking for the Rondebosch turn-off, this working windmill (the only one in sub-Saharan Africa) was built in 1796. Gysbert van Reenen used to own the surrounding wheat fields and built the mill to grind his own flour, naming it after his son-in-law, Sybrand Mostert. It was later acquired by the intrepid Cecil John Rhodes. A trundle through the interior will reveal a few interesting titbits on the history of the propelled marvel and how the whole milling business works. It is run by volunteers, and it's best to phone beforehand to arrange a visit.

★ FREE Rhodes Memorial

Groote Schuur Estate, above UCT **Open** 24hrs daily. **Admission** free.

This grandiose shrine, dedicated to imperialist Cecil John Rhodes, was built on his favourite lookout point in 1912, two years after his death. The monument features a steep set of stairs flanked by eight bronze lions leading up to a pillared faux-Greek chamber housing a bronze bust in his image, featuring an inscription by his friend Rudyard Kipling. These days the steps of the memorial are a popular wedding pic backdrop, while the surrounding grounds make for ideal picnicking. Every so often, you'll see a group of amateur artists set up their easels, capturing the panorama on canvas. The on-site Rhodes Memorial Restaurant & Tea Garden (021 689 9151, www.rhodesmemorial.co.za) is open 9am to 5pm daily for full breakfasts, fresh pasta dishes, baguettes, cake and refreshments.

University of Cape Town

Slopes of Devil's Peak, Rondebosch (021 650 3121/www.uct.ac.za).

South Africa's oldest university, the ivy-blanketed buildings on this English campus have seen their fair share of bright minds since its inception in 1829, including Nobel prize laureate JM Coetzee. The university was internationally recognised for its continued opposition to apartheid, back in the day, before liberalism and race equality were in vogue. UCT's arts and drama faculties are situated in its city satellite, Hiddingh Campus, which has two theatres and a gallery.

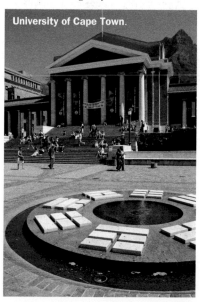
University of Cape Town.

SIGHTS

Southern Peninsula

A crystalline coastline, with warm Indian Ocean currents.

This spectacular, crooked coastline runs from Hout Bay on the west side of the peninsula, past Cape Point, and up the east side to Muizenberg. Perhaps its most appealing virtue is its warmer waters, although sharks do put a slight dampener on the exuberance of beach dwellers. **Hout Bay** is a quaint harbour town, and apart from its beach it is also home to the well-known animal sanctuary, World of Birds. South lies **Cape Point** and its crowning glory, the Cape of Good Hope Nature Reserve, which contains a tangle of hiking trails winding past shipwrecks, lighthouses and secret caves. Next up is the pretty naval alcove of **Simon's Town** – final resting place of the famous seafaring Great Dane, Just Nuisance, and home to a colony of jackass penguins. **Kalk Bay** is the hideaway of choice for cool, arty folk, with a host of top-notch restaurants and cafés, while neighbouring **Fish Hoek** is decidedly less hip but has a great beach. **Muizenberg** is the last stop on the Southern Peninsula stretch, and a prime surfing spot.

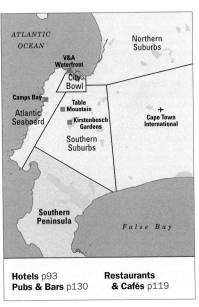

Hotels p93
Pubs & Bars p130
Restaurants & Cafés p119

CAPE POINT

At the tip of the Southern Peninsula lies verdant Cape Point. The vast, beautiful **Cape of Good Hope Nature Reserve** was declared part of the Cape World Heritage Site in 2004. Trails within the park lead to shipwrecks, tidal pools, lighthouses and Antonie's Gat, the hiding place of a slave turned Muslim saint, and you'll be hiking in the company of wildlife including curvy-beaked sugarbirds and cape mountain zebra. If you don't feel like walking, climb aboard the Flying Dutchman funicular that will take you all the way from Cape Point to the upper lighthouse, with its vantage point said to resemble the end of the world.

★ Cape of Good Hope Nature Reserve
Cape Point (021 465 8515/www.capepoint.co.za). **Open** *Oct-Mar* 6am-6pm daily. *Apr-Sept* 7am-5pm daily. **Admission** R60 adults; R10 children. **Credit** AmEx, DC, MC, V.

FREE Cape Point Ostrich Farm
Plateau Road, property number 1051, off M65, opposite entrance to Cape Point (021 780 9294/ www.capepointostrichfarm.com). **Open** 9.30am-5.30pm daily. **Admission** free; R30 guided tours; R10 6-16s. **Credit** AmEx, DC, MC, V.
The weirdest-looking birds, with the longest eyelashes you've ever seen, live at this family-owned ostrich-breeding farm. Each of the 40 pairs have their own private outdoor suite to keep the romance alive (and also to keep a steady supply of eggs coming) and, for a few rands, you can get the inside scoop on the ostrich life cycle. The guided tour takes you through the incubators and breeding rooms, and features interesting titbits on the history of the once-lucrative ostrich-feather trade. There's a coffee shop and a shop selling ostrich leather paraphernalia.

FISH HOEK

The town itself isn't much of a looker (and to make matters worse, alcohol is forbidden here by law) but its lovely sandy beaches make it well worth the drive. **Fish Hoek** and **Clovelly** beaches are family-oriented affairs. There is even a playground for children to tumble around in between ice-creams. It's a great spot for snorkelling too.

Jaeger Walk is named after Fish Hoek's first mayor. The short wheelchair-friendly walkway hugs the False Bay coast, running past boulders and rock pools, from Fish Hoek Beach to **Sunny Cove**. There are cement pavilions along the way, should you decide to sit down and take in the serene surrounds.

HOUT BAY

This harbour town has beach action, a boardwalk and bird-watching opportunities. Nearby Duiker Island is home to a large population of cape fur seals.

Spanning from the beginning of **Chapman's Peak Drive** to the harbour, Hout Bay's kilometre-long expanse of **beach** means that there's space for one and all and sundry, though equestrians and dog walkers are allocated special times. When you've had your fill of the beach, wander across to the Mariner's Wharf bistro for the freshest fishy takeaways; enjoy your chips, crunchy prawns and golden-battered fish on the harbour wall.

Boat Trips to Seal Island

Hout Bay Harbour (021 790 1040/021 790 7278/www.circelaunches.co.za/www.nauticat charters.co.za). **Trips** *Circe Launches* 9.30am, 10.15am daily; all hours, weather permitting Sat, Sun. *Nauticat Charters* 8.45am, 9.45am, 11am, 12.15pm, 2.30pm daily (weather permitting). **Tickets** *Circe Launches* R38 adults; R12 reductions. *Nauticat Charters* R60 adults; R30 reductions. **No credit cards.**
A 40-minute scenic excursion to Duiker Island, home to a squad of blubbery, bewhiskered cape fur seals. Snap away at the doe-eyed pups and their slick and slippery parents barking out warnings. The glass-bottomed boats offer a convenient porthole through which to spy the seals zipping past underwater.

Chapman's Peak Drive ~ab .

Toll road between Hout Bay and Noordhoek (021 790 9163/www.chapmanspeakdrive.co.za). **Cost** R35 minibus (non commercial); R26 light motor vehicles; R17 motorcycle, motor tricycle, motor quad bike. **Credit** MC, V.
Not the best drive to take if you're a passenger prone to car sickness, this long and winding road starts in Hout Bay and bends in and out of the mountain

---

INSIDE TRACK
WHALE OF A TIME

Cape Town offers a multitude of spots from which to spy southern right whales between August and November. Try the **Catwalk** (along the shoreline between Muizenberg and St James), **Jaeger Walk** (between Fish Hoek Beach and Sunny Cove) or simply park off on the **Kalk Bay Harbour** wall. Other top spots are on the coastal road between Fish Hoek and Cape Point, **Chapman's Peak Drive** (toll road between Hout Bay and Noordhoek), **Boyes Drive** between Muizenberg and Kalk Bay (turn into Boyes Drive from Main Road in Muizenberg) or further afield off the R27, the **West Coast coastal road**, between Bloubergstrand and Melkbosstrand.

---

about a hundred times before it ends in Noordhoek. At the time of writing, the Drive was closed until further notice due to rockfalls, but visitors can still drive about halfway up at no charge to enjoy the spectacular views of the bay.

ImiZamo Yethu Township Tours

7263 Mandela Road, ImiZamo Yethu, Hout Bay (083 719 4870/www.suedafrika.net/ imizamoyethu). **Tours** 10.30am, 1pm, 4pm daily. **Cost** R75. **No credit cards.**
A walking tour through this colourful township is just what the doctor ordered if you'd like to explore something slightly out of the area's picture-perfect comfort zone. Visit locals' homes, buy a few snacks

Fish Hoek.

SIGHTS

at the *spaza* shop and play a game of pool at the she-been, with a glass of home-made beer at hand, of course. If you've got any ailments, or simply want to find out more about what the future holds, head to the *sangoma* for a bone-throwing session.
▶ *For more township tours, see p255.*

World of Birds We liked

Valley Road, Hout Bay (021 790 2730/www. worldofbirds.org.za). **Open** *9am-5pm daily. Monkey Jungle 11.30am-1pm, 2-3.30pm daily.* **Admission** R59 adults; R37-R49 reductions. **Credit** AmEx, DC, MC, V.
All squawk and plenty of action, this is the largest bird park in Africa and offers 100 pseudo-tropical walk-through aviaries that'll have bird-lovers in raptures. Over 3,000 species flutter about the place – you'll see everything from quails and cockatoos to owls and ostriches. Around 400 other animal species also live here, the most memorable being the squirrel monkeys getting up to mischief in the open-air cage you can stroll through. If you're not unnerved by the thought of the critters jumping on your head, that is.

KALK BAY nice

Hangout of the hip and happening, this quaint, laid-back harbour town is the ideal place to stop off for a lazy lunch. Around 1pm every day, fleets of local fishing boats return to the busy harbour with everything from snoek and chokka to red romans and yellowtail, all freshly plucked from the surrounding choppy waters. If you're not that adept with a filleting knife, you can have yours beheaded, scaled and gutted by the nimble-fingered on-site fish sellers for a negligible sum. And if you can't be bothered

Hout Bay. *See p69.*

to beer-batter and deep-fry it either, head over to the legendary resident fish-and-chip shop, Kalkies, on the harbour, and dig in.
Recently a water taxi service has started between Kalk Bay and Simon's Town harbours.

KOMMETJIE

FREE Imhoff Farm
Kommetjie Road, Kommetjie (021 783 4545/ www.imhofffarm.co.za). **Open** *9am-5pm daily.* **Admission** free. **Credit** MC, V.
Upon ordering the construction of the Simon's Town refreshment centre in 1743, VOC commissioner Baron von Imhoff heard of a very special lady, widow Christina Diemer, who had been supplying sailors with produce from her farm, Swaaneweide. Suitably impressed with her initiative, he gave her a piece of land near Slangkop, which later became known as Imhoff's Gift. These days the farm is a modern-day Dr Dolittle's Island of ponies, piglets, snakes and camels. It's a commercial enterprise, with animal rides and shops bearing whimsical names such as the Dream Shop, and Over the Mountain and Far Away. Head to the recycling studio and environmental centre and get in touch with your greener side, and complete the holistic picture with a bit of organic, home-made food at one of the restaurants.

Slangkop Lighthouse
Lighthouse Road, Kommetjie (021 783 1717). **Open** *Oct-Apr 10am-3pm daily. Nov-Mar 10am-3pm Mon-Fri.* **Admission** R16 adults; R8.50-R10 reductions. **No credit cards**.
This shimmering ivory tower isn't only the tallest cast-iron lighthouse in the country, it also boasts one of the brightest lights, with a range of 33 nautical miles (around 61km). It first lit up in 1919, and is still operational today. Guided tours are available during the week and include a meander up the steep staircase, as well as intriguing information on the history of lighthouses, including the reason why South Africa is one of the few countries left to employ lighthouse keepers.

MUIZENBERG great surf beach

Muizenberg is a steeped-in-history seaside resort popular with surfer dudes, beach babes and fun-seeking families. Synonymous with killer waves, Muizenberg's Surfer's Corner draws scores of surfers looking to catch that perfect swell. The rest of the beach-front is sadly a shell of its former glamorous self, with relics such as the super-tube and putt-putt course just not holding the same allure they did back when they were still considered a novelty. But if you're after a relaxing, unpretentious day at the beach, this is an ideal spot to let down your hair and soak up the sun. To reach the beach, turn into Atlantic Road from Main Road, pass under the bridge and take the second right to park at the mountain end, or continue straight to the parking area.

The **Catwalk** is a level path between the sea and railway line along the shore between Muizenberg and St James. The walk takes around 40 minutes, but since there's so much to see and explore on your way (it's a great whale-watching hangout during season and the rock pools are lined with anemones) it might take longer. Being so close to the sea, expect to get seriously splashed if you take a stroll at high tide.

Snaking between Muizenberg and Kalk Bay, **Boyes Drive** offers an impressive view of False Bay, and a convenient alternative route if you're seeking to avoid the occasionally bumper-to-bumper seaside road. The drive is stippled with lookout points from which to take in the expansive vistas, as well as starting points for a few hiking routes.

FREE Het Posthuys

180 Main Road, Muizenberg (021 788 7972/021 788 5951/072 041 8074). **Open** 10am-2pm Mon-Fri, or by appointment. **Admission** free; donations appreciated.

Formerly known as Stegmansrust, this inconspicuous, thatched Lego-block of a house is believed to be the oldest building in the False Bay area. Built by the VOC in 1673, it was used as a lookout point by the Dutch during their occupation of the Cape, and later became a toll-house for passing farmers who wanted to sell their produce to ships in Simon's Town (then Simon's Bay). Today it houses a small museum featuring a few interesting bits and bobs about the Battle of Muizenberg (when the house came under fire) and historic photos of a Muizenberg long forgotten. As the museum is run by volunteers, it's best to phone ahead and make an appointment.

FREE Rhodes Cottage

242 Main Road, Muizenberg (021 788 1816/ 072 482 6131/082 425 3092). **Open** by appointment. **Admission** by donation. **No credit cards**.

INSIDE TRACK
BREAKFAST TRAIN

For a scenic Sunday breakfast adventure, buy a train ticket to the end of the Southern Peninsula line. The tracks hug the sea all the way from Muizenberg to Simon's Town, where a slew of great breakfast spots await. Get on at Cape Town or at Newlands station, next to the Newlands Rugby Stadium (the latter is smaller, quieter and has better parking).

Kalk Bay

This seaside chalet is where Cecil John Rhodes breathed his last, leaving behind quite a legacy at the relatively young age of 49. A mine magnate, politician, and firm believer in the superiority of the white, Anglo-Saxon race, he did his darndest to expand the British Empire during his short life, colonising Rhodesia (now Zimbabwe) during his time as prime minister of the Cape Colony (1890-95). He built this house in 1899, only to die here three years later, from tuberculosis. You'll see photos, clippings and caricatures revealing the man behind the un-PC speeches (a treasure trove of which can be found in the well-thumbed copy of his last will and testament).

NOORDHOEK

Stretching all the way from the Tokai side of Table Mountain to the Noordhoek and Sun Valley area overlooking the sea, the **Silvermine Nature Reserve** has trails ranging from easy-peasy to brutal, mountain-biking routes and bird-watching opportunities around every *fynbos*-bedazzled turn. Adrenaline addicts are sure to get their kicks at the rock climbing area near the Silvermine reservoir and the sandstone caves ready for the exploring. The picnic and braai areas offer the easy way out for those wanting the fresh air and panoramic view without all that wearisome walking.

Silvermine Nature Reserve

Ou Kaapse Weg 021 780 9002/www.tmnp. co.za). **Open** *Apr-Sept* 8am-5pm daily. *Oct-Mar* 7am-6pm daily. **Admission** R15 adults; R5 reductions. **No credit cards**.

SIGHTS

ST JAMES

Images of the primary-coloured beach huts at **St James Pool** can be found splashed across the pages of a million tourist guides and postcards, but you still won't be able to resist the temptation of following suit and snapping away. The calm waters of the saltwater pool are great for a leisurely bob-around and also an awesome place to bring the kids for a splash if they're weary of being pounded by waves.

To reach the pool, park near St James Station, then go through the tunnel running under the railway line.

SIMON'S TOWN

Apart from stunning sea views, this quiet naval town possesses a rich cultural heritage.

★ Boulders African Penguin Colony

Kleintuin Road, Simon's Town, parking area in Seaforth Road (021 786 2329/www.tmnp.co.za). **Open** *Oct, Nov* 8am-6.30pm daily. *Dec, Jan* 7am-7.30pm daily. *Feb, Mar* 8am-5.30pm daily. *Apr-Sept* 8am-5pm daily. **Admission** R30; R10 under-12s. **Credit** AmEx, DC, MC, V.

There's something incredibly endearing about these creatures. Maybe it's their unrefined singing

---

Shark Tactics

Just when you thought it was safe to go into the water…

SIGHTS

We can thank Stephen Spielberg and a certain 1975 film for the fact that selachophobia (an irrational fear of sharks) is one of the most common phobias among adults today. But just how irrational is the fear? And is it really safe to go back into the water?

South Africa has an incredibly diverse shark population. A quarter of the world's shark species (98 to be precise) dwell in South African waters and around 40 of these species call the waters around Cape Town home.

According to Alison Kock, a shark specialist at the Save Our Seas Shark Centre, most are completely harmless to humans. In 2008 only four people died of shark attacks and 58 were bitten throughout the world. Statistically, you have a better chance of getting killed by a faulty toaster.

Alison is also director of research at Shark Spotters, an organisation born when a shark attack prompted informal car guard Rasta Davids to borrow a mobile phone and stand lookout at the top of Boyes Drive. With the help of members of the Muizenberg community, the organisation was formalised in 2004. These days there are 14 spotters working all year round (with between five and ten extra spotters in summer) – one stationed on the beach and others higher up on the mountain. Beaches under surveillance include Surfers' Corner in Muizenberg, Danger Beach in St James, Fish Hoek Beach and the Hoek, Noordhoek. Spotters communicate with walkie-talkies and use flags to signal to beachgoers. So, if you're planning a swim, learn the signals:

● Green flag – spotting visibility good; no sharks sighted.
● Black flag – spotting visibility poor; no sharks sighted.
● Red flag – a shark was sighted recently, but it's no longer visible to spotters.
● White flag with a black shark (plus loud siren) – shark sighted; get out of the water.
● No flag – no spotters on duty.

Alison Kock's shark safety tips:
● Familiarise yourself with the area before hitting the water.
● Swim at a beach that has Shark Spotters.
● Don't swim alone or far out (most bites take place beyond the surf break).
● Don't swim when there's fishing activity in the vicinity.

Drop by the new **Save Our Seas Shark Centre** in Kalk Bay (28 Main Road, 021 788 6694, www.saveourseas.com/sharkcentresa, open 10am-4pm Mon-Fri), to learn more about these much misunderstood creatures.

St James.

voices that resemble those of braying jackasses (hence the name) or the fact that their useless wings have left them landbound after millions of years of evolution. Whatever the reason, a meander along the winding boardwalk running through the African penguin colony's breeding ground is a joy. Watch as they waddle about, wade in the choppy water and play peekaboo from their twiggy burrows. For a mere R5 extra, you can spy on slippery sea life or beach babes through the binoculars dotting the walkway.

FREE Bronze Age Art Sculpture House & Foundry

King George Way, Simon's Town (021 786 5090/www.bronzeageart.com). **Open** 8am-4.30pm Mon-Thur; 8am-3pm Fri; by appointment Sat, Sun. **Admission** free.

The slightly sharp smell of molten metal is the first thing that hits you upon walking through the heavy doors of this contemporary foundry-cum-gallery housed in the former Albertyn's Stable. Inside, you can browse through a range of sculptures that span commercial wildlife statuettes and slightly more avant-garde works by renowned artists such as Claudette Schreuder and Norman Catherine. Head up to the mezzanine level and ogle the sweaty strongmen and women through the glass pane as they mould, cast and hammer away in the glow of the foundry. The next-door artists' residency has an inspiring sculpture garden that overlooks the Simon's Town yacht basin.

▶ *See also p176.*

Heritage Museum

King George Way, Simon's Town (021 786 2302/072 214 1425). **Open** 11am-4pm Tue-Fri; 11am-5pm Sun. **Admission** R5. **No credit cards**.

In 1965 Simon's Town was declared a 'whites only' area under the Group Areas Act and saw the forced removal of close to 7,000 'coloured' people from their homes. The Amlay family were the last residents to be evicted from their house, in 1975, and the first to return to it in 1995. Today the Amlay house has

become the Heritage Museum, curated by Zainab Davidson née Amlay, who tells the sad story of this turbulent time in Simon's Town's history. The rooms are filled with photos, press clippings and historical artefacts such as handwritten *kitaabs* (books), bridal and haj attire and cooking utensils, all casting light on the culturally rich heritage of the town's erstwhile Muslim community.

Just Nuisance's Grave

By car *Naval Signal School, Klawer Valley Nature Reserve, off Redhill Drive (look for a sign just past Pine Haven). Simon's Town.*
On foot *Historic Steps, Barnard Street (start of Runciman Drive), Simon's Town.*

Standing atop a steep set of stone steps, this bronze statue overlooking Simon's Town immortalises the spirit of probably the coolest seafarer ever to set foot (paw, in this case) on deck. During the World War II, this beer-guzzling mutt was enlisted as an able seaman in the Royal Navy under the occupation 'Bone Crusher', which entitled him to his own railway pass, free access to all the ships in the harbour and his own bunk. Just Nuisance was a local at all the pubs in Cape Town, and accompanied many of his inebriated shipmates back to their quarters safely. Even though he cut a pretty terrifying figure, this Great Dane was actually a pussycat at heart, and only ever let out a low growl to ward off trouble-makers.

Mineral World Topstones & Scratch Patch

Dido Valley Road, Simon's Town (021 786 2020/ www.scratchpatch.co.za). **Open** 8.30am-4.45pm Mon-Fri; 9am-5.30pm Sat, Sun, public holidays. **Admission** free. *Scratch Patch* R14 for a small bag. **Credit** AmEx, DC, MC, V.

This Technicolor pebbly paradise teeming with tots has been around since 1970. Plonk down and delve through the Scratch Patch: mounds of tumble-polished tiger's eyes, amethysts and crystals; with enough patience, you might even manage to snatch a few of those elusive lapis lazuli from in front of your pint-sized neighbours' little noses. After you've sufficiently looted the land, head over to the Topstones factory shop and see where the stones get their shine.

▶ *If you don't want to trek all the way out to Simon's Town, visit Mineral World's satellite branch at the V&A Waterfront (Dock Road, 021 419 9429), where kids have the added incentive of a round of indoor cave golf.*

Simon's Town Boat Trips

Town Pier, in front of Simon's Town Waterfront Centre, Simon's Town. **Simon's Town Boat Company** *021 786 2136/083 257 7760/www.boatcompany.co.za.* **Trips** daily. **Tickets** *Spirit of Just Nuisance* (40 mins) R40 adults; R20 reductions. *Cape Point* (2 hrs) R350 adults; R200 reductions. *Seal Island* (1.5 hrs) R250 adults; R150 reductions. *Whale Watching* (2.5 hrs) R650 adults; R400 reductions. **Guided Sea Kayak Tours** *082 501 8930/ www.kayakcapetown.co.za.* **Tickets** *Penguin Trip* R250. **No credit cards**.

Whether you're up for a quick trip around the harbour or keen to undertake the full two-hour journey to check out humpback dolphins, seals and white sharks at Seal Island, the Simon's Town Boat Company has got you covered. Go between August and December if you want to get a glimpse of the southern right whales as they frolic about with their babes. If you've got even more time on your hands, take a laid-back cruise around Cape Point and see the scattering of shipwrecks that have been laid to waste by the stormy seas through the years. The penguin-spotting kayak trip takes double kayaks out to Boulder's Beach; the trip includes refreshments, swimming and snorkelling.

Simon's Town Museum

The Residency, Court Road, Simon's Town (021 786 3046/www.simonstown.com/museum).

Boulders African Penguin Colony.
See p72.

Open 9am-4pm Mon-Fri; 10am-1pm Sat; 11am-3pm Sun, public holidays. **Admission** R5; R1-2 reductions. **No credit cards**.

Built in 1777, the Residency has been the home of many of the town's colourful residents, ranging from postmasters to constables, crooks and ladies of ill repute. Today, visitors come here to learn more about Simon's Town's fascinating past: exhibits cover the late Stone Age until the forced removals of the 1960s. Some of them could do with a bit of sprucing up, but most visitors will be able to find a room in the house featuring a topic that interests them – be it the Early History Room with its hunter-gatherer dioramas and comprehensive exposition of the Battle of Muizenberg, the Military Room displaying artefacts from both world wars, or the more light-hearted Just Nuisance Room, featuring his royal dogginess's collar and newspaper clippings covering his antics. For the fear factor, head down to the cells and stare into the abyss of the black hole.

FREE South African Naval Museum

Naval Dockyard, St George's Street, Simon's Town (021 787 4686/www.simonstown.com/ navalmuseum). **Open** 9.30am-3.30pm daily. **Admission** free.

Resist the urge to ring the various brass bells scattered about as you browse through the silent Naval Museum – generally silent, that is, except for the sporadic sputtering of the Morse code machine, operated by two seamen frantically punching buttons on a control panel in the re-created communication branch where it's forever 5.50am. Visitors can contemplate the meaning of life in the naval chapel, which is still used for naval weddings and funerals today; its elaborate mural features Disneyesque characters surveying the lie of the land. Brave the menacingly steep flight of stairs for a look at the inner workings of the old clock tower.

Warrior Toy Museum & Collectors' Shop

St George's Street, Simon's Town (021 786 1395). **Open** 10am-3.45pm Mon-Thur, Sat. **Admission** R5. **Credit** MC, V.

The tongue-in-cheek warning next to the chugging toy train warns: 'No smoking unless you're a train'. It reflects the fun-loving character of Percy van Zyl, the man behind this impressive assortment of collectors' and contemporary toys. Shelves of 'celebrity' toy cars such as a flying Chitty Chitty Bang Bang and Mr Bean's lemony mini stand side by side with older, more valuable examples, and a battalion of toy soldiers wards off an ox-formationed attack of spear-wielding Zulus. Other interesting exhibits include a Nazi parade complete with a saluting Hitler and marching Hitler Youth, an Asah miniature piano, and a circus tent full of acrobatic figures. There's also a frightening number of glassy-eyed porcelain dolls with far-off stares that could give the Bride of Chucky a run for her money.

SIGHTS

Northern Suburbs

Suburbia in all its splendour.

Although the strip of suburbs wedged between the N1 and N7 aren't as exquisite as their counterparts within the City Bowl, there are a smattering of spots worth exploring. The coastal towns of **Blouberg Strand** and **Table View** are notoriously windy, making their respective beaches more popular with windsurfers and kite-flyers than with sunbathers. But come cocktail hour, local drinking holes are teeming with folk appreciating the splendid sunset.

While the neighbouring industrial town of **Milnerton** doesn't offer much in the sightseeing department, it does manage to attract hordes of bargain hunters to its roadside flea market. Meanwhile, **Durbanville** and its surrounding area has an abundance of shopping malls and some of the most beautiful wine estates this side of the Winelands.

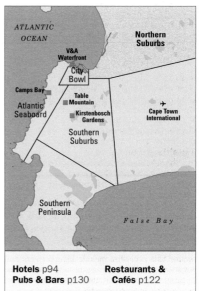

Hotels p94 **Restaurants &** **Pubs & Bars** p130 **Cafés** p122

SIGHTS

BLOUBERG STRAND

The small coastal town of Blouberg is an outpost for both adrenalin junkies and cocktail drinkers. Its **beach** (Otto du Plessis Drive) is the perfect vantage point from which to trace the complete, iconic outline of Table Mountain ('Blouberg' translates as 'Blue Mountain'). It gets its fair share of gale-force winds, which makes it popular with kite surfers. If you're lucky enough to get it on a wind-free day, slather on the suncream and stake off a quiet spot on the sand before braving the icy waves.

DURBANVILLE & SURROUNDS

The prosperous inland town and the area around it are best known for wine production, and the Durbanville Wine Valley. It's also home to the only zoo in the Western Cape.

FREE Durbanville Rose Garden
Durban Road, Durbanville (021 948 1744).
Open 6am-sunset daily. **Admission** free.

This 3.5-hectare rose garden isn't much to look at during the winter season (what with it being the best time to prune and all). But with the advent of spring, it sees a kaleidoscope of blossoming buds making their sweet-smelling debuts. A stroll through the meticulous garden, a very Victorian affair, featuring over 500 blooming varietals, will have you hankering for a parasol and a spot of tea in no time. And, as luck would have it, a spread of cream tea awaits should you pop in to the clubhouse on a Sunday.

Durbanville Wine Valley
083 310 1228/www.durbanvillewine.co.za.
The Durbanville wine route features nine wine estates (some of them with top-notch restaurants), and since the valley's fertile terroir makes for award-winning sauvignon blanc, it's a good idea to stock up on the good stuff as you make your way through them. The estates are Altydgedacht (021 976 1295, www.altydgedacht.co.za), Bloemendal (021 976 2682, www.bloemendal.co.za), D'Aria (021 975 5736, www.daria.co.za), De Grendel (021 558 6280, www.degrendel.co.za), Diemersdal (021 976 3361, www.diemersdal.co.za), Durbanville Hills (021 558 1300,

SIGHTS

www.durbanvillehills.co.za), Hillcrest (021 975 2346, www.hillcrestfarm.co.za), Meerendal (021 975 1655, www.meerendal.co.za) and Nitida (021 976 1467, www.nitida.co.za).
▶ *For more on the wine territories in the region, see p65* **Urban Terroir**.

Tygerberg Zoo
Exit 39, Klipheuwel-Stellenbosch off-ramp, N1 highway (021 884 4494/www.tygerbergzoo.co.za). **Open** 9am-5pm daily. **Admission** R55; R40 reductions. **Credit** MC, V.
Rare and endangered animals are bred in this rural hideaway, so close encounters with seriously curious creatures are guaranteed – think armour-plated armadillos and tongue-wagging anteaters. Some of the more majestic endangered beasts roaming around this enclosure include Bengal tigers and American grizzlies; however, the locals won't allow foreigners to steal all the limelight, and there are also plenty of springbok and zebras. In the children's farmyard, kids can pet and pamper the more docile, cuddly members of the animal kingdom.
▶ *For more on the zoo, see p162.*

MILNERTON

An industrial town, Milnerton's main draw is its weekly market.

Milnerton Market
Otto du Plessis Drive, Paarden Eiland, Milnerton. **Open** 7am-5pm Sat, Sun.
Milnerton Market might be more of a bazaar than a touristy flea market, and the rows upon rows of cars lined next to this dusty stretch should tip you off that this caravan of bakkies (pick-up trucks), boots and tents has a few aces up its sleeve. The market is akin to an open-air general dealer, selling everything from saws, mobile phones and face creams to beautiful crystal spirit decanters and vintage jewellery. Every Saturday sees stylists and publicists scrounging for finds in between tucking into yummy pancakes.

TABLE VIEW

Dolphin Beach (Marine Drive) is hardly the spot for a picnic: wind here is almost as certain as death and taxes. But, looking on the bright side, it makes for great kitesurfing; indeed, the beach is internationally renowned for it). What's more, the views of Table Mountain from here are picture-perfect.

Durbanville Wine Valley.

Consume

Cape Royale. *See p80.*

Hotels

From old-world charm to latter-day luxury.

The accommodation you choose plays an integral role in your experience of a destination – and Cape Town more or less has it all: stylish boutique hotels, five-star hideaways, private villas with jaw-dropping views, intimate guesthouses, backpackers' lodges, and more. The choice is incredibly varied. In addition, rural escapes can be found fairly close to the city, in tree-lined suburbs, or in the Winelands (covered in our Escapes & Excursions section).

You can't turn a corner these days without seeing a construction site for another hotel in Cape Town. With the FIFA 2010 World Cup around the corner the challenge is on to make sure there are enough beds in the city. The most recent notable addition to the luxury scene has been the opening of the **One & Only Cape Town** in the V&A Waterfront, an event that attracted a sprinkling of international celebs. But you don't have to pay the earth for a comfortable and fun stay in this city: there are funky spots galore too, like the quirky **Grand Daddy,** with its unique airstream trailer park on the penthouse.

PRICES AND INFORMATION

The prices given in this chapter refer to the rack rates for standard double rooms, unless otherwise indicated. These rates should give you an idea of what to expect to pay, but prices vary dramatically with the season. Prices rise greatly during the summer high season and rates are also higher on the Atlantic seaboard, but then the views are often worth the price. During winter, bargains can be found, especially via www.capetownonsale.com – the room sale runs from the end of May to end of September. Self-catering accommodation is becoming increasingly popular; for more, *see p80* **DIY divas.**

If you've left booking a little late try www.mtbeds.co.za, while www.sa-venues.co.za is a particularly useful site when looking for accommodation around South Africa.

Note that 'BAR' in listings information stands for Best Available Rate. This rate is dependent on the number of available rooms in a hotel at a given time, as well as at the time of booking. It's computer-generated, so you'll be hard-pressed to haggle a better price.

We've listed a selection of services for each hotel at the bottom of each review, detailing everything from in-room entertainment (including DStv, South Africa's own digital satellite TV provider, which offers local, American, British and European channels) to parking. Prices for internet access and parking are for any given 24-hour period unless stated.

CITY BOWL

Deluxe

★ Mount Nelson
76 Orange Street, Gardens (021 483 1000/ www.mountnelson.co.za). **Rates** R4,285-R9,885. **Rooms** 201. **Credit** AmEx, DC, MC, V. **Map** p276 G5 **❶**

Since it opened in 1899, the city's undisputed grande dame has played host to a slew of dignitaries and stars and it continues to be a hotel of choice for well-heeled travellers. It is imbued with an elegant air that harks back to a time when the pace of life was slower – and one had plenty of staff, of course. The luxury suites, sprawling gardens, large pool and terrace area and swanky new spa make the Mount Nelson a very glamorous place to hang one's hat.

Bar. Business centre. Concierge. Disabled-adapted rooms. Gym. Internet (free wireless,

Mount Nelson.

shared terminals). Parking (free). Pools (2 outdoor). Restaurants (2). Spa. TV: DStv, DVD in some rooms.
▶ *For the Cape Colony restaurant, see p99; for the spa, see p150 Spa for the Course.*

Westin Grand Cape Town Arabella Quays
Convention Square, 1 Lower Long Street, City Centre (021 412 9999/www.westin.com/grandcapetown). **Rates** R3,735-R4,085.
Rooms 483. **Credit** AmEx, DC, MC, V.
Map p275 H3 ❷
Ideally situated a hop and a skip from the Waterfront and adjacent to the always-busy CTICC, this statement hotel has even more to say since its recent image

and name overhaul. Catering to Armani-suited business travellers, stars and their entourages and savvy city visitors who relish its central location, the luxury suites, superior cuisine, great views of the urban melée and fabulous spa (*see p150* **Spa for the Course**) ensure the overall package is worth it.
Bar. Business centre. Concierge. Disabled-adapted rooms. Gym. Internet (free wireless, free terminal). Parking (R25). Pool (1 heated). Restaurant. Room service. Spa. TV: DStv.

Expensive

Cape Cadogan
5 Upper Union Street, Gardens (021 480 8080/www.capecadogan.com). **Rates** R2,125-R4,100.
Rooms 12. **Credit** AmEx, DC, MC, V.
Map p274 F5 ❸
Comprising the original hotel, nearby luxury apartments and the more private Owners Villa, the Cape Cadogan continues to provide stylish sanctuary for city visitors. Elegant interiors and a sense that one is staying in a home rather than a business establishment are certainly factors in the success of this setup. Rooms are spacious and welcoming, with all the desired creature comforts.
Concierge. Internet (free wireless in library, R50 for 5,000 credits on laptop in room). Parking (free off-street; R75 per day underground). Pool (1 outside). Room service. TV: DStv, DVD.

> ### INSIDE TRACK
> ### TRAILER PARK DREAMING
>
> Unleash your secret trailer trash yearnings at the rooftop trailer park of the **Grand Daddy** (*see p83*). Each American Airstream trailer boasts a uniquely themed interior designed by a local artist. To add a spot of authenticity, all trailers come complete with a speck-sized garden and US Postal Service mailbox.

DIY Divas

Self-catering takes on a whole new meaning with these stylish spots.

CONSUME

For those who relish their privacy while on holiday, there are some superb self-catering options to choose from in the city.

Enjoy a beautiful Atlantic Ocean view from your private apartment at **Bali Bay Apartments** (113 Victoria Road, Camps Bay, 021 438 1893, www.balibay.com), or opt for inner-city chic at the swanky serviced apartments, complete with all the expected five-star luxuries and facilities, at **Cape Royale Luxury Hotel & Residence** (47 Main Road, Green Point, 021 430 0500, www.caperoyale.co.za). The **Peninsula All Suite Hotel** (313 Beach Road, Sea Point, 021 430 7777, www.peninsula.co.za), meanwhile, is an ideally central spot for those on extended holiday stays, and families are welcomed with open arms.

For something that's up there in the style stakes, why not book a private villa? **Cape Portfolios** (021 438 4775, www.capeportfolios.com) specialises in Camps Bay villa rental and has a wide choice of accommodation on its books: **Camps Bay Villa** (48 Francolin Road, Camps Bay, 021 438 1144, www.campsbayvilla.com) is a popular bet with visiting film crews and international movers and shakers.

Those who enjoy the cosmopolitan vibe of De Waterkant will feel absolutely at home in any of the properties belonging to **Village & Life** (021 438 3972, www.villageandlife.com) – the company also has properties in the Waterfront, nearby Mouille Point and Camps Bay.

Other recommended swanky private villa rentals on this side of the mountain include **Eleven Sedgemoor Road** (11 Sedgemoor Road, Camps Bay, 021 438 7219) and **Lion's View** (4 First Crescent, Camps Bay, 021 438 1239, www.lionsview.co.za). And **Icon Villas** (086 184 5527, www.icape.co.za) has a phenomenal collection across the peninsula and further off the Western Cape, among them super-swanky properties like **Bridge House** in the leafy Higgovale.

If you'd prefer a quieter stay on the southern side of the peninsula, book a room at the **St James** (108 Main Road, St James, 021 788 4543, www.the lastword.co.za), just a stone's throw from the sea and the St James catwalk, or make a group booking for the architect-designed **Bishop's View** (1 Upper Quarter Deck Road, Kalk Bay, 074 203 4151, www.capevillarental.co.za) in the quaint fishing village of Kalk Bay. Closer to Cape Point Nature Reserve and close to nature, meanwhile, **South Winds** (021 701 5149/074 203 4151, www.capevillarental.co.za) is a charming Cape Cod clapboard home with uninterrupted sea views.

Cape Royale.

★ Kensington Place

38 Kensington Crescent, Higgovale (021 424 4744/www.kensingtonplace.co.za). **Rates** R2,600-R3,900. **Rooms** 8. **Credit** AmEx, MC, V.
Frequently raved about in glam international mags, this urbane establishment puts its guests' comfort above all else – why else would breakfast be served all day? Suites are comfortable and oh-so-chic (Skype phones and iPod docking stations are provided), the views of the city and the mountain are simply gorgeous and the service is thoughtful.
Bar. Concierge. Internet (free on laptops in rooms). Parking (free). Pool (1 outdoor). Room service. TV: DStv, DVD.

Mandela Rhodes Place (Hotel & Spa)

Cnr Wale & Burg Streets, City Centre (021 481 4000/www.mandelarhodesplace.co.za). **Rates** R2,010-R3,470. **Rooms** 108. **Credit** AmEx, DC, MC, V. **Map** p276 G4 ❹
Just a few years old, this inner-city apartment hotel celebrates its position in the heart of the urban regeneration in style: glossy surfaces and luxury details are part of the package. Book yourself into anything from a one-bedroom studio to a two-bedroom deluxe apartment, where you can opt to make your own breakfast in the high-tech kitchen or go for the five-star hotel service deal where everything's done for you. The suites are dotted among a number of buildings in the vicinity that comprise the hotel.
Bars (2). Business centre. Concierge. Disabled-adapted rooms. Gym. Internet (R150 per day wireless). Parking (R50). Pool (1 outdoor). Restaurants (3). Room service. Spa. TV: DStv, DVD.

Moderate

2inn Kensington

21 Kensington Crescent, Oranjezicht (021 423 1707/www.2inn1.com). **Rates** R1,150-R1,980. **Rooms** 10. **Credit** AmEx, DC, MC, V.
City-centric style seekers will love this perfectly placed boutique guesthouse situated just below Table Mountain and an easy stroll away from the city's must-do shops, bars and restaurants. It is housed in a contemporary African-styled and renovated Victorian home with all mod cons and luxury details present, and features a central poolside deck – a boon for sun seekers; in-house spa treatments can also be arranged. The spacious suite is ideal for families or friends travelling together.
Concierge. Internet (free wireless). Pool (1 outside). Restaurant. TV:DStv, DVD.

Alta Bay

12 Invermark Crescent, Higgovale (021 487 8800/www.altabay.com). **Rates** R1,300-R2,700. **Rooms** 7. **Credit** AmEx, DC, MC, V.
This smart and sophisticated guesthouse is situated in a beautifully renovated home under the slopes of

Table Mountain and within easy reach of the buzz of the city. Understated interiors help create a sense of calm and quiet, while the attention to guests' comfort – from the plushest robes and softest sheets to an all-inclusive mini bar – is exemplary.
Business centre. Internet (free wireless). Parking (free). Pool (1 outdoor). Room service. TV: DStv, DVD.

An African Villa

19 Carstens Street, Tamboerskloof (021 423 2162/www.capetowncity.co.za). **Rates** R475-R700. **Rooms** 13. **Credit** AmEx, DC, MC, V. **Map** p274 F4 ❺
Elegant African-inspired surroundings set the scene at this small hotel, comprised of three renovated and interlinked Victorian terraced houses in Tamboerskloof. A home-from-home atmosphere is key to its popularity; facilities include a pool, internet and spacious high-ceilinged rooms.
Internet (free WiFi, free shared terminals). Parking (R25). Pool (1 outdoor). TV: DStv.

Cape Diamond Hotel

Cnr Parliament & Longmarket Streets, City Centre (021 461 2519/www.capediamond hotel.co.za). **Rates** R770-R1,030. **Rooms** 60. **Credit** AmEx, DC, MC, V. **Map** p276 H4 ❻
This inner-city gem is right in the thick of things. Less than five years old, the hotel has some 60 individually decorated suites with all the details you need for a comfortable stay. It's a popular bet for tour and conference groups.
Bar. Disabled-adapted room. Internet (R30 for 15min). Parking (R55). Restaurant. TV: DStv.

Cape Milner

Milner Road, Tamboerskloof (021 426 1101/ www.capemilner.com). **Rates** R1,100-R700. **Rooms** 56. **Credit** MC, V. **Map** p274 F4 ❼
A popular bet with both business and leisure travellers, this hotel is characterised by its contemporary furnishing and convenient location just a few minutes from the CBD. With just 57 rooms (of which ten are luxury suites), a boutique hotel atmosphere prevails.
Bar. Business centre. Concierge. Disabled-adapted rooms. Gym. Internet (wireless, shared terminal R30 per day). Parking (R35). Pool (outdoor). Restaurant. Room service. TV: DStv, DVD on request, pay movies R30.

Fritz Hotel

1 Faure Street, Gardens (021 480 9000/ www.fritzhotel.co.za). **Rates** R500-R850. **Rooms** 13. **Credit** AmEx, DC, MC, V. **Map** p276 G5 ❽
A popular choice with German-speaking visitors, this hotel boasts African decor touches and bright and airy high-ceilinged bedrooms. It's popular with business travellers: the outside terrace is convenient for informal meetings; ADSL and email is free of charge and a fax machine is standard in your room.

CONSUME

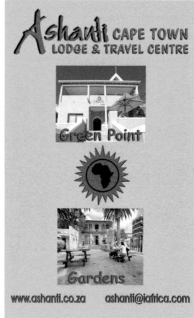

Hot Beds

Cool places to rest your head.

Cape Town is certainly one of the most picturesque cities on the continent, and visitors to the Mother City are spoilt for choice when it comes to interesting or dramatic places to stay. If blow-the-budget experiences are what you're after, check into the swanky **One & Only** (*see p87*). The five-star setup is located in the heart of the V&A Waterfront and boasts magnificent views, impeccable service and two of the most exciting restaurants in the city, Nobu (*see p113*) and Maze (*see p112*).

At the **Airstream Penthouse Trailer Park** (see Grand Daddy, *below*), guests check in to vintage Airstream trailers on top of the four-star Grand Daddy hotel in the heart of the city. Each trailer has been individually decorated by a local artist.

The well-priced **Protea Hotel Fire & Ice**, also know as the Extreme Hotel (*see p84*) is a popular pit stop for thrill-seekers, who use it as a base for adrenaline-based adventures (the external five-storey climbing wall is a dead giveaway). Be sure to swim in the glass-walled pool and take a ride in the 'shark cage' elevator.

At **Tintswalo Atlantic** (*see p93*) in Hout Bay you'd be forgiven for thinking you've washed up on a deserted (albeit

ultra-luxurious) island. Tucked away out of sight under Chapman's Peak, this secret ten-suite lodge boasts exquisite, uninterrupted views of the ocean, sumptuous decor and quality cuisine. And for a true top-of-the-world experience, book a place on the **Hoerikwaggo Trail** (www.sanparks.org). You'll spend a night in a tented camp on Table Mountain, looked after and catered for by your guide.

CONSUME

Concierge. Internet (free wireless, shared terminals). Parking (free). TV: DStv.

★ Grand Daddy

38 Long Street, City Centre (021 424 7247/ www.granddaddy.co.za). **Rates** R945-R1,850. **Rooms** 67; 7 trailers. **Credit** AmEx, DC, MC, V. **Map** p276 H3 **⑨**

Following in the footsteps of its quirky predecessors Daddy Long Legs Boutique Hotel and Daddy Long Legs Self Catering Apartments, this plush hotel offers top-notch accommodation with a twist. The undisputed *pièce de résistance* is the zany 'penthouse trailer park' comprising a collection of seven vintage Airstream caravans, each conceptualised and decorated by a different local talent. *Photo p84*. Bars (2). Internet (R20 for 20mb wireless, free shared terminal). Parking (R30 overnight). Restaurant. Room service. TV.
▶ *For more, see above Hot Beds.*

Hippo Boutique Hotel

5-9 Park Road, Gardens (021 423 2500/ www.hippotique.co.za). **Rates** R1,198-R1,980. **Rooms** 25. **Map** p274 F5 **⑩**

There's something so utterly glamorous about stepping out of one's hotel into the thick of a happening city, and – thanks to its great location – you can do just that at Hippo. On its doorstep are lots of cool bars and restaurants, and staff will keep you in the loop about where to see and be seen. Rooms are on the 'chiconomy' scale – well priced without losing out on good looks – and handily each has its own small kitchen should you ever tire of dining out.
Bar. Business centre. Concierge. Internet (free wireless, terminals in rooms). Parking (free). Pool (1 outdoor). Restaurants (3). Room service. TV: DStv, DVD.

Ikhaya Lodge

Dunkley Square, Wandel Street, Gardens (021 461 8880/www.ikhayalodge.co.za). **Rates** R750-R1,125. **Rooms** 19. **Credit** AmEx, DC, MC, V. **Map** p276 G5 **⑪**

An African theme pervades at this independent traveller's choice on charming Dunkley Square. Guests can choose from an en suite room or a self-catering apartment furnished with all mod cons. The Lodge is a particularly popular bet for visiting film production

Grand Daddy. See p83.

teams, thanks to the storage facilities and the hotel's proximity to film industry-related services.
Bar. Business centre. Internet (R25 per day wireless, R1 per minute shared terminal). Parking (free). Restaurant. TV: DStv, DVD in some rooms.

Protea Hotel Fire & Ice
Corner New Church & Bree Streets (021 488 2555/www.extreme-hotels.com). **Rates** R845-R1,445 BAR. **Rooms** 190. **Credit** AmEx, DC, MC, V. **Map** p276 G4 **⑫**
Designed to cater for fun-loving adrenaline junkies (the 'climber' fixed to the wall outside should be a clue), the design gimmicks here add a fun element to one's overall experience. This is the South African representative of an international sports hotel group, and visitors who come to Cape Town for the big waves, big white sharks and big nights out on the town will love the irreverent approach to hoteliering.
Bar. Concierge. Internet (free wireless, free shared terminal). Parking (R40). Pool (1 outdoor). Restaurant. Room service. TV: DStv.
▶ *See also p83 Hot Beds.*

Protea Hotel Victoria Junction
Cnr Somerset & Ebenezer Roads, Green Point (021 418 1234/www.proteahotels.com). **Rates** R1,445-R2,925. **Rooms** 172. **Credit** AmEx, DC, MC, V. **Map** p276 G2 **⑬**
A popular bet for visiting film crews and movie industry types (they have rooms especially for your equipment and props), this hotel offers convenience, service and good facilities at doable prices. The interiors are designed to mimic various movie sets, from the Out of Africa lounge to the Moulin Rouge booths in The Set restaurant. Gimmicks aside, it's a great bet for urban warriors. Rooms range from standard twin and doubles to more luxurious loft apartments.

Bar. Business centre. Internet (R30 for 30 mins wireless). Parking (R35). Pool (1 outdoor). Room service. TV: DStv, DVD on request.

Southern Sun Waterfront
1 Lower Buitengracht, City Centre (021 409 4000/www.southernsun.com). **Rates** R1,425 BAR. **Rooms** 546. **Credit** AmEx, DC, MC, V. **Map** p276 H3 **⑭**
This South African giant of a hotel brand has a perfectly placed Waterfront site, and its 500-plus rooms mean it's a popular bet with both tourist and conference groups. It has all the hotel conveniences that you'd expect. If you're a regular traveller, enrol in their Frequent Guest programme for extra discounts and privileges.
Bar. Business centre. Concierge. Disabled-adapted rooms. Gym. Internet (R1 per minute wireless). Parking (R30). Pool (1 outdoor). Restaurants (2). Room service. Spa. TV: DStv.

Budget

★ Ashanti Lodge
11 Hof Street, Gardens (021 423 8721/www. ashanti.co.za). **Rates** R135 dorm; R270 single R490 double room. **Rooms** 74 beds in dorms; 22 private. **Credit** MC, V. **Map** p276 G5 **⑮**
Ashanti Lodge is renowned 'party central' for twentysomething visitors to the city. The great rates, extensive facilities (from the swimming pool to the bar, big, clean communal kitchen, barbecue and laundry facilities) and always-buzzing atmosphere ensure its popularity. There are a variety of accommodation options, from dorms to the smarter en-suite double rooms in the nearby Ashanti Guesthouse. There are also single rooms (with double beds) and the teeny tiniest camping area too.
Bar. Business centre. Internet (R25 for an hour wireless, shared terminals). Pool (1 outdoor). Room service. TV in some rooms.

Celebrating the wealth of artistic talent to be found in South Africa, this budget boutique hotel caters for independent travellers and is a haven of innovation in the city, with some 13 individually decorated rooms. For an evening of entertainment, book into the Karaoke Room, or how about playing doctor doctor in the Emergency Room, which comes complete with rubber nurse's outfit? There are also five self-catering apartments available to rent at another Long Street site. *Photo p87.*
Bar. Internet (R20 for 20mb, free shared terminals). Parking (R30). TV: DVD in some rooms.

Long Street Backpackers
209 Long Street, City Centre (021 423 0615/ www.longstreetbackpackers.co.za). **Rates** R100 dorm; R180-R250 room. **Rooms** 60 beds in dorms; 12 private. **No credit cards.** **Map** p276 G4 ⓳
Party people who are travelling through the city tend to congregate at this Long Street backpackers' institution that's as known for its always-buzzing bar as its budget rates and comfy surroundings. Light sleeper and worried about being too close to the Long Street mix? Book a room in the back for a peaceful night's rest.
Bar. TV room.

ATLANTIC SEABOARD
Deluxe

Atlanticview Boutique Hotel
31 Francolin Road, Camps Bay (021 438 2254/ www.atlanticviewcapetown.com). **Rates** R3,500-R4,500. **Rooms** 9. **Credit** AmEx, DC, MC, V. **Map** p273 B9 ⓴
As the name suggests, the views from this perfectly placed intimate hotel are superb. A rim flow pool leads the eye to the azure Atlantic Ocean and floor-to-ceiling windows mean that beautiful seascapes are never out of sight. Guestroom interiors are opulent with Afro touches, while details like daily sundowners and snacks and a well-equipped gym ensure guests' comfort.
Bar. Business centre. Concierge. Gym. Internet (free wireless, shared terminal). Parking (free). Pools (2 outdoor). Spa. TV: DStv, DVD on request.

Cape Grace Hotel
West Quay Road, V&A Waterfront (021 410 7100/www.capegrace.com). **Rates** R4,810-R5,750. **Credit** AmEx, DC, MC, V. **Rooms** 121. **Map** p275 H2 ㉑
With its recently refurbished rooms (121 in total), outstanding restaurant and dining facilities, views of the yacht basin (the hotel has its own luxury boat if cruising's your thing) and superb African-inspired spa, this is certainly one of the best hotels in the city.

Backpack
74 New Church Street, Tamboerskloof (021 423 5555/www.backpackers.co.za). **Rates** R110-R150 dorm; R350 room. **Rooms** 44 beds in dorms; 23 private. **Credit** MC, V. **Map** p274 F5 ⓰
Marketing themselves as a 'boutique backpackers', this budget accommodation is part hostel, part hotel. Up there in the popularity stakes with savvy travellers, it has a selection of dorm, double and double en-suite options. Its status as a five-star backpackers' is ensured by its stylish interior, clean and neat rooms, details like quality linen, hot water bottles for the colder nights and private safes, as well as facilities like the on-site travel centre, café and pool.
Bar. Internet (R30 per hour wireless, shared terminals). Parking (free). Pool (1 outdoor). Restaurant. Room service.

Cape Town Backpackers
81 New Church Street, Tamboerskloof (021 426 0200/www.capetownbackpackers.com). **Rates** R110 dorm; R420-R500 room. **Rooms** 23 beds in dorms; 23 private. **Credit** MC, V. **Map** p274 F4 ⓱
Its convenient situation, Afro-inspired, clean interiors and proximity to the buzz of Long and Kloof streets means that this budget spot is a popular one indeed. All linen is supplied and the accommodation ranges from dorms to en-suite doubles at the adjacent guesthouse (they even have a honeymoon suite). On-site travel facilities (staff can get you a good car hire rate), a breakfast menu and laundry service ensure you'll feel right at home.
Bar. Internet (R10 for half hour wireless, shared terminals). Parking (free). Restaurant (breakfast).

★ Daddy Long Legs
134 Long Street, City Centre (021 422 3074/ 021 424 1403/www.daddylonglegs.co.za). **Rates** R600-R825 hotel; R700-R925 self-catering. **Rooms** 13. **Credit** AmEx, DC, MC, V. **Map** p276 G4 ⓲

CONSUME

Handpicked & Gorgeous

For over twelve years, Icon Villas has been delivering a unique vantage of South Africa, one that suits the traveller who is seeking an exclusive, private experience. Whether it's an iconic modern mansion or a discreetly placed Victorian villa, we discover and rent the most beautiful properties. We give them that elusive quality that breathes "home" and turns the tourist into a welcomed and privileged guest.

"Recommended by Conde Nast Traveler US as the Villa Specialist for South Africa."

Tel: 0861 VILLAS
Int: +27 21 424 0905
Email: res@iconvillas.travel
Web: www.iconvillas.travel

iconVillas*

*allure | concierge | decor | essentials | golf | journeys | unfurnished

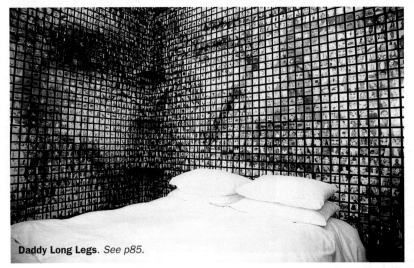

Daddy Long Legs. *See p85.*

A commitment to personalised service ensures its popularity (and a high proportion of return visitors) and it's no surprise that it is a constant on international hotel awards lists. *Photo p88.*
Bar. Business centre. Concierge. Disabled-adapted rooms. Internet (R100 for 24hours wireless, shared terminals). Parking (free). Pool (1 outdoor). Restaurant. Room service. Spa. TV: DStv, DVD on request.
▶ *The hotel's Bascule whisky bar is a must-visit; see p126.*

★ Dock House
Portswood Close, Portswood Ridge, V&A Waterfront (021 421 9334/www.dockhouse. co.za). **Rates** R2,995-R7,495. **Rooms** 6. **Credit** AmEx, DC, MC, V. **Map** p274 G1 ㉒
It's a challenge to remember you're actually in the heart of the Waterfront when you're in this luxe private villa-hotel. Elegant interiors abound and in-room facilities range from a complimentary bar to plasma screen and, always, a swanky bathroom. Butler service, an excellent 24-hour menu, a decadent spa and gym with state-of-the-art equipment, and a prime position in the Waterfront makes it popular with rock stars and heads of state alike.
Bar. Business centre. Concierge. Gym. Internet (free wireless, shared terminals). Parking (free). Pool (1 outdoor). Room service. Spa. TV: DStv, DVD on request.

Ellerman House Luxury Hotel & Villa
180 Kloof Road, Bantry Bay (021 430 3200/ www.ellerman.co.za). **Rates** R4,800-R8,900. **Rooms** 16. **Credit** AmEx, DC, MC, V. **Rooms** 16. **Map** p272 A4 ㉓

Rub shoulders with the international jet set society at this outstanding Relais & Chateaux property that's blessed with gorgeous views and dressed to kill in layers of antiques, fine fabrics and luxury details. Rock stars and tycoons come here for the same reasons, the discreet, top-notch service, the privacy, luxury surrounds and fabulous food.
Bar. Business centre. Gym. Internet (free wireless, shared terminal). Parking (free). Pool (1 outside). Room service. Spa. TV: DStv, DVD.

One & Only
Dock Road, V&A Waterfront (021 431 5888/ www.oneandonlyresorts.com). **Rates** R5,500. **Rooms** 131. **Credit** AmEx, DC, MC, V. **Map** p274 G2 ㉔
Arguably Cape Town's most glamorous hotel, the latest offering from the One & Only international hotel super-group is situated in the heart of the V&A Waterfront, with views of the yacht basin on one side and Table Mountain on the other. Choose from any one of the 131 rooms and relish your position in the midst of the action. With both a Gordon Ramsay and a Nobu restaurant as well as a world-class spa, members of the jet set are sure to feel right at home here.
Bar. Business centre. Concierge. Disabled-adapted rooms. Gym. Internet (free wireless). Parking (free). Pool (1 outdoor). Restaurant. Room service. Spa. TV: DStv, DVD.
▶ *For Maze and Nobu, see pp112-113; see also p83 Hot Beds and p150 Spa for the Course.*

Table Bay Hotel
Quay Six, V&A Waterfront (021 406 5000/ www.suninternational.com). **Rates** R5,250.

CONSUME

Cape Grace Hotel. *See p85.*

Rooms 329. **Credit** AmEx, DC, MC, V.
Map p275 H1 ㉕
Certainly one of the most elegant hotels in town, this impressive site boasts lofty classically inspired interiors and an ideal position in the Waterfront, with great views. The hotel has plush rooms with all the luxury mod cons you'd expect from its five-star status. Excellent dining facilities ensure an all-round lavish experience.
Bar. Business centre. Concierge. Disabled-adapted rooms. Gym. Internet (free wireless, R40 cable). Parking (R40 per night). Pool (1 outdoor). Restaurant (2). Spa. TV: DStv, DVD on request.

★ Twelve Apostles Hotel & Spa
Victoria Road, Camps Bay (021 437 9000/ www.12apostleshotel.com). **Rates** R3,500-R9,100.
Rooms 79. **Credit** AmEx, DC, MC, V.
It's all about location at this five-star hotel and spa that's perched on the rocks above Oudekraal, near Llandudno. Sweeping views of the Atlantic and the mountain abound as do beautiful room interiors, with luxury details at every turn. The Azure restaurant is terrific, while the spa adds to the spoil-me experience. A fabulous honeymoon choice.
Bar. Business centre. Concierge. Disabled-adapted rooms. Gym. Internet (free wireless, cable). Parking (free). Pools (2 outdoor). Restaurants (2). Room service. Spa. TV: DStv, DVD.
▶ *For Azure, see p110; see also p150 Spa for the Course.*

Expensive

Ambassador Hotel
34 Victoria Road, Bantry Bay (021 439 6170/ www.ambassador.co.za). **Rates** R1,560-R2,215

BAR. **Rooms** 96. **Credit** AmEx, DC, MC, V.
Map p272 A4 ㉖
An enviable position above the rocks in Bantry Bay, picture perfect sea (and sunset) views and a selection of accommodation, from double suites to one- and two-bedroom serviced apartments, make this place ideal for everyone from romantic weekenders to business and family travellers. The downstairs bar is the perfect spot to enjoy oysters and champagne, while Salt restaurant is a dining must-do while in the city.
Bar. Concierge. Disabled-adapted rooms. Internet (free wireless). Parking (free). Pool (1 outdoor). Restaurant. Room service. TV: DStv, DVD in some rooms.

Bay
69 Victoria Road, Camps Bay (021 430 4444/ www.thebay.co.za). **Rates** R3,000-R7,600.
Rooms 76. **Credit** AmEx, DC, MC, V.
Map p273 A8 ㉗
It's impossible not to be seduced by the Copacabana-like views of the beach that's just a hop over the road from this popular hotel. Crisp interiors beckon, and with rooms that include the affordable Travellers' Rooms for 'millionaire backpackers', this is a hotel that makes living on the beach an achievable reality. Kick back and relax at any of the pools or hang out sipping cocktails at the pavement Camps Bay Beach Club. There's also a Wellness Centre for me-time and massages.
Bar. Business centre. Concierge. Disabled-adapted rooms. Internet (R60 for 1hour, wireless, cable). Parking (free). Pools (4 splash, 1 heated). Restaurants (2). Room service. Spa. TV: DStv, DVD.
▶ *For the Salt restaurant, see p114.*

O on Kloof

*92 Kloof Road, Bantry Bay (021 439 2081/
082 568 2784/www.oonkloof.co.za).* **Rates**
R2,400-R3,880. **Rooms** 8. **Credit** AmEx, MC, V.
Map p272 B4 ②

One of the city's best boutique hotels (and voted one
of the best 101 hotels of the world by *Tatler*), this
spot has exquisitely captured luxury and tranquillity in a space that offers so much more than the
weary traveller has hoped for, with heated indoor
pool, fully equipped gymnasium, wireless internet,
hammocks, sun decks and more. As if the extras
weren't surprise enough, majestic views of the ocean
and mountain come as standard, as do the services
you come to expect from a top-class boutique hotel.
*Bar. Business centre. Gym. Internet (free wireless,
shared terminals). Ipod docking station. Parking
(free). Pool (1 indoor, heated). Room service.
Spa. TV: DStv, DVD.*

Moderate

Primi Seacastle

*15 Victoria Road, Camps Bay (021 438 4010/
www.primi-seacastle.com).* **Rates** R1,090-R3,610.
Rooms 10. **Credit** AmEx, DC, MC, V.
Map p273 A7 ②

Perfectly positioned on the Camps Bay beachfront,
this well-priced small hotel has ten rooms, ranging
from a standard double up to a honeymoon suite,
as well as a family room – plus a swimming pool.
There are barbecue facilities if you want to cook
dinner for yourself and a whole range of dining
options to choose from too, from self-service breakfast buffets to pre-ordered dinners. Winter special
rates are a boon for those who travel at this time
of the year.
*Bar. Business centre. Concierge. Internet
(free wireless). Parking (free). Pool (1 outdoor).
Room service. TV: DStv, DVD.*

Winchester Mansions

*221 Beach Road, Sea Point (021 434 2351/
www.winchester.co.za).* **Rates** R1,525-R1,970.
Rooms 76. **Credit** AmEx, DC, MC, V.
Map p272 C2 ③

This charming property combines old world details
with a thoroughly modern understanding of what
one wants from a hotel stay. Guests can choose from
classic- or contemporary-styled suites, and with just
76 rooms, a personalised level of service is ensured.

CONSUME

Twelve Apostles Hotel & Spa.

The hotel's proximity to the Sea Point promenade, with Table Mountain behind it, is a big selling point for the Winchester Mansions.

Bar. Bus. Concierge. Disabled-adapted rooms. Internet (R60 for 1hour wireless, shared terminal). Parking (R40 per night). Pool (1 outdoor). Restaurant. Room service. Spa. TV: DStv, DVD in some rooms.

▶ *For Harvey's at the Mansions, see p111 and p127. Sunday breakfast jazz sessions are an institution here.*

Budget

House on the Hill

5 Norman Road, Green Point (021 439 3902/ www.houseonthehillct.co.za). **Rates** R550-R625 B&B; R350-R400 self-catering. **Rooms** 9. **Credit** MC, V. **Map** p274 F2 ③①
Travelling on a budget but not up to the whole backpackers' scene? This Green Point property is a happy compromise, offering budget accommodation in clean, comfortable surroundings. Afro-inspired interiors, newly renovated rooms and a friendly family atmosphere ensures its popularity with international travellers and extended-stay visitors.
TV.

Sunflower Stop

179 Main Road, Green Point (021 434 6535/ www.sunflowerstop.co.za). **Rates** R110-140 dorm; R450 room. **Rooms** 14 beds in dorms; 12 private. **Credit** MC, V. **Map** p274 F2 ③②
Sunflower Stop is a perennial favourite on the budget and backpackers' scene, and you'll easily spot the yellow painted Green Point landmark on the Main Road. Whether you opt for a bed in a dorm or prefer the privacy of an en-suite double, you'll enjoy the little details that make one's stay here a pleasure: weekly barbecues, handy shuttle service into and around the city and loads of advice as to where to go and what to do in the city. Fills up quickly in the summer months, so best to book in advance.
Bar. Internet (R25 per hour). Pool (1 outdoor). TV room.

SOUTHERN SUBURBS

Deluxe

★ Cellars Hohenort

93 Brommersvlei Road, Constantia (021 794 2137/www.cellars-hohenort.com). **Rates** R1,750-R3,300. **Rooms** 53. **Credit** AmEx, DC, MC, V.
For a sophisticated stay in pristine semi-rural surroundings, this Constantia hotel set in a historic manor house is ideal. Elegant interiors, thoughtful in-room luxuries, manicured gardens and outstanding service together create an outstanding package. The hotel also has two private villas for rent, including the two-storey Madiba Villa, complete with its

own pool and 24-hour butler service. The hotel's Martini bar and lounge is a comfortable place to while away an hour or two, and the on-site spa is superb. Not to mention the Greenhouse, Conservatory Bistro and The Cape Malay restaurants, all serving great food, with executive chef Peter Tempelhoff at the helm. *Photo p92.*

Bar. Business centre. Concierge. Disabled-adapted rooms. Internet (free wireless, shared terminals). Parking (free). Pools (2 outdoor, heated). Restaurants (2). Spa. TV: DStv, DVD.

▶ *For the hotel's restaurants, see p115 (Cape Malay) and p117 (Greenhouse at the Cellars); see also p150 Spa for the Course.*

Constantia

Spaanschemat River Road, Constantia (021 794 6561/www.theconstantia.com). **Rates** R3,900-R5,500. **Rooms** 8. **Credit** AmEx, DC, MC, V.
A member of a luxury guesthouse/boutique hotel group, this property in Constantia encompasses the luxury of privacy (there are just six suites) with the benefits of five-star service and facilities. Attention to detail and personalised service as well as elegant surroundings keep visitors coming back for more. There are a number of sister establishments with the same level of service and facilities dotted around the peninsula.
Bar. Business centre. Internet (free wireless). Parking (free). Pool (1 outdoor). TV: DStv, DVD.

Expensive

Constantia Uitsig

Spaanschemat River Road (021 794 6500/ www.constantia-uitsig.com). **Rates** R1,750-R6,450. **Rooms** 16. **Credit** AmEx, DC, MC, V.
Guests here enjoy the benefits of rural surroundings (the hotel is on a working vineyard) with sophisticated facilities. Accommodation is in private cottages; there are five in total, ensuring quiet and privacy. The top-notch spa and award-winning restaurants mean you don't have to leave for an all-round pampering experience.
Bar. Internet (R100 per hour wireless, shared terminals). Pool (1 outdoor). Restaurant (3). Room service. Spa. TV: DStv, DVD on request.

▶ *For the restaurants, see p116 (Constantia Uitsig), p117 (La Colombe) and p118 (River Café). For the vineyard itself, see p62.*

★ Steenberg Hotel & Spa

10802 Steenberg Estate, Tokai Road, Tokai (021 713 2222/www.steenberghotel.com). **Rates** R1,935-R5,985. **Rooms** 24. **Credit** AmEx, DC, MC, V.
Views of the vineyards and False Bay, along with impressive suites, ensure a memorable experience in this luxury home-from-home. The hotel is quite small, with 21 rooms, but the three Heritage Suites

are the jewels in the crown. Each is decorated according to a specific period in South African history and combines pricey antiques and high-tech facilities. Of course, golf-lovers relish the proximity to a quality course, while the dining at Catharina's is excellent too.

Bar. Business centre. Concierge. Internet (free wireless, shared terminal). Parking (free). Pool (1 outdoor). Restaurant. Room service. Spa. TV: DStv, DVD on request.

▶ *For the vineyards, see p63; for the restaurant, Catarina's, see p115.*

★ Vineyard Hotel & Spa

Colinton Road, Newlands (021 657 4500/ www.vineyard.co.za). **Rooms** 175. **Credit** AmEx, DC, MC, V.

The Vineyard Hotel & Spa is a popular bet thanks to its convenient location, lovely sprawling gardens and excellent conferencing facilities. The 175-room hotel was once the home of Lady Anne Barnard and there are displays of antiques and historical paraphernalia in the reception areas. Contemporary styled suites, some very good facilities such as two swimming pools, the outstanding Angsana spa and the Square and Myoga restaurants make it popular with both day visitors and out-of-towners.

Bar. Business centre. Concierge. Disabled-adapted rooms. Gym. Internet (free wireless). Parking (free). Pools (1 indoor, 1 outdoor). Restaurants (4). Spa. TV: DStv.

▶ *For the hotel's restaurants, see p117 (Myoga) and p119 (the Square).*

Moderate

25 Banksia Boutique Hotel

14 Banksia Road, Rosebank (021 689 2992/ www.banksiaboutique.co.za). **Rates** R1,050 per person sharing. **Rooms** 8. **Credit** DC, MC, V.

Located conveniently close to both the city and the southern suburbs, this elegant boutique hotel has a selection of luxurious suites that help make even a two-day business trip feel like a relaxing holiday. An on-site conference facility enhances its appeal for the business sector while the attention to detail (such as the artworks, DVD library and refined home-style breakfasts) make it an appealing option for everyone.

Bar. Concierge. Internet (free wireless). Parking (free). Pool (1 outdoor). Room service on request. TV: DStv, DVD.

Medindi Manor

4 Thicket Road, Rosebank (021 686 3563/ www.medindi.co.za). **Rates** R670-R1,710. **Rooms** 15. **Credit** AmEx, MC, V.

Set in a beautifully restored Edwardian homestead, this popular guesthouse is conveniently located in

the heart of the southern suburbs and is popular with both tourists and business travellers (there's a small conference room). The guesthouse comprises seven spacious rooms in the house, and there are a further eight situated in the gardens.

Internet (R50 for 500mb wireless). Parking (free). Pool (1 outdoor). Room service. TV: DStv.

SOUTHERN PENINSULA

Deluxe

★ Tintswalo Atlantic

Chapman's Peak Drive, Hout Bay (087 754 9300/www.tintswalo.com). **Rates** R7,100. **Rooms** 12. **Credit** AmEx, DC, MC, V.

Being right on the lip of the Atlantic, each of the ten luxury island-themed suites (the Robben Island one sporting its very own prison-bar bathroom door) has views that'll have you humming 'Cocomo' in no time. Follow the winding wooden boardwalk to the main lodge for a leisurely splashabout in the pool or a bit of classy nosh in the dining room (sporting an interactive kitchen, no less). If all that communal bonding proves a bit taxing, kick back on your own private deck, glass in hand, and take in the scenery.

Bar. Concierge. Internet (R150 for 85mb, free terminals). Pool (1 outdoor). Restaurant. Room service. TV: DStv, DVD.

Expensive

Hout Bay Manor

Baviaanskloof, off Main Road, Hout Bay (021 790 0116/www.houtbaymanor.com). **Rates** R1,800-R4,950. **Rooms** 21. **Credit** AmEx, DC, MC, V.

A recent overhaul has injected new life and Afro soul into this small and personable hotel. Its size – there are just 21 rooms, each decorated in a different contemporary ethnic style – ensures a personalised approach to service. The Manor's proximity to Hout Bay beach and surrounds makes it ideal for those wishing to base themselves in this suburb. The restaurant, Pure, offers sophisticated dining.

Bar. Business centre. Concierge. Disabled-adapted rooms. Internet (free wireless, shared terminal). Parking (free). Pool (1 outdoor). Restaurant. Room service. TV: DStv.

★ Rodwell House

Rodwell Road, St James (021 787 9880/www. rodwellhouse.co.za). **Rates** R1,500-R5,000. **Rooms** 8. **Credit** MC, V.

An ideal position opposite St James tidal pool and the catwalk that winds its way all the way to Muizenberg ensures that those who love the sea are in their element here. This magnificent mansion is awash with local artwork and original teak interior detailing. There are just eight spacious suites, each

Cellars Hohenort. *See p91.*

with a sea or mountain view and, thanks to the owner's Epicurean tastes, guests are treated to great wine and food too. A host of services can be arranged for guests, ranging from bird-watching expeditions on the nearby mountains to wine tasting from the hotel's cellar.

Bar. Business centre. Gym. Internet (free wireless, shared terminal). Parking (free). Pool (1 outdoor). Restaurant. Room service. TV: DStv, DVD.

Moderate

Boulders Beach Lodge & Restaurant

4 Boulders Place, Boulders Beach, Simon's Town (021 786 1758/www.bouldersbeach. co.za). **Rates** R950. **Rooms** 14. **Credit** AmEx, DC, MC, V.

Situated in the picturesque seaside village of Simon's Town in the southern reaches of the peninsula, this laid-back lodge enjoys its position right above the beach as well as its reputation as an excellent place in which to kick back and relax. Choose from the Courtyard, Upper Deck (with sea views) or Family Suite for your stay and relish the fact that you're just a stone's throw from the sea and well and truly away from it all. A visit to the nearby penguin colony is a must-do while in the city and the on-site restaurant, with its wooden deck overlooking the ocean and fusion-inspired menu, is highly recommended.

Bar. Internet (R50 per day, wireless). Restaurant.
▶ *For more on Simon's Town, see p72; for more on the beach, see p161.*

Chapman's Peak Hotel

Chapman's Peak Drive, Hout Bay (021 790 1036/www.chapmanspeakhotel.com). **Rates** R550-R2,450. **Rooms** 36. **Credit** AmEx, DC, MC, V.

Its prime position overlooking Hout Bay beach is a major asset for Chapman's Peak, and a series of newly completed, contemporary-style rooms have breathed a much-needed new lease of life into the hotel. Rooms vary from the likes of the affordable Original Room to the sophisticated Penthouse Suite, with sweeping ocean views.

Bar. Parking (free). Restaurant.
▶ *For the hotel's worthwhile restaurants, see p120.*

Budget

British Hotel Apartments

90 St George's Street, Simon's Town (021 786 2214/www.britishhotelapartments.co.za). **Rates** R500 (sleeps 2)-R2,700 (sleeps 6). **Rooms** 16. **Credit** DC, MC, V.

An old-school seaside hotel atmosphere makes this place the antithesis of Cape Town's swanky modern lodgings, but the charm factor is unbeatable. Choose from the small serviced Courtyard Suite or any of the apartments (sleeping up to six people) and relish the old-fashioned surroundings (roll-top baths, faded Persian carpets and imposing colonial four-poster beds). The Sunday carvery makes weekend stays a pleasure.

Internet (free wireless). TV: DStv.

NORTHERN SUBURBS

Moderate

Lagoon Beach Hotel
Lagoon Gate Drive, Milnerton (021 528 2000/
www.lagoonbeachhotel.co.za). **Rates** R1,380-
R2,160. **Rooms** 232. **Credit** AmEx, DC, MC, V.
Picture-perfect views of Table Bay and Table
Mountain seduce all who check into this sizeable
hotel, popular with groups. Inside, it's all about the
shiny contemporary surroundings. In summer,
when the wind makes beach walks impossible, retire
to the Camelot Spa for some R&R. There are also a
number of restaurants on-site.
Bar. Business centre. Concierge. Disabled-adapted
rooms. Gym. Spa. Internet (R50 per hour
wireless, cable). Parking (free). Pools (2 outdoor).
Restaurants (3). Room service. TV: DStv, DVD
on request.

Protea Hotel Tyger Valley
Hendrik Verwoerd Drive, Welgemoed (021 913
2000/www.proteahotels.com). **Rates** R810-
R1,010. **Rooms** 100. **Credit** AmEx, DC, MC, V.
Relatively cheap and cheerful, this three-star hotel is
part of a chain and a good place to lay one's hat when
visiting the Northern Suburbs. The Point of View
restaurant is a recent addition.

Bar. Business centre. Disabled-adapted rooms.
Internet (R30 for 30min wireless, shared
terminals). Parking (R15). Pool (1 outdoor).
TV: DStv.

TOWNSHIPS

Kopanong B&B
C329 Velani Crescent, Khayelitsha (021 361
2084/www.kopanong-township.co.za). **Rates**
R530. **Rooms** 4. **No credit cards**.
Rated by township tour guides as one of the better
guesthouses for providing an authentic township
experience, this comfortable guesthouse has acco-
modation in three double suites, two of which are
en suite. Owner Thope is on hand to welcome
guests and, together with her daughter Mpho, will
happily prepare an authentic African dinner for
you and your party.
Internet (price on request). Disabled-adapted
room. Restaurant.

Vicky's B&B
C-685A Kiyane Street, Site C, Khayelitsha
(082 225 2986/www.cape-town-hotels.travel).
Rates R190-R230 pp incl. dinner and breakfast.
Rooms 6. **No credit cards**.
Vicky's B&B is the most well-known guesthouse
on the township tour circuit. Your host, Vicky, was
the first to spot a gap in this sector of the tourist
accommodation market and in ten years has grown
her brand to include a self-sustaining sewing
centre across the way from her guesthouse.
Guests stay in any of the three rooms in her origi-
nal township shack.
Bar. Internet (R10 for 1 hour). Pool (1 outdoor).
Restaurant. TV: DVD.
▶ *For more hotels outside Cape Town, see the*
Escapes & Excursions chapter (see pp211-246).

CONSUME

Vineyard Hotel & Spa.

Restaurants & Cafés

From classic European cuisine to distinctive South African dishes.

Turn back the clock some 350 years to when the Cape colony was established as a refuelling station. Thanks to fertile lands and prolific fresh produce, there was plenty with which to supply the passing ships en route to the spice lands. The region still produces bountiful produce, and Cape Town diners are feeling the benefit more than ever, with menus incorporating local produce and cooking methods.

Fresh fish and shellfish are ubiquitous. Serving only sustainable seafood is a priority – to check whether the fish on the menu has the green light for eating, text the name to 079 499 8795 and you'll receive an instant answer. Other local flavours reflect Cape Town's unique heritage, and come in the form of mildly spiced, aromatic and fruity Cape Malay curries, or traditional African samp (chopped corn kernels), beans and meat.

Throughout this chapter, budget venues have been labelled **R**.

CITY BOWL

95 Keerom
95 Keerom Street, City Centre (021 422 0765/ www.95keerom.com). **Open** 7am-late Mon-Wed, Sat; noon-2pm Thur, Fri. **Main courses** R100. **Credit** AmEx, DC, MC, V. **Map** p276 G4 ❶ **Italian**
Authentic Italian food meets refined dining at this sophisticated City Centre restaurant. Beef carpaccio is a perfect way to kick off the meal, while mains include light and delicate home-made pastas served with a range of fresher than fresh sauces and the famous New York-style seared tuna with anchovies, capers, olives and tomatoes. The *gelato* is, in a word, heaven.
▶ *New gourmet sibling Carne (see p99) is just across the road.*

R Addis in Cape
41 Church Street, City Centre (021 424 5722/ www.addisincape.co.za). **Open** noon-2.30pm, 6-11pm daily. **Main courses** R90. **Credit** DC, MC, V. **Map** p276 G4 ❷ **Ethiopian**
See p96 **Hello Africa**.

Africa Café
Heritage Square, Shortmarket Street, City Centre (021 422 0221). **Open** 6.30-11pm Mon-Sat. **Main courses** R220. **Credit** MC, V. **Map** p276 G3 ❸ **African**
See p96 **Hello Africa**.

Anytime Trattoria
44 Long Street, City Centre (021 422 1106/ www.anytimerestaurant.net). **Open** 11am-11pm Mon-Sat. **Main courses** R100. **Credit** MC, V. **Map** p276 H3 ❹ **Italian**
This white and bright restaurant in the New Space theatre complex is all about authentic Italian food. The menu features dishes such as melted mozzarella and anchovy-topped crostini for quick and easy munching, authentic pastas and the likes of go-for-broke Parma ham-topped veal Saltimbocca alla Romana if you're ravenous. Pizzas and salads too.

Aubergine
39 Barnet Street, Gardens (021 465 4909). **Open** noon-2pm, 5-10pm Wed-Fri; 5-10pm Mon, Tue, Sat. **Main courses** R160. **Credit** AmEx, DC, MC, V. **Map** p276 G5 ❺ **French**

INSIDE TRACK ABOUT A BRAAI

Nothing is more South African than lighting up a braai. The word can be used both as a noun and a verb and pertains to a type of barbecue, where a wood fire is left to burn down and the meat is then cooked over the charcoal. It's as much a social ritual as a cooking method, and the country is so enamoured with it that it celebrates National Braai Day on 24 September.

Award-winning chef Harald Bresselschmidt conjures up worldly, sophisticated fare at this elegant restaurant, where elite ingredients such as truffles and foie gras often feature on the menu. Think melt-in-the-mouth tender ostrich fillet with orange and balsamic butter or an opulent rabbit with onion and mustard soubise, truffle infused pea purée and white cabbage salad. Not to mention the excellent wine list. Dine on the cheap between 5pm and 7pm, on special menus.
▶ *See p116* **French Revolution**.

Biesmiellah's
2 Wale Stree, cnr Pentz Street, Bo-Kaap (021 423 0850/www.biesmiellah.co.za). **Open** 10.30am-11pm Mon-Sat. **Main courses** R77. **Credit** DC, MC, V. **Map** p276 G3 ⑤ Cape Malay
See p96 **Hello Africa**.

Birds Boutique Café
127 Bree Street, City Centre (021 426 2534). **Open** 7am-4pm Mon-Fri; 8am-2pm Sat. **Main courses** R62. **Credit** MC, V. **Map** p276 G4 ⑦ Café
Don't go expecting an ordinary dining excursion – this offbeat eaterie plays a soothing soundtrack of bird calls, serves its meals in wonky, home-made crockery and sports ceramic swan light fittings. The food is home-made and wholesome, featuring fluffy spinach and feta omelettes, quiches with wholemeal pastry, and legendary chicken pies. Finish with honey-and-cream-drenched pancakes or the hearty warm apple crumble.

★ R Bizerca Bistro
15 Anton Anreith Arcade, Foreshore (021 418 0001/www.bizerca.com). **Open** 7-11am, noon-3pm,

---

Hello Africa

Explore the continent's unique tastes and flavours.

Cape Town offers adventurous eaters tastes from across the African continent, be it Xhosa fare like *samp* (crushed maize used in porridge) and *marog* (African spinach), spongy *injeras* (flatbreads) from Ethiopia, or Cape Malay cuisine.

For an authentic taste of Cape Malay food, head to **Biesmiellah's** (*see p96*) for samosas, potato half moons and chilli bites, followed by meat-in-spicy-sauce mains like lamb *denningvleis* or mild chicken *kalya*. Since wine is traditionally taboo, accompany the spicy dishes with a glass of rose-flavoured *falooda* – a drink made of rose syrup with vermicelli and tapioca.

For dishes from across the spectrum of local food, try **Nyoni's Kraal** (*see p106*), which serves *braaivleis* (barbecue), Malay curries, *amangina* (chicken feet) and smileys (sheep's heads).

For something more universally appealing, try the **Africa Café** (*see p95*), where you'll not only rub shoulders with your fair share of Birkenstocked tourists but also have your pick of everything from Xhosa spinach patties and Mozambican peri-peri prawns to Ethiopian lamb.

Mama Africa (*see p105*) is another Pan-African treat, boasting a live (and loud) Congolese band and as much meat from feathered, scaled and furry beasts as you can eat, all served with a side of *samp* and *pap* (mealie meal porridge). There's more African food at **Marco's African Place** (*see p105*), also popular with tourists. The menu includes specialities like Zwelethu's

Favourite Chicken (simmered with onions and peppers) and a platter of pan-fried springbok, ostrich and kudu fillets. End your meal with the tongue-in-cheek Group Areas dessert, comprised of white and dark chocolate mousses.

You can taste the food of Ethiopia at the beautiful and authentically decorated **Addis in Cape** (*see p95*), where you are encouraged to eat with your hands, mopping up every drop sauce with pieces of *injera* (flatbread).

Africa Café.

CONSUME

Boo Radley's.

6.30-10pm Mon-Fri; noon-3pm, 6.30-10pm Sat. **Main courses** R125. **Credit** MC, V. **Map** p276 H3 ❽ **French**
Award-winning chef Laurent Deslandes has brought his philosophy of Gallic dining to Cape Town. The menu changes every six weeks and offers daily specials depending on availability. The rabbit cassoulet and venison are well worth looking out for and the more adventurous will enjoy the braised pig's trotter with seared scallop and truffle oil.
▶ *See p116* **French Revolution**.

R Boo Radleys ⟵nice
62 Hout Street, City Centre (021 424 3040/ www.booradleys.co.za). **Open** 11am-11pm Mon-Fri; 5-11pm Sat. **Main courses** R70. **Credit** MC, V. **Map** p276 H3 ❾ **Bistro**
New York City style hits Cape Town with this elegant bistro that's dressed to kill in classy leather banquettes, Parisian café chairs and a black and white checked floor. Seating just 50, the restaurant serves the likes of garlicky mussels, bouillabaisse and that all-time retro favourite, prawn cocktail with avocado. Pop in for a pre- or post-theatre meal (the restaurant is situated near the New Space theatre complex), or take it slowly and linger over one or more of the famed minty mojitos.

★ Brewers & Union
St Stephen's Church, 110 Bree Street, City Centre (021 422 2770). **Open** 11am-11pm Mon-Thur; noon-late Fri, Sat. **Main courses** R65. **Credit** AmEx, MC, V. **Map** p276 G3 ❿ **Bar**
This beer salon serves up a range of artisan-made beers along with a selection of eats that include smoked chorizo, grilled sausages, cheeses, homemade crisps and breads served on utilitarian breadboards. Throw in an elegant brasserie-style interior, enthusiastic staff, cool tunes and a clientele of shiny, happy, well-dressed people and you've got the ideal urban retreat.

★ Bukhara
33 Church Street, City Centre (021 424 0000/ www.bukhara.com). **Open** noon-3pm, 6-11pm Mon-Sat; 6-11pm Sun. **Main courses** R150. **Credit** AmEx, DC, MC, V. **Map** p276 G4 ⓫ **Indian**
Heavenly tandoori dishes and fragrant curries await you at this popular establishment. Study the extensive menu while nibbling on the complimentary poppadoms and, once you've ordered, watch the chefs work their magic through the frosted kitchen glass for some pointers on how to make the legendary butter chicken, tandoori lamb chops and lamb rogan josh.

Café du Cap
76 Church Street, City Centre (021 424 4008). **Open** noon-4pm Mon, Tue; noon-4pm, 6pm-late Wed-Fri. **Main courses** R70. **Credit** DC, MC, V. **Map** p276 G4 ⓬ **Belgian**
Tried and tested Belgian bistro favourites abound on the unfussy menu of this modern, yet intimate eaterie. Expect authentic eats like *vispannetje*, croquettes or frites, and the occasional French influence, with the likes of pâté and terrines. The tender, aged cuts of meat are any carnivore's dream.

Café Gainsbourg
64 Kloof Street, Gardens (021 422 1780). **Open** 7.30am-10.30pm Mon-Fri; 9am-10.30pm Sat, Sun. **Main courses** R73. **Credit** DC, MC, V. **Map** p274 F5 ⓭ **Café**
This coffee spot has a distinctly upmarket feel, with a dark interior, screed floors and art deco-style pendant lamps; no wonder it's so popular among laptop-addicted businessmen. Don't go expecting a rush job – it's all about slow food here. Breakfasts of thick white toast slathered with Nutella or croque monsieur will necessitate some belt loosening; lunches of gourmet sandwiches and salads take a healthier route.

CONSUME

★ Cape Colony

Mount Nelson Hotel, 76 Orange Street, City Centre (021 483 1948). **Open** 6.30-10.30pm daily. **Main courses** R133. **Credit** AmEx, DC, MC, V. **Map** p276 G5 ⓮ **French/Asian**

Whether you opt for the classical or modern Asian-inspired menu, the food at Mount Nelson's signature restaurant won't disappoint. The traditional menu lists favourites such as beef Wellington. On the Asian side are newfangled creations like Vietnamese black-lacquered rack of lamb. The grand vaulted ceilings and opulent decor make this elegant restaurant ideal for special occasions.

▶ *See also p78 for more on The Mount Nelson Hotel and p122* **Time for Tea**.

R Cape to Cuba

227 Long Street, City Centre (021 424 2330). **Open** 9am-late daily. **Main courses** R80. **Credit** AmEx, MC, V. **Map** p276 G4 ⓯ **Cuban**

This left-of-centre tribute to Che Guevara was a favourite Kalk Bay hangout that's now opened up in the city. Fire up the taste buds with a plate of chilli poppers as they're meant to be enjoyed – with friends and ample cocktails, or move on to greater things with flavourful paella, enchiladas with guacamole or fresh seafood and steaks.

Other locations Main Road, Kalk Bay (021 788 1566).

R Carlyle's On Derry

17 Derry Street, Vredehoek (021 461 8787). **Open** 6-10.30pm Tue-Sun. **Main courses** R70. **Credit** MC, V. **Pizza**

Laid-back locals seek refuge from Vredehoek's notorious gale force winds at this neighbourhood haunt. The thin-crusted pizzas are the stuff legends are made of, and include mouth-watering combos such as blue cheese and fig preserve, and Thai chicken with tomato and coriander. If pizzas aren't your thing, the fall-off-the-bone lamb-shank is a tried and tested favourite.

★ Carne

70 Keerom Street, City Centre (021 424 3460). **Open** 6.30pm-late Mon-Sat. **Main courses** R115. **Credit** AmEx, DC, MC, V. **Map** p276 G4 ⓰ **Meat**

Restaurateur Giorgio Nava is famously passionate about provenance and the result is a farm producing his own Italian-South African beef, which he serves at Carne, the sister to his stylish flagship Italian restaurant 95 Keerom. The menu features plenty of cuts not always seen on steakhouse menus, from ribeye to hanger steaks – the cult cut favoured by many a top-notch chef these days. If you're not into blood on your plate, there's always chicken or ostrich, just don't expect fanciful fripperies – the presentation is pared down and accompaniments are kept to the bare minimum. *Photo p100.*

▶ *See also p95 for more on 95 Keerom.*

Cape to Cuba.

★ Caveau Wine Bar & Deli

92 Bree Street, Heritage Square, City Centre (021 422 1367/www.caveau.co.za). **Open** 7am-10.30pm Mon-Sat. **Main courses** R80. **Credit** AmEx, DC, MC, V. **Map** p276 G3 ⓱ **Tapas, bistro**

The prime seats at this wine bar in historic Heritage Square are definitely on the terrace facing Bree Street – an ideal spot for a long, boozy lunch. For more secluded dining, opt for the seating in the newly opened courtyard. The constantly changing blackboard menu features great tapas as well as bistor dishes like calamari with chilli, steak with béarnaise sauce and steak tartare. Excellent wine lists, with lots available by the glass.

Other locations Josephine Mill, 13 Boundary Road, Newlands (021 685 5140).

▶ *See p45 for more information about Heritage Square.*

INSIDE TRACK
WINTER SPECIALS

Winter is Cape Town's secret season, when prices drop along with the temperature. Some of the city's best restaurants run pocket-friendly winter specials, including award-winning culinary darling **La Colombe** (*see p117*).

CONSUME

Carne. *See p99.*

R Chef Pon's Thai & Asian Kitchen

12 Mill Street, Gardens (021 465 5846). **Open** 6-10.30pm daily. **Main courses** R75. **Credit** AmEx, DC, MC, V. **Map** p274 G5 ⑬ **Asian**

This informal Mill Street stalwart's comprehensive Asian menu offers tempting dishes from Thailand, China, Japan and Mongolia, marked according to their levels of spiciness; the Jungle duck curry being the most famous fire-starter. Begin with crispy vegetarian spring rolls or calamari tempura, and move on to the Thai curries or sticky duck pancakes, if your tastes lean towards the mild side.

★ Col'Cacchio   *boring*

Shop 2, The Spearhead Building, 42 Hans Strijdom Avenue, Foreshore (021 419 4848/ www.colcacchio.co.za). **Open** noon-11pm Mon-Fri; 6-11pm Sat, Sun. **Main courses** R75. **Credit** AmEx, DC, MC, V. **Map** p276 H3 ⑲ **Pizzas**

If you're generally unable to make up your mind in restaurants, the 50 different pizza toppings on offer at this famous franchise will have you breaking into a slight sweat. If the pressure gets too much, however, you could always just build your own. Favourites include the indulgent *tre colori* with smoked salmon, crème fraîche and caviar, and the Fantasia, with caramelised onion, brie and sesame seeds. If pizza doesn't take your fancy there are also great pasta, gnocchi and salad offerings. **Other locations** throughout the city.

Doppio Zero

Mandela Rhodes Place, Corner St George's Mall and Church Street, City Centre (021 424 9225/ www.doppio.co.za). **Open** 7am-10pm daily. **Main courses** R90. **Credit** DC, MC, V. **Map** p276 G4 ⑳ **Italian**

This successful franchise has just opened its newest branch in the prime location of Mandela Rhodes's Atrium, incorporating a bakery (the artisan ciabatta has received a nod of approval from many a bread-junkie), restaurant (with a very popular range of pizzas) and *gelateria* (featuring almost 30 flavours of the real deal). The atmosphere is relaxed and cosy, with musicians putting in the odd appearance. Tuck into a moreish spread of tried and true comfort food such as veal pizzaiola and spaghetti meatballs like you wish your mama could make.

Fork

84 Long Street, City Centre (021 424 6334/ www.fork-restaurants.co.za). **Open** noon-11pm Mon-Sat. **Main courses** R45. **Credit** MC, V. **Map** p276 G4 ㉑ **Tapas**

Do the in-vogue thing and indulge in a spot of communal eating. Each beautifully composed plate features four mouthfuls; plates range from super-affordable *patatas bravas* to pricier dishes such as pancetta-wrapped tiger prawns and kudu fillet with tomato purée – all ideal for sharing and swapping. *Photo p102.*

CONSUME

Something Fishy

The freshest ocean fare.

Some of the world's finest tuna can be found off South Africa's shores and luckily for us, before it's shipped to Japan, our local chefs snap some of it up. If there's tuna on the menu it's better if it's fresh rather than frozen; order it just-seared – anything more and the flavour will be destroyed.

The prawns you'll find on local menus are generally well priced and portions plentiful – ask for yours peri-peri, the spice makes all the difference. We're big on line-caught fish here and if yellowtail or cob is on offer, be sure to order it. But try to steer clear of kingklip, as it's on the soon-to-be-threatened list. Restaurants are increasingly aware of eco-friendly seafood choices and if you're not sure that the special of the day is above board, simply text the fish name to 079 499 8795 and you'll get an SMS response giving the red (no), orange (maybe) or green (yes) status of the fish you're thinking of ordering. This clever initiative comes from SASSI (Southern African Sustainable Seafood Initiative) and it's helping to spread awareness among consumers.

Not sure where to start? If you're watching your wallet, the cheap and

cheerful offerings of the **Ocean Basket** chain are ideal (www.oceanbasket.co.za; branches around the city). **Nobu** (*see p112*) is on the opposite end of the price scale, but a culinary and seafood experience par excellence, as is **Baia** (*see p110*). **Miller's Thumb** (*see p105*) in the City Bowl is a family favourite, with the freshest fare treated with care. **Willoughby & Co** (*see p114*), at the V&A Waterfront, remains one of the city's most popular sushi and seafood destinations, while you can't go wrong with fish and chips from **Texies** on Grand Parade.

Ginja

121 Castle Street, City Centre (021 426 2368). **Open** 7-10pm Mon-Sat. **Set dinners** R99 1 course; R190 2 courses; R220 3 courses. **Credit** AmEx, DC, MC, V. **Map** p276 G3 ㉒
Contemporary
Award-winning chef Mike Bassett whips up conceptual culinary creations that look almost too good to eat. Navigate your way through the corridor into the red-walled haven and pick and choose from exciting starters including tasting spoons from around the world, and sumptuous mains like melt-in-the mouth rack of lamb or springbok Wellington.

Greens on Park

5 Park Road, Gardens (021 422 4415). **Open** 8am-5pm Mon; 8am-11pm Tue-Sat. **Main courses** R75. **Credit** AmEx, DC, MC, V. **Map** p274 F5 ㉓ Café, bistro, pizza
Enjoy an eyeful of life on Kloof Street from the terrace here. The extensive breakfast menu is legendary and the wood-fired pizzas are more than enough reason to become a loyal patron, featuring interesting topping combos like prawn and chilli, and salmon, crème fraîche, caviar and dill. The gourmet burgers are equally addictive.

Other locations Shop 7, High Constantia Centre, Constantia Main Road, Constantia (021 794 7843); Shop 1A, Intaba Building, cnr Protea and Corwen Roads, Claremont (021 674 5152); Shop 8A, Plattekloof Village, Plattekloof Road, Plattekloof (021 558 0855).

Haiku

58 Burg Street, City Centre (021 424 7000). **Open** noon-2.30pm, 6-11pm Mon-Sat; 6-11pm Sun. **Main courses** R120 lunch, R170 dinner. **Credit** AmEx, DC, MC, V. **Map** p276 G4 ㉔ Asian
Grab a bunch of friends and work your way through the range of Asian tapas including fried, boiled and steamed dim sum (filled with everything from spinach and cream cheese to seared scallops) or spicy lamb, sushi, *robata*, stir-fries and wok dishes. The Peking duck is phenomenal and the banana chocolate spring rolls with coconut ice-cream are the perfect way to end your meal. Communication is sometimes hampered by the music, so you might have to raise your voice to be heard over the din.

Headquarters

Heritage Square, Bree Street, City Centre (021 424 6373). **Open** 11am-10.30pm

CONSUME

Mon-Sat. **Main courses** R140. **Credit** AmEx, DC, MC, V. **Map** p276 G3 ㉕ **Meat**
When they said 'keep it simple, stupid', the owners of this place (HQ for short) took the message literally. They serve only seared sirloin, salad and frites. Take it or leave it. Great for those who struggle with decision-making: all you need to worry about is how you'd like your steak cooked and what you're going to drink.

▶ *See also p45 Heritage Square.*

★ Jardine
185 Bree Street, City Centre (021 424 5640). **Open** 7-10pm Mon-Sat. **Set dinners** 2 courses R240; 3 courses R280. **Credit** AmEx, DC, MC, V. **Map** p276 G4 ㉖ **Contemporary**
Come hungry, begin the gastronomic adventure and you'll soon see what all the fuss is about. Starters include the likes of crayfish bouillon, duck-confit terrine and beetroot tart, while mains feature epics such as tender Chalmar beef fillet with oxtail, and tomatoey West Coast crayfish risotto. Or go big and indulge in the sublime tasting menu. The interior is intimate and features an ever-changing collection of contemporary artwork, perfectly complementing the cutting-edge fare.

▶ *The bakery downstairs does brisk business in artisan breads, pastries, and man-size sandwiches. See also p103* **Well-Bread***.*

Josephine's
The Piazza, Parliament Street, City Centre (021 469 9750; www.josephineboulangerie.com). **Open** 6.30am-4pm Mon-Fri; 6.30am-noon Sat. **No credit cards**. **Map** p276 H4 ㉗ **Café**

Fork. *See p101.*

In the heart of Cape Town lies a pretty pink slice of Paris. Josephine's dishes out girly treats, from brioche and croissants to *pain de campagne* croquemonsieur and macaroons. Everything is beautifully presented, too. There are also Chinese teas, Belgian coffee, and home-made jams.

R Kubo's Little Japan
48 Riebeek Street, City Centre (021 421 4360). **Open** noon-2pm, 6-10pm Mon-Fri; 6-10pm Sat. **Main courses** R93. **Credit** AmEx, DC, MC, V. **Map** p276 H3 ㉘ **Japanese**
Not exactly the type of place you'd see splashed across the pages of an interiors magazine, this little hole-in-the-wall offers innumerable super-fresh sushi options, but if you don't dig the raw stuff, there is also great cooked Japanese food, including tasty beef-and-mushroom skewers and soothing miso and clam soup.

La Petite Tarte
Shop 11A. Cape Quarter, De Waterkant Street, De Waterkant (021 425 9077). **Open** 8am-5pm Mon-Fri; 8am-3pm Sat. **Main courses** R44. **Credit** DC, MC, V. **Map** p276 G3 ㉙ **Café**
Imagine yourself at a little Parisian café as you take a seat on the pavement outside this quaint coffee shop. The interior is equally chic, sporting bits and bobs from the Continent and setting the scene for sophisticated French bites like fruit tarts and croque monsieurs. Also good for an after-work tipple.

Lazari Food Gallery
Corner Upper Maynard Street and Vredehoek Avenue, Vredehoek (021 461 9865). **Open** 7.30am-5pm Mon-Fri; 8am-4pm Sat; 8am-2.30pm Sun. **Main courses** R45. **Credit** AmEx, MC, V. **Café**
Sink back into one of the retro armchairs of this small and vibey City Bowl nook and watch the world go by. The breakfast croissants with plentiful fillings are the perfect way to start the day; the selection of wraps, sarnies and pittas also makes the place a popular lunchtime haunt. No visit is complete without an obligatory pink chocolate-topped cupcake that'll teleport you straight back to childhood.

R Loading Bay
30 Hudson Street, Hudson Building, De Waterkant (021 425 6320/1). **Open** 7am-5pm Mon-Fri; 8am-4pm Sat. **Main courses** R41. **Credit** AmEx, DC, MC, V. **Map** p276 G3 ㉚ **Lebanese/Café**
This stylish industrial space is kitted out in concrete, wood, black and splashes of neon, and features a trendy boutique on its mezzanine level. The food is a modern take on Lebanese fare, including filling salads, fresh pastas and moreish *man'ouche* (flatbread) with milky *labneh* and *za'tar*, a tangy condiment.

▶ *For the boutique, see p145.*

CONSUME

Profile Well-Bread

The art of the artisan baker.

'It was all a fluke,' explains Jason Lilley when asked how he ended up baking bread for a living. Now at the helm of the city' hippest artisan bakery, Jardine (Cnr Bloem and Bree Streets, City Bowl; 021 424 5644), it does seem that Lilley's career has had some element of coincidence about it.

After graduating from the Swiss Hotel School in Randburg in 2000, Jason kicked off his chef's career at the Cellars Hohenort in Cape Town's Constantia Valley, where he met chef George Jardine – an encounter that would prove auspicious – before moving on to becoming a successful pastry chef at Table Bay Hotel and the Arabella Sheraton (now the Westin Grand Cape Town Arabella Quays). Later, during a stint at the illustrious Pezula Resort and Spa Hotel in Knysna, fate stepped in when he met artisan baker Markus Farbinger at a local food festival. Farbinger agreed to teach him the fine art of crafting handmade bread.

Lilley took to bread-making like a duck to à l'orange, and when pal George Jardine made him the offer of opening a bakery adjacent to his award-winning restaurant Jardine (*see p102*), he jumped at the chance, bringing 'Henry', his bread starter (master dough culture), along for the ride.

With a lineage that can be traced back to the King Arthur Flour Company in Vermont, America, Henry the Bread Starter has been Jardine Bakery's good luck charm since its opening. Lilley got it from one of Markus's mentors, Jeffrey Hammelman, during a bread-making course and has been lovingly feeding and watering it ever since – using it in everything from his French-style sourdoughs to nutty ryes.

Word about the bewitching bread has certainly got around and in its two years of existence the bakery has gained a loyal following, with customers addicted to the range of scrumptious sarmies and pastries) as much as its buzzing sidewalk-café culture.

'There's a group of regulars who order the same thing every single day,' says Lilley of his cult following. 'It's a great way of keeping us on our toes, as we're only as good as our last croissant and cup of coffee.'

MORE BREAD

Josephine's
Beautiful *pain campagne*, brioche, croissants and more. *See p102.*

Doppio Zero
One of a successful franchise, with bakery incorporated. Great artisan ciabatta. *See p100.*

CONSUME

CAFE & CHOCOLATIER

Enjoy a truly exquisite South African high tea experience at Myatt Café & Chocolatier, situated at Cape Town's most popular shopping centre, the V&A Waterfront.

This stylish café will take you to new heights of sophistication where you can give into every temptation. Treat your senses with a gastronomic experience of special blended teas, pastries, mini croissants, delectable sandwiches and scones. MARY chocolates, imported from Belgium, handcrafted cakes and delicate macaroons can be enjoyed at this trendy café or wrapped beautifully as the ultimate gift. Crockery from Villeroy and Boch, designer Vitra chairs and Eileen Grey tables adds to this quintessential fine dining experience. Indulge in excellence with Myatt Café & Chocolatier.

Myatt Café & Chocolatier is open for breakfast, lunch, tea and dinner.

V&A Waterfront, Upper Level, Shop 6244, Cape Town, South Africa.
Tel: +27 21 418 8844   www.myattcafe.com

R Maharajah
230 Long Street, City Centre (021 424 6607).
Open 12.30-3pm Mon-Fri; 6.30-10.30pm Mon-Sat.
Main courses R78. **Credit** AmEx, DC, MC, V.
Map p276 G4 30 ③ **Indian**
This Indian restaurant attracts a fair following of curry devotees. The menu is extensive, with curries ranging from mild to singeing. The tomatoey fish curry has just the right touch of spice and the lamb on the bone is amazing. Just be sure to keep those soft rotis coming to mop up every last delicious drop.

Mama Africa
178 Long Street, City Centre (021 426 1017/ www.mamaafricarest.net). **Open** 11am-4pm Tue-Fri; 7am-11pm Mon, Sat. **Main courses** R95. **Credit** AmEx, DC, MC, V. **Map** p276 G4 ㉜ **African**
► *See p96* **Hello Africa**.

★ Manna Epicure
151 Kloof Street, Gardens (021 426 2413).
Open 9am-6pm Tue-Sat; 9am-4pm Sun. **Main courses** R83. **Credit** DC, MC, V. **Café**
A white and shining beacon on the hilly Kloof Street coffee shop stretch, Manna Epicure's bright and airy interior features quirky touches like teapots that appear to sprout from the wall. Breakfasts range from sensible to self-indulgent and the lunch of delicately poached salmon trout with salsa verde and potato wedges is highly recommended.

Marco's African Place
15 Rose Lane, Bo-Kaap (021 423 5412/ www.marcosafricanplace.co.za). **Open** noon-11pm Tue-Thur; noon-midnight Fri, Sat; 3-11pm Sun. **Credit** AmEx, DC, MC, V. **Map** p276 G3 ㉝ **African**
► *See p96* **Hello Africa**.

★ R Masala Dosa
167 Long Street, City Centre (021 424 6772/ www.masaladosa.co.za). **Open** 11.30am-10pm Mon-Sat. **Main courses** R52. **Credit** AmEx, MC, V. **Map** p276 G4 ㉞ **Indian**
Head for the white, patent leather booth seats and make your choice from the wacky, over-the-top faux Bollywood-poster menus. The dosa (a thin rice-and-lentil pancake) is the undisputed star of the show here and comes with divine, mildly spiced fillings such as butternut and lamb curry, and coconut chicken. They are all accompanied by bowls of spicy dipping sauces. Sweet tooths can indulge in the chocolate dosa or the silky cardamom-infused semolina pudding. *Photo p106.*

R Melissa's
94 Kloof Street, Gardens (021 424 5540/www. melissas.co.za). **Open** 7.30am-8pm Mon-Fri; 8am-8pm Sat, Sun. **Main courses** R50. **Credit** AmEx, DC, MC, V. **Map** p274 F5 ㉟ **Café**

The mother ship of a franchise that's seen satellites sprouting left, right and centre, this Kloof Street institution offers window seats and bar stools from which to survey the goings on of the City Bowl. The bountiful buffet table groans with treats and the blackboard menu changes daily. The shelves are choc-a-block with home-made Melissa's products, ranging from jams and quiches to custards and vinegars.
Other locations throughout the city.

R Mesopotamia
Cnr Long and Church streets, City Centre (021 424 4664/www.mesopotamia.co.za). **Open** 7pm-late Mon-Sat. **Main courses** R80. **Credit** AmEx, DC, MC, V. **Map** p276 G4 ㊱ **Kurdish**
This Kurdish restaurant is great for large groups looking for a bit of bread-breaking and belly dancing. There's a lip-smacking selection of mezze including *kinder* (pumpkin with tahini and garlic yoghurt) and *ciger* (fried lambs' liver with onions and parsley), ideal with a few side orders of naan bread. The decor is like something out of *Aladdin*, with kelim-draped walls, oil lamps and low copper tables.

Miller's Thumb
10B Kloof Nek Road, Gardens (021 424 3838). **Open** 6.30-10.30pm Mon, Sat; 12.30-2pm,

Manna Epicure.

CONSUME

Masala Dosa. *See p105.*

6.30-10.30pm Tue-Fri. Closed July. **Main courses** R117. **Credit** AmEx, DC, MC, V. **Map** p274 F5 ⊛ **Seafood**
This cosy neighbourhood hangout serves fresh fish (there are usually three line-caught fish options) in several delicious guises – Cajun style, perhaps, or Cape Malay. For something different, try the dorado or tuna with sweet chilli, lime and lychee. Or there's hefty *espetada* or rich beef drenched in bordelaise sauce. The Mississippi mud pie is worth the weight gain.

Nova
70 New Church Street, City Centre (021 422 3585). **Open** 7pm-late (last orders as 10pm) Mon-Sat. **Main courses** R100. **Credit** AmEx, DC, MC, V. ⊛ **Contemporary**
Award-winning chef extraordinaire Richard Carstens plies his gastronomically adventurous trade at this chic, white-painted little spot. Expect the freshest local ingredients given an accomplished twist – with a good dollop of lighthearted playfulness thrown in. If you feel like being adventurous, try the tasting menu, with Carstens' signature dishes that incorporate his molecular gastronomy flair.

Nyoni's Kraal
98 Long Street, City Centre (021 422 0529/ www.nyoniskraal.co.za). **Open** 8am-11pm Mon-Sat; 4-11pm Sun. **Main courses** R100. **Credit** AmEx, DC, MC, V. **Map** p276 G4 ⊛ **African**
▶ *See p96* **Hello Africa***.*

Nzolo Brand Café
48 Church Street, City Centre (021 426 1857). **Open** 8am-4.30pm Mon-Fri; 8am-3pm Sat. **Main courses** R60. **Credit** MC, V. **Map** p276 G4 ⊛ **Café**
If it's a sunny day, it would be a sin not to sit outside under the decorated tree, sporting a few zany plastic chickens to boot. It's a great spot from which to watch the bustle of the little side street frequented by antique seekers and art-lovers as you tuck into your choice of gourmet sandwiches or African-inspired meals. If you're lucky enough arrive on time, the moist, nutty, flavour-packing carrot cake with cream cheese topping is guaranteed to put a smile on your dial.

★ Origin
28 Hudson Street, De Waterkant (021 421 1000/ www.originroasting.co.za). **Open** 7am-5pm Mon-Fri; 9am-2pm Sat. **Main courses** R30. **Credit** AmEx, MC, V. **Map** p276 G3 ⊛ **Café**
Coffee junkies flock to this converted tobacco house for their daily bean fix. The artisan roastery stocks coffee from across the African continent as well as prime coffee producers like Colombia, Guatemala, Indonesia and India. If you're a bit of a novice, fear not – the über-enthusiastic baristas will talk you through all of the choices.
▶ *See also p112 Nigiro Tea.*

★ R Royale Eatery & Royale Kitchen
273 Long Street, City Centre (021 422 4536). **Open** noon-11.30pm Mon-Sat. **Main courses** R55. **Credit** AmEx, DC, MC, V. **Map** p276 G4 ⊛ **Burgers**
This hipster hangout is all about the gourmet burger – whether it's the gargantuan classic beef Royale, the Googamooly with its guacamole doused vegetarian lentil and chickpea patty, or the perennially popular Norwood, with mushroom, three cheeses and green peppercorn sauce. All burgers come with a choice of American-style fries, potato wedges or sweet potato chips. The downstairs area is kitted out with retro booths and quirky contemporary artwork; the upstairs Royale Kitchen is an *Amélie*-inspired wonderland of antique props and sheet-music wallpaper. The super thick shakes for dessert are a must.
▶ *See p126 Waiting Room.*

INSIDE TRACK
A ROYALE TIME

If Hollywood actress Salma Hayek is to be believed, **Royale** (*see p106*) makes the best burgers in the whole wide world. She even professed her love for the place live on US talk show *Late Night* with Conan O'Brien.

CONSUME

★ Saigon

Cnr of Kloof and Camp streets, Gardens (021 424 7670/7669). **Open** noon-2.30pm, 6-10.30pm Mon-Fri; 6-10.30pm Sat. **Main courses** R70. **Credit** AmEx, DC, MC, V. **Map** p274 F5
Vietnamese

This Vietnamese restaurant has been around for some ten years, and is still as popular as ever. Yummy starters include crystal spring rolls and DIY lettuce wraps with noodles, prawns and chilli sauce; follow with legendary mains like sizzling seafood hotplate (flambéed dramatically in front of the diner) with creamy curried peanut sauce, and barbecue duck with chilli sauce. There's also plenty for vegetarians – like the Buddhist curry with sweet potato that'll take you straight to nirvana.
▶ *During summer months you can have a ten-minute massage at your table – a novel way to relax into the evening.*

Savoy Cabbage

101 Hout Street, City Centre (021 424 2626/ www.savoycabbage.co.za). **Open** noon-2.30pm, 7-10.30pm Mon-Fri; 7-10.30pm Sat. **Main courses** R155. **Credit** AmEx, DC, MC, V. **Map** p276 G3 **Bistro, contemporary**
All pared-down, industrial glass-and-steel chic in a historic building, this place is a haven for lovers of all things meaty. Indulge in the sautéed brains with capers, parsley and charred butter, or opt for the Chalmar beef fillet with melted marrow, mushroom and Guinness sauce. The signature tomato tart is famed throughout the city.

INSIDE TRACK VINTAGE VIBES

You'll find retro Americana with a Cape Malay twist at the 1950s-style fast-food institution that is the **Wembley Roadhouse** (23 Belgravia Road, Belgravia, Athlone, 021 697 1430/www.wembleygroup. co.za). Waiters come out to your car to take your order – the Wembley Whopper is legendary.

Shoga

121 Castle Street, City Centre (021 426 2369). **Open** 7-10pm Mon-Sat. **Main courses** R103. **Credit** AmEx, DC, MC, V. **Map** p276 G3
Asian, contemporary

This hipper sibling of downstairs restaurant Ginja (*see p101*) has a more laid-back atmosphere and features unfussy, but delicious Asian-influenced fare. There's a great tapas selection of tasty treats and main courses, including the likes of prawn risotto and other special treats; meanwhile, the decadent chocolate and macadamia brownie will give chocoholics their fix for the day.

R Showroom Café

38 Long Street, City Centre (021 424 7247/ www.theshowroomrestaurant.co.za). **Open** 6.30am-11pm Mon-Sat; 7am-8pm Sun. **Main courses** R65. **Credit** AmEx, DC, MC, V. **Map** p276 H3 **Contemporary**

CONSUME

Royale Eatery & Royale Kitchen.

Part of the Grand Daddy hotel, this cosmopolitan café sees a steady trade of media and advertising types sandwiched in among the tourists. With a menu by the award-winning Bruce Robertson, expect pared down sophisticated fare – from the best Caesar salad ever to gourmet sandwiches and wraps, rib-sticking pastas and a particularly good burger.

Societi Bistro

50 Orange Street, Gardens (021 424 2100/ www.societi.co.za). **Open** noon-11pm daily. **Main courses** R50-R198. **Credit** AmEx, DC, MC, V. **Map** p276 G4 **㊼ Bistro**

City slickers will be glad to hear that this popular hotspot has recently relocated from the Waterfront to Gardens. Breakfasts are brilliant, with scrummy offerings including eggs Benedict. The pizza bianco is also a winner, with toppings of Parma ham and artichokes and mascarpone; springbok carpaccio with chilli and crème fraîche is also successful. The roasts are superbly hearty, be they the tender red wine and tomato lamb shank or the oven-roasted fish with herbed butter and new potatoes.

▶ *The bistro has great meal and movie specials in conjunction with the Labia cinema across the road; see p167* **Queen of the Big Screen**.

Subarshi

Shop 1, The Spearhead, 42 Hans Strijdom Avenue, Foreshore (021 421 3366). **Open** noon-10pm Mon-Fri; 5pm-10pm Sun. **Main courses** R70. **Credit** AmEx, DC, MC, V. **Map** p276 H3 **㊽ Sushi**

Pop into this bright and tiny spot for your urban sushi fix, chosen from the conveyor belt. With its comfy bar seats, you're sure to want to linger here for several platefuls. If you're after something different, try a sushi sandwich.

Sundance Gourmet Coffee Co.

59 Buitengracht Street, Gardens (021 424 1461/ www.sundancecoffeeco.com). **Open** 6.30am-4.30pm Mon-Fri. **Main courses** R34. **Credit** AmEx, DC, MC, V. **Map** p276 G3 **㊾ Café**

With stores dotted around the city, you'll never be in danger of missing out on your caffeine hit – simply

Lip-smacking local food

Your glossary to a gamut of homegrown dishes.

Beskuit (Rusks): Bone-dry rectangular biscuits that are best enjoyed dipped into a piping hot cuppa and then slurped in a style that eludes sophistication.

Biltong: The preferred snack of sports enthusiasts, these dried, salty strips of beef are perfect when washed down with liberal lashings of beer.

Bobotie: This fragrant, slightly spicy Cape Malay dish is comprised of curried mince with dried fruit such as raisins, topped with an egg custard, which is then baked.

Boerewors: No self-respecting braai should be without this spiced beef sausage. Slap on a long bread roll, slather with tomato sauce or chutney, and hey presto, you have a boerewors-roll.

Bunnychow: Hollow out half a loaf of white bread, fill with curry and dig in. Elegant it ain't, but damn, it's good.

Chakalaka: Ranging from a bit-of-a-bite to hot-as-hell, this tomato-based vegetable relish is usually served with pap (mealie-meal porridge) and meat dishes.

Koeksisters: Sinfully sweet plaits of dough, which are deep-fried before being drenched in a cinnamon-sugar syrup. Not a healthy snack.

Koeksister: Not to be confused with *koeksisters*, this sweet Cape Malay snack is more like a small, fragrant doughnut, soaked in syrup and dipped in coconut.

Potjie: The key components to preparing the perfect potjie stew are simple enough: you need a cast-iron pot known as a *potjie*, a decent fire, a little stirring and a lot of patience. The choice of ingredients relies very much on the *potjie* master, but stews usually includes meat and vegetables.

Smiley: Describing this township delicacy as an acquired taste would be a definite understatement. It's a boiled sheep's head.

look out for the creamy, latte colours of the awnings and step into a world where gourmet grinds are the order of the day. From caffe marrochinos to frappacinos and straight up and down cappuccinos, they've got it sorted. There are also yummy sandwiches. **Other locations** throughout the city.

★ Vida e Caffè
Shop 1, Mooikloof, 34 Kloof Street, Gardens (021 426 0627/www.caffe.co.za). **Open** 7am-5pm Mon-Sat; 8am-5pm Sun. **Credit** AmEx, DC, MC, V. **Map** p276 G4 ⑩ **Café**
Vida is mushrooming at an astronomical rate, and you'll understand why when you take your first sip of its hallowed coffee. A golden thread running through all the chain's branches is the friendly, chatty staff who make a grand occasion out of any order. The eats are correspondingly Portuguese, with rolls and muffins brimful of authentic ingredients and – of course – the custardy *pasteis de nata*. *Photo p110.*
Other locations throughout the city.

Yum
2 Deer Park Drive, Vredehoek (021 461 7607). **Open** 4-11pm Mon-Thur; noon-11pm Fri; 9am-11pm Sat, Sun. **Main courses** R80. **Credit** AmEx, DC, MC, V. **Bistro**
Breakfasts are very big at this funky, laid-back pavement diner and include fry-ups and feather-light omelettes (the salmon, cream cheese and dill mustard is fab), as well as original spins on the first meal of the day, including a tropical coconut pancake with pineapple and muesli. The rest of the menu consists of wraps, burgers and moreish pastas.

ATLANTIC SEABOARD

221
Shop 221, Victoria Wharf, V&A Waterfront (021 418 3633/www.221waterfront.co.za). **Open** noon-11pm Mon-Sat; noon-10pm Sun. **Main courses** R100. **Credit** AmEx, DC, MC, V. **Map** p275 H1 ⑩ **Contemporary, global**
A truly jaw-dropping panoramic view awaits you in this modern, glass-panelled establishment, and the food isn't bad either. Black mussels in Thai green curry sauce are spiced just right, while the deep-fried prawns in kadaifi pastry with Cajun butter sauce are a crunchy treat. Mains are equally elegant, with seafood taking centre stage (salsa verde-topped line fish on braised baby marrow and butternut mash, say) and meat coming in at a close second with dishes like duck breast glazed with lavender honey and peppercorns, served with braised celery and apple.

1800°
Cape Royale Luxury Hotel and Residence, 47 Main Road, Green Point (021 430 0796). **Open** 6.30-10.30am, noon-3pm, 6-11pm daily. **Main courses** R115. **Credit** AmEx, DC, MC, V. **Map** p274 F2 ⑫ **Meat**
Another spot that's tapping into the trend for all- or mostly-meat menus, this upmarket grillroom is part of the plush Cape Royale Hotel and sees a steady trade in besuited businessmen and other carnivores. Get into the mood with a martini, then move on to a menu that's full of steak, gourmet salts (and rubs) and sauce choices – the latter ranging from Madagascan peppercorn to Indonesian coffee. There are venison cuts too, and a good wine list.

Vida e Caffè. *See p109.*

CONSUME

Azure

12 Apostles Hotel & Spa, Victoria Road, Camps Bay (021 437 9000/www.12apostleshotel.com). **Open** 7-10.30am, 12.30-3.30pm, 6-9.30pm daily. **Main courses** R160. **Credit** AmEx, DC, MC, V. **Fusion**
Be sure to rock up early for dinner and catch the exquisite sunset from the upmarket, stylish dining room. Incorporating ingredients from the surrounding vegetation and the hotel's garden, the fare is fine-dining fusion at its best. Expect local ingredients, used in dishes like smoked snoek tart, as well as classic continental dishes like slow-roasted duck. Those wanting to tip the scales of indulgence are well advised to try the chef's 'four of the best' dessert plate.
▶ *See also p88 Twelve Apostles.*

Baia

Shop 6262, Upper Level, Victoria Warf, V&A Waterfront (021 421 0935/6/7). **Open** noon-3pm, 7-11pm daily. **Main courses** R260. **Credit** AmEx, DC, MC, V. **Map** p275 H1 ⑤ **Seafood, contemporary**
Not surprisingly, this Waterfront restaurant specialises in seafood in all its guises, with an added bit of Portuguese flair (the fillet *trinchado* and Mozambican prawn curry being *muito delicioso*). The menu selection is substantial, but headliners include a bouillabaisse and a duet of quail stuffed with goat's cheese and preserved fig, sozzled in a white wine and chive sauce. The desserts are equally decadent, especially the roasted banana and Amarula panna cotta.

Balducci

Shop 6162, Victoria Wharf, V&A Waterfront (021 421 6002/3/www.balducci.co.za). **Open** 9am-late

daily. **Main courses** R120. **Credit** AmEx, DC, MC, V. **Map** p275 H1 ⑤ **Contemporary**
Get your people-watching fix in between mouthfuls at this much-loved café/bar/restaurant. The sushi is in a league of its own, the duck spring rolls are tasty and perfectly crisp, and the marinated beef carpaccio is paper-thin perfection. The gourmet pizzas are also a hit; the Scandinavian does justice to its name, with ingredients including Norwegian salmon, and caviar.

Belthazar

Shop 153, Victoria Wharf, V&A Waterfront (021 421 3753/6/www.belthazar.co.za). **Open** noon-11pm daily. **Main courses** R165. **Credit** AmEx, DC, MC, V. **Map** p275 H1 ⑤ **Meat**
Polished wood and brass abound in this lush establishment, making it very popular with the suit squad (well, that and the fact that it offers the biggest wine list in the world). Meat is master here – from the gravy-drenched *boerewors* to prime cuts of fillet and rib-eye steaks. Starters include retro treats like avocado Ritz and peri-peri chicken livers.

Beluga

The Foundry, Prestwich Street, Green Point (021 418 2948/ www.beluga.co.za). **Open** 11.30am-11pm daily. **Main courses** R134. **Credit** AmEx, DC, MC, V. **Map** p276 G2 ⑤ **Sushi, Contemporary**
Hide-out of the media mavens, this chic establishment has become synonymous with its sushi specials and its happy hour. The dishes are fresh and flavourful fusion creations, with seafood featuring prominently (sesame-crusted ahi tuna with wasabi mayo, for example). There's a separate Pacific Rim menu featuring tasting plates with everything from satays to spring rolls.

Caffe Neo

V. good. [handwritten]

South Seas building, 129 Beach Road, Mouille Point (021 433 0849). **Open** 7am-7pm daily. **Main courses** R40. **Credit** AmEx, DC, MC, V. **Map** p274 E1 ❺❼ **Café**

Opposite the Mouille Point lighthouse, this popular spot is the perfect pit-stop on the promenade. There's a tasty selection of Greek mezze to nibble on, as well as well-stuffed sarmies. Solitary snackers can choose a good read from the 'library' in the centre of the café.

R Café Sofia

Villa Rosa, 267 Main Road, Sea Point (021 439 7993/www.cafesofia.co.za). **Open** 8am-late daily. **Main courses** R45. **Credit** AmEx, MC, V. **Map** p272 C2 ❺❽ **Tapas**

Order a jug of sangria and watch the pretty people come and go in this cool bar-slash-eatery. The tapas aren't to be sneezed at either, and for a R100 you get a whopping ten substantial Mediterranean nibbles to swap and share with your friends. The silky orange and almond chicken livers positively melt in the mouth.

Other locations throughout the city.

Caturra Coffee

39 Regent Road, Sea Point (021 434 5160/ www.catura.co.za). **Open** 7.30am-midnight daily. **Main courses** R40. **Credit** AmEx, MC, V. **Map** p272 B3 ❺❾ **Café**

Still going after all of these years, this Sea Point stalwart has never lost sight of its desire to show the unitiated the way and the truth of good coffee. It does all the espressos, cappuccinos and the like and it does them properly (though the selection has expanded to include the 'fluffy' options like freezerchinos and flavoured coffees). Stock up on the Arabica/Robusta in-house blend for brewing at home.

R The Cedar

The Courtyard Building, 100 Main Road, Sea Point (021 433 2546). **Open** 11am-3pm, late Mon-Sat. **Main courses** R75. **Credit** AmEx, DC, MC, V. **Map** p272 C2 ❻⓿ **Lebanese**

This hidden gem on the Main Road stretch of Sea Point serves some of the best Lebanese fare south of Beirut. The restaurant is family-run and intimate, and the food is best shared with a large, jovial group of friends. Notable dishes include baked *kofta* (a

---

INSIDE TRACK
BARGAIN BREAKFASTS

Kloof Street is king for cheap breakfasts. Find full English breakfasts going for a song at eateries like next-door neighbours **Arnold's** (60 Kloof Street, Gardens, 021 424 4344/www.arnolds.co.za) and **Café Sofia** (*see p111*).

---

spicy meatball) with a tart pomegranate sauce and a fragrant *batata harra*, perfectly marrying potato, cauliflower and nuts with a spicy sauce.

Geisha

Cape Royale Luxury Hotel and Residence, 47 Main Road, Green Point (021 439 0533). **Open** noon-11pm daily. **Main courses** R80. **Credit** AmEx, DC, MC, V. **Map** p274 F2 ❻❶ **Asian tapas**

The menu is for sharing and sampling – make up a meal from the half-portion mains of Asian tapas, noodles and wok dishes. Salmon can be seared with *edamame* purée or encrusted in *shichimi* (a spicy mix), served with udon noodles and lemongrass *dashi* (soup). Those with a sweet tooth should finish with the seven-course tapas dessert menu.

Harveys at the Mansions

Winchester Mansions, 221 Beach Road, Sea Point (021 434 2351/www.winchester.co.za). **Open** 7am-10.30pm daily. **Main courses** R93. **Credit** AmEx, DC, MC, V. **Map** p272 C2 ❻❷ **Classic**

Winchester Mansions is a poster child of a bygone era – from the gabled façade and heavy wooden revolving doors to the crisp, clean interior. It should come as no surprise, then, that this is where the well-to-do come for a bit of posh nosh. Starters include prawn ravioli with a brandy-infused shellfish bisque; mains feature the likes of fish amandine (dill- and almond-crusted), accompanied by smoked salmon and chive soufflé, and beef Rossini served with potato and root rösti with onion marmalade.

Il Leone Mastrantonio

22 Coburn Street, cnr Prestwich Street, Green Point (021 421 0071). **Open** noon-3pm, 6.30-10.30pm Tue-Sun. **Main courses** R85. **Credit** AmEx, DC, MC, V. **Map** p276 G2 ❻❸ **Italian**

Enjoy the best of contemporary and traditional Italian eats at this relaxed spot. The pasta, tortellini, ravioli and gnocchi are all made from scratch. The spaghetti with raw tomatoes, capers and olives is simple faultlessness incarnate; the moreish risotto is made to order. Fish and meat dishes are also done well, as is the calorie-laden dessert menu.

Manos

nice [handwritten]

39 Main Road, Green Point (021 434 1090). **Open** noon-10.30pm Mon-Sat. **Main courses** R85. **Credit** AmEx, DC, MC, V. **Map** p274 G2 ❻❺ **Bistro**

The buzzy smart vibe makes this restaurant a favoured city hangout of older hipsters. Meals are hearty and reasonably priced: try the pink, almost-translucent beef carpaccio dressed with a squirt of lemon, or get your kicks from the spicy chicken livers. For mains, the fillet with bearnaise is popular, as is the smoky vegetable cassoulet. Fresh fish is always a good choice too.

have pudding at ice cream shop next door [handwritten]

★ Maze

Dock Road, V&A Waterfront (021 431 5222/ www.onenadonlyresorts.com). **Open** 6.30-10.30am, noon-3pm, 6-11pm daily. **Main courses** R200. **Credit** AmEx, DC, MC, V. **Map** p274 G2 ⑥⑥
Contemporary

The South African extension of celebrated UK chef Gordon Ramsay's award-winning London restaurant of the same name, it's all about understated contemporary style and a menu of tasting-size dishes with a distinctly South African flair, overseen by Michelin award-winning chef Jason Atherton. Diners can expect a plethora of exquisitely presented dishes featuring locally sourced seafood, game and organic fresh produce. Maze is also home to the largest wine collection in South Africa.

Meloncino

Shop 259, Upper Level, Victoria Wharf, V&A Waterfront (021 419 5558/www.meloncino. co.za). **Open** 11.30am-11pm daily. **Main courses** R90. **Credit** AmEx, DC, MC, V. **Map** p275 H1 ⑥⑦ **Italian**

This one's a gem. The menu boasts an extensive selection of dishes, all cooked up by Italian chefs. Try the *spaghetti scoglio in sarta fata* – spaghetti with seafood, tomatoes and chilli, in a transparent wrapping – or one of the dreamy desserts. Attentive managers and the hip orange, white and black decor contribute to a memorable night out.

★ Miss K Food Café

Shop 1, Winston Place, 65 Main Road, Green Point (021 439 9559). **Open** 8am-4.30pm Tue-Sat; 8.30am-1pm Sun. **Main courses** R54. **Credit** MC, V. **Map** p274 F2 ⑥⑧ **Café**

Modern and airy, with a touch of funkiness, this coffee shop is fast becoming a new favourite among Green Point gadabouts. The breakfasts alone make the place worth a visit, especially the heaven-sent hangover cure of eggs with baked cannellini beans, chorizo and cornbread. Lunches are light, with buffet salads, grills, stir-fries and a gob-stopping chicken pie, if you're lucky. The selection of fresh cakes, including syrupy orange polenta cake and velvety lemon tart, has also found favour with regulars.

Newport

47 Beach Road, Mouille Point (021 439 1538). **Open** 6.30am-10pm daily. **Main courses** R35. **Credit** AmEx, DC, MC, V. **Café**

INSIDE TRACK
ONE LUMP OR TWO?

At tea house and specialist tea merchant **Nigiro** (*see p112*), tea lovers get the opportunity to take part in a tea ceremony with tea master Mingwei Tsai.

This beachfront deli offers the whole kit and kaboodle, ranging from straight-from-the-oven cookies and freshly baked breads to cured meats, international cheeses, organic chocolates and French champagne. Take in the sea view over a scrummy sandwich and finish off your lunch with a scoop of Italian-style *gelato* or a refreshing smoothie.

★ Nigiro Tea

28 Hudson Street, De Waterkant (021 421 1000/ www.nigirotea.co.za). **Open** 7am-5pm Mon, Wed-Fri; 7am-4pm Tue; 9am-2pm Sat. **Main courses** R35. **Credit** AmEx, MC, V. **Map** p276 G3 ⑥⑨ **Café**

Once you've joined Mingwei Tsai and his team and learned about the intricacies of the Japanese tea ceremony and the subtleties of different teas, you're likely to be more than a little inspired to bring the tea appreciation ritual into your own life. The sibling company to coffee specialists Origin Roasting (and situated in the same building), this is the spot where those who are passionate about their tea fix stock up on their favourites or browse the 80-plus range of teas and blends for something new to take home. *Photo p114.*

▶ *See also p106 Origin and below* **One Lump or Two.**

★ Nobu

Dock Road, V&A Waterfront (021 431 5111/ www.onenadonlyresorts.com). **Open** 6pm-midnight daily. **Main courses** R200. **Credit** AmEx, DC, MC, V. **Map** p274 G2 ⑦⑩ **Japanese fusion**

The famous chain has been a hit in South Africa. Expect impossibly beautifully prepared offerings, from raw shellfish and seafood with Nobu's trademark sauces to perfect sushi and specialities like *wagyu* beef and sea urchin tempura. A gourmet dining destination of note.

La Perla

Cnr Church and Beach roads, Sea Point (021 434 2471/www.laperla.co.za). **Open** 9am-11pm daily. **Main courses** R120. **Credit** AmEx, DC, MC, V. **Map** p272 B3 ⑥④ **Italian**

Step back in time to a place where the old-school starched-collared service and the choice of dishes have remained more or less the same for 30-odd years. Fire things up with the simple chilli and garlic fried squid or dig into plates piled high with pasta. The varied fresh seafood grill options have stood the test of time, and the veal saltimbocca is worth a nibble too.

Pepenero

Two Oceans House, Shop 1, Beach Road, Mouille Point (021 439 9027/ www.pepenero. co.za). **Open** noon-late daily. **Main courses** R120. **Credit** AmEx, DC, MC, V. **Seafood, Italian**

Wine and Dine

The Cape Winelands is a serious gourmet destination.

Terroir

In the past a visit to South Africa's Winelands was all about tasting the product and stocking up at ex-cellar prices. Over the last decade, however, it has become much more of an epicurean experience, with top restaurants on wine estates. Close to Cape Town lies the Nitida Estate, home to **Cassia** (*see p122*), where rustic dishes are given a sophisticated twist – a great, lazy lunchtime stop.

At Constantia Uitsig estate, you can choose from laid-back countrified bites at the **River Café** (*see p118*), Italian specialities at **Constantia Uitsig** (*see p115*) and sophisticated French cuisine with Asian twists at the award-winning **La Colombe** (*see p117*). Estate wines are served at each.

There's more great food out towards Stellenbosch. **Terroir** (*see p223*) on Kleine Zalze wine estate has a menu of refined rustic offerings, while popular stalwart **96 Winery Road** (*see p223*) marries winemaker and owner Ken Forrester's liquid offerings with a much-loved menu of country cuisine.

Style warriors head for **Overture** (*see p223*) on the Hidden Valley wine estate, lair of super talent Bertus Basson. Here they can drink in the views while savouring perfectly presented, innovative cooking. They're also partial to **Cuvée** (*see p222*), where the interiors are as impeccably dressed as the plates.

Just before the mountain pass to Franschhoek lies **Tokara** (*see p224*), the outstanding restaurant on the eponymous wine estate, with magnificent views and food. And in Franschhoek the easy-going **Bread & Wine** (*see p215*) on the Môreson estate features home-cured charcuterie as well as a host of filling country choices. The estate's bubbly is excellent value.

This swish, sexy restaurant is heaven sent for seafood lovers, who adore the excellent salsa verde squid and crayfish-stuffed ravioli. Meat eaters are well-looked-after too; the steak *tagliata* with rocket, parmesan and avocado being a prime example. There's also a substantial selection of pastas and grills for those with less adventurous palates.

Pigalle
57 Somerset Road, Green Point (021 421 4848). **Open** noon-3pm, 7pm-late Mon-Sat. **Main courses** R120. **Credit** AmEx, DC, MC, V. **Map** p276 G2 🐧 **Portuguese**
Embrace the inner retro in this plush velvety diner and spin your date around on the dancefloor while the jazz band belts out big band standards. Seafood is big here, and ranges from sublime garlic or peri-peri prawns to table-buckling platters. The steaks are equally good and served with a creamy mustard mash and stir-fried veg.

★ R Posticino
No. 3 Albany Mews, 323 Main Road, Sea Point (021 439 4014/www.posticino.co.za). **Open** 11am-10.30pm daily. **Main courses** R60. **Credit** AmEx, DC, MC, V. **Map** p272 C2 🐧 **Italian**

A real home from home in Sea Point, this laid-back trattoria offers thin-crust pizzas (which some say are the best in Cape Town) alongside tried and trusted favourites like chicken livers and caprese salad. The authentic veal and pasta dishes are also sure-fire comfort staples, while the welcome is genuinely warm. A local gem.

★ Roundhouse Restaurant
The Glen on Kloof Road, Camps Bay (021 438 4347/072 277 2236/www.theroundhouse restaurant.com). **Open** 11am-2.30pm, 6-9.30pm Tue-Sun. **Set menus** 3 courses R330, 4 courses R440, 5 courses R550. **Credit** MC, V. **Map** p273 B7 🐧 **Contemporary**
What was once Lord Charles Somerset's 'shooting box' has been tastefully renovated into a contemporary restaurant. A setting on the slopes of the Lion's Head means that diners can take in the Camps Bay vista while making up their minds what to choose from the modern French menu. For starters you'd be well advised to try the citrus-cured salmon with a tempura of mussel and garlic aioli, or the grilled quail. For mains, tempting options include a mouth-watering roast fillet of beef served with pinotage jus, or pepper-encrusted tuna, served with prawn risotto.

CONSUME

CONSUME

Nigiro Tea. *See p112*.

Salt
Ambassador Hotel, 34 Victoria Road, Bantry Bay (021 439 7258/www.saltrestaurant.co.za). **Open** 12.30-3pm, 7-10.30pm daily. **Main courses** R110. **Credit** AmEx, DC, MC, V. **Map** p272 A4
74 Contemporary
Cosmo cool with a killer view to boot, this award-winning restaurant serves contemporary South African food. Chic starters include honey-roasted quail, lentil and herb salad; a popular choice for mains is the deliciously tender slow-roasted pork belly with pickled cabbage and roast pear. A good thing to know beforehand is that the portions are quite substantial, so be sure to pace yourself for the list of yummy desserts.

★ Sevruga
Shop 4, Quay 5, Victoria Wharf, V&A Waterfront (021 421 5134/www.sevruga.co.za). **Open** 11.30am-11pm daily. **Main courses** R130. **Credit** AmEx, DC, MC, V. **Map** p275 H1
75 Sushi, meat
The younger sister of caviar namesake, Beluga (*see p110*), this swish harbour-front restaurant is equally adept at making killer sushi. The vast space somehow remains intimate, with an impressive array of wines adorning the walls. Those with meatier appetites will be sated by winners like slow-braised lamb with soft polenta, whole roasted garlic and tomato chutney. A welcome Waterfront addition.

★ Wakame
nice food but noisy.
1st Floor, cnr Surrey Place and Beach Road, Mouille Point (021 433 2377/www.wakame. co.za). **Open** noon-3pm, 6-10.30pm Mon-Thur;

noon-3.30pm, 6-11pm Fri, Sat; noon-3.30pm, 6-10pm Sun. **Main courses** R115. **Credit** AmEx, DC, MC, V. **Asian**
Seafood reigns supreme at this polished Asian restaurant: the moist and delicate tea-smoked salmon with lime and shrimp beurre blanc far outdoes its cult reputation. Another fishy favourite is the sesame-seed-encrusted tuna fillet, which is perfectly complemented by a side serving of sweet-potato chips, thus putting a proudly South African spin on an Asian classic.

Willoughby & Co
Shop 6132, Lower Level, Victoria Wharf, V&A Waterfront (021 418 6116). **Open** noon-9.45pm daily. **Main courses** R110. **Credit** AmEx, DC, MC, V. **Map** p275 H1. **Seafood**
Watch the mall rats go by as you indulge in the fresh fare of this sushi stalwart. Prawn laksa is another Asian-style favourite, while those who prefer their fish battered and fried can get theirs in a quaint copper pan with a side serving of chips. The scallops and substantial paella are also worth looking out for.

SOUTHERN SUBURBS

Bihari
25 Westlake Lifestyle Centre, Westlake Drive, Tokai (021 702 2975/www.bihari.co.za). **Open** noon-10.30pm daily. **Main courses** R107. **Credit** DC, MC, V. **Indian**
The Hindu god Ganesh greets you upon entering Bihari's opulent interior of rich reds and Taj Mahal murals. The menu features dishes with rich sauces

served in shiny copper pots. Tear off piece after piece of the delectable buttery garlic naan and mop up the spoils of greats like rogan josh, prawn korma, crab curry or punch-packing lamb vindaloo. Vegetarians will be super-chuffed with the list of paneer, dhal and biryanis.

Buitenverwachting

Buitenverwachting Wine Farm, Klein Constantia Road, Constantia (021 794 3522/www.buitenver wachting.co.za). **Open** *Summer* noon-2pm, 7-9.30pm Tue-Sat. **Main courses** R140. **Credit** AmEx, DC, MC, V. Classic

This restaurant – with truly amazing views – offers a very popular three-course wine-accompanied lunch menu for a surprisingly humble amount. But if you're looking to pull out the big guns, go for the tasting menu (in three or five courses): you'll be treated to posh nosh including glazed quail with braised chicory, and grilled beef in a bone marrow crust.

▶ *There's more on Buitenverwachting in the Sightseeing section, see p62.*

Cape Malay

Cellars-Hohenort, Constantia (021 794 2137/ www.cellars-hohenort.com). **Open** 7-10.30pm Mon, Thur-Sun. **Main courses** R200. **Credit** AmEx, DC, MC, V. Cape Malay

Eating at this Cape Malay restaurant housed in the Cellars-Hohenort is no dine and dash affair. The four set menus (rotated every week) list perfectly plated Malay-style eats like snoek, tomato bredie, curries and bobotie, all given a gourmet treatment that transforms them into something spectacular.

▶ *See also p117 Greenhouse at the Cellars and p91 Cellars-Hohenort.*

Cargills

20 Station road, Rondebosch (021 689 2666). **Open** 12.30-2pm, 6.30pm-late Tue-Fri; 6.30pm-late Sat. **Main courses** R100. **Credit** AmEx, DC, MC, V.

See p116 **French Revolution**.

★ Catharina's at Steenberg

Steenberg Hotel, Tokai Road, Constantia Valley (021 713 2222/www.steenberghotel.com). **Open** 7am-10pm daily. **Main courses** R125. **Credit** AmEx, DC, MC, V. South African

The elegant interior, with its old wooden beams, thick stone walls, starched linens and glittering chandeliers, sets the appropriate mood for a spot of fine dining. The fare is South African-inspired but classic, incorporating favourites like ostrich carpaccio and tartare, Namibian truffle risotto, slow-roasted springbok shank and roasted warthog belly. Topping them all off are myriad sauces, jus, salsas, oils and foams, adding that sophisticated bit of culinary *je ne sais quoi.*

▶ *See also p63 Steenberg Vineyards and p91 Steenberg Hotel.*

R Chai-Yo

95 Durban Road, Little Mowbray (021 689 6156/7). **Open** noon-2.30pm, 6-10.30pm daily. **Main courses** R55-R82. **Credit** AmEx, DC, MC, V. Thai

Get some fire in your belly and prepare for truly eyebrow singeing Thai curries in this relaxed spot. Start with a bowl of piquant tom yum, satay with creamy peanut sauce or a crispy prawn spring roll. The aromatic red, green and yellow curries are all made with your choice of poultry, beef, pork, seafood or vegetables, and there's also a variety of tofu and sprout stir-fries and excellent curries for vegetarians.

★ R Chandani Indian & Vegetarian Restaurant

85 Roodebloem Road, Woodstock, Salt River (021 447 7887/www.chandani.co.za). **Open** noon-3pm, 6-10.30pm Mon-Sat. **Main courses** R67. **Credit** MC, V. Indian

Elaborately decorated with authentic Indian furniture, this upmarket restaurant specialises in North Indian cuisine but also features a few Goan options. Vegetarians are very well catered for with a range of lip-smacking dishes, the most notable of which is paneer bhurjee, a combination of mashed paneer, onions, tomato and spices. Lamb rogan josh is flavourful and hearty; those craving something from the sea will enjoy *machchi* Goan curry, kingklip in coconut with curry leaves and mustard seeds.

Constantia Uitsig

Constantia Uitsig Wine Farm, Spaanschemat River Road, Constantia Valley (021 794 4480/ www.constantia-uitsig.com). **Open** noon-2.30pm, 7-9.30pm daily. **Main courses** R120. **Credit** AmEx, DC, MC, V. Bistro

Worldly and award-winning cuisine takes centre stage against an eye-popping backdrop of mountains and vineyards. The late chef patron, Frank Swainston, has left quite a culinary legacy and his influence is still very visible on the menu. Chef

INSIDE TRACK
THE GREAT GATSBY

The Gatsby (*see p121* **Streetwise Snacking**) is meant to be shared. So park yourself on the grass in the Company's Garden, and be prepared to get your hands dirty with all those fries and oily sauces. You can buy one at Miriam's Kitchen (101 St George's Mall, 021 423 0772/ www.miriamskitchen.co.za). Or, to sample some of the best Gatsbys in the Cape, drive all the way to the legendary Golden Dish in Athlone (Gatesville Shopping Centre, Klipfontein Road, Gatesville Athlone, 021 633 7864).

Clayton Bell creates layered, delicate tastes and textures from top-notch seasonal produce – the sweetbread marsala, tripe Fiorentina and Karoo lamb flavoured with Provençal herbs are the (food)stuff legends are made of. Equally enamouring starters include tuna carpaccio, tomato tart and a classically creamy Caesar salad.

► See also p62 and p117 La Colombe.

R Fat Cactus Cafe
47 Durban Road, Little Mowbray (021 685 1920). **Open** 11am-11pm daily. **Main courses** R40-R100. **Credit** AmEx, DC, MC, V. **Mexican**
Buy into the fiesta-siesta philosophy of life with a visit to this perfectly unpretentious Mexican mainstay. The nachos and tacos are as crunchy as they come and the burritos, enchiladas, quesadillas and fajitas can be filled with your choice of chilli con carne, gaucho beans, coyote chicken or grilled vegetables – all of them bursting with smoky, sticky, spicy goodness. And then there's the sublime assortment of authentic Tex-Mex tipples to accompany everything.
Other locations 5 Park Road, Gardens (021 422 5022).

Greek
78 Durban Road, Little Mowbray (021 686 4314). **Open** 9am-10pm Tue-Sun. **Main courses** R80. **Credit** AmEx, DC, MC, V. **Greek**
This unfussy Greek eaterie offers a rib-sticking feast of flavours. Begin with the moreish mezze platter with dips including *skorthalia* (garlicky potato

French Revolution

Classic cuisine is being given a new twist in the Mother City.

Bizerca Bistro.

Most chefs will tell you that one can't put a price on classical French training, and happily there are plenty of talents in Cape Town whose slick sauces, artfully crafted plates and carefully conceived wine lists showcase the classic style. Increasingly, though, Cape Town has seen a shift from haute cuisine to peasant- and bistro-style food.

Take the **Foodbarn** (*see p120*) in Noordhoek, lair of super talent Franck Dangereux. His *pan bagna*, complete with garlicky bread and runny poached egg, sells up a storm, though the famous prawn, avocado and aubergine tian is an undoubted winner too.

At **Bizerca Bistro** (*see p96*), you can sample Gallic chef Laurent Deslandes' delightfully laid-back yet exquisitely crafted cuisine. It's all about bistro favourites – from home-made sausage or braised pigs' trotters to the ultimate roasted leg of lamb with all the (French) trimmings, and desserts that taste just as good as they look.

Pastis (*see p118*) in Constantia is another laid-back establishment, acting as bistro and watering hole for a great many locals – many of whom can't get through a week without their *croque monsieur* or *moules marinière* fix. The teeny tiny **Cargills** (*see p115*) in Rondebosch is another unassuming gem, one that serves a duck à l'orange second to none.

Another Constantia favourite is **La Colombe** (*see p117*), where chef Luke Dale-Roberts marries his classic training with a penchant for the East. The result is lip-smackingly delicious: his kudu tartare with mirin and sesame seeds is not to be missed. Meanwhile, at award-winning **Aubergine** (*see p95*) in the City Bowl, chef Harald Bresselschmidt sends out plate after plate of gorgeous offerings, some with an Asian twist.

La Colombe.

purée), *melitzanasalata* (smoky aubergine tapenade), tzatziki and taramosalata, and perfectly flaky pastries like *spanakopita* and *tiropita* (three-cheese filo pastry triangles). Mouth-watering mains feature seductively tender lamb dishes including lamb filo cigars and a schwerma royale.

★ Greenhouse at the Cellars

Cellars-Hohenort, 93 Brommersvlei Road, Constantia (021 794 2137/ www.cellars-hohenort.com). **Open** 7-10.30am, 12.30-2.30pm, 7-10.30pm daily. **Main courses** R130. **Credit** AmEx, DC, MC, V. **Contemporary**
Indulge in the five-star silver-serviced swishness and take in the opulent view of beautifully knotted 300-year-old camphor trees at this Winelands restaurant. Executive chef Peter Tempelhoff waves his gourmet wand, conjuring up unforgettably creative eats. A signature starter is duck and porcini *pastilla*, while mains include a slow-roasted crispy duck with honey ginger jus. You'll be spoiled for choice with sumptuous dessert options such as Grand Marnier soufflé with cardamom ice-cream, Belgian chocolate soufflé with garden spearmint ice-cream and almond soufflé with marzipan ice-cream. The adjoining Conservatory Bistro serves lighter daytime fare.
► *See also p115 Cape Malay and p91 Cellars-Hohenort.*

R Home Bar & Restaurant

53 2nd Avenue, Harfield Village (021 683 6066). **Open** 7-11pm Mon-Sat. **Main courses** R70. **Credit** AmEx, DC, MC, V. **Bistro**
A garden shed's worth of shovels and spades have been incorporated into a wrought-iron security door, drawing lounge lizards into the warm orange glow of the bar. The chalkboard specials vary from peri-peri chicken livers and home-made burgers to more exotic fare like Asian duck.

★ La Colombe

Constantia Uitsig Wine Farm, Spaanschemat River Road, Constantia (021 794 2390/ www.constantia-uitsig.com). **Open** *Summer* 12.30-1.30pm, 7.30-8.30pm daily. *Winter* 12.30-1.30pm, 7.30-8.30pm Mon-Sat; 12.30-1.30pm Sun. **Main courses** R160. **Credit** AmEx, DC, MC, V. **Contemporary**
Yet another multi-award-winner in the Constantia Uitsig stable, this swanky restaurant, with chef Luke Dale-Roberts at the helm, wows foodies from across the globe. Try the hand-chopped kudu (a kind of antelope) tartare for starters and move on to the likes of springbok medallions with celeriac purée in a rich port and truffle sauce, or sweetbreads glazed in truffle jus with almond and cardamom cream. Look out for the great winter lunchtime specials. This is a true gourmet destination.
► *See also p116* **French Revolution** *and p113* **Wine and Dine**.

Magica Roma

8 Central Square, Pinelands (021 531 1489). **Open** noon-2pm, 6-10pm Mon-Fri; 6-10pm Sat. **Main courses** R95. **Credit** AmEx, DC, MC, V. **Italian**
One of the few restaurants to survive the suburban tedium that is Pinelands. The food is perfectly executed classic Italian fare – the pasta is cooked al dente and the dishes incorporate simple, traditional ingredients. The antipasti are a must, as are the fresh seafood and tender veal dishes.

Myoga

Vineyard Hotel and Spa, Colinton Road (off Protea Road), Newlands (021 657 4545/www. myoga.co.za). **Open** 11.30am-3pm, 7-10.30pm Mon-Sat. **Main courses** 1 course R109, 2 courses R199, 3 courses R235, 5 courses R265, 6 courses R350. **Credit** AmEx, DC, MC, V. **Contemporary**
Take a seat at one of the plush orange high-backed chairs and prepare to be blown away by the food here. The trio of prawns starter is lip-lickingly lavish as are the tender meat choices, including beef fillet and pepper coriander springbok. A dessert that deserves an A for originality is the heavenly white chocolate soup with Turkish delight sponge, rose geranium sorbet, violet ice-cream and dissolved candy floss.
► *See also p118 Square Restaurant & Sushi Bar and p92 Vineyard Hotel.*

Mzoli's

Shop 3, NY 115, Gugulethu (021 638 1355). **Open** 9am-6.30pm Mon-Thur; 9am-8pm Fri-Sun. **Main courses** R50. **No credit cards.** **Meat**
Let your hair down and get into the Gugs groove at the homely tavern that's a hit among locals and kombi-busloads of tourists alike. Not exactly a haven for vegetarians, this hangout specialises in *tshisanyamas* (braais), so expect plates of chops, *wors* and chicken charred to perfection by the braaimasters out back. A side order of pap (mealie meal porridge) or a half loaf of bread is essential to help soak up Mzoli's delicious secret sauce.

Olive Station

Rondebosch Village centre, level 1, Main road, Rondebosch (021 686 8224/www.theolive station.co.za). **Open** 10am-7pm Mon-Fri; 8am-2pm Sat. **Main courses** according to weight R46. **Credit** AmEx, DC, MC, V. **Café**
A much-loved hangout for Capetonian vegetarians, even the breakfast at the Olive Station is a bounty of Lebanese and Mediterranean fare: tuck into Lebanese-French toast with a piquant aubergine-ginger jam and olive pesto-zesto, or ciabatta, hard-boiled egg, labneh and all the trimmings. For lunch, the Leb lamb burger is a must. Otherwise, mix and match to your heart's content from the abundant meze spread.

CONSUME

Orchid

23 Wolfe Street, Chelsea Village, Wynberg (021 761 1000). **Open** 8.30am-5pm Mon-Fri; 8.30am-2pm Sat. **Main courses** R50. **Credit** MC, V. **Café**

Carly Porter's quaint café is all rusty pink and wood interior meets home-style rib-sticking comfort food and pretty teatime treats. Think French toast with berries or fluffy scrambled eggs and crispy bacon twists on home-style bread for breakfast, and creamy savoury tarts and still-warm spongy muffins for lunch. Once you've sampled the fig, white chocolate and custard tartlets, or the buttery madeleines, teatime will forever seem incomplete without them.

Pastis Bistro Brasserie

Shop 12, High Constantia Centre, Groot Constantia Road, Constantia (021 794 8334/ www.pastisbrasserie.co.za). **Open** 8.30am-10pm daily. **Main courses** R89. **Credit** AmEx, DC, MC, V. **French**

The cosy-hearthed bar is the ideal spot for a few pre-dinner hot toddies during the dreary winter months. The bistro's starter selection is reassuringly traditional and includes creamy sage chicken livers, garlic escargot, real-deal frites and French onion soup, while mains include bowls of mussels and seasonal offerings like oxtail.

▶ *See p116* **French Revolution***.*

★ Queen of Tarts

213 Lower Main Road, Observatory (021 448 2420). **Open** 8.30am-4.30pm Mon-Fri; 8.30am-2.30pm Sat. **Main courses** R53. **Credit** MC, V. **Café**

Alice and the white rabbit would feel at home in this quaint 1950s-style teashop. The brekkies include the full English affair, as well as a yummy maple-drizzled flapjack, nut and banana ensemble. Tarts boast decadent fillings including potato, pesto and bacon, and butternut with gorgonzola, and sweets include the likes of chocolate swirl meringues, almond and pear tart, and chocolate fairy cakes. Take home something delicious too.

▶ *Queen of Tarts also has a stall at the Saturday morning Neighbourgoods Market in Woodstock.*

River Café at Constantia Uitsig

Constantia Uitsig Wine Farm, Spaanschemat River Road, Constantia (021 794 3010/www. constantia-uitsig.com). **Open** 8.30-11am, 12.30-3pm, 3-5pm daily. **Main courses** R90. **Credit** AmEx, DC, MC, V. **Bistro**

Enjoy a spot of fun and sun in this conservatory-like restaurant in the lovely Constantia valley. The cooking is appropriately wholesome, country-kitchenesque, with great eggy breakfasts and substantial sarmies. Or opt for the lamb burger or chicken and leek pie, and finish with a deliciously spongy Cape vinegar pud.

▶ *See also p117 La Colombe, p115 Constantia Uitsig Restaurant and p62 Constantia Uitsig.*

Simon's at Groot Constantia

Groot Constantia Estate, Groot Constantia Road, Constantia (021 794 1143/www.simons.co.za). **Open** noon-late daily. **Main courses** R80. **Credit** AmEx, DC, MC, V. **Bistro**

Far from the stuffy establishment you'd associate with an award-winning wine estate, the mood here is family-friendly and the is food accessible and modern. There's a certain something about the beauty of the surrounds that sends the appetite into overdrive, and luckily it will be more than sated by the satisfying spread. Expect the likes of moreish fishcakes, steamed mussels and blackened calamari for starters, and mains that will have the carnivorous salivating.

▶ *See also p63 Groot Constantia.*

R Simply Asia

61 Rosmead Avenue, Kenilworth (021 674 5175/ www.simplyasia.co.za). **Open** 11am-10pm daily. **Main courses** R50. **Credit** MC, V. **Asian**

Expect healthy, authentic Thai street food – flash-fried and deliciously crunchy, with flavours of basil, garlic, galangal, chilli and coconut. Tuck into everything from satays, broths and seafood to oodles of noodles. Vegetarians won't be disappointed with the range of tofu, bean sprout and bamboo-shoot stir-fries, either.

The Square Restaurant & Sushi Bar

Vineyard Hotel, Colinton Road, Newlands (021 657 4500/www.vineyard.co.za). **Open** 7-10.30am, 12.30-3pm, 6-10pm daily. **Set meals** 1 course R105; 2 courses R165; 3 courses R195. **Credit** AmEx, DC, MC, V. **Asian, South African**

The chic minimalist interior of this contemporary establishment is perfectly suited to the pared-down flavours of the Asian cuisine served here. Not surprisingly, the sushi and sashimi are favoured starters, and mains include other eastern delights such as dim sum, seared tuna with Asian greens, and a crispy duck and mango salad. To add a bit

---

INSIDE TRACK FISH & CHIPS

Craving good old fish and chips? Get your fingers greasy at **Kalky's** (*see p120*) at the Kalk Bay harbour or the **Wharfside Bistro** (*see p122* **Wharfside Grill**) at Hout Bay harbour. Don't let the latter's name deceive you – this is a good old-fashioned takeaway joint with outside benches and plastic forks. Both establishments offer sea-fresh fare; but come prepared to leave your pretensions at the door.

CONSUME

Harbour House. *See p120.*

of South African flair to the mix, there are also the likes of Karoo lamb and springbok, which are complemented by sauces with local flavour.

▶ *See also p117 Myoga and p92 Vineyard Hotel.*

Wang Thai
High Constantia House, cnr Constantia & Groot Constantia roads, Constantia (021 794-0022/ www.wangthai.co.za). **Open** noon-11pm daily. **Main courses** R90. **Credit** AmEx, DC, MC, V. **Thai**
This authentic Thai restaurant is garnering loyal followers faster than you can say pad thai. The expert combination of flavour and texture is key to food that is sure to satisfy even the fussiest Thai cuisine fan. Stellar starters include glass noodle salad with prawns, calamari and chicken in a lemon, chilli coriander dressing, and spicy beef salad with onion, cucumber, celery and tomato. The extensive range of curries takes centre stage, though, and features the likes of lychee duck with panang base, and a pineapple and mussel red that's well worth the teary eyes.
Other locations throughout the city.

The Wild Fig
Valkenberg Estate, Liesbeeck Avenue, Observatory (021 448 0507). **Open** noon-3.30pm, 6.30-10.30pm Mon-Fri, Sun; 6.30-10.30pm Sat. **Main courses** R82. **Credit** AmEx, DC, MC, V. **Bistro**
This friendly country kitchen on the banks of the Liesbeeck River puts a contemporary spin on classic bistro dishes. The ingredients are fresh and seasonal, the preparation to the point, and the plating pure elegance. Expect signature dishes such as shredded lamb filo parcel or roast duck in Van der Hum sauce. And depending on availability, local line-caught fish, beef, lamb and venison all feature on the menu.

SOUTHERN PENINSULA

Black Marlin
Main Road, Miller's Point, Simon's Town (021 786 1621/www.blackmarlin.co.za). **Open** 8am-10pm daily. **Main courses** R150. **Credit** AmEx, DC, MC, V. **Seafood**
Even though it can look like tourist headquarters on a sunny day, Black Marlin is actually an outstanding fish and seafood restaurant. The lobster bisque and black marlin carpaccio are favoured starter staples, and freshly caught fish hog the limelight on the mains menu. The kingklip-on-the-spit is an evergreen crowd pleaser, as is the massive prawn platter.

★ R Café Roux
270 Chapman's Peak Drive, Noordhoek Farm Village, Noordhoek (021 789 2538/www.cafe roux.co.za). **Open** 8.30am-5pm daily. **Main courses** R60-R80. **Credit** AmEx, DC, M, V. **Bistro**
A kid-friendly venue without the sparklers and screaming, this hangout is down home with delicious eats to boot. Salads are crammed with just-picked goodies, sandwiches are substantial and the home-made burgers hunger-busting. The breakfast (the eggs Benedict deserving a lift of the cap) is a sure-fire draw.
▶ *The Thursday night braais during summer are legendary.*

C'est la Vie
Rosmead Road, Kalk Bay (083 676 7430). **Open** 7.30am-3pm Wed-Sun. **Main courses** R40. **No credit cards.** **Café**
This Kalk Bay spot is a lovely local indeed. It has garnered a reputation among caffeine junkies as one of the best coffee stops in the peninsula (it serves

CONSUME

Illy), but bread-heads love it too for the artisan breads, buttery croissants and light and lovely madeleines – ideal for dipping in a latte. It's a delightful breakfast destination too (try the boiled egg with slices of baguette).

Chapman's Peak Hotel

Chapman's Peak Drive, Hout Bay (021 790 1036/ www.chapmanspeakhotel.co.za). **Open** noon-11pm Mon-Sat; noon-10pm Sun. **Main courses** R90. **Credit** AmEx, DC, MC, V. **Bistro**

Dine in style on the time-tested terrace and drink in the amazing view stretching from Hout Bay to the Sentinel. This family-owned establishment is known for its seafood – the fresh-from-the-sea pan-fried calamari rings, fish nuggets and prawns are all served with chips, veggies and peri-peri sauce. Meat eaters should definitely try the spice-crusted rare lamb chops.

▶ *See also p94.*

Empire Café

11 York Road, Muizenberg (021 788 1250). **Open** 7am-4pm Mon-Wed, Sat; 7am-9pm Thur, Fri; 8am-4pm Sun. **Main courses** R75. **Credit** AmEx, DC, MC, V. **Café**

If laid-back surfer chic is your thing, you'll love this unpretentious café, which borrows from Mediterranean cuisine and features saucy pastas, rump steak with wilted spinach, fresh line-caught fish, and great ciabatta steak rolls.

★ The Foodbarn

Noordhoek Farm Village, Village Lane, Noordhoek (021 789 1390/www.thefoodbarn. co.za). **Open** noon-4pm Mon, Sun; noon-4pm, 7-9.30pm Tue-Sat. **Main courses** R90. **Credit** MC, V. **French/fusion**

Informal by day, candle-lit and cosy by night, this thatched barn with its lovely old-school *stoep* serves top-notch global fare without the bank-breaking bill. Renowned chef Franck Dangereux sends the masses salivating with his eclectic fusion cuisine and masterfully inventive sauces. His set three-course winter lunch menus are renowned and feature some of his signature dishes, including kofta parcels with harissa, tahini and cumin dipping sauces for starters, and spicy Moroccan lamb cutlets or steak au poivre for mains. The poached quince tarte tatin is amazing if you're lucky enough to be there when quinces are in season.

▶ *See p116* **French Revolution**

★ Harbour House

Kalk Bay Harbour, off Main Road, Kalk Bay (021 788 4133/www.harbourhouse.co.za). **Open** noon-4pm, 6-10pm Mon-Sat; noon-4pm, 6.30-10pm Sun. **Main courses** R140. **Credit** AmEx, DC, MC, V. **Seafood**

It's a case of out-of-the-boat-and-into-the-pan at this popular restaurant on the lip of the Southern Peninsula. The prawn and avocado tian is a popular choice for starters, and the spicy calamari isn't bad either. Things are kept simple for the main courses, with the fresh line-caught fish the star and chermoula prawns packing a flavourful punch. If you prefer land-bound delights, there's ribeye steak. This place is right on the rocks so expect some super-snappable sunsets. *Photo p119.*

R Kalky's *great eat!*

Kalk Bay Harbour, Kalk Bay (021 788 1726). **Open** 10am-8pm daily. **Main courses** R31. **No credit cards.** **Seafood**

Arguably the best fish and chips in the Cape is served at this humble Kalk Bay harbourside eaterie. Choose from fried or grilled hake, snoek, stumpnose, tuna or whichever fish has just been pulled from the sea. This place revels in the unpretentious, and suitably the dinnerware doesn't disappoint – all meals are served on metal plates accompanied by plastic cutlery.

Klipkantien

Majestic Village, Main Road, Kalk Bay (021 788 2848/www.klipkantien.co.za). **Open** 9am-late Tue-Sat; 9am-5pm Sun. **Main courses** R97. **Credit** AmEx, DC, MC, V. **Seafood, meat**

Watch the comings and goings of the harbour from this quaint restaurant. Tapas include sardines, mussels, tuna fishcakes and vinaigrette-dressed cauliflower; mains are the likes of line-caught fish and steak, and there are even a few German favourites like bratwurst, schnitzel and *wienerli* (traditional potato salad).

Knead *great breakfast!*

82 Beach Road, Surfer's Corner, Muizenberg (021 788 2909). **Open** 8am-6pm daily. **Main courses** R45. **Credit** DC, MC, V. **Café**

Join the throngs of Muizenberg surfers for some upper-crust bread, rolls, pastries, pies and pizzas – all fresh from the oven. You can compile your own platter with a choice of nine breads and toppings, or go the easy route and order the ready-made rolls with satisfying fillings such as roast chicken, roast tomato and red onion.

Other locations Wembley Square, North building, Gardens (021 462 4183).

La Cuccina

Shop 1, Victoria Mall, cnr Victoria and Empire roads, Hout Bay (021 790 8008/www.lacuccina. co.za). **Open** 7am-5pm Mon-Wed, Sun; 7am-5pm, 7pm-late Thur-Sat. **Main courses** buffet by weight (R120/kg). **Credit** AmEx, DC, MC, V. **Café**

This place is positively pumping with patrons at the weekends, especially for the buffet lunch table, where you can loot and load to your heart's content. Popular choices include fresh-baked lasagnes, curries, casseroles and salads.

Streetwise Snacking

Food on the go, with a local flavour.

So much can be understood about a culture by the food one finds on the street, bought still sizzling from informal vendors or market stallholders. Cape Town is no exception. Here, the corner café (convenience store) is key to getting to grips with street food. In the city, many of the local convenience stores have been owned and operated by the same families for years and the cooked food they sell is integral to their success.

Take the **Rose Street Café** (corner of Rose & Wale streets) in the Bo-Kaap for example – here you'll find that traditional Cape Malay stalwart, the samosa, in a variety of delicious, spicy forms. The triangular deep-fried pastry that's filled either with curried mince or vegetables is synonymous with South Africa and they are particularly good here. The rotis (a pancake-like flatbread filled with a slow-cooked curry – often mutton or beef) are also worth checking out.

On weekend nights, Long Street is abuzz and here you'll find *boerewors* rolls for sale at street stalls. As South African as they come – a 'boerie roll' consists of a generous piece of cumin and coriander-spiced barbecued sausage on a roll with lashings of fried onions, tomato sauce, mustard or Mrs Balls chutney (a well-known South African peach chutney).

If you pay a visit to a local township, you'll find plenty of examples of local street food. Here, the best braai (barbecue) masters are distinguished by the queues at their stalls. Simply choose a piece of meat and wait for yours to be sizzled to perfection. For the adventurous, there's 'walkie talkies' to try. Granted, roast chicken feet and beaks aren't to everyone's taste. But most of those who try a 'smiley' (a boiled sheep's head) swear it's absolutely delicious. One street food treat that's absolutely particular to the Cape is the Gatsby – a two–foot-long bread roll filled with oily fries, spicy sauces, mountains of cold meats, cheese, curries and salad. On-the-hoof food at its best.

★ Live Bait

Kalk Bay Harbour, Kalk Bay (021 788 5755).
Open noon-10pm daily. **Main courses** R100.
Credit AmEx, DC, MC, V. **Seafood**
Catering to both the cultivated and the chilled out, this straight-outta-Santorini seafood haven is the perfect destination for those lazy, windless Kalk Bay days. For those with champagne tastes there is fresh sashimi, pan-fried spice-dusted calamari, and seafood platters that'll have the table groaning, For beer budgets there is the equally scrumptious battered fish and chips.

★ Olympia Café & Deli

134 Main Road, Kalk Bay (021 788 6396).
Open 7am-9pm Mon-Sat. **Main courses** R65.
Credit AmEx, DC, MC, V. **Café**
A Kalk Bay legend among laid-back hipsters, the breakfast at this informal deli is an institution, be it the fluffy scrambled eggs, flaky croissants or mushrooms on toast. The blackboard lunch menu is short, changes from day to day and features specialities like West Coast oysters, tuna tartare, line-caught fish, creamy mussels and seafood linguine.
► *The bakery section has moved around the block to a separate outlet.*

Polana

Kalk Bay Harbour, Kalk Bay (021 788 7162).
Open noon-4pm, 6-10pm daily. **Main courses** R140. **Credit** AmEx, DC, MC, V. **Mozambican**
Kick up the spice factor a notch and indulge in the Mozambican/Portuguese inspired fare at this laid-back lounge-slash-eatery. Noteworthy faves include chorizo and calamari pan, chermoula prawns and smoky peri-peri chicken roll. Those wanting a snack can choose from the tapas menu. which features a totally tempting seafood platter.
► *This is a smoking venue.*

Pure

Hout Bay Manor, Baviaanskloof, off Main Road, Hout Bay (021 790 0116/www.houtbay manor.co.za). **Open** 6.30-9.30pm Tue-Sat;

noon-3pm Sun. **Main courses** R140. **Credit** AmEx, DC, MC, V. **Contemporary**
The dramatic, eclectic decor, combining chandeliers, driftwood screens and mother-of-pearl curtains, sets the scene for equally complex locally inspired dishes. Starters feature a guinea fowl consommé with oxtail, while mains include a showstopper of pan-fried springbok with sweet potato nut crust and fig chilli jam. Those wanting the whole Pure experience should order the seven-course tasting menu.

Rioja
Solole Game Reserve, Wood Road, Noordhoek (021 785 5123/www.roija.co.za). **Open** noon-3pm, 6-9pm Tue-Sat; noon-3pm Sun. **Main courses** R72-R115. **Credit** AmEx, DC, MC, V. **Tapas, Mediterranean**
The best of the bush for those who don't like bundu-bashing (roughing it), the Kommetjie local, Rioja, has relocated to the Solole Game Reserve. The tapas selection is as scrumptious as ever and includes Mediterranean-inspired nibbles like potato wedges with a spicy tomato sauce, calamari tentacles and grilled sardines. The mains feature great steaks, fresh line-caught fish and flavourful vegetarian Thai curry.

R Salty Sea Dog
6 Wharf Street, Simon's Town (021 786 1918). **Open** 10am-9pm Mon-Sat; 8.30am-4.30pm Sun. **Main courses** R50. **Credit** AmEx, DC, MC, V. **Seafood**
When nothing but a plate of fish and chips will do, this unaffected Simon's Town haunt is just what the doctor ordered. Owned by Simon's Town's ex-magistrate, an avid fisherman, the restaurant provides the freshest spoils of the sea. Check out the views of the marina as you enjoy starters like deep-fried squid tentacles or *smoor snoek* (flaked snoek mixed with potatoes and peas). Mains offer a choice of battered or grilled hake, kingklip, geelstert or kabeljou, all served with chips, mushy peas and pickled onions.

Wharfside Grill at Mariner's Wharf
Mariner's Wharf, The Harbour, Harbour Road, Hout Bay (021 790 1100/www.mariners wharf.com). **Open** 9-11am, noon-9.30pm daily. **Main courses** R75-R115. **Credit** AmEx, DC, MC, V. **Seafood**

INSIDE TRACK
TIME FOR TEA
Scary colonial but lovely

Get ready to arch your pinky: the **Mount Nelson Hotel** (*see p99* **Cape Colony**), known by locals as the Pink Palace, boasts the best afternoon tea in the world – and a host of international foodies and travel writers agree.

Sailor-suited waiters bid you 'ahoy' at this family-friendly harbour restaurant. Signature starters include oak-smoked snoek pâté and seafood chowder. Ask the sailor-servers for their recommendation of the catch of the day (it can range from grilled Cape salmon to char-grilled game fish) and prepare to get stuck in.
▶ *The takeaway bistro downstairs does excellent fish and chips if you're after something to eat after a walk on the beach.*

NORTHERN SUBURBS

Blowfish
1 Marine Drive, Bloubergstrand (021 556 5464). **Open** 6.30-10.30am, noon-10pm daily. **Main courses** R96. **Credit** AmEx, DC, MC, V. **Seafood**
A location right on Dolphin Beach provides this upmarket seafood joint with a view of the Blouberg (Table Mountain) in all its postcard splendour. It's known for its first-rate fish and sushi (watch it going round and round on the conveyor belt). Seasonal line-caught fish are grilled, deep-fried or prepared tempura style, and given a feisty kick with some Cajun spices. Non-fishy dishes include a done-to-perfection crispy duck with orange and cardamom sauce.

Blue Peter
Blue Peter Hotel, 7 Popham Road, Bloubergstrand (021 554 1956/www.bluepeter.co.za). **Open** 10am-10pm daily. **Main courses** R30-R200. **Credit** AmEx, DC, MC, V. **Café**
Sipping sundowners at the Blue Peter has been a Cape Town institution for decades, and you'll see why when you arrive during the twilight hours. Casual eats include crowd-pleasing staples like hamburgers, pizzas and fish and chips. The hotel dining room, meanwhile, showcases retro fare like Parma-wrapped melon and garlicky snails, with mains of chicken, seafood and meat.

★ Cassia
Nitida Wine Farm, M13 off Racecourse Road, Durbanville (021 976 0640). **Open** noon-3pm Tue-Sun; 6.30pm-10pm Tue-Sat. **Main courses** R80-R120. **Credit** DC, MC, V. **Contemporary**
See the un-suburbanised side of Durbanville from the tranquil, bucolic setting of the Nitida wine estate. The interior of the restaurant is all high-ceilinged, pared-down minimalism, and serves as the perfect muted backdrop for the colourful contemporary creations. Foie gras and lentil terrine with brioche and onion marmalade works well, while warm duck salad with Nitida grapes, pancetta and sherry vinegar is the perfect, moreish marriage of salty and sweet. Dark chocolate beignets and orange cardamom *affogato* are the perfect way to round it all off.
▶ *Nitida also does excellent takeaway picnics, perfect for families.*

Pubs & Bars

Chilled pints and cool cocktails.

It's not surprising that Capetonians love to drink – after all, the city is in the heart of one of the best wine-producing regions in the world. There is a huge variety of settings in which to enjoy a tipple. Start with a long lunch that blends into a sundowner, which is just a short hop from an all-night party. Glam it up and do it in style, or dress down and go casual, whether it's barefoot from the beach or somewhere dark and mysterious in the city. There are beachfront bars for summer, and cosy fireside places for winter. Whatever the weather, whatever the mood and whoever the company, Cape Town has the bar you have been searching for your whole life.

CITY BOWL

Asoka Son of Dharma
68 Kloof Street, Tamboerskloof (021 422 0909/ www.asokabar.co.za). **Open** 5pm-2am daily. **Credit** AmEx, DC, MC, V. **Map** p274 F5 ❶
Simply fabulous cocktails are made with pride, passion and flair here by the well-trained barmen. Be sure to ask for their current specialities, which keep up with cocktail trends. The Pornstar, with vanilla vodka and a shot of sparkling wine on the side, is highly recommended. There's also a full menu of yummy tapas to stave off the hunger pangs, and music of the chilled lounge beat variety on most evenings. The place is famous for its olive tree that thrives inside the premises, enhancing Asoka's tranquil atmosphere.
▶ *For more on Asoka's music, see p185.*

Baghdad Café
190 Long Street, City Centre (084 234 4000). **Open** 8pm-4am Tue-Sat. **No credit cards**. **Map** p276 G4 ❷
It looks so tiny from the street but there's a surprising amount of space inside where you can lounge around on cushions and puff on many-flavoured hubblies like the Caterpillar in *Alice In Wonderland*. The vibe is relaxed and chilled, with DJs spinning R&B and house over the weekends, and karaoke nights on Thursdays.

Blooz Bar
108 Kloof Street, Gardens (021 426 5042). **Open** 11am-2am daily. **Credit** AmEx, DC, MC, V. **Map** p274 F5 ❸

This newly opened bar is aimed at a young student crowd, with special student nights on Thursdays. But a music policy covering eras from the 1980s to the present day makes it accessible for all ages, with DJs playing at weekends and a small stage for live music. Summertime easy living is epitomised on the outside deck, with its sweeping view of Table Mountain. There's a pool table, and light dishes like schnitzels, jacket potatoes and salads are served.

Catú Irish Bar
Corner Burg & Hout Street, City Centre (021 424 7453/www.catu.co.za). Open 10am-2am Mon-Sat. **Credit** AmEx, MC, V. **Map** p276 H3 ❹
An Irish pub in the midst of high-rises, its name derives from the Gaelic phrase 'Conas Ata Tu', meaning 'How are you'. Classically kitted out with a beautiful bar and cold draughts (perhaps a pint of Guinness from the tap), this is a place to relax in after a long day's work. Being off the main drag means it's never unbearably packed. Irish music and sing-along tunes will keep you going. There's good pub grub, from bangers and mash to the popular

| **INSIDE TRACK** |
| **PERSEVERANCE TAVERN** |

Have a beer with the ghosts of Cape Town past: historic local figures (like Cecil John Rhodes) have all slugged back a pint at the city's oldest bar (*see p125*). On the walls you'll find some of Cape Town's earliest electric streetlamps.

Friday night braais on the veranda, or simply pop in to watch your favourite sport on the big screen.

Che Bar
227 Long Street, City Centre (021 424 2330). **Open** 9am-7pm Mon, Tue, Thur; 9am-midnight Wed, Fri; 4pm-midnight Sat. **Credit** AmEx, MC, V. **Map** p276 G4 ❺
The Cuban-style bar brings a tropical taste of Havana to Cape Town, with Panama hats, carved pillars and ornate mirrors. Bartenders are dressed in berets and T-shirts depicting the famous revolutionary for whom the bar is named, as they serve a large range of cocktails with style and flair. A classic mojito is an absolute must.

Daddy Cool
38 Long Street, City Centre (021 424 7247/ www.granddaddy.co.za). **Open** 4-11pm Mon-Thur; 4pm-1am Fri; 2pm-1am Sat. **Credit** AmEx, DC, MC, V. **Map** p276 H3 ❻
The spiritual home of the city's kings of bling, this hip hangout situated at the Grand Daddy hotel turns the notion of hotel bar on its head. Decorated to thrill in gold galore, with ultra cool white leather couches and chairs, you can soak up the music while surfing the crowd. And if you've made a night of it and you're too drunk to drive? Check into the Sugar Daddy Suite and make your Mama proud.
► *See p83 for the Grand Daddy.*

Dubliner @ Kennedy's
251 Long Street, City Centre (021 424 1212/ www.thedubliner.co.za). **Open** 11am 4am daily. **Credit** AmEx, MC, DC, V. **Map** p276 G4 ❼
This Irish-style pub is one of the most popular, busy and crowded places in Long Street, every night of the week. It's loud and raucous and you're likely to be flirted with at least once on your way through the throng to the bar. Drinks are a bit on the expensive side, especially as they increase in price by 20%

after 10pm. Guinness and Pilsner are on tap. There's live music every night too, with sing-along-friendly cover versions. Daytime punters can cheer their sporting teams on, with all the big matches shown on flat-screen TVs.

★ Fireman's Arms
25-27 Mechau Road, cnr Buitengracht Street, City Centre (021 419 1513). **Open** 11am-2am Mon-Sat. **Credit** AmEx, DC, MC, V. **Map** p276 H3 ❽
One of the oldest pubs in Cape Town, the Fireman's Arms has held out against all the development going on around it and remains defiantly nestled between skyscrapers and loft apartments. It hardly gets more traditional than this, with 13 beers on tap and fabulous pub grub. Home-made meaty pies are a speciality, particularly the 'really, really, really' hot Fireman's Pie laden with chilli. The less adventurous can tuck into bangers and mash, liver and bacon or a pizza from the wood-fire oven while watching the rugby or cricket.

Friendly Society & Salsa Lounge
125A Waterkant Street, De Waterkant (021 421 6969/ www.friendlysociety.co.za). **Open** 4pm-2am Mon-Thur; 9am-4am Fri, Sat. **Admission** varies. **Credit** MC, V. **Map** p276 G3 ❾
As the name suggests, a friendly place to hang out after a hard day on the beach, shopping or sightseeing. Knock back a cocktail or an icy beer in the upstairs lounge bar to the accompaniment of a tinkling baby grand piano, or put your feet up on the shaded patio with its waterfall. Light meals are served at all times. The downstairs bar at Friendly Society springs into life from about 9pm with live performances by local artists – in particular the simply fabulous resident Odidiva every Saturday night. DJs and vocalists play on other nights of the week.
► *This is a gay-friendly venue, see p178.*

Jo'burg
218 Long Street, City Centre (021 422 0142/ www.joburgbar.com). **Open** 10am-late Mon-Sat; 6pm-late Sun. **Credit** AmEx, DC, MC, V. **Map** p276 H3 ❿
It's loud and noisy, with hip hop blaring, and remains one of the stalwart favourites of Long

INSIDE TRACK
WHO WANTS TO BE A
MILLIONAIRE?

Quiz nights are increasingly popular, with the **Fireman's Arms** (*see p124*) hosting one on Thursday evenings and **Neighbourhood** (*see p125*) on alternate Thursdays. Be sure to grab your cleverest friends – competition is fierce.

CONSUME

Street, filling to overflowing later in the night and wee hours of the morning. There's a small dance floor, a pool table at the back, and the neighbouring Pretoria – accessed by a secret side passage – keeps its dancefloor pumping all night. Also part of the Jo'burg empire is L/Bs, which you'll find behind a plain wooden door and up a set of very steep stairs just next door. It's not always open, but look out for it – you'll be glad you did.

▶ *Jo'burg hosts monthly 'wedding parties', see p194* **Inside Track**.

★ Julep
Alley off Long Street, nr Green Street, City Centre (021 423 4276/www.julep.co.za). **Open** 5pm-2am Tue-Sat. **Credit** DC, MC, V. **Map** p276 G4 ⑪
This is one of Cape Town's best-kept secrets. If you find it, you deserve it. It's a gorgeous little place with bare brick walls, comfy couches and a spectacular selection of cocktails featuring what is without a doubt the best dry Martini in the city. There are happy hours on week nights and a full range of tapas to stop the tummy growling. It's mellow and chilled and simply fabulous. Look out for special, intimate live music performances by local artists like Dave Ferguson and Wonderboom frontman Cito.

★ Neighbourhood Restaurant, Bar & Lounge
163 Long Street, City Centre (021 424 7260/ www.goodinthehood.co.za). **Open** 4pm-2am Mon-Thur; 3pm-4am Fri; 2pm-4am Sat. **Credit** MC, V. **Map** p276 G4 ⑫
It's a spacious venue but the layout, with a number of interleading rooms, lends a feeling of intimacy, and the balcony is always packed even on a so-called quiet night. There's great food to be had: burgers, chicken wings, nachos, chilli poppers, pastas and waffles. To accompany it, sample from one of the largest selections of local and imported bottled beers. This is the perfect place to begin your Long Street pub crawl.

Opal lounge
30 Kloof Street, City Centre (021 422 4747). **Open** 6pm-late Mon-Sat. **Credit** AmEx, DC, MC, V. **Map** p276 G4 ⑬
Divided into a number of exotic lounges, each serving a themed menu (Persian, Oriental and Colonial) and suitably dressed in an exquisite selection of collectibles, this is a popular spot for all-night drinks. Service can be on the slow side.

Perserverance Tavern
83 Buitenkant Street, Gardens (021 461 2440/ www.perseverancetavern.co.za). **Open** Noon-late Mon-Sat. **Credit** AmEx, MC, V. **Map** p276 H5 ⑭
Dating back to 1836, this is the oldest pub in Cape Town. Travellers disembarking from ships at Cape Town's Castle, affectionately known as Persies,

stayed at the Perseverance Tavern, in what was then Slave's Walk, as far back as 1808. The history-steeped pub, which received its liquor licence in 1836, has been lovingly restored. A pub in the true sense of the word, it is a place for beer and fish and chips at incredibly reasonable prices.

★ Planet Bar
Mount Nelson Hotel, 76 Orange Street, Gardens (021 483 1948/www.mountnelson.co.za). **Open** 5pm-late Mon-Thur, Sat, Sun; 3pm-late Fri. **Credit** AmEx, DC, MC, V. **Map** p276 G4 ⑮
The grand old colonial dame that is the Mount Nelson tucks up her famous pink skirts and shows a thoroughly modern bit of leg at her sexy Planet Bar. It's fabulous in summer when you can sit on the terrace and enjoy the Nellie's lush garden while sipping real-deal champagne or something from the huge cocktail menu and nibbling complimentary olives and pretzels. There's a full bar menu for bigger appetites, with cigars for afters. The hotel and bar is a favourite for celebrity-spotting.
▶ *See p78 for the Mount Nelson.*

★ Rafiki's
13B Kloof Nek Road, Tamboerskloof (021 426 4731/www.rafikis.co.za). **Open** 8am-2am daily. **Credit** AmEx, DC, MC, V. **Map** p274 F5 ⑯
The wraparound balcony is enormously popular whatever the weather, and attracts hordes of locals and backpackers for sundowners or the fabulous prawn and pizza specials. Inside there are fireplaces to cosy up to in winter, and it's a fab destination if

Planet Bar.

Relish.

you're into watching sporting events on big screens. The menu has expanded to include breakfast and tapas, and you can keep in touch with the world in this wireless hotspot.

Relish
70 New Church Street, City Centre (021 422 3584/www.relish.co.za). **Open** 5pm-late Mon-Sat. **Credit** AmEx, DC, MC, V. **Map** p274 F4 ⑰
This three-storey building with restaurant, bar and top deck takes full advantage of the glorious mountain view with floor-to-ceiling glass, and it rocks during the summer when DJs spin the party tunes. There's a huge range of pizzas from the traditional wood-fired oven, ideal with a jug of sangria or other cocktails. If you're visiting out of season, look out for winter specials.

The Shack
45 De Villiers Street, Zonnebloem (021 461 5892). **Open** 1pm-4am Mon-Fri; 6pm-4am Sat, Sun. **Credit** MC, V. **Map** p276 H5 ⑱
A true Cape Town legend this, and the scene of many a messy late night – or early morning. There's a small bar and pool table downstairs, and more up top in a warren of cosy interconnecting spaces. Be careful of the stairs because drinks from the friendly barmen at the five bars are strong enough to put a wobble in your knees before you know it. The kitchen is open from 6pm till 3am serving burgers, toasted sarmies and the famous Papa Luke's chilli poppers. Highly recommended for a night out that's casual and informal, and extremely high on the fun scale.

Speedway Café
105 Roodehek Terrace, off Hope Street, Gardens (084 577 2418). **Open** 5pm-late Tue-Sun; 10am-late Sun. **Credit** AmEx, DC, MC, V. **Map** p276 G5 ⑲

The home of twin boys-about-town Paul and Dave van der Spuy, this grungy bar and restaurant is emblazoned with car and biking memorabilia – the ideal canvas for the themed Harley, Vespa and collector car get-togethers held here. With a menu from the adjacent German Club (think schnitzels and bratwurst), it's all about no frills good times. Regular band nights keep those good times rolling.

★ Waiting Room
273 Long Street (above Royale eatery), City Centre (021 422 4536/www.royaleeatery.co.za). **Open** 6pm-2am Mon-Sat. **Credit** AmEx, DC, MC, V. **Map** p276 G4 ⑳
You'll need to look for a plain, unmarked door and climb a steep stairway to find the Waiting Room. It's well worth it. It's a cosy, unpretentious bar with retro chairs and lighting of the kind that your granny might have had. There's also a stunning roof deck for hanging out on those hot summer nights. Check out live bands every Tuesday and DJs spinning laid-back beats from Wednesday through to Saturday. This was originally the place where you waited for your table downstairs at the gourmet burger joint Royale Eatery, but it has become a venue of choice in its own right.

ATLANTIC SEABOARD

Baraza
The Promenade, Victoria Street, Camps Bay (021 438 1758/www.blues.co.za). **Open** 5pm-2am Mon-Fri; noon-2am Sat, Sun. **Credit** AmEx, DC, MC, V. **Map** p273 A8 ㉑
It's the Swahili words for 'meeting place' and a favourite hang-out in Camps Bay, with its elevated view of the beach, sunsets and passing parade of beautiful people, Harley Davidsons and open-top sports cars. DJs play laid-back, chilled beats on most nights during summer, and you can order something to eat from the small menu provided by parent restaurant Blues next door. Cocktails are the order of the day, and there's also a good range of local and imported bottled beer.

★ Bascule
Cape Grace Hotel, West Quay Road, V&A Waterfront (021 410 7100/www.capegrace.com). **Open** 10am-midnight daily. **Credit** AmEx, DC, MC, V. **Map** p275 H2 ㉒
During the day, unwind with a light meal from Café Bascule, which is open until 4pm, and soak up the gorgeousness of the yachts in the marina and the view of Table Mountain. Later, the place morphs into a glamorous whisky bar, with nearly 500 whiskies from around the world – and some of the most expensive and desirable. Locals love it for after-work drinks on a Friday when they loosen their ties and let down their hair to get a head start on the weekend.
► *For the Cape Grace, see p85.*

CONSUME

Speedway Café.

Café Caprice *buzzy good breakfast*
*37 Victoria Road, Camps Bay (021 438 8315/
www.cafecaprice.co.za).* **Open** 9am-late (kitchen
closes 10pm). **Credit** AmEx, DC, MC, V.
Map p273 A8 ㉓
Possibly the trendiest spot on the Camps Bay strip,
where all the beautiful people – and a celebrity or
two – like to hang out after a hard day on the beach.
It's the place to see and be seen and pavement
tables are at a premium. The pace doesn't let up
after sunset, with DJs playing the hottest dance
music until late into the night. Caprice serves up
fabulous breakfasts, tapas, salads, sandwiches,
burgers and pastas, though ooking at the sleek,
toned crowd in their bikinis and baggies you'd be
forgiven for thinking they never eat.

Dizzy's
*41 The Drive, Camps Bay (021 438 2686/
www.dizzys.co.za).* **Open** noon-4am daily.
Credit AmEx, DC, MC, V. **Map** p273 A8 ㉔
When the beachfront in Camps Bay gets a little too
hectic and too pretentious, dial it back a notch and
head for Dizzy's, where the restaurant serves pizzas,
seafood and sushi until late at night. The adjoining
pub/cigar bar and lounge pumps out live music
Wednesday to Sunday; Tuesday is the legendary
karaoke night.

Harvey's at the Mansions
*Winchester Mansions, Beach Road, Sea Point
(021 434 2351/www.winchester.co.za).* **Open**
7am-11pm daily. **Credit** AmEx, DC, MC, V.
Map p272 C2 ㉕
The hotel bar is quaint and the central courtyard is
breathtakingly beautiful in a New Orleans kind of
way, with central fountain and lush foliage. The
other option is to grab one of the veranda tables
with a view of the ocean. There's a small selection

of cocktails and an excellent range of wines available by the carafe at very reasonable prices.
► *For Winchester Mansions, see p89.*

Leopard Bar
*Twelve Apostles Hotel, Oudekraal (021 437
9000/www.12apostleshotel.com).* **Open** 7am-1am
daily. **Credit** AmEx, DC, MC, V.
A little bit off the beaten track, the bar inside the
Twelve Apostles Hotel rewards with its stretch of
wild coastline. If you're lucky you'll spot some
Southern Right whales frolicking during the winter
months. There are comfy couches with plump cushions, and a fireplace inside, where you can enjoy
live music on Monday, Tuesday, Wednesday and
Friday. The large outside deck affords 180-degree
views of the Atlantic. Cocktails are classy and
service is impeccable.
► *See the Twelve Apostles, see p88.*

La Med
*Glen Country Club, Victoria Road, Clifton (021
438 5600/www.lamed.co.za).* **Open** noon-late
Mon-Fri; 9am-late Sat, Sun. **Credit** AmEx, DC,
MC, V. **Map** p273 A7 ㉖
This is the ultimate Cape Town summer experience,
with hordes of tourists and locals stopping off
directly from the beach for buckets of beer and pizza.
La Med overlooks sports fields where paragliders
land, and it's a stone's throw from the ocean, where

INSIDE TRACK
MOTORHEAD HEAVEN

Car and bike fanatics can grab a beer at
Speedway Café (*see p126*), Cape Town's
answer to London's famous Ace Café.

CONSUME

CONSUME

INSIDE TRACK
VINTAGE BOWLING

The oldest wooden bowling alley in Cape Town is available for hire at the **Speedway Café** (see p126), so round up a few friends and come give it a roll. The venue comes complete with pin boys, to set everything up manually, and a bar to add cheer. The lanes are a bit wonky, but it all adds to the atmosphere.

---

the same paragliders have been known to land as well from time to time. Although it heaves in summer, in winter La Med stokes up the roaring fires, lays on the red wine and invites you to come watch rugby on the big-screen TVs.

Mitchell's Brewery
East Pier Road, V&A Waterfront (021 419 5074/ www.waterfront.co.za). **Open** 10am-2am daily. **Credit** AmEx, DC, MC, V. **Map** p274 G1 ㉗
The original Mitchell's Brewery opened in picturesque Knysna on the Garden Route in the early 1980s, before spreading its wings to this branch on the V&A Waterfront. The range of unpasteurised live ales includes Bosun's Bitter, Forester's Draught, Raven Stout and Ninety Shilling Ale. Work your way through as many of them as you can, and when you've had enough there's a good selection of single malt whiskies. There's also a rib-sticking range of typical pub food, from man-sized pizzas and baskets of deep-fried munchies to pies and chips.
▶ *If you're in Knysna, pop into the Mitchell's Brewery there for a tour and a tasting (see p233).*

La Vie
205 Beach Road, Sea Point (087 808 2456). **Open** 9am-11.30pm daily. **Credit** MC, V. **Map** p272 C2 ㉘
Technically a restaurant, La Vie does a brisk trade in the late afternoon for sundowners and cocktails, and DJs play lazy, loungy beats on Friday evenings. After a few rounds of shooters things can quickly get into a party mood. On this side of the Peninsula, there's still the advantage of a glorious ocean sunset, but without the crowds that you find further along in Camps Bay. There are big lawns with swings and things across the road for children of all ages to frolic. Pizzas and snack platters to share will tide you over and there are all sorts of events taking place, from poker evenings to book launches.

Vista Bar
Dock Road, V&A Waterfront (021 431 5888/ www.onenadonlyresorts.com). **Open** 6am-late daily. **Credit** AmEx, DC, MC, V. **Map** p274 G2 ㉙
Situated between Maze and Nobu restaurants, the larger-than-life Vista Bar has magnificent views of

Table Mountain, which guests can enjoy while sipping on martinis or perfectly chilled champagne. Contemporary interiors with a touch of Mid-Century Modern and playful takes on scale are suitable easy on the eye and the perfect foil for the eight-metre high 'window wall'.

★ Wafu
1st floor, Corner Beach Road and Surrey Place, Mouille Point (021 433 2377/www.wakame. co.za). **Open** noon-11.30pm daily. **Credit** AmEx, DC, MC, V.
You'll find this place by entering Wakame restaurant and ascending the stairs to the upper level. There's a large inside area but what you're really after is the wooden deck, with its plump, deep couches, umbrellas and fabulous view. Order speciality cocktails or a bottle of wine, and sample the Asian tapas and dim sum. It can be relaxed during the da but come sundowner time, it generally gets packed. So get there early to grab one of those coveted couches.

SOUTHERN SUBURBS

★ Caveau at the Mill
13 Boundary Road, Newlands (021 685 5140/ www.caveau.co.za). **Open** 7am-midnight Tue-Sat; 10.30am-5pm Sun. **Credit** AmEx, DC, MC, V.
If you're serious about your wine – and the Cape winelands offer some of the best in the world – you can get a one-stop wine-route experience in the heart of the leafy suburb of Newlands. This second Caveau (the original is a favourite spot in Heritage Square in town) is situated inside the national landmark of Josephine Mill. You can sample the huge selection of wine, buy some to take home, or linger for lunch or dinner. There's live acoustic music on Friday evenings from 7pm.
▶ *For Josephine Mill, see p64.*

Cybar
28 Main Road, Rondebosch (021 685 5356/ www.cybar.biz). **Open** 10am-2am Mon-Sat; 10am-midnight Sun. **Credit** AmEx, MC, V.
In the heart of vibrant Rondebosch, Cybar is the new hip, cool and cosmopolitan bar and eaterie, a place for a quick drink with mates or a very late one with strangers.

Forrester's Arms
52 Newlands Avenue, Newlands (021 689 5949). **Open** 11am-11pm Mon-Thur; 11am-midnight Fri; 10am-11pm Sat; 10am-6pm Sun. **Credit** AmEx, DC, MC, V.
Affectionately known as Forries, this place is a legend in its own happy hour, for everything from student drinking, sports-watching and post-match drinks to after-work wind-downs and hearty food. You won't want to miss the carvery, which is available every day in winter and over weekends in summer.

Home Bar

53 Second Avenue, Harfield Village (021 683 6066). **Open** 7pm-11pm Mon-Sat. **Credit** AmEx, DC, MC, V.

A small, cosy place tucked away in a converted house in the suburbs that attracts a loyal crowd of regulars who come back time and again for the relaxed, homely vibe and great meals from the restaurant. **Other locations**: Home Again Derry Street, Vredehoek (021 465 8463).

★ Martini

Cellars Hohenort Hotel, 93 Brommersvlei Road, Constantia (021 794 2137/www.cellars-hohenort.com/martini). **Open** 7.30am-midnight daily. **Credit** AmEx, DC, MC, V.

An utterly gorgeous hotel bar, elegantly sophisticated and luxuriously decorated with brightly coloured polka dots over neutrals and bold geometric patterns softened with flowers. As the name suggests, the martini is a signature drink, but there are more than 150 on the menu. There are also several other cocktails, champagne by the bottle or glass, and the best wines from the Constantia Valley.

▶ *For the Cellars Hohenort, see p91.*

★ Oblivion

22 Chichester Road, Harfield Village (021 671 8522/www.oblivion.co.za). **Open** 11.30am-2am daily. **Credit** MC, V.

It bills itself as a funky, friendly, European-style wine bar for the over-23s, but with a multicoloured lit-up dancefloor, who can resist a bit of a boogie? If that's not for you, there are plump leather couches, fireplaces and board games, so you can have a relaxed night out just hanging with friends. The menu offers light meals and snacks to have with wine, cocktails or shooters. Bear in mind that although the bar trades until 2am, the doors close at midnight.

Peddlars On The Bend

13 Spaanschemat River Road, Constantia (021 794 7747). **Open** 11am-11pm daily. **Credit** AmEx, DC, MC, V.

Boozy Bites

Eats to go with your drinks.

When you drink, you want to eat. The worst thing you can do is leave it too late and have to resort to the infamous 'garage pie'. There are plenty of places around Cape Town that serve great meals of the pizza/burger/tapas variety that go so well with wine and beer. And many places, usually the more upmarket bars in hotels, will hand out complimentary snacks such as olives, biltong bites, pretzels and crisps. **Julep** (*see p125*) off Long Street does great tapas, served until 11pm, as does **Asoka** (*see p123*) on Kloof Street and the **Caveau** (*see p128*) wine bars in the city centre and Newlands – perfect for when you don't have a big appetite but just need something to soak up the alcohol.

For burgers and pizzas, try **Neighbourhood** (*see p125*), while places like Forries (**Forrester's Arms**, *see p128*), Persies (**Perseverance Tavern**, *see p125*) and the **Fireman's Arms** (*see p124*) are where you should be heading for traditional pub grub like bangers and mash or fish and chips.

For something completely different, no Long Street bar crawl is complete without a stop at Mohammed's street schwerma stand. He's there from 8pm until 4am, music blaring, selling wonderfully messy and delicious *boerewors* rolls, vegetarian pitas and schwermas. Smile sweetly and he'll sneak you cookies and biscuits and a cup of strong coffee.

Neighbourhood.

CONSUME

The Cape Town area is very fortunate to have several wine routes and this place is right in the middle of the Constantia Valley, which produces some of South Africa's finest wines. When visiting the wine farms, make a point of stopping in here too, either at the main restaurant, the pretty garden or the bar. In summer you're going to want to be at beachfront places but it's good to remember that Peddlars has a fireplace for those stormy winter days.

Springbok Pub Newlands

1 Sport Pienaar Road, Newlands Station,
Newlands (021 671 4251/www.springbokpub.com).
Open noon-4am Mon-Sat. **Credit** MC, V.
With five bars and four entertainment areas and things like Tequila Tuesdays and jug specials on a Thursday, this place is always a good bet for getting completely trashed. Just like back in the day when it was Springfields. It's right across from Newlands Stadium so you can safely expect a sports-mad crowd who either watch the game there, or watch it live and come for celebratory drinks afterwards. A DJ plays a mixture of pop, rock, dance and hip hop every night.

SOUTHERN PENINSULA

★ **Brass Bell**
Main Road, Kalk Bay (021 788 5455/www.brass
bell.co.za). **Open** 11am-11pm Mon-Fri; 8.30am-
11pm Sat, Sun. **Credit** AmEx, DC, MC, V.
The Brass Bell has been around for just about forever and you really can't get closer to the water than this – the waves literally break over the wall. The restaurant specialises in seafood, as you would expect with the fishing boats pulling into the harbour next door, and the bar area has been the scene of many raucous Saturday and Sunday afternoons, with live music.

Dunes

1 Beach Road, Hout Bay (021 790 1876). **Open** *Summer* 9am-midnight daily. *Winter* 10am-11pm daily. **Credit** AmEx, DC, MC, V.
Make this a pit stop on your circuit of the Peninsula as you meander to or from Cape Point over Chapman's Peak. Right on Hout Bay beach and operating first and foremost as a restaurant, it's also hugely popular at weekends for afternoons drinking

---

INSIDE TRACK
KARATE WATER

Brandy and coke is a favourite local tipple, known colloquially as 'Klippies and coke', after popular local brandy, Klipdrift. Another local name for it is Karate Water (because consumption is said to induce drunken bravado).

---

in the sun. It's very child-friendly, so expect dozens of rug rats tearing around and playing in the sand. The menu offers seafood, hamburgers, sandwiches and fresh salads.

Red Herring

Corner of Beach & Pine roads, Noordhoek (021
789 1783). **Open** 5pm-midnight Mon; 11am-
midnight Tue-Sun. **Credit** AmEx, DC, MC, V.
The Red Herring bar and its à la carte restaurant draw a very beach- and family-orientated crowd, and more than their fair share of sun-bleached surfers. Dogs are welcome too. There's a garden area and the upstairs deck overlooks the kilometres of pristine white sand and turquoise ocean of Noordhoek beach. There are happy hours on Wednesday and Friday, and live music on Sunday evenings.

NORTHERN SUBURBS

Blue Peter Lower Deck

Blue Peter Hotel, 7 Popham Road, Blouberg
(021 554 1956/www.bluepeter.co.za). **Open**
10am-10pm daily. **Credit** AmEx, DC, MC, V.
The sloping lawn outside the downstairs bistro and bar is the perfect place to be on a warm afternoon with a few ice-cold beers. There are tables with umbrellas but who doesn't like lolling about on the grass? Pizzas are a great accompaniment at this casual, relaxed and friendly venue. It's only about 30 minutes from the city centre and well worth the drive.

Cock 'n Tail

67-70 Edward Street, Tyger Valley (021 919
5028/www.edwardstreet.co.za). **Open** 6pm-4am
Thur-Sat. **Credit** MC, V.
Cock 'n Tail serves Portuguese food during the day but by night becomes the party destination of choice in the northern suburbs. The crowd is young and there are things like foam parties and R5 drinks specials – and barely legal teenage boys take their shirts off in exchange for alcohol – so you get the idea. There's a huge bar to cope with it all, and an elevated VIP area. Summer nights can be enjoyed in an outside area. Bands play on Fridays.

Doodles Beachfront

110 Beach Boulevard, Table View (021 554 1080/
www.doodles.co.za). **Open** 9am-late daily. **Credit**
AmEx, DC, MC, V.
This popular bar – with a sweeping picture-postcard view of the ocean and Table Mountain in the distance – has been going for nearly two decades, with free-flowing drinks, a full menu and vibrant party atmosphere, any time of the day. As much as we love summer, winter is a reality and the outside deck can be enclosed during cold weather. There are smoking and non-smoking sections, loads of draught on tap, live music on Tuesdays and Sundays, DJs on Fridays, happy hours and big screens for sport. What more do you need?

Shops & Services

Shop till you drop for edgy fashion, creative craft and gems galore.

Though beach, dining, adventure and cultural experiences are most certainly part of the Cape Town package, savvy visitors know to come with a half-empty suitcase ready to fill up with well-priced buys for themselves, friends and families. Start your shopping expedition with a browse-before-you-buy attitude and you're on your way. If it's African mementoes you're after, visit the **Pan African Market** and **Greenmarket Square** for a real-deal bargaining experience, or look out for the more formalised African craft stores dotted throughout the city. Between them, **Canal Walk** and the **V&A Waterfront** cover high street and

high-end fashion while the smaller malls like **Cavendish Square** and **Willowbridge Lifestyle Centre** are as much about the see-and-be-seen factor as the shopping. Long Street remains a charming bastion of fashion, book, music and antique stores, while **Kloof Street** and **De Waterkant** have the design scene wrapped up. Go boutique hopping in **Newlands Main Street**, bric-a-brac buying in **Kalk Bay** and, if you're after a bit of bling, don't forget that South African-bought diamonds are among the best value in the world.

CONSUME

General

MALLS

★ 210 on Long
210 Long Street, City Centre (082 391 3878).
Open 10am-6pm Mon-Fri; 10am-4pm Sat.
Map p276 G3.
This edgy emporium hits the mark for those who like some consciousness with their consumerism. Stop in at Hemporium for clothes and accessories manufactured from the wonder plant, wander over to the Green Shop, home of eco-friendly toys and gadgets and be sure to take a look at Galleria Gibello, with haunting photographs taken throughout Africa. Saturday markets (11am-3pm) are abuzz with wine tastings and fashion and craft sales. *Photo p131.*

Canal Walk
Century Boulevard, Century City, Milnerton, Northern Suburbs (021 555 4444/www. canalwalk.co.za). **Open** 9am-9pm daily.

About the author
Vicki Sleet *is a freelance lifestyle journalist with a special interest in design, shopping and food.*

One of the most extensive shopping experiences in the city, this mock Italianate complex delivers on two levels – big and bigger. Some 400 shops cater for every fashion, shoe, accessory, electronics, grocery, book and furniture whim you may have, while the arena-sized food court provides fuel for your shopping expeditions. Plenty to keep kids occupied too – from holiday shows and activities to places like the MTN Science Centre.

INSIDE TRACK
DESIGNER TOTS

Stock up on hip threads for your brood at the weekly **Kindergoods market** at the Old Biscuit Mill. You'll find all sorts of local designer goods for little ones – including nifty treats like Bob Marley baby-grows and vintage wind-up toys (Neighbourgoods Market, the Old Biscuit Mill, 373-375 Albert Road, Woodstock, 021 448 1438, www.neighbourgoods market.co.za). For more on both, *see* p135 **Love Thy Neighbour.**

210 on Long. See p131.

This community-orientated centre is a beacon for the northern suburbs regulars who use it as their local shopping and socialising haunt. Whether picking up groceries or meeting the gals for lunch, there is a host of ways to spend one's dosh here. Great clothing, jewellery and accessories stores ensure it's always a hit.

Victoria Wharf
V&A Waterfront, Atlantic Seaboard (021 408 7600/www.waterfront.co.za). **Open** 9am-9pm Mon-Sat; 10am-9pm Sun. **Map** p275 H1.
The city's waterside mall, this dockside destination has everything and more for those who love nothing better than a shopping, eating and entertainment spree. High-end and luxury stores are a large part of the tenant crowd although the big name brands and supermarkets also feature. A favourite with tourists looking for chic purchases to take home, the new Link Mall is a glam addition that plays host to a selection of top-notch brands like Louis Vuitton and Gucci.

Cavendish Square
1 Dreyer Street, Claremont, Southern Suburbs (021 657 5600/www.cavendish.co.za). **Open** 9am-7pm Mon-Sat; 10am-5pm Sun.
A visit or two a week to this glam mall is a fixture for many a style-savvy resident of the southern suburbs. Glossy stores filled with right on trend fashions and accessories, gift and decor stores galore, plus shoe displays that'll make you drool. Expect high-end offerings at high-end prices.

Constantia Village
Cnr Main Road and River Road, Constantia, Southern Suburbs (021 794 5065/ www.constantiavillage.com). **Open** 9am-6pm Mon-Fri; 9am-5pm Sat; 9am-1pm Sun (Woolworths and Pick 'n Pay open later).
Yummy mummies meet here for their morning coffee at the Seattle Coffee Co, then make their way to Pick n' Pay or Woolies to pick up groceries for their clan. A local centre that has everything you need, just with a sophisticated sheen.

Gardens Centre
Mill Street, Gardens, City Bowl (021 465 1842/ www.gardensshoppingcentre.co.za). **Open** 9am-7pm Mon-Fri; 9am-5pm Sat; 9am-2pm Sun. **Map** p274 G5.
This buzzing little local centre stocks all kinds of groceries, gifts and gadgets. An excellent German deli is a lunchtime draw, while there is a smattering of fashion and gift outlets are worth visiting. They also have branches of some of the main banks.

Tygervalley Shopping Centre
Cnr Willie van Schoor and Bill Bezuidenhout avenues, Durbanville, Northern Suburbs (021 914 1822/www.tygervalley.co.za). **Open** 9am-7pm Mon-Sat; 9am-5pm Sun.

Willowbridge Lifestyle Centre
39 Carl Cronjé Drive, Tygervalley, Northern Suburbs (021 914 7218/www.willowbridge. co.za). **Open** *Summer* 9am-7pm Mon-Fri; 9am-6pm Sat; 9am-5pm Sun & public holidays. *Winter* 9am-6pm Mon-Sat, 9am-5pm Sun and public holidays.
This vibey piazza-style mall is lined with cool eateries and coffee stops, a Woolworths and an @home lifestyle store, edgy boutiques and high end accessories shops. A boon for stylemongers who come here for both a strut and a shop.

MARKETS
Church Street Antique Market
Church Street, City Centre. **Open** 9am-4pm Mon-Sat. **No credit cards. Map** p276 G3.
This well-established market is a strong part of the heart and soul of charismatic Church Street and for years has been the source of many a bargain-hunter's and collector's best finds. Vintage is the key word, from funky clothing and costume jewellery to books, porcelain and brocante. Grab a coffee and shop till you drop, weather permitting.
▶ *For more on Church Street, see p44.*

★ Greenmarket Square
Cnr Shortmarket and Burg streets, City Centre (www.greenmarketsquare.com). **Open** 9am-4pm Mon-Sat. **No credit cards. Map** p276 H4.
Given that this has to be one of the most beautiful and architecturally interesting city squares in the southern hemisphere, no trip to Cape Town is complete without some quality bonding time on this historical gem. Come here for a full range of African folk art plus well-priced CDs and souvenir clothing. An added bonus is the Pan African character of the vendors (who welcome bargaining), especially on Fridays

Greenmarket Square.

when they don traditional garb. Enjoy the array of groovy places at which to refresh and people-watch.

Green Point Market
Parking lot, Bowling Green, Green Point, Atlantic Seaboard (021 439 4805). **Open** *9am-6pm Sun.* **Map** *p274 F1.*
Think Cameroon meets Camden Town. This market, which has been part of the Green Point landscape for years and years now, has a new home in the city and features a selection of curio and African crafts stalls as well as an attractive range of bric-a-brac stalls. It's a wonderful spot to work off a long Sunday brunch.
▶ *For more on Green Point, see p58.*

★ Neighbourgoods Market
373-375 Albert Road, Old Biscuit Mill, Woodstock, Southern Suburbs (021 462 6361/www. neighbourgoodsmarket.co.za). **Open** *Old Biscuit Mill Shops 9am-4pm Mon-Fri; 9am-2pm Sat. Neighbourgoods Market 9am-2pm Sat.*
With the current proliferation of farmers' markets specialising in all things artisanal, the meteoric rise and success of this two-year-old organic village fête for the Volvo/four-wheel-drive set is hardly surprising. Rub shoulders with bohos and bon vivants while you shop, champagne flute in hand, for pastry, preserves and a plethora of prepared foods. Don't leave without a bunch or two of lush local flora, the best fresh produce in Cape Town and even a supply of free-range meat. Market innovators Justin Rhodes and Cameron Munro are to be commended for this income-generating initiative. It has become the highlight of many locals' week and many a visitor's stay.
▶ *See also p135* **Love Thy Neighbour.** *And check out the slew of art galleries that have opened in the Woodstock area.*

★ Pan African Market
76 Long Street, City Centre (021 426 4478/ www.panafrican.co.za). **Open** *Summer 8.30am-5.30pm Mon-Fri; 8.30am-3.30pm Sat. Winter 9am-5pm Mon-Fri; 9am-3pm Sat.* **Credit** AmEx, DC, MC, V. **Map** *p276 H4.*
Situated in the heart of central Cape Town's art-and-antiques precinct, the Pan African Market is uniquely attractive for a number of reasons. The lobby is a gem of Victorian tiling, while the first and second floors are a beehive of traders in new and old folk art, with representatives from most locales in West, sub-Saharan and southern Africa. Once you've ordered your custom-tailored garment, and finally chosen your mask among the many thousands, enjoy a coffee or a Swahili-infused lunch on the oh-so-quaint first-floor terrace. Bargaining is welcomed.
▶ *See also p49.*

Specialist
BOOKS & MAGAZINES
★ A is for Apple
16B Kloof Nek Road, Tamboerskloof (021 424 5409/www.aisforapple.co.za). **Open** *9am-5pm Mon-Fri; 9am-2pm Sat.* **Credit** DC, MC, V. **Map** *p274 F5.*
In an age where computers are introduced in toddlerhood, how encouraging that A is for Apple is fighting the good fight to keep books and their magical allure alive among the early literacy set. The look is candy-coloured Dr Seuss-meets-anime and a weekly storytelling hour in a comfy nook nurtures the wordsmiths of the future. With a decaf coffee bar and retro zoo biscuits for the older kids, bookshops don't come cooler than this.

Baobab Books

210 Long Street, Baobab Mall, City Centre (021 422 3894). **Open** 10am-6pm Mon-Sat. **Credit** DC, MC, V. **Map** p276 G4.

Tucked away in a grow-your-own retail arcade on Cape Town's trendy Long Street, Baobab Books is the city's best-kept between-the-covers secret. Discover amazing rarities among collections of South Africana, history and militaria. Serious literature and volumes on material culture (visual, tribal, furniture, costume etc.) further attest to a discerning selectivity at the helm. A bibliophile's dream.

★ Biblioteq

30 Hudson Street, Loading Bay, De Waterkant, City Bowl (021 422 0774/www.biblioteqbooks. com). **Open** 9.30am-5.30pm Mon-Fri; 9.30am-3pm Sat. **Credit** DC, MC, V. **Map** p276 G3.

Don't be intimidated by the über-chic style of the place. Nor should the staggering price tags of some of the volumes deter you. Biblioteq's niche is 'the book as limited-edition artwork'. Housing an impressive collection featuring mainly titles on visual art, popular culture, design and the like, this shop is an excellent source of special-event gifts for the friend who has everything.

★ Book Lounge

71 Roeland Street, City Centre (021 462 2425). **Open** 8.30am-7.30pm Mon-Fri; 9.30am-6pm Sat; 10am-4pm Sun. **Credit** MC, V. **Map** p276 H5.

A slow turn around this carefully created, two-storey bookshop in Cape Town's ascendant East City leaves you with the unmistakable impression that the Book Lounge was created by book-lovers for book-lovers. While all the predictable departments are represented, it is the median quality of

books on the shelves that convinces. No pulp fiction here; rather plenty of comfy seating and even coffee and nibbles in the basement.

▶ *Regular launches and Saturday morning kiddies' storytime has ensured loyal support from authors and book-lovers alike.*

Clarke's Bookshop

211 Long Street, City Centre (021 423 5739/ www.clarkesbooks.co.za). **Open** 9am-5pm Mon-Fri; 9am-1pm Sat. **Credit** AmEx, DC, MC, V. **Map** p276 G4.

The gold standard among the city's book vendors, Clarke's is to local literati what the Shakespeare & Company bookstore is to Paris. Clarke's is wonderfully laden with new, second-hand and rare books, maps and other published material. A long-time champion of local authors and a fund of academia, this is one of Cape Town's most esteemed resources.

Exclusive Books

Shop 6160, Lower Level, Victoria Wharf, V&A Waterfront, Atlantic Seaboard (021 419 0905/ for other branches 011 798 0000/www.exclusive books.com). **Open** 9am-10.30pm Mon-Thur; 9am-11pm Fri, Sat; 9am-9pm Sun. **Credit** AmEx, DC, MC, V. **Map** p275 H1.

The big daddy of bookstores with a catalogue to match. You will not only find the newest and biggest selection of current books and magazines, but also slick stationery and a damn fine cup of coffee too (in the larger branches).

Other locations throughout the city.

★ Kalk Bay Books

124 Main Road, Kalk Bay, Southern Peninsula (021 788 2266/www.kalkbaybooks.co.za).

CONSUME

Clarke's Bookshop.

Love Thy Neighbour

A talented duo has transformed the local food shopping scene.

At the first light of dawn on a Saturday morning, most of us are snoring deeply beneath our duvets. Not Justin Rhodes and Cameron Munro – they're already hard at work setting the stage for the city's hippest weekly shopping event: Woodstock's Neighbourgoods Market.

The Rhodes and Munro story starts years ago, when the frayed suburb of Woodstock was still synonymous with hookers and gang wars and, needless to say, utterly without gourmet organic goodies. That's about the time that South African Munro met New Yorker Rhodes in the Big Apple. The pair fell in love, came back here and opened up a cupboard-sized gallery, What if the World, in the East City, which fast blossomed into a premier platform for emerging artists. This success sprouted the seeds for a gourmet food market – the pair found a dilapidated warehouse in an old biscuit factory in Woodstock and the rest is history.

'We wanted to create a platform for organic farmers, micro producers and speciality fine food purveyors,' says Rhodes. 'While also getting an amazing selection of quality food items together under one roof,' adds Munro. For six months the duo drove around sourcing traders; going on recommendations from people in the food industry. 'There was a bit of convincing to do,' admits Munro – many people thought they were crazy to start a gourmet food market in a dodgy neighbourhood like Woodstock. But the pair pulled it off, in a big way, and today the market houses 120 stalls (with over 1,000 traders on the waiting list). A separate design market is choc-a-bloc with jewellery, ceramics, furniture and clothing by emerging local designers. There's also a market for the little ones – plying kiddies' wear and vintage toys.

Just what can newbies expect when visiting? 'It's an amazing opportunity to taste the fruits of the Western Cape – 99.5 per cent of the produce is local and comes from within a 400-kilometre radius,' says Munro. 'It's also nice to experience the communities of Cape Town meeting on a Saturday morning – there's quite a social element to it which is interesting.'

'People love coming down and interacting with the vendors,' adds Rhodes. 'Nowadays people want experiences, rather than just walking into a grocery store, and the market offers the opportunity to meet the guy who's making your bread and ask what goes into it.'

When pressed to single out stalls, they mention Trevor Daly, 'the bread guy' who bakes artisan loaves in an old shipping container in the mountains of Worcester in the Winelands, and Romena, 'the fantastic vegetable lady' whose family has been trading vegetables at the Salt River market for three generations. 'She sources the most amazing selection of weird and wonderful vegetables and fruits, from Japanese oranges to ten different types of lemongrass,' says Munro. There's also Charles, 'the vintage guy', Luke who does savoury tarts, and Jane who sells big wheels of artisan cheeses. The list goes on...

The pair wax lyrical about their home town. 'There's something really accessible about it,' muses Rhodes. 'It's big enough but also small enough. Whereas a city like New York can really eat you up and swallow you, Cape Town has a nice neighbourly feel to it. I think it'll always be a home for me no matter where we end up living.'

Let's hope their wanderlust stays dormant for now – our Saturdays would be pretty miserable without them.

CONSUME

DIAMONDS
No better place,
no better time

Over time, you will come to cherish the memory of your stay in South Africa; the climate, the spirit of the people and their cultural diversity, perhaps the thrill of tracking the Big Five in a top game reserve, the cuisine and the excitement of a world class sporting event.

Nothing will recall these extraordinary moments more vividly than if you return home with an exquisitely crafted piece of diamond jewellery from Shimansky.

You not only take with you a piece of Africa itself, a stone born billion years ago deep

diamond laboratories. Each stone is carefully selected to match a design concept. Who will wear it now - and for generations to come?

Shimansky's unique diamond designs such as the most sought-after engagement ring in South Africa, The Millennium

Every Shimansky diamond is laser inscribed with it. unique certificate number for your peace of mind

within the earth, but you preserve an unforgettable emotion. In the receiving of a diamond set in precious metal, you become its new custodian. The jewellery in turn, becomes a symbol of love, passion, a life partnership, a milestone, or an heirloom.

No-one understands the significance of this exchange, more than Shimansky does.

The journey of a Shimansky diamond begins with an uncut stone sourced directly from South African mines and certified by independent

Diamond Ring and the internationally patented My Girl™ diamond cut, travel the world. But no matter where the diamond ends its journey, a laser-inscribed certificate number along with the carat weight, olour and clarity no bigger than a few micron on the girdle, tie the owner to the stone. They become inextricably linked for all time, a signature of provenance.

That is why when international celebrities, statesmen and stars visit South Africa, Shimansky invariably becomes part of their itinerary. Katie Melua wears an 18k white and yellow gold flower pendant with sapphires, inspired by the national flower of her birth country, Georgia. James Blunt's Shimansky-designed 18k yellow and white monkey pendant studded with 5.50cts of diamonds is a treasured keepsake and reminder of his successful tour of South Africa. Lionel Richie returned home with not only an elephant hair and 18k yellow gold cuff but with a priceless gift for his grand-daughter, 2 year old Harlow Winter Kate Richie Madden. Harlow's keepsake, an internationally patented My Girl™ diamond set in a pendant, will be kept for a special moment in her life. It is these moments, that Shimansky value most.

Natural diamonds from the African soil and tanzanite, the rarest gem of all, set in platinum or gold, form only part of a selection of jewellery designed for glamorous occasions, celebrations and naturally, romance. Diamonds still represent the ultimate expression of love, passion and commitment for an engagement or anniversary.

There is no better place, no better time to visit the flagship store at Sandton City, Johannesburg where the décor and jewellery pieces offer you a refined shopping experience Those visiting Cape Town are invited to the Shimansky head office for a personally guided tour of the jewellery showroom at The Clock Tower, Waterfront. View first-hand award winning designs handcrafted in their on-site Jewellery Manufacturing workshop and the art of Diamond Cutting and Polishing. Discover the history of diamonds in the only Diamond Museum in Cape Town. Visiting any of the of the Shimansky outlets is highly recommended.

If it is one line from Shakespeare that expresses every day what Shimansky sees every day as their jewellery pieces begin their new journey of a lifetime, it is this: 'They do not love that do not show their love'.

The Clock Tower, Waterfront,
Cape Town Tel: 021 421 2788
Other retail outlets:
Cape Town: V&A Waterfront;
Canal Walk;
Cape Town International Airport.
Gauteng: Sandton City,
Johannesburg;
Brooklyn and Menlyn Mall,
Pretoria.
Durban: The Pavilion, Westville.
www.shimansky.co.za

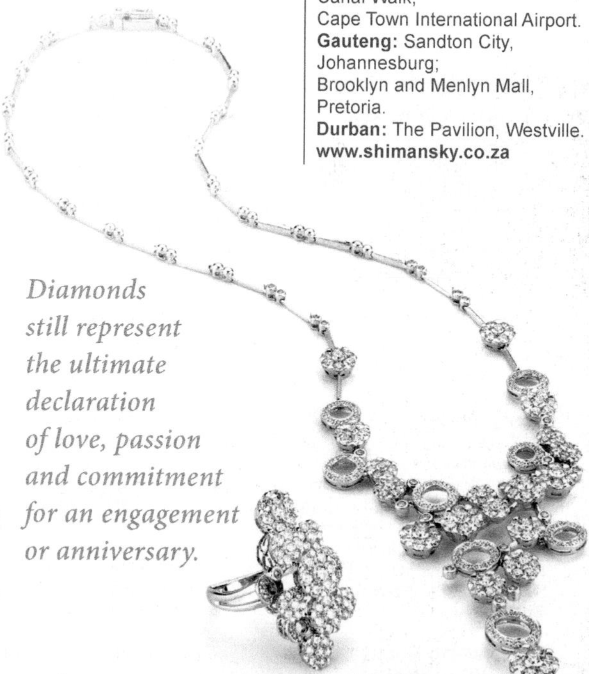

Diamonds still represent the ultimate declaration of love, passion and commitment for an engagement or anniversary.

SHIMANSKY

Naartjie

Open 9am-6pm daily in summer; 9am-5pm daily in winter. Credit AmEx, DC, MC, V.

This quaint reader's haven, owned by former magazine editor Ann Donald, comes straight out of central casting (Think *Notting Hill*, *84 Charing Cross Road* and so on). Sniff among cavernous shelves for timeless reads as well as a quality selection of newer titles.

Quagga Art & Books

84 Main Road, Kalk Bay, Southern Peninsula (021 788 2752/ www.quaggabooks.co.za). Open 9.30am-5pm Mon-Sat; 10am-5pm Sun. Credit MC, V.

The coolest and most authentic of Cape Town's antiquarian bookshops, Quagga Art & Books is the provenance to which many literary treasures can be traced. Africana, art and history are three areas for which this store is well loved. Maps, pictures and objets d'art create a unique ambience. Caution: ensure the one you have your eye on is for sale before you bond.

Reader's Den

Shop G10, Stadium on Main, Main Road, Claremont, Southern Suburbs (021 671 9551/ www.readersden.co.za). Open 10am-5pm Mon-Fri; 9am-2pm Sat. Credit MC, V.

On entering this haven for lovers of graphic novels and comic books, you're immediately struck by how established this genre of literature has become. Super heroes, manga and the like are represented with impressive depth.

Wordsworth Books

Shop 7103, Lower Level, Victoria Wharf, V&A Waterfront, Atlantic Seaboard (021 425 6880/for other branches 021 797 5664).

Open 9am-10pm Mon-Sat; 10am-9.30pm Sun. Credit AmEx, DC, MC, V. Map p275 H1.

The smaller of the national book chains, this worthy alternative nevertheless carries a serious selection of current, classic and coffee table volumes. South African interest, cookery and gay titles are specialities, with well-stocked departments, and staff are outstanding.

Other locations throughout the city.

▶ *Visit the Traveller's Bookshop store-within-a-store here for a host of local and international city and country guidebooks and maps.*

CHILDREN

Fashion

★ Crazy About Cape Town

Shop 132, Lower Level, Victoria Wharf, V&A Waterfront (021 419 9474). Open 9am-9pm daily. Credit AmEx, DC, MC, V. Map p275 H1.

Visitors to the city head for this Waterfront stall with its distinctive gear for little people decorated with the friendly Chalk Man motif. Stock up on tees and sweaters that'll remind them just how cool Cape Town is.

Earthchild

Shop 112, Lower Level, Victoria Wharf, V&A Waterfront (021 421 5033/www.earthchild.co.za). Open 9am-9pm Mon-Sat; 10am-9pm Sun. Credit AmEx, DC, MC, V. Map p275 H1.

If you're loath to clothe your precious bundle in artificial textiles and garish chain store numbers, head for this store, which specialises in 100% cotton gear for little girls and guys. Lots of room to move and fashionable cuts too, making them a great bet for stylish wardrobe basics.

CONSUME

Fairy Shop

311 Main Road, Kenilworth, Southern Suburbs (021 762 1546/www.fairyshop.co.za). **Open** 9am-5.30pm Mon-Fri; 9am-1.30pm Sat. **Credit** DC, MC, V.

Fill up the dress-up box, stock up on children's birthday presents in bulk and find that ultimate fairy outfit (from wand to wings) for the flutterbug in your life. You'll find everything from dresses to shoes, hair bands, bags and fairyfied babywear too.

Jessica's Kidsware

Shop 52, Constantia Village, Main Road, Constantia, Southern Suburbs (021 794 2223/ www.jessicas.co.za). **Open** 9am-6pm Mon-Fri; 9am-5pm Sat; 9am-1pm Sun. **Credit** MC, V.

Stylish buys for kids (from babyhood up) – great shoes, boys' gear that's not all khaki and gorgeous party dresses too. They also carry the Cherry Melon range of maternity gear for fashionable mums-to-be.

Kapow

Shop 6192, Lower Level, Victoria Wharf, V&A Waterfront (021 421 3364). **Open** 9am-9pm daily. **Credit** AmEx, DC, MC, V. **Map** p275 H1.

Though some of the displays are more in the way of adult fun (furry handcuffs, French maid's outfits et al), this is a great stop for kiddies' dress-up gear as well as those fairy tchotchkes that little girls can never seem to get enough of.

Kids Emporium

Factory A, Unit 4, Honeywell Road, Tokai, Southern Suburbs (021 701 5835/www.kids emporium.co.za). **Open** 8.30am-5pm Mon-Fri; 9am-2pm Sat. **Credit** MC, V.

Yowser! Who knew kids were such big business? A treasure trove for the busy (and style savvy) mum – shop for maternity wear, essential nursery gear, unusual toys, essential travel gear for kids on the move, nappy bags, essential décor items… you get the picture. If it's for little people, you'll find it here.

Naartjie

Shop 136, Victoria Wharf, V&A Waterfront (021 421 5819). **Open** 9am-9pm Mon-Sat; 10am-9pm Sun. **Credit** AmEx, DC, MC, V. **Map** p275 H1.

This South African kids' clothing success story adds colour and charm to any wardrobe, thanks to their trademark prints, worn-in cottons and comfy cuts for boys and girls. Their baby gear is too cute for words, their girls' dresses and stretch cotton leggings with the cutest frills are loved by all ages, and their boys' printed sweaters and heavy-duty cargoes are right on the money.

Other locations Shop F62, Cavendish Square (021 683 7184); Shop 437, Upper Level, Canal Walk (021 551 6317); 46 Victoria Avenue, Hout Bay (021 790 3093).

Pumpkin Patch

Shop 251, Lower Level, Canal Walk, Century City, Northern Suburbs (021 555 4632). **Open** 9am-9pm daily. **Credit** AmEx, DC, MC, V.

Something of a cult with fashion conscious mums, this brand of cute and colourful gear for babies and kids has loads of eye candy for filling up wardrobes. Look out for their preppy gear for little boys (think Argyle sweaters and denim jackets) and plenty of mix and match options for little fashionistas in the making. Good fabrics and great cuts.

ELECTRONICS & PHOTOGRAPHY

Look & Listen

Shop 14, Upper Level, Cavendish Square, Claremont, Southern Suburbs (021 683 1810/ www.lookandlisten.co.za). **Open** 9am-7pm daily. **Credit** AmEx, DC, MC, V.

This large music and DVD store also carries a good range of iPods and MP3-specific accessories – ranging from travel speakers in a bag to the Bose docking systems.

Other locations Shop 85, Lower Level, Canal Walk (021 551 4647); Shop 35 Willowbridge, 39 Charl Cronjé Drive, Tygervalley (021 914 0760).

★ Orms

Shop 5, Roeland Square, cnr Roeland & Canterbury streets, City Centre (021 465 3573/www.orms.co.za). **Open** 8am-6pm Mon-Fri; 8am-1pm Sat. **Credit** AmEx, DC, MC, V. **Map** p276 H5.

Secret Room. *See p141.*

Rub shoulders with the city's photography set, professional or otherwise at this buzzing East City precinct store. From the biggest Megapixel digicams on the market to big name SLR cameras, tripods, camera bags, albums and even photography paper, this shop has really got it all. The place to bring cameras for services, staff will also help you troubleshoot. It is one of the best printing photographic houses in the city.

FASHION
Ladieswear

Callaghan Collezioni
Shop G46, Ground Floor, Cavendish Square, Claremont, Southern Suburbs (021 683 1716). **Open** 9am-7pm Mon-Sat; 10am-5pm Sun. **Credit** AmEx, DC, MC, V.
Label slaves love this lair in the heart of Cavendish where they find the latest fashions from the likes of Calvin Klein, Chloe, Prada and Diane von Furstenburg, whose wrap and cocktail dresses are a perennial hit. They're known for wooing their customers with hands-on service and frothy cappuccinos, which is just as well considering this season's must-haves may leave a serious dent in your wallet.

Cigar Clothing
12B Prospur House, Cavendish Street, Claremont, Southern Suburbs (021 683 3582/www.cigar women.co.za). **Open** 9am-5.30pm Mon-Thur; 9am-3pm Sat. **Credit** AmEx, DC, MC, V.
French contemporary leisure wear is the watchword here, though you'll find smarter stuff for evening do's too. Always a good bet for those perfect wardrobe basics – the white T (in stretch cotton that keeps its shape), linen gear for summer, colourful cardis and sparkly tops for adding some oomph. **Other locations** 72 Waterkant Street, Waterkant (021 418 4846).

Esprit
Shop 7201, Upper Level, Victoria Wharf, V&A Waterfront, Atlantic Seaboard (021 418 0942/ www.esprit.com). **Open** 9am-9pm Mon-Sat; 10am-9pm Sun. **Credit** AmEx, DC, MC, V. **Map** p275 H1.

Millionaire's Mile

Haute couture comes to town.

Savvy shoppers know that an overseas ticket is no longer what's required for a taste of international fashions. The V&A Link Mall, also dubbed 'Millionaire's Mile' is home to a plethora of top-notch swanky fashion stops. At **Apsley 2** (021 418 0061), brands such as Christian Louboutin rub shoulders with the likes of Ralph Lauren and Hermès in eye-catching fashion and homeware displays.

At **Ben Sherman** (021 425 8996) lads about town stock up on the brand's trademark shirts and cutting-edge T-shirt designs, while at **Burberry** (021 425 8933) fresh-off-the-boat seasonal offerings keep fashion slaves fed. Visit **Byblos** (021 418 8744) and soak up the styles that have kept this brand at the forefront of fashion since the 1970s, and if you're looking for that classic fashion or jewellery accessory item that's for keeps, **Dunhill** (021 425 3190) remains the brand to buy. Lovers of a bit of bling always feel at home at **Gucci** (021 421 8800) and this store is definitely worth a peep.

As cult label **Louis Vuitton** (021 405 9700) releases seasonal items on the same day around the world you know you're in the fashion frontline at this

impressively swish store, while lovers of Italian mega brand **Maxmara** (021 418 9447) are spoiled for choice with pieces from each of their high fashion, leisure and sporty ranges. **Jimmy Choo** (021 418 8506) feeds shoe devotees with sky-scraper must-have heels.

Treat yourself with stripy covetables from **Paul Smith** (021 418 0007), order a James Bond-style suit from **Hugo Boss** (021 418 8328) and, if effortlessly casual wear is your thing, then **Pringle of Scotland** (021 418 5282) is an essential stop on your tour.

The famous brand that's great for stylish basics returned to these shores after a long hiatus in 2008. Look out for their trademark laid-back gear with a fashionable twist. Good for streetwear-inspired must-haves, and the bags are always a good buy.

★ Lulu Tantan

Shop 7218, Upper level, Victoria Wharf, V&A Waterfront, Atlantic Seaboard (021 418 8535). **Open** 9am-9pm daily. **Credit** AmEx, DC, MC, V. **Map** p275 H1.

Owner Inge Peacock trawls the world looking for independent designers not scared of making a statement, and her selections are showcased in this jewellery box of a store where seriously stylish women shop for one-off pieces and ensembles that help them to stand out from the crowd. An Asian influence means the store is lined with fashions like Sai So kimono coats as well as lines form both Indian and Malaysian big names.

Mango

Shop 7202, Upper Level, Victoria Wharf, V&A Waterfront (021 418 0916/www.mango.com). **Open** 9am-9pm Mon-Sat; 10am-9pm Sun. **Credit** AmEx, DC, MC, V. **Map** p275 H1.

The cult Spanish brand has finally made its way to the tip of Africa and not a moment too soon. This sparkling store on the fringes of the V&A Waterfront's 'Platinum Mile', is filled with rail after rail of fashionable high-street must-haves. The twenty-something party girl's fashion life saver.

Nicci Boutique

Shop G47, Cavendish Square, Claremont, Southern Suburbs (021 683 9458). **Open** 9am-7pm Mon-Sat; 10am-5pm Sun. **Credit** AmEx, DC, MC, V.

What do southern suburbs socialites, yummy mummies and razor-sharp businesswomen have in common? They all frequent this Claremont shop for feminine, well-cut and sexy (but not slutty) clothing. A selection of imported and own-label items – from party tops to Met frocks and trousers with the perfect cut.

Riga

8 Cavendish Street, Claremont, Southern Suburbs (021 674 4394). **Open** 9am-5pm Mon-Sat. **Credit** AmEx, DC, MC, V.

Fresh-off-the-plane fashions ensure you'll always be one step ahead of your friends. This elegant boutique is manned by enthusiastic and knowledgeable staff who know just how to put together a look that's perfectly you. It specialises in Max Mara – from catwalk must-haves to streetwear leisure gear.

Second Time Around

196 Long Street, City Centre (021 423 1674). **Open** 9am-5pm Mon-Fri; 9am-2pm Sat. **No credit cards**. **Map** p276 G4.

Astore. *See p144.*

Though it's become more and more difficult to find real vintage these days, the owner of this previously-owned-clothes pitstop has a knack of ferreting out real finds. Loads of clothes and accessories that you wouldn't (shouldn't?) be seen dead in – Abba-esque jump suits and dresses that would go up in flames in an instant – but every now and then you'll find a real gem. The staff are fantastic.

▶ *You can also hire clothes for fancy-dress parties.*

★ Secret Room

14 Cavendish Street, Claremont, Southern Suburbs (021 683 7607/www.thesecret room.co.za). **Open** 9.30am-5.30pm Mon-Fri; 9.30am-4pm Sat. **Credit** AmEx, DC, MC, V.

Imported and local garments feature here, all with a trademark glam girlie boho look – bright, jewel colours, ephemeral fabrics, sparkly trims and don't-be-afraid-to-flaunt-it cuts. A good bet for evening events, wedding outfits and party gear that makes a statement. *Photo p139.*

Slate

Shop 232, Upper Level, V&A Waterfront, Atlantic Seaboard (021 421 2554). **Open** 9am-9pm Mon-Sat; 10am-9pm Sun. **Credit** AmEx, DC, MC, V. **Map** p275 H1.

The folks here have their fingers on the pulse of what's happening in the pages of *Vogue* and on international catwalks and their ranges of imported

CONSUME

fashions and accessories are right on trend. Great for seasonal statement pieces – like that great winter coat, summer nights party dress and must-have bag.

Studio 8
2 Cavendish Street, Claremont, Southern Suburbs (021 683 1666/www.studio8shop.com). **Open** 9am-5pm Mon-Fri; 9am-4pm Sat. **Credit** AmEx, DC, MC, V.

This inspirational jewellery box is the creation of local style arbiter Marcelle Savage – her love of exquisite craft, intoxicating fabrics and unashamed femininity leaps off every rail and hanger. Find here that special-occasion or core wardrobe piece from labels such as Dosa, Shirin Guild, Girbaud and Marlene Birger. If you're looking for disposable or ephemeral fashion, go elsewhere; many of Cape Town's best-dressed women have been wearing their timeless Studio 8 purchases for years.

Lingerie

Inner Secrets
Shop 23 Piazza St John, Main Road, Sea Point, Atlantic Seaboard (021 433 1029). **Open** 9am-6.30pm Mon-Fri; 9am-2pm Sat. **Credit** AmEx, DC, MC, V. **Map** p272 B3.

Their payoff line says they're all about making a woman feel good and at this lingerie and swimwear specific store, they're intent on doing just that. Swimwear that covers your lumps and bumps and shows off your better assets, and lingerie that's good enough to be seen in public.

★ Kink
3 Park Road, Gardens, City Bowl (021 424 0758/ www.kink.co.za). **Open** 10am-6pm Mon; 10am-midnight Tue-Sat. **Credit** MC, V. Map p274 F4.

Unleash your inner vixen at this sexy inner-city store where beautiful imported underwear (both naughty and nice), gadgets and gizmos and a host of other goodies are guaranteed to make your toes curl.
▶ *A popular destination for racy pole-dancing demos and bachelorette parties.*

★ Storm in a G Cup
Shop 4, Cavendish Street, Claremont, Southern Suburbs (021 674 6629/www.storminagcup. co.za). **Open** 9.30am-5.30pm Mon-Fri; 9am-2pm Sat. **Credit** DC, MC, V.

Most clothing specialists agree that it all starts with what's under the garment and at this elegant boutique they couldn't agree more. A professional fitting service ascertains your cup size. The swimwear service is outstanding – staff will happily alter different sized tops and bottoms to fit your shape, will take in full piece swimsuits to fit and its all part of the price. They also stock special bras for those occasions where you need lift but need a hidden contraption to do it.

Temptations
Shop 557, Upper Level ,Canal Walk, Century City (021 551 9731/www.temptations.co.za, Northern Suburbs). **Open** 9am-9pm daily. **Credit** AmEx, DC, MC, V.

A good place for high-street lingerie at great prices – the products here may not be made from Chantilly lace but as far as on-trend colours, impromptu 'girls just wanna have fun' buys and bachelorette gifts go, it fills a gap in the market perfectly.

Woman's Secret
Shop 7249, Upper Level, Victoria Wharf, V&A Waterfront, Atlantic Seaboard (021 421 1414/ www.womansecret.com). **Open** 9am-9pm daily. **Credit** AmEx, DC, MC, V. **Map** p275 H1.

Spaghetti Mafia. *See p145.*

CONSUME

The name may sound like a derivative of that other international brand but the stock it carries is all its own – all the way from Spain. Shop for pretty basics, the latest season's must-haves in both lingerie and swimwear and corsetry for those hot dates to remember.

Menswear

★ Astore

Mooikloof Centre, 34 Kloof Street, Tamboerskloof (021 422 2888/www.astoreisgood.com). **Open** 9am-6pm Mon-Fri; 9am-3pm Sat; 10am-2pm Sun. **Credit** AmEx, DC, MC, V. **Map** 276 G4.
Specialising in limited-edition and unusual sports footwear, small-run T-shirts and cult literature on design and popular culture, this achingly trendy and pared-down store is a shrine for the urban cowboy. Buy the sunglasses, join the cult. *Photo p141.*
Other locations 13 Vineyard Road, Claremont (021 671 1693).

★ Bluecollar Whitecollar

Shop G21, Lifestyles on Kloof, 50 Kloof Street, Tamboerskloof (021 426 1921/www.bluecollar whitecollar.co.za). **Open** 9am-6pm Mon-Fri; 9am-3.50pm Sat. **Credit** MC, V. **Map** p24 F5.
The design-and-branding maven Paul van der Spuy (Frank B Ernest, Wylde Oscar) has whisked this white rabbit out of his mercurial top hat. As the name suggests, his decades of experience in menswear here juxtaposes industrial- and uniform-inspired workwear with the sartorially swankier and more corporate look.

Cape Storm

Shop 104, Lower Level, Canal Walk, Century City, Northern Suburbs (021 555 0655/www. capestorm.co.za). **Open** 9am-9pm daily. **Credit** AmEx, DC, MC, V.
You don't have to be an outdoorsy type to cotton on to this most practical, durable and serviceable of apparel vendors. This local-is-lekker label has a wide range of gear from jackets and fleece hoodies to climate-control tops that'll serve you well whether you're climbing the Hottentot's Holland or attempting the Himalayas.
Other locations throughout the city.

Cape Union Mart

Quay Four Adventure Centre, V&A Waterfront, Atlantic Seaboard (021 425 4559/www.cape unionmart.co.za). **Open** 9am-9pm Mon-Thur, Sun; 9am-11pm Fri, Sat. **Credit** AmEx, DC, MC, V. **Map** p275 H1.
Whether your look is Out Of Africa or Camp (in the old-fashioned sense), this time-honoured brand of adventure wear remains a benchmark of quality and relaxed practicality. Mixing made-to-fade cottons in a Savannah palette with perennial microfibres, Cape Union Mart is an institutional cornerstone in the wardrobe of country houses to beachside braaiers.
Other locations throughout the city.

Energie

Shop 6281, Upper Level, Victoria Wharf, V&A Waterfront, Atlantic Seaboard (021 418 8189). **Open** 9am-9pm Mon-Sat; 10am-9pm Sun. **Credit** DC, MC, V. **Map** p275 H1.
Arbiters of post-*Apollo 13* chic, this is a one-stop fantasy chest for those trendists who aspire to an international high-street look. Apply here for signature jeans, statement tops and other cutting-edge style accessories. This Italian brand has legs.

★ Fabiani

Shop 272, Upper Level, Victoria Wharf, V&A Waterfront (021 425 1810). **Open** 9am-9pm daily. **Credit** AmEx, DC, MC, V. **Map** p275 H1.
A favourite among the razor-edged international set and a long-time staple among DBDs (Dapper Black Diamonds), Fabiani is the go-to institution for high-end wardrobe construction. The shop is top-heavy with labels (Armani, G Star, Etro) and the house signature is candy colour, impeccable craft and tailoring and ABC-deluxury. Prepare to cough up. Big time.

Loading Bay

30 Hudson Street, De Waterkant, City Bowl (021 425 6320/www.loadingbay.co.za). **Open** 9am-5pm Mon-Fri; 8am-4pm Sat. **Credit** AmEx, DC, MC, V. **Map** p276 G3.
Both the proprietor, JP Bolus, and the contents of this delectable, industrial-styled men's outfitters can be described in two words: handsome and desirable. Plump, sumptuous hoodies, fantasy knitwear and damn fine shirts and trousers will bring tears to the eyes of any aspirant Ivy Leaguer.
▶ *You can also dig into a hearty sandwich at the café that shares the space.*

Mali South

90 Long Street, City Centre (021 426 1519). **Open** 7am-7pm daily. **Credit** MC, V. **Map** p276 G4.
A unique source of authentic but eminently wearable ethnic-inspired ensembles, master tailor Meiga (from Mali) will kit you out in your very own bespoke hand-embroidered outfit. Allow time for

CONSUME

delivery, but be bowled over by the beauty and the affordability of these distinct costumes. This house celebrates African style.

★ Shelf Life

119 Loop Street, City Centre (021 422 3931/ www.shelflife.co.za). **Open** 10am-5.30pm Mon-Fri; 10am-2.30pm Sat. **Credit** MC, V. **Map** p276 G4.
We hope that this new kid on the block survives fickle fad and fashion because it does drop-dead skater- and hip-hop-inspired urban streetwear with a conviction that has yet to be matched. Stylish and passionate frontman Jason has sourced T-shirts, hoodies, sneakers and, yes, an encyclopaedic range of spray cans for graffiti that threaten to propel this fresh local label into instant cult status.

Spaghetti Mafia

199 Loop Street, City Centre (021 424 0696). **Open** 9am-6pm Mon-Fri; 10am-3pm Sat. **Credit** MC, V. **Map** p276 G4.
Just what is it about the Italians? They unfailingly turn out the most wearable, durable, stylish and flattering ready-to-wear. Owners Giovanni and Laura are patient and generous with wardrobe-building advice. The recent opening of a next-door vintage (but unworn) store takes bargain-hunting and '80s nostalgia to new levels. This is Cape Town's most reliable resource for mouth-watering sportswear and tailored key pieces. *Photo p143.*

YDE

Shop 225, Upper Level, Victoria Wharf, V&A Waterfront, Atlantic Seaboard (021 425 6232/ www.yde.co.za). **Open** 9am-9pm Mon-Sat; 10am-9pm Sun. **Credit** AmEx, DC, MC, V. **Map** p275 H1.
For always fresh, hipper-than-hip apparel, this playground for the Facebook generation continues to pioneer the mass-marketing of edgy. YDE continues to garner kudos for the relentless promotion of local is lekker – and now houses almost 100 local designers' ranges.
Other locations throughout the city.

FASHION ACCESSORIES
Shoes

Aldo Shoes

Shop G50, Ground Floor, Cavendish Square, Claremont, Southern Suburbs (021 671 2333/ www.aldoshoes.com). **Open** 9am-7pm Mon-Sat; 10am-5pm Sun. **Credit** AmEx, DC, MC, V.
High-street footwear fashions are the name of the game here – sparkly impossibly high heels are an all-round staple, knee-high boots in winter and pumps and thongs for the summer months. Their men's ranges solve any fashion dilemmas the man in your life might have.
Other locations throughout the city.

Nina Roche

Shop G45A, Ground Floor, Cavendish Square, Claremont, Southern Suburbs (021 671 3533/ www.ninaroche.co.za). 10am-5pm Sun. **Credit** AmEx, DC, MC, V.
Ooh la la ladies – satisfy your footwear fetish at this cult shoe store where the biggest name brands (think Tods, Hogans, Giuseppe Zanotti – the list goes on) lie in wait to tempt you. Forget diamonds darling – shoes are always a girl's best friend.

★ Nine West

Shop 252, Upper Level, Victoria Wharf, V&A Waterfront, Atlantic Seaboard (021 418 7164/ www.ninewest.com). **Open** 9am-9pm daily. **Credit** AmEx, DC, MC, V. **Map** p275 H1.
You'll always find the hottest seasonal look in shoes, bags and purses at this famous American brand footwear store. Heels are unbelievably comfortable, while shoes in general are well cut and last well beyond one season.
Other locations throughout the city.

Spitz

Shop G29, Ground Floor, Cavendish Square, Claremont, Southern Suburbs (021 683 4435/ www.spitz.co.za). **Open** 9am-7pm Mon-Sat; 10am-5pm Sun. **Credit** AmEx, DC, MC, V.
Footwear fashionistas have been shopping at this store for years and with good reason; it's always stocked with must-haves from a variety of big name brands. If you're looking for the quintessential work shoe in the season's hottest colour, the perfect knee-high boot and heels that'll get you noticed, you know where to go.

★ Tsonga Shoes

Shop 48, Constantia Village, Constantia, Southern Suburbs (021 794 8827/083 494 8025/www.tsonga.com). **Open** 9am-6pm Mon-Fri; 9am-5pm Sat; 9am-1pm Sun. **Credit** AmEx, DC, MC, V.
This South African success story specialises in suede and leather hand-tooled footwear in a paint-box range of colours: from loafers to elegant Ugg-esque boots and the comfiest slip-ons.

FOOD & DRINK
Delis

Andiamo Deli & Restaurant

Shop C2, Cape Quarter, Waterkant Street, De Waterkant, City Bowl (021 421 3688/www. andiamo.co.za). **Open** 9am-10.30pm daily. **Credit** AmEx, DC, MC, V. **Map** p276 G3.
A foodie beacon in de Waterkant, this laid-back Italian setup is a restaurant and deli in one, and if you're stocking up on goodies for your pantry at home you'll find everything you need, from your favourite coffee blends to imported oils and other

CONSUME

ingredients for replicating that speciality dish. Aside from breads and baked treats there's plenty at the deli counter in the form of cured meats, imported cheeses and Italian antipasti favourites to fill up the fridge.

Carluccis
22 Upper Orange Street, Oranjezicht, Gardens (021 465 0795/www.carluccis.co.za). **Open** 8am-8pm daily. **Credit** AmEx, DC, MC, V.
Regulars struggle to get through a day without a cappuccino or build-your-own sandwich from this haunt near the Company's Gardens, which is always brimming with pre-cooked specialities (lasagnes, pastas, curries, veggie bakes et al) as well as all the goodies you'll need to make up your own smörgasbord. Stock up at the cheese and meat counter or browse the selection of pre-made carpaccio, salad and antipasti offerings. They also do dry goods like pastas, and have a wide wine selection and imported chocolates galore.

★ Giovanni's Deliworld
103 Main Road, Green Point, Atlantic Seaboard (021 434 6893). **Open** 7.30am-9pm daily. **Credit** AmEx, DC, MC, V. **Map** p274 F2.
The original Cape Town Italian deli is crammed with mouthwatering food and deli products from floor to ceiling. A cheese and meat counter does a roaring trade with patrons needing their fix of parma and parmigiano, there's also a cooked food section that's popular with the can't-cook-won't-cook brigade, while the pantry shelves are laden with tempting baked and imported speciality goods. Plenty of pre-packed heat-and-eat meals as well as salad goodies for impromptu picnics and, of course, a buzzing espresso bar.

Markets

Foodlover's Market
Icon Building, cnr Loop Street & Hans Strijdom Avenue, City Centre (021 425 2814). **Open** 7am-6.30pm Mon-Fri; 9am-3pm Sat. **Credit** AmEx, DC, MC, V. **Map** p276 H3.
This modern food emporium is bound to change the lives of many a Capetonian foodie. Like a supermarket, only better, the market incorporates a bakery, deli, butcher and fresh produce galore, but also offers a café and sushi bar where you can park off and rest in-between shopping sprees.

Newport Market & Deli
47 Beach Road, Green Point (021 439 1538). **Open** 6.30am-10pm daily. **Credit** DC, MC, V.
Much loved by the Promenade set who use it as their pit stop before and after their morning or evening walks, this is a good place to pick up deli-style sandwiches to go, a range of pâtés and pre made salads, good fruity and veg and biscuits and pastries too.

Speciality foods

Jaqui Dyer
205 Main Road, Newlands, Southern Suburbs (021 685 5383). **Open** 8am-8pm Mon-Fri; 8am-6pm Sat, Sun. **Credit** AmEx, DC, MC, V.
Well loved by southern suburbs foodies who adore the owner's commitment to stocking artisan-style offerings and an extensive range of interesting and speciality products.

Main Ingredient
Shop 5, Nedbank Centre, 15 Kloof Road, Sea Point, Atlantic Seaboard (021 439 5169/083 229 1172/www.mainingredient.co.za). **Open** 10am-6pm Mon-Fri; 9.30am-1pm Sat. **Credit** AmEx, DC, MC, V. **Map** p272 B3.
Owned and run by a passionate husband and wife team who, in between their regular tastings, find the time to source unusual and hard-to-find food products from all the corners of South Africa and indeed the globe. Come Saturday mornings the shop is abuzz with wine fundis comparing tasting notes.

Melissa's The Food Shop
94 Kloof Street, Tamboerskloof (021 424 5540/ www.melissas.co.za). **Open** 7.30am-8pm Mon-Fri; 8am-8pm Sat, Sun. **Credit** AmEx, DC, MC, V. **Map** p274 F5.
Cape Town's biggest foodie success story continues its commitment to preservative- and additive-free produce that looks as delicious as it tastes. From quiches and pies to ganached cakes, crammed health bread sandwiches and of course their famous lunch buffet, there is seemingly no end to the extent of their freshly made wares. Browse the deli fridge for pâtés, cheeses et al and while away some time choosing a beautifully packaged sweet treat to give as a gift. **Other locations** throughout the city.

Oakhurst Farm Stall
284 Main Road, Kenilworth (021 762 1827). **Open** 8.30am-5.30pm Mon-Fri; 8.30am-2pm Sat. **Credit** AmEx, DC, MC, V.
Browse the central island of home-bakes that range from quiches to muffins, sausage rolls and pies and biscuits. They also have a counter of pre-made dishes to pick and choose from, an organic fruit and veg section and a catering menu.

INSIDE TRACK
SPICE BAZAAR

Celebrate Cape Town's heritage as spice route stop-over by visiting **Atlas Trading** in the Bo-Kaap. Inside you'll find a spicy smörgasbord of colours, scents and flavours (94 Whale Street, Bo-Kaap, 021 423 4361).

CONSUME

Jewellery trail

All things bright and beautiful.

The African continent is rich in both precious gemstones and metals, as well as jewellery design talent. If a visit to the V&A Waterfront is on the cards, there are plenty of slick jewellery spots to visit. At **Shimansky** (Clock Tower, 021 421 2788, www.shimansky.co.za) you can order a bespoke piece, which they'll have made up for you in just a few days. The plush interior at **Christoff** (021 421 0184, www.christoff.co.za) has designophiles feeling right at home; the stunning contemporary diamond and precious stone-encrusted pieces are a dazzling sight. Situated nearby is the swanky **Chopard Boutique** (021 421 4296), while **Charles Greig** (021 418 4515) and **Uwe Koetter** (shop 14, 021 425 7770) remain two of the most respected local brands. At **Tanzanite International** (shop 118, 021 421 5488), the rare and precious blue tanzanite stone can be found in everything from earrings to over-the-top statement pieces.

At **Diamond Works** (Metro Life Building, Cnr Long & Coen Steytler streets, 021 425 1970, www.thediamondworks.co.za) close to the CTICC, you can take your pick of conflict-free diamonds for investment or custom-made jewellery pieces. Visit **Afrogem** (64 New Church Street, Gardens, 021 424 0848) for a fascinating factory tour and insight into the jewels that come from the continent, and to browse for that special piece or stone to take home.

Contemporary jewellery-lovers feel right at home at bastion of local design **Tinsel** (021 448 6183, www.tinsel.co.za) at the Old Biscuit Mill in Woodstock, featuring cutting-edge pieces by a mixed bag of designers. **Olive Green Cat** (79 Kloof Street, Gardens, 021 424 1101, www.olivegreencat.com) is the shared shop and studio of young guns Ida-Elsje and Philippa Green, and a must-stop for those who like to stay on the cutting edge of jewellery design.

And for an all-in-one experience, visit the newly opened **Jewellery Avenue** (021 446 4600) in the heart of the city (corner of Hout and Burg streets), with more than 20 stores carrying everything from Afro-chic crafty items to custom-made pieces and bargain diamond buys.

Wine

Caroline's Fine Wine Cellar

Shop 44, Matador Centre, 62 Strand Street, City Centre (021 419 8984/www.carolineswine.com). **Open** 9am-5.30pm Mon-Fri; 9am-1pm Sat. **Credit** AmEx, DC, MC, V. **Map** p276 H3.
With over 1,500 wine, brandy and bubbly finds from the Cape winelands, as well as some of the best wine-producing regions in Europe, aficionados are spoilt for choice here. Visitors can book a one-on-one tasting to discover the joys of the Cape of grapes. Tastings and events keep regulars coming back for more while out-of-towners make good use of the wine shipping and delivery service.
Other locations Shop 8 King's Warehouse, Victoria Wharf, V&A Waterfront (021 425 5701).

Lisa's Little Wine Shop

48 Main Road, inside Artvark Gallery, Kalk Bay, Southern Peninsula (021 788 9116/www.taste matters.co.za). **Open** 10am-5pm Mon-Fri; 9am-5pm Sat. **Credit** MC, V.

What this gem lacks in size, it more than makes up for in passion and enthusiasm for local small winery offerings. Owner Lisa Griggs is mad about wine and her Saturday morning tastings are a hit on the local social calendar. Specialising in small runs of interesting lesser-known wines, it also stocks prosecco.
▶ *Read Lisa Griggs's blog and sign up for her regular, informal wine tasting courses and wine and food evenings on her website.*

Manuka Wine Boutique

Noordhoek Farm Village, Noordhoek, Southern Peninsula (021 789 0898/www.manuka.co.za). **Open** 10am-5.30pm Mon-Fri; 9am-5pm Sat; 10am-5pm Sun. **Credit** AmEx, DC, MC, V.
This small chain of wine shops is becoming something of a phenomenon. Visit this branch in the Noordhoek Farm Village and browse the extensive selection of hit South African wines.

Vaughan Johnson's Wine & Cigar Shop

Dock Road, V&A Waterfront, Atlantic Seaboard (021 419 2121/www.vaughanjohnson.com).

CONSUME

Open 9am-6pm Mon-Fri; 9am-5pm Sat; 10am-5pm Sun. **Credit** AmEx, MC, V. **Map** p275 H1.
Expertise and enthusiasm are the watchwords at this inviting store at the V&A Waterfront. A passion for showcasing South African wines is paramount and Vaughan's Top 100 list is an excellent guide for making one's wine selection. Good collectors as well as value-for-money buys and an international shipping service too.

Vino Pronto
42 Orange Street, Gardens (021 424 5587/ www.vinopronto.co.za). **Open** 10.30am-8pm Mon-Fri; 10.30am-5pm Sat; 3pm-8pm public holidays. **Credit** MC, V. **Map** p276 G5.
Small but crammed with excellent local finds, end of bin runs and specially sourced boutique offerings, this little wine shop is a great stop when looking for that unusual wine. Regular tastings and a Wine of the Month club where great wines go for even better prices ensure a loyal clientele.

★ Wine Concepts
Shop 15, Lifestyles on Kloof Centre, 50 Kloof Street, Gardens (021 426 4401/www.wine concepts.co.za). **Open** 10am-7pm Mon-Thur; 10am-8pm Fri; 9am-5pm Sat. **Credit** DC, MC, V. **Map** p274 F5.
Well laid out, with attractive displays and passionate staff too, the Wine Concepts brand is a growing one, thanks to the excellent wine choices, ranging from popular big hitters to little-known boutique offerings. A strong emphasis on food pairing is a big advantage for those determined to wow their guests. **Other locations** Cardiff Castle Building, cnr Main Street & Kildare Road, Newlands (021 671 9030).

Winesense
Shop B2 Mandela Rhodes Place, cnr Wale & Burg streets, City Centre (021 422 0695). **Open** 10am-7pm Mon-Fri. **Credit** AmEx, DC, MC, V. **Map** p276 G4.
It's a great concept: simply make your decision from the wines displayed in the 'filling station', swipe an electronic card and it'll automatically fill up your glass with your tipple of choice so that you can 'try before you buy'. Mixed bottle cases are a hit, while the online shopping service is an added bonus. It also sells Riedel glassware, olive oils and premium spirits.
Other locations throughout the city.

GIFTS & SOUVENIRS
Baraka
Shop A13, Cape Quarter, Dixon Road, De Waterkant (021 425 8883). **Open** 10am-5.30pm Mon-Sat; 11am-3.30pm Sun. **Credit** AmEx, MC, V. **Map** p276 G3.

This eclectic shop should be your first port of call when going gift hunting. There is something for all tastes, ranging from wire woven baskets, cacti and pop-art pics to authentic African masks and beautifully bound Indian leather notebooks.

Heartworks
Shop 51, Gardens Centre, Gardens (021 465 3289). **Open** 9am-7pm Mon-Fri; 9am-5pm Sat; 9am-2pm Sun. **Credit** AmEx, DC, MC, V. **Map** p274 F5.
The name says it all – this place is a beehive of colour, texture and abundance, abuzz with a broad range of local crafts hailing from locations as diverse as rural Africa and cutting-edge urban studios. Owner Margaret Wuhrman makes intuitive selections for her stores but the linking thread remains strong: hand-crafted objects imbued with love and soul. Great for take-home gifts.

★ Imagenius
117 Long Street, City Centre (021 423 7870/ www.imagenius.co.za). **Open** 9.30am-4.30pm Mon-Fri; 9.30am-1pm Sat. **Credit** AmEx, DC, MC, V. **Map** p276 G4.
In a fitting tribute to one of the city's Victorian gems, this shop is a stylish horn of plenty, fusing neo-Rococo with modern third-world knick-knacks, flamboyant jewellery and a host of other idiosyncratic adornments for the home. They threw away the mould when they created this one.

HEALTH & BEAUTY
Beauty services

Elements on Kloof
2nd floor, 39 Kloof Street, Gardens, City Bowl (021 426 2459 /www.elementsonkloof.co.za). **Open** 9am-7pm Mon-Fri; 9am-5pm Sat. **Credit** DC, MC, V. **Map** p274 F5.
Exactly what stressed out city slickers need – a place to unwind and let someone else take care of you. This spa salon has a smörgasbord of body treatments waiting – from specialised facials to non-surgical facelifts, massages from around the world and a dedicated Man Space for beauty conscious men about town. Their packages offer great value for money.

Urban Sanctuary
3 Cardiff Castle Centre, Cnr Main Street and Kildare Road, Newlands, Southern Suburbs (021 683 7593/www.urbansanctuary.co.za). **Open** 8am-8pm Mon-Fri (winter 9am-6pm); 9am-6pm Sat; 9am-5pm Sun. **Credit** AmEx, DC, MC, V.
A name change has done nothing to quell the popularity of this southern suburbs beauty- and body-centric escape. As good for popping in for a pedi as for all-day top-to-toe treatments, the Sanctuary is staffed by unobtrusive professionals. Indigenous essential oil products and late opening times are a bonus.

CONSUME

Vino Pronto.

Wellspa

Lifestyles on Kloof, 50 Kloof Street, Gardens,
City Bowl (021 487 5454/www.wellness
warehouse.com). **Open** 9am-7pm Mon-Fri; 9am-
5pm Sat; 9am-3pm Sun. **Credit** AmEx, DC, MC,
V. **Map** p274 F5.
Choose from a variety of face and body treatments
at this spa housed in the larger-than-life Wellness
Warehouse *(see below)*. The Wellbalanced signature
for face and body is a two-hour journey of relaxation
back to a rather beautiful new you. *See also p150*
Spa for the Course.

Cosmetics, skincare & perfume

Body Shop

Shop G54, Ground Level, Cavendish Square,
Claremont, Southern Suburbs (021 671 1082/
www.thebodyshop.co.za). **Open** 9am-7pm Mon-
Sat; 10am-5pm Sun. **Credit** AmEx, DC, MC, V.
What would life be without Body Shop's Body
Butter or their fresher than fresh fragrances? In a
world where being kind to the environment counts
more than ever, it's great that there are quality prod-
ucts that do good, too.
Other locations throughout the city.

MAC Cosmetics

Shop 6140, Lower Level, Victoria Wharf,
V&A Waterfront, Atlantic Seaboard (021 421
4886/www.maccosmetics.com). **Open** 9am-9pm
Mon-Sat; 10am-9pm Sun. **Credit** AmEx, DC, MC,
V. **Map** p275 H1.
Don't be intimidated by the impeccably made up, all-
in-black staff at this cult make-up brand store – staff

are here to help you with all your makeup needs –
from applying foundation the right way to perfecting your liquid eyeliner flip, they've got it sussed.
From hot seasonal shades to staple go-with-every-
thing faves, this is a delicious escape from the real
world. Book a make-over and offset it against your
make-up, brush or fragrance purchase.
Other locations throughout the city.

Red Square

Shop 6206, Upper Level, Victoria Wharf, V&A
Waterfront, Atlantic Seaboard (021 419 8766/
www.edgars.co.za). **Open** 9am-9pm Mon-Thur,
Sun; 9am-10pm Fri, Sat. **Credit** AmEx, DC, MC,
V. **Map** p275 H1.
You'll find yourself dancing from counter to counter
of beautifully packaged fragrances, beauty products
and make-up at this Waterfront store-within-a-store.
Bonus: you can buy to your heart's desire on your
Edgars card and there are always plenty of 'buy this
and get this free' offers.
Other locations throughout the city.

★ Wellness Warehouse

Lifestyles on Kloof, 50 Kloof Street, Gardens,
City Bowl (021 487 5454/www.wellness
warehouse.com). **Open** 9am-7pm Mon-Fri; 9am-
5pm Sat; 9am-3pm Sun. **Credit** AmEx, DC, MC,
V. **Map** p274 F5.
This enormous store has an excellent range of products good enough to use on your delicate skin. Stock
up on Guinot (this is one of the few places to sell it
other than beauticians), Dr Hauschka, Decleor,
Dermalogica, Ahava and local legends Africology
and Theravine.

Other locations Shop F80 Cavendish Connect, Cnr Dreyer & Main Road, Claremont (021 673 7216).

HOUSE & HOMEWARES

African Image
52 Burg Street, City Centre (021 423 8385/ www.african-image.co.za). **Open** 9am-5pm Mon-Fri; 9am-2pm Sat. **Credit** MC, V. **Map** p276 G3. Proprietors Harry and Sipho bring a generation's love, knowledge and fieldwork to this unique store. African Image has come to define the juxtaposition of antique Africana (trade beads and Southern African beadwork) with modern transitional pieces

that make novel use of contemporary and recycled materials. An amusement park of pattern, print, colour and visual rhythms; perfect for local and international shoppers alike. *Photo p153.*

★ Africa Nova
Shop C3, Cape Quarter, 72 Waterkant Street, De Waterkant, City Bowl (021 425 5123/ www.africanova.co.za). **Open** *Summer* 9.30am-5pm Mon-Fri; 10am-5pm Sat; 10am-3pm Sun. *Winter* 10am-5pm Mon-Fri; 10am-3pm Sat. **Credit** DC, MC, V. **Map** p276 G3. This encyclopedic treasure chest of pan-African *objets*, local ceramic art and high-end indigenous craft sets the gold standard far above banal curio.

Spa for the Course

Relax and unwind at these palaces of pampering.

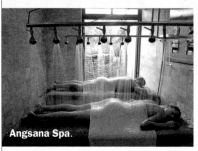

Angsana Spa.

CONSUME

Cape Town has all the ingredients for an alluring city break: sun, sea, shopping and thankfully, if hedonism's your bag, quality spas too. Here's our round-up of the best rest and relaxation spots.

A recent style overhaul and refurb has breathed new life into the **Arabella Spa** (Convention Square, 1 Long Street, 021 412 8200, www.westin.com/grand capetown) – and it remains one of the city's best. Drink in the panoramic city views and let their superb staff ease out your kinks with their specialised luxury treatments (they use the famed Ligne St. Barth and Anne Semonin ranges).

At the conveniently situated **S.K.I.N** (Dock Road, V&A Waterfront, 021 425 3551, www.skinonline.co.za), they'll take care of any stray hair dilemmas, sort you out with a post-beach facial or massage your cares away.

The multi award-winning **Sanctuary Spa** (Victoria Road, Camps Bay, 021 437 0677, www.12apostleshotel.com) is deserving of its position in the polls and a day spent in

their underground grotto, enjoying time in the Rasul chamber, hot and cold plunge pools and hydrotherapy bath will leave you feeling invigorated. Their menu of indigenous essential oil-based treatments is delicious too. They've also recently opened a branch at tranquil Majeka House, just outside Stellenbosch (021 880 1549, www.majekahouse.co.za) providing a stylish and sophisticated body and beauty offering.

The perfectly placed **Elixir Spa** (87-91 Beach Road, Mouille Point, 021 439 2266, www.elixirspa.co.za) fulfils the needs of urban gals and guys who appreciate its accessibility and revel in the clean, contemporary lines of the space. 'Sparties' – birthday or hen parties – are a speciality, while staff also offer a number of high-tech skin rejuvenation techniques. **Equinox Spa at Cape Royale** (021 430 0511, www.cape royale.co.za) in Green Point features elegant Parisian-inspired interiors and a team of specialists waiting to ease out your kinks with a number of multi-treatment packages.

For true Thai relaxation, visit **Angsana Spa** (Colinton Road, off Protea Road, Newlands, 021 674 5005, www.angsana spa.com) where specialists trained by the international spa group are on hand to offer a selection of Asian speciality treatments as well as their famed facials and body treatments. Massages here are sure to ease out the very stiffest of knotted muscles.

The feminine design and hushed surrounds of the **Librisa Spa** (Mount Nelson Hotel, 76 Orange Street, 021 483 1000, www.mountnelson.co.za) ensures an unparalleled sense of being spoilt. Staff here are a study in professionalism and the

Weaving an intoxicating mix of contemporary and tribal design, this ravishing platform enduringly delights the senses. The perfect destination for special and unique pieces for interior designers, international visitors and collectors. *Photo p154.*

Carrol Boyes Shop

Shop 6180, Lower Level, Victoria Wharf, V&A Waterfront, Atlantic Seaboard (021 418 0595/ www.carrolboyes.com). **Open** 9am-9pm Mon-Sat; 10am-9pm Sun. **Credit** AmEx, DC, MC, V. **Map** p275 H1.

Carrol Boyes's signature production has established itself as a perennial brand not least for the standard of craft, her always prolific and fresh range of pewter and stainless-steel home accessories and her instinct for knowing what people want to own.
▶ *Pottery by renowned ceramicist Barbara Jackson and beadwork by Monkeybiz is sold here.*

Clementina Ceramics

Shop 101B, The Old Biscuit Mill, 375 Albert Road, Woodstock (021 447 1398/www. clementina.co.za). **Open** 9am-5pm Mon-Fri; 9am-3pm Sat. **Credit** AmEx, DC, MC, V.

Ceramics paragon Clementina van der Walt's gallery feeds the addictive needs of 20 years of devoted followers, and new ones too. Functional and one-off art pieces enhance an ethnically accented home without dominating. A must for pottery lovers.

Librisa Spa.

OneWellness Spa.

CONSUME

products used range from big-name brands to specially sourced local finds (they also sell a wide range of products for home beautification). The jet-lag treatment is sure to revitalise the weariest of travellers and the renovated Victorian home setting adds to the sense of tranquillity, while the treatment rooms are a visual feast.

Visit **OneWellness Spa** (Radisson Hotel, Beach Road, Granger Bay, 021 441 3000, www.onewellness.co.za) where the comprehensive spa facilities are as seductive as the range of treatments. The eight-step OneJourney concludes in a specially appointed sleep room for making the most of your blissed- out state, and the hot stone massage is one of the best in town. The latest kid on the spa block is the **One&Only Spa** (021 431 5810,www.one andonlyresorts.com) at the newly opened One&Only Hotel in the V&A Waterfront. Set amid waterways and gardens, it's set to become a favourite spa destination, with every possible spa indulgence catered for and a range of signature treatments.

What the achingly chic **Paris Spa** (Cellars-Hohenort, 93 Brommersvlei Road, Constantia, 021 794 5434, www.paris spa.co.za,) lacks in size it makes up for with the extensive list of offerings – from facials (try the 24-carat gold La Prairie facial for the ultimate in indulgence) to specialist massages. The ginger and lime body scrub is pure pampering at its best.

If you are staying in the inner city, try these fabulous urban regeneration spots: **Camelot Spa** (Mandela Rhodes Place Hotel & Spa, Cnr Burg & Wale street, 021 422 2144, www.camelotspa group.com). Facilities here include a double treatment room for stressed-out couples, a floatation pool for a meditative bob-around and a Turkish steam room for a pore-cleansing pick-me-up. Or spend the day at **Emporio Valenti** (the Spearhead, 42 Hans Strijdom Avenue, 0861 367 6746, www.emporiovalenti.co.za), a swanky new salon where the expert teams will have you primped, plucked and preened to perfection in no time.

Imiso Ceramics

*Unit A102, The Old Biscuit Mill, 375 Albert
Road, Woodstock (021 447 7668/www.imiso
ceramics.co.za).* **Open** 9am-4pm Mon-Fri; 9am-
3pm Sat. **Credit** MC, V.
Ceramics whiz kid Andile Dyalvane is rapidly
amassing a cult following. Start collecting while you
still can, as these exquisitely hand-crafted vessels –
some functional and others unashamedly decorative
– are as red-hot as the kilns in which they are fired.
With pieces ranging from tiny teacups to tall, tubular, hand-built urns and vases, the hardest task is
picking which one to give a home to.

Klooftique

*87 Kloof Street, Gardens, City Bowl (021 424
9458/www.klooftique.co.za).* **Open** 9am-5pm
Mon-Fri; 9.30am-1pm Sat. **Credit** AmEx, DC,
MC, V. **Map** p274 F5.
The strong points here are the impeccable cabinet-
work of the wood, glass and veneer tables and storage units, and the upholstery of the art deco-inspired
lounge suites and club chairs. Seasoned owners
Jerome and Marianna Furman have an impeccable
eye for form and function that dovetails perfectly
with a sleek, pared-down urban look. Garnish with
contemporary glass and Africana, *et voilà*!

LIM

*86A Kloof Street, Gardens, City Bowl (021 423
1200/www.lim.co.za).* **Open** 9am-5pm Mon-Fri;
9.15am-1pm Sat. **Credit** AmEx, DC, MC, V.
Map p274 F5.
Owner Pauline Mutlow has an uncanny and foolproof
eye for home and lifestyle accessories, whose distinction is endless compatibility. Functional pieces (by
indigenous stars Clementina van der Walt, Anthony
Shapiro, Wonki Ware) cohabit seamlessly with choice
tribal pieces, leather-bound albums, handcrafted
glass and modular furniture. Great for gifts and paradise for modern and new homeowners.

Loft Living

*122 Kloof Street, Tamboerskloof (021 422 0088/
www.loftliving.co.za).* **Open** 9am-5pm Mon-Fri;
9.30am-1.30pm Sat. **Credit** AmEx, DC, MC, V.

This trend-setting home decor store is synonymous with sleek, stylish and sophisticated urban
living. Bring your newly acquired pied-à-terre to
life with ease and aplomb with goods that you'll
find here: upholstered furniture, scatter cushions,
ornamentation and home accessories that are both
distinctive and versatile.

L'Orangerie

*7 Wolfe Street, Wynberg (021 761 8355/
www.lorangerie.com).* **Open** 9am-5pm Mon-Fri;
9.30am-1.30pm Sat. **Credit** AmEx, DC, MC, V.
Reminiscences of 1920s ocean liners and beach
houses in Cap Ferrat and Brighton permeate this
serene space. Ecru, cream and white linens and nos-
talgic home appointments in glass, wood and pottery will have you renting *Gosford Park* and dusting
off the card table for a spot of weekend bridge.
Other locations Kildare Centre, Kildare Road
(021 674 4284).

Okha

*109 Hatfield Street, Gardens, City Bowl (021 461
7233/www.okha.com).* **Open** 8.30am-5pm Mon-
Fri; 9am-1pm Sat. **Credit** AmEx, DC, MC, V.
Map p276 G5.
Think interiors for the Prada/Hermes/Gucci set:
sleek monochromes, impeccable craft and a heady
cocktail of natural and industrial materials. Here,
you'll find home accessories for the wood, steel and
stone, architect-designed dream home.

Pa Kua

*Shop 6117, Lower Level, Victoria Wharf, V&A
Waterfront, Atlantic Seaboard (021 418 8528/
www.pakua.co.za).* **Open** 9am-9pm daily. **Credit**
AmEx, DC, MC, V. **Map** p275 H1.
The preserve of distinctive and wow-factor
crafter's art, glassware and ceramics, Pa Kua carries a wide range of generously scaled statement
pieces to anchor rooms in resort homes. Those looking for high-end gifting ideas will be well-served
by Pa Kua's impressive range of scented candles
and room fragrancers.

★ Pierre Cronje

*Jarvis Street, De Waterkant, City Bowl (021 421
1249/www.pierrecronje.co.za).* **Open** 7am-4.15pm
Mon-Thur, 7am-noon Fri. **No credit cards**.
Map p276 G3.
This established furniture business has built up a
devoted clientele for its speciality: top-quality hand-
crafted furniture in three signature styles, namely
Country, Classic and Contemporary. Here you will
find no gimmicks, only durable, sturdy antiques of
tomorrow and a no-holds-barred celebration of the
timeless allure of wood.
Other locations Shop 71, Lower mall,
Cavendish Square, Claremont (021 674 4530);
Shop 45 Willowbridge Lifestyle Centre,
Tygervalley (021 914 5252).

CONSUME

Story

*221A Upper Buitenkant Street, cnr Vredehoek
Avenue, Vredehoek (021 462 4889).* **Open** 9am-
5pm Mon-Fri; 9.30am-1.30pm Sat. **Credit** MC, V.
Map p275 H5.

With shapes inspired by lava lamps and an eggshell
palette tinged with antique turquoise and olive,
Story is a whimsical postcard with a grown-up
Alice's backward glance at the looking glass.
Souvenirs for your home of period ceramics, sparkly
trinketry and evocatively reconditioned furniture
create a timeless dreamscape.

TWIICE International

*70-72 Bree Street, City Centre (021 487 9060/
www.twiice.com).* **Open** 8.30am-5pm Mon-Fri.
Credit AmEx, DC, MC, V. **Map** p276 G3.

This design temple of new and established post-war
design superstars – Charles and Ray Eames, Jean
Prouwe, Philippe Starck and Zaha Hadid – is an
unsurpassed resource for corporate and high-end
domestic furniture. Service and style are of international calibre.

Zulu Azania

56A Church Street, City Centre (021 424 4510).
Open 10am-4pm Mon-Fri; 10am-3pm Sat. **Credit**
AmEx, DC, MC, V. **Map** p276 G3.

The owners of Zulu Azania have collected tribal
artefacts from a wide range of geographical areas in
Africa. What distinguishes this gallery from the
recent proliferation of curio shops is its devotion to
quality and authenticity, as well as its preference for
a larger scale of pieces, making it ideal foraging for
collectors and decorators alike. Beadwork, carving
and breathtaking terracotta drinking and water vessels are hallmarks of the gallery's aesthetic. While
prices bespeak their rare provenance, the space is
relaxed and invites appreciative browsing.

Antiques

Burr & Muir

*82 Church Street, City Centre (021 422 1319/
www.burrmuir.spinner.co.za).* **Open** 9.30am-
4.30pm Mon-Fri; 9.30am-1pm Sat. **Credit** AmEx,
MC, V. **Map** p276 G4.

Geoff Burr and Graham Muir are internationally
renowned authorities on art nouveau, art deco and
post-war glass, as their treasure trove on picturesque
Church Street attests. Don't be deterred by the catalogue prices; the proprietors welcome 'just looking'.

Hans Niehaus Antiques & Collectables

*37 Vineyard Road, Claremont, Southern Suburbs
(021 674 3901).* **Open** 9am-5pm Mon-Fri;
10.30am-2pm Sat. **No credit cards**.

This eclectic mix of China, household *objets* and
period and modern furniture reflects the proprietor's quirky but impeccable eye. There is always
something interesting and unique, which is why

African Image. *See p150.*

Africa Nova. See p150.

dealers and collectors alike continue to make a bee-line to this place. Hans's humane attitude to pricing is an added attraction.

Long Street Antique Arcade
127 Long Street, City Centre (021 423 3585).
Open 9am-4.30pm Mon-Fri; 9am-2pm Sat.
Credit Varies. **Map** p276 G4.
The initiators of this rabbit warren of small and varied dealers have succeeded in their aim: to create a veritable theme park for the antique enthusiast. Feel the hours roll on as you browse the always-rich pickings of collectibles (including jewellery, books, militaria, china and silver). The atmosphere is relaxed and browsey; a coffee shop offers succour to the weary while they admire their trophies.

Lütge Gallery
53 Church Street, City Centre (021 424 8448).
Open 9.30am-1pm, 1.30-4.30pm Mon-Fri; 10am-1pm Sat. **Credit** AmEx, DC, MC, V.
Map p276 G3.
Specialising in genuine and reconstituted Cape furniture, these rooms are a goldmine for decorators looking for the pared-down, Modern-Cape look. An unfussy and accessible emporiums.

Plush Bazaar
Unit A103, Old Biscuit Mill, 375 Albert Road, Salt River (021 447 6495). **Open** 9am-4.30pm Mon-Fri; 8am-2.30pm Sat. **Credit** AmEx, DC, MC, V. **Map** p274 G2.

This jewellery box showcases André Crouse's spectacular cornucopia of sensual delights. The mix of French country, Victorian and tongue-in-cheek tat is a heady one that reliably yields conversation pieces for the loft, cottage or baroque pied-à-terre.

Railway House Décor & Collectables
23 Main Road, Kalk Bay, Southern Peninsula (021 788 4761). **Open** 9am-5pm Mon-Sat; 10am-5pm Sun. **Credit** AmEx, DC, MC, V.
This bargain-hunter's paradise consistently yields treasures for the collector of ephemera, curiosities and 20th-century antiques. The stock is suffused with overtones of the colonial, nautical and generally quaint – and the prices are affordable.
▶ *One warning: beware the house parrot; he has been known to bite before!*

Shipwreck Shop
Hout Bay Harbour, Hout Bay, Southern Peninsula (021 790 1100/www.marine rswharf.com). **Open** 9am-5.30pm daily.
Credit AmEx, DC, MC, V.
With over 20,000 bits of maritime bric-a-brac and booty, this nautical nook is the biggest of its kind in South Africa. Sea souvenirs include an impressive collection of scrimshaw, ship's equipment, militaria, coins and brassware. Enough to shiver your timbers.

Whatnot & China Town
70 Main Road, Kalk Bay, Southern Peninsula (021 788 1823). **Open** *Summer* 9am-5pm daily.
Winter 10am-4pm daily. **Credit** MC, V.
This mecca of the mismatched and miscellaneous is where shabby chic comes to die. Tread warily around shelves and tables and, yes, whatnots, of Anglophile household China and ornamental pieces to find the missing sugar bowl from Granny's set. Do not, however, anticipate bargains.

MUSIC & ENTERTAINMENT

★ African Music Store
134 Long Street, City Centre (021 426 0857/ www.africanmusicstore.). **Open** 9am-6pm Mon-Fri; 9am-2pm Sat. **Credit** MC, V.
Map p276 G4.
This is a unique doorway into the music of a continent, which plays a seminal role in so many of the sounds we regard as part of our aural wallpaper. The atmosphere is relaxed and upbeat. It's all here: from world-music crossovers (Ali Farka Touré, Youssou N'Dour, Salif Keita) to local luminaries (Freshlyground, Judith Sephuma and the lamented Lucky Dube). The golden oldies catalogue is also full of nuggets: Sipho Hotstix Mabusa, Stimela and Cesaria Evora to name a few.

High 5
Shop no.5, Mooikloof Centre, 34 Kloof Street, City Centre (021 422 5455/6/www.xupa.co.za).

Open *Winter* 9am-5pm Mon-Fri; 9am-3pm Sat; 10am-2pm Sun. *Summer* 9am-6pm Mon-Fri, weekends are the same as in winter. **Credit** MC, V. **Map** p274 F5.

Owing to its unique mix of merchandise, this trend-setting store is fast becoming a landmark on Cape Town's radioactive Kloof Street. The quick turnover collection of quirky and provocative T-shirts, hoodies and denims are an attractive diversion from the main event: rare B and cult movies, special-interest DVDs, vintage vinyl, a dazzling and impressive collection of house and a plethora of other limited-appeal rarities. A splendid source of faux trailer trash knick-knacks.

Mabu Vinyl

2 Rheede Street, Gardens, (021 423 7635/www. mabuvinyl.co.za). **Open** 9am-8pm Mon-Thur; 9am-7pm Fri; 10am-6pm Sat; 11am-3pm Sun. **Credit** MC, V. **Map** p274 F5.

As charming as the frayed LP covers, Mabu Vinyl is the aficionado's choice for pre-played records, CDs and cassettes, if you don't mind the old curiosity shop feel. Root around for vintage pressings of 1960s favourites (Jimi Hendrix, Carole King, Janis Joplin, Motown), local nostalgia (Springbok hits, Gallo Africa) and a wide selection of dance, hip-hop, electronica and trance.

Musica Megastore

Dock Road Complex, Dock Road, V&A Waterfront, Atlantic Seaboard (021 425 6300/ www.musica.co.za). **Open** 9am-9pm daily. **Credit** AmEx, DC, MC, V. **Map** p275 H1.

If you like your music-shopping with a 'mega' attached, this is Eldorado. All that is audio-visual (CDs, DVDs, gaming) is well represented here. Their current-releases inventory is of international standard, while their classical department carries, for example, operas from *Aida* to *Zaide* and is the go-to destination for Cape Town's serious music pundits. Also a good conduit for ordering out-of-stock rarities. **Other locations** throughout the city.

TICKETS

Computicket
083 915 8000/www.computicket.co.za.

Artscape Dial-a-Seat
Tickets 021 421 7695; information 021 421 7839.

TRAVELLERS' NEEDS

Frasers
Lower level, Victoria Wharf Shopping Centre, V&A Waterfront, Atlantic Seaboard (021 418 0718). **Open** 9am-9pm daily. **Credit** AmEx, DC, MC, V. **Map** p275 H1.

With more than 100 years' experience under its stylish leather belt, Frasers has gained a reputation for

---

INSIDE TRACK
HOLY SMOKE

Sturk's Tobacconists has stood on the edge of Greenmarket Square since 1793. This historic family-run tobacco shop oozes vintage appeal, and is worth a peek even if you don't light up. The shop's speciality is sourcing hand-blended tobaccos from all over the world. It also stocks cigars and other smoking paraphernalia (54 Shortmarket Street, City Centre, 021 423 3928).

---

kitting out sophisticated travellers in bags, briefcases and wheelie suitcases of the utmost quality. Designer labels in their stable include GUESS, Nine West and Busby.

Premier Shoes & Luggage

155 Kloof Street, City Bowl (021 424 4904). **Open** 8.30am-5pm Mon-Fri; 8.30am-1pm Sat. **Credit** MC, V. **Map** p274 F5.

This family-run establishment has been a Kloof Street institution for ages and has a loyal following among locals. Apart from resoling threadbare shoes, dying and dry-cleaning garbs, and breathing new life into loved-up handbags, they also boast a range of affordable luggage.

Story. *See p153.*

CONSUME

MaxMara
V&A Waterfront
Cape Town
Ph 021 418 9447

MaxMara
Hyde Park
Johannesburg
Ph 011 325 5760

Riga Fashion Salon
Claremont
Cape Town
Ph 021 674 4394

MaxMara

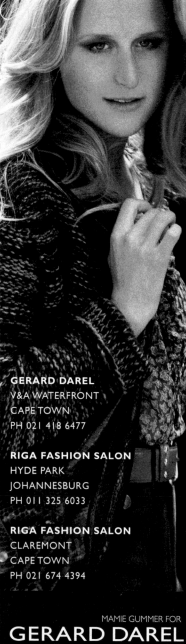

GERARD DAREL
V&A WATERFRONT
CAPE TOWN
PH 021 418 6477

RIGA FASHION SALON
HYDE PARK
JOHANNESBURG
PH 011 325 6033

RIGA FASHION SALON
CLAREMONT
CAPE TOWN
PH 021 674 4394

MAMIE GUMMER FOR
GERARD DAREL

Arts & Entertainment

Jimmy Dludlu. *See p185.*

Calendar

From wine-tasting to kite-flying, something for every occasion.

There's always something happening in Cape Town, but it's not always possible to say when. In true laid-back Mother City fashion, plans are made and cancelled on a whim. This adds to the improvisatory feel of the place, but does make forward planning rather difficult. Thus many of our Calendar events are pencilled in, rather than set in stone.

During the summer Capetonians are treated to a range of outdoorsy festivals and events, be they sports-, culture- or music-related. Be sure to keep an eye on the local press for updates, or phone the Cape Town Tourism Bureau for the latest on what's going on. There are more events listed throughout the Arts & Entertainment section too.

SUMMER

Kirstenbosch Sundowner Concerts

Rhodes Drive, Newlands (021 799 8783/ www.sanbi.org). **Date** Late Nov-early Apr.
Beat the Sunday blues with a few good bottles of wine and a sunset backdrop during the popular weekly Kirstenbosch sundowner concerts. These performances have become a summer institution among Capetonians, so get there early if you want a grassy patch from which to see hot local talents like Freshlyground, the Parlotones and Fokofpolisiekar.
▶ *For more on Kirstenbosch, see p64.*

OBZ Festival

Various locations in Observatory (www.obzfestival.co.za). **Date** Late Nov-early Dec.
Each year the slightly grungy 'burb of Obz transforms into a hotspot of cultural happenings for this street festival. Top local musos pump the jams from a number of stages and a market sells local and imported threads as well as its fair share of food.

Cape Town Minstrel Carnival

City Centre. **Date** 1-2 Jan.
There's something about the luminous multi-coloured satin suits and frenetic banjo-strumming of the Cape Minstrels that puts Capetonians in the party mood. The tradition has roots in the practices associated with slavery, when 2 January was given as a holiday to the slaves. Today singers and musicians still march through the streets of the Mother City (usually along Wale Street) complete with face paint, twirling parasols and some infectious beats, while ringing in the *tweede nuwejaar* (second new year).

Shakespeare at the Maynardville Open-Air Theatre

Date Early Jan-late Feb.
See p206.

Design Indaba Expo

CTICC, Convention Square, 1 Lower Long Street, City Centre (021 465 9966/www.designindaba expo.com). **Date** Late Feb-March. **Map** p276 H3.
Local architects, decorators, designers and a host of other illuminated thinkers showcase cutting-edge creations during this annual expo.

AUTUMN

Cape Town International Jazz Festival

CTICC, Convention Square, 1 Lower Long Street, City Centre (021 422 5651/www. capetownjazzfest.com). **Date** Early Apr. **Map** p276 H3.

Celebrating its tenth anniversary in 2009, the Cape Town Jazz Festival is now one of the top-five jazz events in the world. Over 40 local and international talents improvise the toe-tapping beats.

▶ *For more on jazz in the city, see pp184-86.*

Taste of Cape Town
Jan van Riebeeck Sports Fields, De Hoop Avenue, City Bowl (www.tasteofcapetown.com). **Date** Early Apr.
Nibble your way though stalls of sophisticated nosh brought to you by the Cape's top restaurants. Or park yourself on a conveniently placed couch and sip some suitable tipple along with your gourmet delicacies.

Cape Times V&A Waterfront Wine Affair
V&A Waterfront, Dock Road, Foreshore (021 408 7600/www.waterfront.co.za). **Date** Early May. **Map** p275 H1.
Probably the easiest way to drink your way through the Winelands without leaving the city, this Waterfront tipple spectacular showcases the wares of over 75 Western Cape wine estates in one convenient sip-and-saunter venue.

Good Food & Wine Show
CTICC, Convention Square, 1 Lower Long Street, City Centre (021 797 4500/www.gourmetsa.com). **Date** Late May. **Map** p276 H3.
Eat, drink and get ready to be overwhelmed at the heady smells of hundreds of restaurant and food stalls all putting their best culinary feet forward. When you've eaten your fill, head to one of the state-of-the-art demo kitchen theatres where you'll spot BBC chefs comparing knife sizes with the local master cooks.

WINTER

Cape Town Book Fair
CTICC, Convention Square, 1 Lower Long Street, City Centre (021 418 5493/www.capetownbookfair.com). **Date** Mid-June. **Map** p276 H3.
A world-class assembly of local and international book stores and publishing houses showcasing everything from Swiss comic books to fairy tales from France. Add to the mix a host of renowned authors, illustrators and publishers sharing nuggets of wisdom and you've got the perfect fix for any self-respecting book junkie.

Cape Town Fashion Week
CTICC, Convention Square, 1 Lower Long Street, City Centre (021 422 0390/www.capetownfashionweek.co.za). **Date** Early Aug. **Map** p276 H3.
Channel your inner Heidi Klum and ooh and aah at the haute couture creations floating past you during this Capetonian Project Runway. The proudly SA fashion show sports threads by local designers.

SPRING

Cape Town International Kite Festival
Zandvlei, Muizenberg (021 447 9040/www.capementalhealth.co.za/kite.htm). **Date** Late Oct.
The sky's the limit as far as designs go at Africa's biggest kite festival. Larger-than-life South Park characters dip and dive along with giant octopi and Chinese dragons on Muizenberg's Zandvlei grounds.

Khayelitsha Festival
OR Thambo Hall, Khayelitsha (021 442 9628/www.khayelitshafestival.co.za). **Date** Late Oct.
Shake your groove thang at this new festival celebrating the vibrant community of Khayelitsha. Apart from a large expo showcasing local businesses, NGOs and corporate companies, there's a stage dedicated to live music, fashion shows boasting local design talents, and a storytelling *boma* that promises a fair amount of yarn spinning.

FNB Whisky Live Festival
CTICC, Convention Square, 1 Lower Long Street, City Centre 021 880 0180/www.whiskyfestival.co.za). **Date** Early Nov. **Map** p276 H3.
Whether you indulge in the odd dram or have an extensive range of single malts, you'll get your

Kirstenbosch Sundowner Concerts.

money's worth out of this tipple fest. There are over 180 top brands from stalwart master blenders in Scotland and Ireland to lesser-known spirit makers from Japan and Wales.

Outside Cape Town
SUMMER
Franschhoek Cap Classique & Champagne Festival
Various locations in Franschhoek (021 876 3603/www.franschhoek.org). **Date** Early Dec.
So, what's the difference between Methode Cap Classique and champagne? Grab a glass and start sampling the barrage of bubblies at this fabulous affair to find out. There are gourmet offerings from the area's restaurants too.

Spier Arts Festivals
Spier Estate, R310 Lynedoch Road, Stellenbosch (021 809 1100/www.spier.co.za). **Date** Feb-Oct.
This three-in-one arts extravaganza held in the cultural hub of Stellenbosch runs through most of the year. The initiative promotes South African and pan-African artists in a range of events encompassing an open-air poetry festival, a performing arts festival and a music festival.

AUTUMN
Tulbagh Goes Dutch
Various locations in Tulbagh (023 230 1348/ www.tourismtulbagh.co.za). **Date** Late Mar.
This festival, which celebrates all things Dutch, is probably the only time of the year when wooden clogs are fashionable. The raucous Saturday night Dutch Courage party is always good fun, and Sunday's Cape Dutch Breakfast is the ideal way to get over the previous night's overindulgence.

SA Cheese Festival, Franschhoek
Bien Donné, R45 between Paarl & Franschhoek (021 975 1444/www.cheesefestival.co.za). **Date** Late Apr.
Cheese and cheer abound at this outdoorsy bacchanal of gourmet food and fine wines. The festival features a marquee brimming with cheesy delights and a live music area – a must for cheese-lovers.

Riebeek Valley Olive Festival
Riebeek Valley (022 448 1584/www.riebeek valley.info). **Date** Early May.
The quaint villages of Riebeek Kasteel and Riebeek West team up for the biggest olive festival in the country. In between olive and olive-oil tastings, visitors can explore the olive groves, go on wine-cellar tours or pick and mix fresh produce at the local farmers market. Or simply kick back and listen to live music.

Franschhoek Literary Festival
Various locations in Franschhoek (021 876 2861/www.flf.co.za). **Date** Mid-May.
Novelists, publishers and hordes of bibliophiles from here and abroad converge on the touristy but oh-so-lovely town of Franschhoek during this relatively new literary festival started by award-winning author Christopher Hope. Apart from book and poetry readings, there are also plays and music to help set the cultured mood.

WINTER
Wacky Wine Weekend
Various wineries in Robertson (023 626 3167/ www.wackywineweekend.com). **Date** Early June.
Go crazy with the help of a few bottles of vino, courtesy of over 45 regional wineries, and take part in the range of zany activities including the likes of vineyard quad biking, wine diving and Italian pole climbing.

SPRING
Out the Box Festival
Various locations in City Bowl (www2.unima.za. org/festival.html). **Date** Early Sept.
A celebration of puppetry .
See p208.

Rocking the Daisies
Cloof Wine Estate, Darling (www.rockingthedaisies.co.za). **Date** Mid-Sept.
A young, annual festival where some of the country's biggest rock, blues, pop and folk bands play alongside lesser-known artists. Make sure your camping gear is sorted. Pack warm clothes, and avoid blow-up mattresses and open shoes as the devil thorns in the area truly are from hell.

Hermanus Whale Festival
Various locations in Hermanus (www.whalefestival.co.za). **Date** Late Sept.
Hermanus is at its most happening when the southern right whales come out to play. See how many blubbery beauts you can spot amid the festivities that include an art gallery ramble, live music, stand-up comedy, boules championship and half-marathon.
► *For more good places to spot whales, see p69* **Inside Track**.

Voorkamerfest
Various locations in Darling, outside Cape Town (022 492 3427/www.voorkamerfest-darling.co.za). **Date** Early Sept.
Performers come from as far afield as Belgium and India to take part in this unique arts festival that's hosted in the *voorkamers* (front rooms) of venues that include everything from small township shacks to large Victorian manor houses.

ARTS & ENTERTAINMENT

Children

Keeping the kids busy won't be an issue in the Mother City.

The best holidays are about making memories –
and Cape Town has a catalogue of child-friendly
attractions that seem designed for the purpose.
Riding a camel on a beach? Getting up close and
personal with crocodiles, lions, sharks and
monkeys? Running around the biggest back garden
you've ever seen? All these and more are possible
for your children.

Most travel companies have options for families
(except for car hire companies, which universally
fail to think of car seats), and most Cape Town
attractions have elements that cater specially for
youngsters, with most providing free entry for very small children. There's no
shortage of activities, then. But the memory-making is up to you.

RESOURCES

A good place to go if you're looking for ideas
of things to do with the children is the **Cape
Town Tourism's Visitor Centre** (021 426
4260, www.tourismcapetown.co.za).

ANIMAL ENCOUNTERS

★ Boulders Beach

South of Simon's Town (021 786 2329). **Open**
Oct, Nov 8am-6.30pm daily. *Dec, Jan* 7am-7.30pm
daily. *Feb, Mar* 8am-5.30pm daily. *Apr-Sept* 8am-
5pm daily. **Admission** R30; R10 under-12s.
Credit AmEx, DC, MC, V.
Cape Town's biggest penguin colony makes its home
here in a protected cove, with visitors getting the rare
opportunity of swimming alongside them. There are
so many penguins that even if you arrive after the
gates have closed, you'll still spot plenty of penguins
sunning themselves on the rocks.
► *For more on the birds, see p73.*

Butterfly World

*R44, Klapmuts (021 875 5628/www.butterfly
world.co.za).* **Open** 9am-5pm daily. **Admission**
R35 adults; R30 reductions; R20 children; under-
3s free. **Credit** MC, V.

South Africa's biggest free-flying butterfly park
doesn't just have butterflies – there are also mar-
moset monkeys, iguanas and spiders – but they are
the main attraction. There are 24 species in total, all
of which are contained in the large indoor garden.

Cape Town Ostrich Ranch

*Vanschoorsdrift Road, off the N7, Philadelphia
(021 972 1955/www.ostrichranch.co.za).* **Open**
9am-5pm daily. **Admission** R55 adults; R30
reductions; R45 children (6-16s); R15 under-6s.
Credit MC, V.
It may not be as impressive as Oudtshoorn, but at
least it's just 45 minutes drive from the city. The
ranch encourages visitors to interact with the
ostriches, allowing little children to feed the birds.
Kids are also allowed to sit on an ostrich.

Drakenstein Lion Park

*Old Paarl Road, near Klapmuts, NE of Cape
Town (021 863 3290/www.lionrescue.org.za).*

**INSIDE TRACK
STORYTIME**

The city's favourite bookstore, the **Book
Lounge**, has children's storytelling
sessions each Saturday morning. Browse
the shelves with a cup of coffee and a
cupcake, while your little ones enjoy the
stories (71 Roeland Street, City Centre,
021 462 2425).

About the author
Mark van Dijk *is the deputy editor of* Men's
Health *magazine, and his post-kids exercise
routine consists mostly of running after his
young daughters on Fish Hoek beach.*

Open 9.30am-5pm daily. **Admission** R40 adults; R20 children. **Credit** MC, V.

Want to see real-life lions? Here's the place. And while, not surprisingly, it lacks the hands-on interactivity of a petting zoo, the Drakenstein Lion Park does offer a whole bunch of captive-born lions mooching around in the sun, seemingly content in the fact that they will never be reintroduced to the wild.

► *For more on the big cats, see p218.*

Imhoff Farm

Kommetjie Road, Kommetjie (021 783 4545/ www.imhofffarm.co.za). **Open** 9am-5pm daily. **Credit** MC, V.

Imhoff Farm is an all-in-one farmyard/snake park/petting zoo, situated on the south peninsula, near Cape Point. It provides pretty much everything from craft shops to camel rides. Yes, that's 'camel rides'... on the beach.

Le Bonheur Crocodile Farm

Babylonstoren Road, R45 between Paarl & Franschhoek (021 863 1142/www.lebonheur crocfarm.co.za). **Open** 9.30am-5pm daily. **Admission** R28 adults; R15 3-18s; R5 under-3s. **Credit** MC, V.

Le Bonheur is home to about 1,000 crocodiles and, if you're in the area, it's a recommended detour for families, particularly those with young boys. The walkways take you just close enough (but not too close) to the lazy reptiles, while the on-site restaurant offers such delights as crocodile pie.

► *For some more scary animals, see p72* **Shark Tactics**.

Monkey Town

Mondeor Road, Somerset West (021 858 1060/ www.monkeys.co.za). **Open** 9am-5pm daily. **Admission** R60; R40 students; R35 pensioners; R25 under-12s. **Credit** AmEx, DC, MC, V.

About 40km (25 miles) out of the city, Monkey Town is worth popping into: the park is home to 230 primates of 27 different species, ranging from hamadryas baboons, lemurs and lion-tailed macaques to African favourites like vervet monkeys and chimpanzees. Check the website for updated feeding times.

► *If you're travelling up the Garden Route, visit Monkeyland near Plettenberg Bay, see p235.*

Spier Wine Estate

On the R310 towards Stellenbosch, outside Cape Town (021 809 1100/www.spier.co.za). **Open** 10am-5pm daily. **Admission** *Cheetah Outreach* R10. *Eagle Encounters* R40. **Credit** AmEx, DC, MC, V.

Though it might seem strange to include a Stellenbosch wine estate on a kiddies' holiday list, Spier earns its place by being one of the few destinations in the winelands that actually thinks to cater for the younger generation. The estate offers a

Cheetah Outreach, an aviary for birds of prey, and a large lakeside picnic area with horse rides.

► *See also pxx Restaurants.*

★ Two Oceans Aquarium

Dock Road, V&A Waterfront (021 418 3823/ www.aquarium.co.za). **Open** 9.30am-6pm daily. **Admission** R82 adults; R65 14-17s; R38 4-13s; under-4s free. **Credit** AmEx, DC, MC, V. **Map** p274 G2.

A Mother City must-see, the Two Oceans Aquarium offers a watery home to about 3 000 marine beasties, ranging from turtles to crabs to rays to seals to penguins, plus – of course – fishes great (like the sharks) and small (like the Nemo-esque clownfish). You'll want to time your visit to coincide with the 3.30pm 'lunch time' at the Predator Exhibit.

Tygerberg Zoo

Exit 39, Klipheuwel-Stellenbosch off-ramp, N1 (021 884 4494). **Open** 9am-5pm daily. **Admission** R55 adults; R40 children (2-14). **Credit** MC, V.

All right, we're not going to lie: although it's Cape Town's only 'proper' zoo, Tygerberg is very much on the rustic side, so don't go if you're looking for the whole glitzy African Safari experience. What makes this particular one cool though is that it sports some of the animal kingdom's weirder beasts, including llamas, potbellied pigs and armadillos.

World of Birds

Valley Road, Hout Bay (021 790 2730/ www.worldofbirds.org.za). **Open** 9am-5pm daily. **Admission** R59 adults; R37-R49 reductions; free under-3s. **Credit** AmEx, DC, MC, V.

A network of walk-through aviaries allows you to get up close and personal with over 3,000 feathered friends and smallish animals, ranging from peacocks to flamingos to exotic-looking species like spoonbills and turacos.

World of Birds

CHILDMINDING

While most local babysitting companies are safe and reliable, it's always wise to make a point of checking the sitter's references. Also, note that some operators charge extra for babysitting in hotels, and most charge extra for babysitting after midnight. **Sitters4U** (083 691 2009, www.sitters4u.co.za) and **Super Sitters** (021 552 1220, www.supersitters.net) are good options.

EATING OUT

Barnyard Farmstall
4 Steenberg Road, Tokai (021 712 6934). **Open** 8.30am-5pm Mon, Tue, Sun; 8am-7pm Wed-Fri. **Main courses** R30-R80. **Credit** AmEx, DC, MC, V.
This charming country-style restaurant is set in a small farmyard – striking just the right balance between a petting zoo and an outdoor eaterie.

Café Roux
Noordhoek Farm Village, Noordhoek (021 789 2538/www.caferoux.co.za). **Open** 8.30am-11.15am, noon-3.30pm daily. **Main courses** R54-R98. **Credit** AmEx, DC, MC, V.
Let the children loose on the jungle-gym or trotting around on the big-bellied ponies while you tuck into one of the killer brekkies – the eggs benedict and fluffy omelettes are fantastic.

Deer Park Café
2 Deer Park Avenue, Vredehoek (021 462 6311). **Open** 8am-8pm daily. **Main courses** R44-R89. **Credit** AmEx, DC, MC, V.
A City Bowl eaterie that opens on to a safe public park (Rocklands Park), the Deer Park Café is great for breakfasts and lunches. The menu is good (it caters for children and grown-ups), but the tastiest part of it all is that big patch of toddler-friendly grass.

EDUTAINMENT

Iziko Planetarium
25 Queen Victoria Street, Gardens (021 481 3900/www.iziko.org.za). **Screenings** *Current feature* 2pm Mon-Fri; 1pm, 2.30pm Sat, Sun.

Children's show 2pm Sat, Sun. **Admission** R20; R10 adults going to a children's show; R6-R8 reductions. **Credit** MC, V. **Map** p276 G4.
Here's a rare chance, in our light-polluted modern time, to see all the stars in the Cape's night sky. The Planetarium offers a range of shows, with many designed specifically for children.

Iziko South African Museum
25 Queen Victoria Street, Gardens (021 481 3800/www.iziko.org.za). **Open** 10am-5pm daily. **Admission** R15; free under-16s. **Credit** MC, V. **Map** p276 G4.
While they'll probably run (or yawn) their way through the social history exhibits, children will enjoy the natural history stuff… especially the Whale Well and the dinosaur section. The Cluttered Hall of Stuffed Animals (you'll know it when you see it – we're not sure what else to call it) is a great way to show little kids what the animals in their story-books look like in (almost) real life.

MTN ScienCentre
Shop 407, Canal Walk, Century City (021 529 8100/www.mtnsciencentre.org.za). **Open** 9am-6pm Mon-Thur, Sun; 9am-9pm Fri, Sat. **Admission** R22; R28 3-18s; R86 family (2 adults, 2 children). **Credit** AmEx, DC, MC, V.
This interactive discovery centre, situated in the Canal Walk shopping mall (along with Boogaloos Skatepark and Place of Play), offers daily workshops during school holidays, along with 280 permanent displays, taking in fun-with-science activities like brainteasers and mini laboratories.

Warrior Toy Museum
St George's Street, Simon's Town (021 786 1395). **Open** 10am-3.45pm Mon-Thur, Sat, Sun. **Admission** R5. **Credit** MC, V.
This museum is packed with about 4,000 model cars, 500 dolls and teddy bears, plus miniature dolls' houses, toy soldiers, and pretty much any other toy you can think of, including two fully operating railroads.

INDOOR ENTERTAINMENT

Bizzy Bodies
Westlake Business Park, Westlake (021 702 0505/www.bizzybodies.co.za). **Open** 10am-5pm Tue-Sat (during school term); 10am-5pm Mon-Sat (during school holidays); 10am-2pm public holidays. **Rates** *Children over 2* R35 (1st hour), then R30 per hr. *Children under 2* R30 (1st hour); then R25 per hr. **Credit** MC, V.
A large indoor play gym, Bizzy Bodies offers an active playtime for children aged from one to 12 years. The area is geared around getting the kids to run, climb, swing and slide on soft, padded obstacles – and the coffee corner gives parents a chance to get a quick rest in between.

ARTS & ENTERTAINMENT

Cave Golf

*At Scratch Patch, 1 Dock Road, V&A Waterfront
(021 419 9429).* **Open** 9am-5pm daily.
Admission R10. **Credit** AmEx, DC, MC, V.
Map p274 G1.
The 18 holes at this indoor mini-golf (or 'putt-putt')
course provide a good blend of difficulty and enjoyment.

GrandWest Casino & Entertainment World

*1 Vanguard Drive, Goodwood (021 505 7777/
www.grandwest.co.za).* **Open** *Ice Rink* 10am-
midnight Mon-Fri; 9am-midnight Sat; noon-
midnight Sun. *Ten-pin bowling* 11am-11pm
Mon-Thur, Sun; 10am-1am Fri, Sat. **Admission**
both R30. **Credit** AmEx, DC, MC, V.
Look past the roulette wheels and slot machines,
and you'll find one of the city's most child-friendly
entertainment centres. Facilities here include
ice-skating at the Ice Station (021 535 2260,
www.icerink.co.za), along with arcade games, go-
karting, mini-golf and fun rides (like a carousel for
little girls and a runway train for little boys) at the
Magic Company (021 534 0244).

Kenilworth Karting

*Cnr Warrington & Myhof roads, Kenilworth
(021 683 2670/www.karting.co.za).* **Open**
1-11pm Mon-Thur; 11am-11pm Fri; 10am-
midnight Sat, Sun. **Admission** *10-lap race*
R50; R40 under-16s. **Credit** MC, V.
A hard-to-find indoor go-karting circuit, Kenilworth
Karting has a 310m (1 020ft) track which offers 10,
15-, 20- or 30-lap races… depending on what you
book and how busy the circuit is. It's relatively safe,
too: the marshals keep a close eye on dangerous driving (and, unfortunately, on cheats). Drivers must
be at least 1.5m (4.9ft) tall, and helmets and hair nets
are provided.

Laserquest

*Lower level, Stadium on Main, Claremont
(021 683 7296/www.laserquest.co.za).* **Open**
10.30am-10pm Mon-Thur; 10.30am-11pm Fri-Sun.
Admission R55 before 6pm; R45 after 6pm.
Credit MC, V.
It's like paintball… only indoors, in the dark, and
with painless laser beams instead of little paintball
bullets. Games are timed and are well regulated, and
the winner is the one who shoots the most opponents
the most often. Dads will want to join in too.

Place of Play

*Shop 43, Canal Walk Shopping Mall, Century
City Boulevard (021 555 0303/www.place
ofplay.co.za).* **Open** 9.30am-6pm daily.
Admission *Children over 2* R20 Mon-Fri;
R40 Sat, Sun. *Children under 2* R25 Mon-Fri;
R40 Sat, Sun. Parents free. **Credit** AmEx,
DC, MC, V.

This large (we're talking 2,000sq m or 22,000 sq ft)
indoor venue provides a variety of play facilities,
with descriptive names such as the Magnetic
Climbing Wall, Lazermaze, Slippery Slide and
Three-Storey Jungle Gym. Place of Play puts a big
emphasis on safety, with each child given a wrist-
band to ensure that they can't leave the premises
without being noticed.

Planet Kids

*3 Wherry Road, behind False Bay Station,
Muizenberg (021788 3070/www.planetkids.
co.za).* **Open** 10am-6pm daily. **Rates** R30/hr.
No credit cards.
Let the little ones run amok at this Trekkie-themed
indoor play centre featuring a UFO jumping castle
complete with inflatable alien inhabitants and space
cars. Parents can either refuel at the Flying Saucer
Café or make use of the convenient drop-off service.
The centre is wheelchair friendly and customised to
accommodate children with all abilities. Kids must
be two or older.

Stadium on Main

*3rd Floor, Main Road, Claremont (021 671
3665/021 683 9061).* **Open** 9am-midnight
Mon-Fri; 8am-5pm Sat, Sun. **Credit** AmEx,
DC, MC, V.
Stadium on Main has a top-storey entertainment
area that offers indoor cricket, netball and soccer
courts. Social and league games are offered throughout the week, so you'll have to book ahead of time if
you fancy getting a game.

OUTDOOR ENTERTAINMENT

Action Paint Ball

*Tokai Forest (021 790 7603/www.action
paintball.co.za).* **Open** 9.30am-12.45pm, 1.30-
4.45pm daily. **Rates** R110 for 100 balls.
No credit cards.
The kids will love this. Of course, by 'kids' we mean
older teenage boys because 'kids' under 11 are
strictly not allowed to play. The game is closely
monitored for safety, but – as with any war game
where guns and play bullets are involved – some
'kids' tend to get a bit carried away.

Boogaloos Skate Park

*Shop 531, Canal Walk Shopping Centre,
Century City Boulevard (021 555 2895/
www.boogaloos.com).* **Open** 9am-9pm daily.
Credit DC, MC, V.
This skatepark (or 'designated skateboarding area',
to use it's official name as decided by the city coun-
cil) is situated on the outer roof of the Canal Walk
Shopping Centre, and offers plenty of open space,
ramps and rails for Cape Town's fearless skaters
to practise and perfect their grinds, flips and ollies.
There are BMX-only sessions on Tuesday and
Thursday evenings.

Scratch Patch
*Dido Valley Road, Simon's Town (021 786
2020/www.scratchpatch.co.za).* **Open** 8.30am-
4.45pm Mon-Fri; 9am-5.30pm Sat, Sun, public
holidays. **Credit** AmEx, DC, MC, V.
*Dock Road, V&A Waterfront (021 419
9429/www.scratchpatch.co.za).* **Open** 9am-
5.30pm daily. **Credit** AmEx, DC, MC, V.
Crawl around and collect bright and shiny semi-
precious stones – tiger's eye, agate amethyst and
more – and put them into small bags (R11) or bigger containers (R65). What you put into your container is up to you but you'll probably want to stick
to the brighter semi-precious stones, and avoid the
duller quartz pebbles.
▶ *See also p73.*

THEME PARKS

★ Ratanga Junction
*Canal Walk, Century City, Sable Street exit, N1
(086 120 0300/group bookings 021 550 8504/
www.ratanga.co.za).* **Open** Western Cape school
holidays 10am-5pm daily. **Admission** R120
above 1.3m (4.2ft) tall; R60 under 1.3m (4.2ft) tall;
R35 fun pass. **Credit** AmEx, DC, MC, V.
Cape Town's only theme park has a hard-to-predict
schedule (it's usually closed in winter, except for
sometimes in the school holidays), but tends to come
out of hibernation just in time for summer. Fun rides
include the Cobra, the Slingshot and Monkey Falls,
along with a number of new rides and attractions
with names that speak for themselves.

ARTS & ENTERTAINMENT

Running Away to the Circus

These kids aren't clowning around.

'After almost two decades, our travelling
circus finally found a place to call home. It
arrived in pieces on 18 March 2008,' Zip-
Zap Circus School's co-founder Laurence
Estève laughs when describing the arduous
process of setting up the huge tent that's
now a permanent fixture in the city centre.

Estève, who hails from France, met
acrobat husband Brent van Rensburg at a
holiday resort in the Caribbean 20 years
ago. The two were soon travelling the world
as a flying trapeze act, and when the circus
season ended, van Rensburg suggested a
visit to his home country, South Africa.

'By the end of our holiday, we were
completely broke,' she reminisces, 'so we
did what we knew best, and started
teaching the trapeze to tourists.'

The 'holiday' was extended indefinitely
after a stint at the V&A Waterfront where
they encountered a group of children who
couldn't afford to join in the excitement.

The solution to the sullen little faces
seemed simple enough at the time –
establishing a free circus school for kids

from all walks of life. But the execution
hasn't been without challenge; the search
for a permanent practice venue having
been only one of the many obstacles.

Many of the students come from
disadvantaged backgrounds, where issues
like violence, crime and drug abuse are
prevalent, so the school isn't run like a
military operation. 'The beauty of Zip-Zap is
that it attracts kids who don't necessarily
fit in anywhere else,' says Estève. 'We let
them play and be who they are, and
eventually they find their own way.'

The only rule, it seems, is courtesy. Estève
says the values they instil not only help the
children to perform better as a team, but
also arm them for the real world. 'Life is
very much like circus school,' she says.
'You've got your five minutes of fame, and
the rest of the time you're a stage hand.'

Zip-Zap Circus School
Practice times *Apr-Sept* 9am-10.45pm Sat
for 6-8s; 11am-12.45pm Sat for 9-11s.
Phone ahead to book place. **Admission** free.

Film

The big releases are joined by local favourites in Cape Town.

At first glance, it looks as if Hollywood blockbusters dominate Cape Town's cinema listings – it's easier to find a screen showing the new Brad Pitt movie than it is to track down one showing a South African-produced film. But dig a little deeper and you'll find that there is some allternative and arthouse cinema on show as well.

When it comes to deciding where to see a film, the choice is between the retro allure of the oddly named **Labia** and the more swish multiplexes of the **Ster-Kenekor** or **Nu Metro** chains. Nu Metro is the country's second-largest cinema, and though mainly devoted to the mainstream, it sometimes screens films that are out of the ordinary. For unusual cinematic experiences, there is the luxury of dinner and a film at the **Twelve Apostles** hotel in Camps Bay, or an out-of-town film show at Franschhoek's **Screening Room**.

RESOURCES

Animation junkies should pop by the monthly **Animation xChange** (083 787 1342, www.animationsa.org) – an underground social gathering where animators share their work and talk shop over a glass of wine, while film buffs who prefer to get their fix from the comfort of their couch should visit **DVD Nouveau** (166 Bree Street, 021 422 4984, www.dvdnouveau.co.za) for a quality dose of celluloid overload. If you can't decide on a venue, the **South African Movie Site** (www.moviesite.co.za) is an excellent resource for checking cinema listings and getting an overview of what's on show.

VENUES

Multiplexes

★ Cinema Nouveau
Cavendish Square, 1 Dreyer Street, Claremont (021 657 5600/www.cavendish.co.za). V&A Waterfront Lower level, V&A Waterfront (0861 300 444/www. waterfront.co.za). **Map** p275 H1.
Both **Open** *Box offices* 9.15am-8.30pm Mon-Sat; 11.30am-8.30pm Sun. **Tickets** R45; R24 reductions. **Credit** AmEx, DC, MC, V.
Ster-Kinekor's dedicated arthouse cinema is a film buff's dream. It even brings out its own magazine, profiling all the latest releases. It's run in partnership with Jameson whiskey, which means that together the duo have enough dosh to put on a top-notch selection of new cutting-edge films.

Nu Metro
Canal Walk Shopping Centre, Century Boulevard, Century City, Milnerton (021 555 2510/www. canalwalk.co.za). **Open** Box office 8.30am-11pm daily. **Tickets** R33 adults; R23 reductions. **Credit** AmEx, DC, MC, V.
Although mainstream fare is the name of the game here, the country's second largest cinema chain also has a few surprises up its sleeve. Their Canal Walk branch, the star of the show, is the biggest with a staggering 17 cinemas to choose from and a regular selection of Bollywood romps to spice up the schedule. They also have a more upmarket Cinema Privé screen that invites patrons to enjoy big budget blockbusters in style. This state-of-the-art cinema has its own business class lounge area where you can order a drink or two before the show.
Other locations V&A Waterfront, upper level (021 419 9700/www.waterfront.co.za).

Ster-Kinekor
Information & bookings through Ticketline (082 16789/www.sterkinekor.com).
South Africa's biggest cinema chain is divided into separate branches, including the cheaper Ster-Kinekor Junction and the more expensive Ster-Kinekor Classic (*see below*).

Ster-Kinekor Classic
Cavendish Square *1 Dreyer Street, Claremont (021 657 5600/www.cavendish.co.za).*
Longbeach Mall *Sunnydale Road, Sun Valley (021 785 5955).*
Tyger Valley Shopping Centre *Willie van Schoor Avenue, Bellville (021 914 1822/ www.tygervalley.co.za).*
All Open *Box offices* 9am-11pm Mon-Sat; 11am-8.30pm Sun. **Tickets** R45; R24 reductions. Half-price for all Tue. **Credit** AmEx, DC, MC, V.
To make up for the heftier price tag, more snack options like nachos and coffee are available at Ster-Kinekor's 'Classic' cinemas. Half-price Tuesdays

for movie club members does help to lessen the financial blow, however. This deal makes Tuesday the cinema's most popular night, so it's best to book in advance.

Independents

Cine 12
Twelve Apostles Hotel & Spa, Victoria Road, Camps Bay (021 437 9000/www.12apostles hotel.com). **Tickets** R255 for dinner and movie. **Credit** AmEx, DC, MC, V.
This is as decadent as it gets. Enjoy a four-course meal at spectacular seaside hotel Twelve Apostles'

Queen of the Big Screen
Discover a local movie-house legend.

Google 'Labia' and cinemas won't be top of the list. But despite the kinky name, the Mother City's oldest independent cinema isn't *that* kind of cinema.

Most Capetonians have fond childhood memories of going to the Labia to watch *ET*, *Bambi* or *The Aristocats*. The grand dame, with her wood-panelled walls and vintage ticket booth seems simply magical; a last remnant of cinema's golden age. Where else can you still buy your popcorn packaged in a brown paper bag? Or get your chocolate fix in the form of a steaming mug of whisky-spiked cocoa? And then there's the quality programming, of course.

Originally, this voluptuously curved building was the plush ballroom of the Italian Embassy. Princess Labia had other plans for it, and in 1949 opened the space as a theatre. A cinema screen followed in the '70s, and for the next few years the venue played host to both film screenings and theatre performances. When current owner Ludi Kraus bought it in 1989, the Labia as we know it today was born. But the years had taken their toll on our favourite starlet. 'It was very run-down at that stage,' recalls Kraus. Luckily for us the theatre was lovingly given a new lease of life, and three screens were added.

These days the cinema is at the centre of Cape Town's independent film culture. On a Friday night the tables spilling out on to the courtyard are abuzz with wine-wielding film buffs, winding down the week with an independent flick. It hosts regular festivals on topics ranging from slasher movies to Judaism. Eye-opening documentaries accompanied by Q&A sessions with experts are also on the menu.

The city's best-loved independent movie house has come a long way since her waltzing days and her charms have stood the test of time. Do drop by next time you're in the neighbourhood. It sure beats the gaudy glare of the mall. And if you want better screen resolution and sound, simply head up around the corner to the Kloof Street baby sister.
▶ For listings, *see p168.*

super swanky restaurant, Azure. Then sit back with some gourmet snacks – including real movie treats like ice-creams, popcorn, candy and hot chocolate – and watch a film in its luxury, state-of-the-art 16-seater cinema. The film schedule changes weekly, but if you book out the venue for a private screening you have a ginormous selection of about 300 films to pick from.

Labia
68 Orange Street, Gardens (021 424 5927/ www.labia.co.za). **Open** Box office 11.30am-10.30pm daily. **Tickets** R25 adults; R20 reductions. **Credit** MC, V.
See p167 **Queen of the Big Screen**.
Other locations Lifestyles on Kloof Centre, 50 Kloof Street, Gardens.

Screening Room
Le Quartier Français, 16 Huguenot Road, Franschhoek, outside Cape Town (021 876 2151/www.lequartier.co.za). **Open** 9am-6pm Wed-Sat. *Private screenings* Mon, Tue. **Tickets** R45 inc glass of wine and snacks. **Credit** DC, MC, V.
The picturesque winelands hamlet of Franschhoek seems an unlikely place to find a movie theatre. Sink into leather chairs while sipping on fine wine and enjoying anything from cinematic classics to arthouse films at this privately owned intimate 24-seater cinema
▶ *Le Quartier Français is also home to the Tasting Room; see p216.*

FESTIVALS

Suidoosterfees
Artscape Theatre, cnr DF Malan Street & Hertzog Boulevard, Foreshore (021 421 7839/021 406 2835/www.artscape.co.za/ www.suidoosterfees.co.za). **Bookings** Computicket or Dial-a-seat. **Credit** AmEx, DC, MC, V. **Map** p275 I3. **Date** 26-31 Jan 2010.
A multicultural festival named after the Mother City's feisty south-easterly wind, which is famous for playing havoc on the streets, chasing runaway skirts and acrobatic plastic bags. The festival aims

to promote the art world's Big Five – dance, music, theatre, film and fine art. Offerings range from mainstream to arthouse with a special focus on productions in Afrikaans.

Cape Winelands Film Festival
Oude Libertas Amphitheatre, Stellenbosch, outside Cape Town (021 809 7380/www. oudelibertas.co.za). Bookings Computicket. **Credit** AmEx, DC, MC, V. **Date** Mar.
This promising new festival, which shows award-winning short films, features and documentaries from across the globe, was inaugurated in 2009. The picturesque Oude Libertas Theatre outside Stellenbosch served as the home base, with other screenings at smaller venues throughout the town. Films were divided into categories: these ranged from world cinema to eco cinema, cinema of conscience and food on film, as well as a category for South African premieres.

Encounters South African International Documentary Festival
Nu Metro, V&A Waterfront (021 465 4686/ www.encounters.co.za). **Credit** AmEx, DC, MC, V. **Date** July. **Map** p275 H1.
Encounters is an annual highlight for film buffs and documentary junkies, who get to pick from an array of local and international productions by emerging and established filmmakers. In 2009 more than 49 films were showcased. The festival has done much to raise the bar for South Africa's documentary-making industry. Initiatives also include taking the festival to the townships and running workshops.

TRI Continental Film Festival
Cinema Nouveau, V&A Waterfront (021 788 5462/www.3continentsfestival.co.za). **Credit** AmEx, DC, MC, V. **Date** 22-31 Aug 2009. **Map** p275 H1.
This global initiative connects filmmakers from the Americas, Asia and Africa who are striving to use the power of film for social change. All the narrative, documentary, feature and short films on show have strong socio-political messages, addressing topics like human rights, equality and freedom. Various workshops, township and rural screenings, discussion forums and seminars are employed to get the message across.

Out in Africa: South African Gay & Lesbian Film Festival
Nu Metro, upper level, V&A Waterfront (021 461 4027/www.oia.co.za). **Credit** AmEx, DC, MC, V. **Date** Sept. **Map** p275 H1.
Now in its 16th year, South Africa's annual gay and lesbian film festival showcases the hottest new shorts, series, doccies and features.
▶ *For more on gay events and gay culture in Cape Town, see pp177-181.*

Galleries

Cape Town gets creative with a slew of great galleries.

Cape Town's art landscape is booming. With two university fine arts departments on its doorstep and a host of galleries to pick from, art aficionados are well catered for. So much so, that the city launched its first biennale, CAPE, in 2007. Despite a few labour pains, the event marked an exciting new turn for the local contemporary art scene.

If you're pressed for time, but still want a taste of what the city's top galleries have to offer, head over to the suburb of Woodstock. The gritty district on the edge of the city is experiencing regeneration and transformation into a one-stop contemporary art stop.

About the author

Ilze Hugo is a fine arts graduate and freelance writer, who specialises in travel and the arts.

INFORMATION

For up to date information about galleries and shows, check the websites of **Art South Africa** (www.artsouthafrica.com), **Artthrob** (www.artthrob.co.za) and **Cape Contemporary African Culture** (021 461 2325, www.capeafrica.org).

If you're keen on a literary window into the local scene, pick up a copy of the revered quarterly visual arts magazine *Art South Africa* (available at selected galleries and major newsagents) or browse its digital equivalent, www.artthrob.co.za.

GALLERIES

City Bowl

★ Association for the Visual Arts

35 Church Street, City Centre (021 424 7436/ www.ava.co.za). **Open** 10am-5pm Mon-Fri; 10am-1pm Sat. **Credit** AmEx, DC, MC, V. **Map** p276 G4.

You'll find one of the country's oldest galleries housed in a stately Cape Dutch building. A non-profit organisation, the AVA first opened here in 1971 – its main aim to promote and advance South African art and artists (both emerging and established). Apart from organising exhibitions the AVA also runs an outreach fund, providing grants for studio space and materials for emerging artists. It's the ideal place to stock up on the work of talented young guns before they make it big. There's also a smaller, informal gallery space-cum-office area, which has work from previous exhibitors on sale.

Atlantic Art Gallery

25 Wale Street, City Centre (021 423 5775). **Open** 10am-4.30pm Mon-Fri; 9.30am-1pm Sat. **No credit cards.** **Map** p276 G4.

The brushstrokes that mark the entrance to this, one of Cape Town's oldest galleries, read '25'. Step through the gate on to the royal-blue carpeting, and you're surrounded by walls dripping with colour. Riva Cohen has run Atlantic since its inception and rubbed shoulders with respected names like the late Maggie Laubser and Marjorie Wallace. Her gallery has moved three times since setting up shop in 1973; from Burg to Church and, finally, Wale Street. The collection includes names like Bester and Slingsby.

Cape Gallery

60 Church Street, City Centre (021 423 5309/ www.capegallery.co.za). **Open** 9.30am-5pm Mon-Fri; 10am-2pm Sat. **Credit** AmEx, DC, MC, V. **Map** p276 G4.

A historic apricot-coloured building with creaky wooden floors and retro signage has housed the gallery since the 1970s and the work inside is mostly by Cape-based artists. Unlike its neighbour, the AVA (*see above*), Cape tends to favour a more traditional aesthetic approach, including a wealth of landscapes, still lifes and figurative studies. Regular names on the roster include Judy Woodburne, Frederike Stokhuyzen and Max Wolpe.

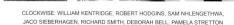

Erdmann Contemporary/ Photographers Gallery ZA

63 Shortmarket Street, City Centre (021 422 2762/072 356 7056/www.erdmann contemporary.co.za). **Open** 10am-5pm Mon-Fri; 11am-1pm Sat. **Credit** AmEx, DC, MC, V. **Map** p276 G3.

Run under the experienced eye of art purveyor Heidi Erdmann, this gallery fills a much-needed niche in the local art scene. the focus is on promoting South African fine art photography and comic art – and all the biggest names in the field have shown their work in this petite space. You can also expect to find the odd conceptual piece, painting, drawing and sculpture by critically acclaimed fine artists such as Nicola Grobler.

Focus Contemporary

2 Long Street, cnr Hans Strijdom (entrance on Loop Street), City Centre (021 419 8888/072 912 2929/www.focuscontemporary.co.za). **Open** 9am-5.30pm Mon-Fri; 10am-2pm Sat, public holidays. **Credit** MC, V. **Map** p276 H3.

You'll find a fresh mix of mainly photographic works by hip young up-and-comers and middleweights alike here. Originally intended as a platform for photography alone, Focus has gradually broadened its horizons to include work by folk like emerging fine art graduates Ingrid Nurse and Peter Jenks. Work lighting up the walls can include shots by Kenyan photographer Mimi Cherono and photos of Picasso by Frenchman André Villiers.

IArt

71 Loop Street, City Centre (021 424 5150/ www.iart.co.za). **Open** *Winter* 10am-5pm Mon-Fri. *Summer* 9am-6pm Mon-Fri; 10am-2pm Sat. **Credit** AmEx, MC, V. **Map** p276 G4.

IArt was founded in 2000 as an art consultancy, catering mainly to private and corporate collectors. While the gallery remains an investor's dream – come here

to fork out on work by high-flying hits like Paul Emsley and Colbert Mashile – the space has since evolved. It features a traditional gallery upstairs for serious buyers with a more contemporary space downstairs where the focus is on edgier exhibitions.

João Ferreira Gallery

70 Loop Street, City Centre (021 423 5403/ www.joaoferreiragallery.com). **Open** 10am-5pm Mon-Fri; 10am-2pm Sat. **Credit** AmEx, DC, MC, V. **Map** p276 G4.

Art dealer João Ferreira has been on the scene for a while now and has a fine collection of contemporary artists under his wing. His gallery is tiny but is still much revered by the key figures of Cape Town's contemporary art scene, and the quality of work on show more than makes up for the lack of floor space. Artists on Ferreira's books include accolade-reaping art stars such as Alan Alborough, Paul Edmonds, Bridget Baker and Stephen Inggs.

Johans Borman Fine Art Gallery

In-Fin-Art Building, Upper Buitengracht, City Centre (021 423 6075/www.johansborman.co.za). **Open** 10am-6pm Mon-Fri; 9am-2pm Sat. **Credit** AmEx, DC, MC, V. **Map** p274 F4.

This stately space purveys work of the country's old masters, textbook favourites like Stern, Sekoto, Pierneef and Boonzaaier. Come here to invest for a rainy day or for a history lesson. Not all their artists are six feet under though – they also showcase a few pieces from more contemporary folk like David Reade and Marlene von Dürckheim.

Salon91

91 Kloof Street (082 679 3906/www.salon91 art.co.za). **Open** 10am-6pm Tue-Fri; 10am-2pm Sat or by appointment. **Credit** MC, V. **Map** p274 F5.

Owner Monique du Preez has created an intimate gallery space with a unique personality that eschews

IArt.

ARTS & ENTERTAINMENT

the notion of a gallery as blank canvas or empty white space. It was born out of a need to address the lack of exhibition space for talented fine arts graduates and other emerging creatives before they hit it big, and has a preference for sculptural work.

3rd I Gallery

95 Waterkant Street, De Waterkant (021 425 2266). **Open** 9am-5pm Mon-Fri or by appointment; 10am-1pm Sat, closed last Sat of every month. **Credit** MC, V. **Map** p276 G3.

The exposed walls and thick wooden beams of this 18th-century warehouse make the 3rd I the perfect canvas for a vibrant collection of art. Gallery owners Chantal Coetzee and Sharon Peers are both artists in their own right, Coetzee specialising in colourful pop paintings embedded with spiritual iconography, while Peers's striking photography explores sacred geometries.

34 Long

34 Long Street, City Centre (021 426 4594/ 082 354 1500/www.34long.com). **Open** 10am-5pm Tue-Fri; 10am-2pm Sat; public holidays by appointment. **Credit** AmEx, MC, V. **Map** p276 G4.

Long, at number 34 Long Street, is tightly squeezed in between two straight-laced office blocks and adorned with naughty-looking gargoyles. Although the exhibition space inside this narrow historical treasure isn't much bigger than you might find inside a walk-in closet, the gallery has staged – and continues to stage – some top-notch art. Exhibitions have included work by international art superstars like Takashi Murakami and Jeff Koons as well as local heavyweights like Willie Bester, Marlene Dumas and Norman Catherine.

VEO Gallery

28 Jarvis Street, De Waterkant (021 421 3278/ 021 423 7069/www.veo.co.za). **Open** 10am-5pm Mon-Thur; 10am-4pm Fri; 10am-2pm Sat; or by appointment. **Credit** AmEx, DC, MC, V. **Map** p276 G3.

The focus at VEO is mainly on accessible pieces to liven up your living space. Also on offer is a framing and interior decorating consulting service. Wander in from the kerb and take in work by the likes of Uwe Pfaff, David Kuijers and Richard Scott.

INSIDE TRACK
KUCHA KUCHA KOO

Cape Town now hosts its own **Pecha Kucha Nights**. These entertaining art and design networking events were started in Tokyo by architectural firm Klein-Dytham before spreading across the world (www.pecha-kucha.org/cities/cape-town).

Salon91. *See p171.*

Worldart

54 Church Street, City Centre (021 423 3075/ www.worldart.co.za). **Open** 10am-5pm Mon-Fri; 10am-2pm Sat. **Credit** AmEx, DC, MC, V. **Map** p274 G3.

Ambling down Church Street, past Afropop coffee shops and antique vendors, you'll spy a slick white cube of a gallery with a glass-walled shop front. Inside is a host of happening offerings – from colourful odes to pop art by Richard Scott to Kurt Campbell's archival pigment prints.

Atlantic Seaboard

Everard Read Gallery

3 Portswood Road, V&A Waterfront (021 418 4527/www.everard-read-capetown.co.za). **Open** 9am-6pm Mon-Fri; 9am-1pm Sat; or by appointment. **Credit** AmEx, DC, MC, V. **Map** p274 G1.

Sink your feet into plush carpets as you explore works by established artists such as painters Beezey Bailey and wildlife sculptor Dylan Lewis (whose work made headlines two years ago when 75 of his sculptures where auctioned by Christie's for £1.9 million). The luxurious space with its stately fireplace is the sister gallery of one of South Africa's oldest galleries, Everard Read's in Johannesburg, that has been around since 1913.

Die Kunskamer

3 Portswood Road, Waterfront (021 419 3226/ www.kunskamer.co.za). **Open** 8.30am-5pm Mon-Fri; 9.30am-1pm Sat. **Credit** AmEx, DC, MC, V. **Map** p274 G1.

Pull on the palm of a hand with a skull sprouting from a fingertip to open the macabre bronze gate (by artist David Brown) and step inside this double gallery space, housing both Die Kunskamer and Everard Read. Die Kunskamer deals in old South African masters like Scully, Sekoto and Stern, with works by a few younger artists.

Rose Korber Art

48 Sedgemoor Road, Camps Bay (021 438 9152/083 261 1173/www.rosekorberart.com). **Open** 9am-5pm Mon-Fri; weekends and public holidays by appointment. **Credit** AmEx, DC, MC, V. **Map** p273 B8.

A former art lecturer, critic and writer, Korber started dealing in art from her home in 1990. Her collection features the cream of the South African art crop (William Kentridge, Claudette Schreuders), as well as a few lesser-knowns. The gallery is a must-visit for anyone wanting to get a broad overview of the South African contemporary art landscape.

Southern Suburbs

★ Bell-Roberts

Ground Floor, Fairweather House, 176 Sir Lowry Road, Woodstock (021 465 9108/ www.bell-roberts.com). **Open** 9am-5pm Mon-Fri; 10am-1pm Sat. **Credit** MC, V. **Map** p275 J4.

The focus at Bell-Roberts is on prize-winning Cape-based art stars, with hip names such as Nigel Mullins, Cameron Platter and Kevin Brand all making a turn to coat the Colgate-white walls with their creative musings. Apart from running a gallery, Bell-Roberts also has her fingers in a host of other pies – such as a publishing house, art bookshop, book design studio, art framing workshop, and a small design and projects gallery.

▶ *See also right* **Woodstock**.

Blank Projects

113-115 Sir Lowry Road, Woodstock (072 198 9221/www.blankprojects.blogspot.com). **Open** opening nights and by appointment. **No credit cards. Map** p275 J4.

Artists Liza Grobler and Jonathan Garnham started Blank Projects with a gallery no bigger than a janitor's storage closet. It's since put on some weight (the pair got hold of the empty space next door and expanded), but the work on offer is still as fresh and experimental as ever. The duo is filling a much needed gap by providing a space for established contemporary artists to let their hair down, free from the usual restrictions of the bigger galleries, while at the same time making room for exhibitions by emerging art stars.

▶ *See also right* **Woodstock**.

Carmel Art

66 Vineyard Road, Claremont (021 671 6601/ www.carmelart.co.za). **Open** 9am-5pm Mon-Fri; 9am-1pm Sat. **Credit** AmEx, DC, MC, V.

Shop till you drop at the Cavendish Square mall, then cross the road for a bit of culture at this Claremont favourite. Boasting a whopping 60-plus artists on its books, Carmel Art stocks paintings by popular artists including Pieter van der Westhuizen and Hannetjie de Clercq; come here for affordable pieces.

Curious, Whetstone & Frankley Exhibitionists

87A Station Road, Observatory (021 448 8780/ www.curiouswhetstoneandfrankley.com). **Open** 11am-2pm Wed-Fri; 10am-2pm Sat during shows. **Credit** MC, V.

Discover this matchbox-sized gallery in between a bridge and a martial arts studio in eccentric Observatory. Scuffle inside to stock up on hip indie art, craft and design at good prices – everything from interactive art events to tongue-in-cheek jewellery, kooky crockery, quirky paintings and illustrations.

★ Goodman Gallery Cape

3rd Floor, Fairweather House, 176 Sir Lowry Road, Woodstock (021 462 7573/www.goodman gallerycape.com). **Open** 9.30am-5.30pm Tue-Fri; 10am-4pm Sat. **Credit** AmEx, DC, MC, V. **Map** p275 J4.

The Goodman Gallery is a contemporary art stalwart. Its creator, Linda Givon, has made the careers of the biggest names in South African art today – including Willie Bester and William Kentridge. Givon has recently handed over the reins, but the space still upholds its reputation as one of the country's top players. At the helm – and assisted by curator Storm Janse van Rensburg – is Emma Bedford, who garnered much acclaim for her curatorial skills while working at the National Gallery.

▶ *See also right* **Woodstock**.

★ Michael Stevenson Gallery

Ground floor, Buchanan Building, 160 Sir Lowry Road, Woodstock (021 462 1500/www.michael stevenson.com). **Open** 9am-5pm Mon-Fri; 10am-1pm Sat. **Credit** AmEx, DC, MC, V. **Map** p275 J4.

Enter the swanked-up old loading garage that leads into one of Cape Town's most respected contemporary galleries. Rubbing shoulders with a cluster of gallery heavyweights in hip suburb Woodstock, this swish, industrial-looking space boasts a variety of maze-like interlocking exhibition spaces, including a room packed with photographic prints, a side gallery for showcasing young artists and a ritzy courtyard. Curator Sophie Perrier was the founding editor of esteemed art read, *Art South Africa*. These days she spends her time sourcing and showcasing a truly international collection of contemporary art, including Mustafa Maluka and Pieter Hugo.

▶ *See also right* **Woodstock**.

What If the World

Gallery *1st Floor, Albert Hall, 208 Albert Road (021 448 1438/084 414 4554/www.whatifthe world.com).* **Open** Mon, Sun by appt; 10am-4.30pm Tue-Fri; 10am-2pm Sat. **Credit** AmEx, MC, V.

Design Studio *11 Hope Street, City Centre (084 550 1037/www.whatiftheworld.com).* **Open** noon-5pm Tue-Fri; 10am-2pm Sat. **No credit cards.**

Woodstock

A gritty suburb is fast becoming Cape Town's new art centre.

At the foot of Devil's Peak, the tattered suburb of Woodstock is gradually rising from the ashes. Worn Victorian buildings are getting new licks of paint, while derelict warehouses are being transformed into swish art galleries. Not too long ago the area's gang-ridden reputation branded it a no-go territory for the affluent. Today, it boasts a buffet of cultures and income brackets. Children play soccer in the street, and art students rub shoulders with immigrants and advertising execs.

The gallery names lining the streets read like a who's-who of the local contemporary art scene – the biggest guns in the business have recently moved to this side of the tracks. Indie outfit **What if the World** (*see p174*) was the first to take the plunge; other stalwarts soon followed, with the **Goodman Gallery Cape** (*see p174*) pioneering the migration and **Michael Stevenson** (*see p174*) and **Bell-Roberts** (*see p174*) following hot on its heels.

The Michael Stevenson space, housed in an former factory, boasts high ceilings and sweeping exhibition spaces. According to gallery director Sophie Perrier, the volume of space and the sheer quantity of square metres that the gallery could get for its money were the biggest draws influencing the move. Emma Bedford, director at the Goodman Gallery Cape, concurs: 'Where else can you find the fabulous spaces we have, the great volumes and ample parking so close to the city centre?'

Bell-Roberts owner, Suzette Bell-Roberts, had been on the lookout for a gallery space before discovering the new venue in Woodstock. 'There aren't many blank canvases like this to work with in the CBD,' she muses, 'unless one is prepared to spend outrageous amounts on refurbishing.'

Bedford loves the suburb's mix of creative, residential and industrial elements, second-hand shops and corner cafés, the sense of history, and the fact that people still hang out in the streets to conduct their business or just chat. And the best part about working here? 'The view!' she exclaims. 'I must have the best corner office in the city, with wrap-around windows that encompass the entire mountain range from Devil's Peak to Signal Hill and my beloved Cape Town below. It knocks everyone's breath away. Foreign visitors can't believe it.'

She also loves the fact that she can just pop downstairs if she wants to see what the other galleries are up to. 'There's been a snowball effect and the presence of the larger galleries has encouraged smaller galleries to set up here.' Perrier confirms this: 'The proximity of other galleries is a positive development for all of us, as visitors are able to make an outing of it.' Bell-Roberts agrees: 'Visitors now have the convenience of visiting six galleries within the same block and one or two others not too far away.'

ARTS & ENTERTAINMENT

New Yorker Justin Rhodes and his South African partner Cameron Munro started What if the World with a tiny gallery in the East City Precinct. The idea was to create a community-conscious platform for emerging young artists to strut their stuff, while also playing host to workshops, art events and collaborative initiatives. The duo has since moved on to bigger things with a sexy new gallery space in rising art hub, Woodstock. Their old premises were converted into a burgeoning design studio showcasing work by up-and-comers like Adriaan Hugo; the Woodstock space celebrates the likes of conceptual art collective Avant Car Guard and whimsical illustrator Michael Taylor.
▶ *For more on Justin Rhodes and Cameron Munro, see p135* **Love Thy Neighbour**; *for more on Woodstock, see p175.*

Southern Peninsula

Bronze Age Art Sculpture House
King George Way, Simon's Town (021 786 5090/www.bronzeageart.com). **Open** 8am-4.30pm Mon-Thur; 8am-3pm Fri; weekends by appointment. **Credit** AmEx, DC, MC, V.
A sculpture gallery and foundry situated smack in the centre of naval haven Simon's Town. Visitors can watch the foundry at work from the second-storey balcony or stock up on bronze beauties by some of SA's top sculptors (all pieces are signed limited editions). The foundry specialises in mould making, patination, casting and mounting. They also do restoration work, take on corporate and private commissions and run foundry courses.
▶ *For more on the gallery, see p72.*

Hout Bay Gallery
71 Victoria Avenue, Hout Bay (021 790 3618/www.houtbaygallery.co.za). **Open** 10am-5pm daily. **Credit** AmEx, DC, MC, V.

What If the World. See p174.

There's more to the quaint harbour town of Hout Bay than fish and chips and sweeping sea vistas. Take the Hout Bay Gallery, established in 1984, that purveys a selection of picturesque fare by local artists like David Kuijers, Tay Dall and Richard Scott. Also on offer is a collection of imported furniture and hand-spun wool carpets.

Kalk Bay Modern
Above Olympia Café, 134 Main Road, Kalk Bay (021 788 6571). **Open** 9.30am-5pm daily. **Credit** MC, V.
Kalk Bay Modern's new home above local hangout Olympia Café is bigger and better, with stunning views over False Bay and Kalk Bay's colourful harbour – and the Olympia's scrumptious pastries are nearby to boot. Browse a selection of colourful craftwork and design pieces like satirical conceptual hotshot Brett Murray's famous plastic lights, brightly coloured Afropop textiles and embroidered Nguni cows needled by a local grassroots collective. The walls are adorned with work from local artists like Colbert Mashile and Max Wolpe.
▶ *For the Olympia Café, see p121.*

Northern Suburbs

Art b. Gallery
Library Centre, Carel van Aswegen Street, Bellville (021 918 2301/021 918 2287/ www.artb.co.za). **Open** 9am-4.30pm Mon-Fri; 9am-noon Sat. **No credit cards**.
Apart from being heaven for bookworms, Cape Town's biggest public library is home to a top-notch gallery. Run by the Arts Association of Bellville (with help from the city of Cape Town) on a pro bono basis, it aims to generate public awareness of art and provide a platform for both established and emerging local artists. Community workshops and art classes are run downstairs, while the upstairs gallery boasts a smaller vestibule, often used for ceramic, jewellery and glassware exhibitions, as well as a main space for contemporary exhibitions in a wide range of disciplines.

Rust-en-Vrede Gallery
10 Wellington Road, Durbanville (021 976 4691/ www.rust-en-vrede.com). **Open** 8am-4.30pm Mon-Fri; 9am-12.30pm Sat. **No credit cards**.
While the Rust-en-Vrede Gallery has been around since the early 1980s and is very well-respected among the area's arty set, its Cape Dutch façade dates back to 1840 when the building housed a prison and police headquarters. These days the space plays host to group and solo exhibitions by both emerging and established artists like Elizabeth Gunther and Christo Basson. There are also art studios, a clay museum where a host of mainly contemporary clayware, representing various construction techniques, is displayed, and a café dishing up Mediterranean fare.

Gay & Lesbian

Pink and proud of it.

Ask a Capetonian about being gay in the city and he or she will tell you that it's the queer capital of South Africa – or even, some may suggest – the southern hemisphere. Newcomers are always wowed by the free spirit and generous hospitality of the locals, and South Africa's long years of struggle have resulted in one of the most liberal constitutions in the world. The country's protection of gay rights includes the outlawing of homophobia (hate speech on the grounds of sexual orientation is illegal) and the legalisation of same-sex marriages.

Despite the overall relaxed atmosphere, however, visitors do need to keep in mind that certain social conduct is still frowned upon by less accepting members of the public – so don't let your guard down just because you're a visitor. And please remember to play it safe… the AIDS pandemic is more widespread in Africa than on any other continent.

THE LIE OF THE LAND

Cape Town's unofficial gay village is contained in one of the city's quaintest areas, **De Waterkant**. Rows of brightly coloured cottages and villas jostle for their prime camping spot with über-chic restaurants, bars, boutiques and speciality stores.

The **Triangle Project** (general enquiries 021 448 3812, helpline 021 712 6699, www. triangle.org.za) cares for the gay, lesbian, bisexual and transgendered community in Cape Town by providing professional counselling, medical services, confidential HIV testing plus counselling, workshops, support groups and more.

Community and religious groups include the **Good Hope Metropolitan Community Church** in Zonnebloem (www.goodhope mcc.org), **Cape Town Family Fellowship Church** in Gardens (Garret 021 715 8510), the **Inner Circle – Queer Muslim Organisation** (www.theinnercircle.org.za) and the LGBTI Jewish group **Jewish Outlook** (www.jewishoutlook.org.za).

About the author

*Cape Town-born **Jean-Pierre de la Chaumette** specialises in reporting on gay life in the Mother City and is a regular contributor to international publications on all things lifestyle-related.*

Besides any issues of faith or community, all these groups will be able to advise you on same-sex marriages in South Africa.

Gay and gay-friendly tour operators include **Cape Fusion Tours** (021 461 2437, www.capefusiontours.com), specialists in delicious gourmet tours of the Cape and Winelands; **Cape Info Africa** (021 425 6461, www.capeinfoafrica.co.za), in the heart of the gay village, has all the bells and whistles of a professional travel and tourism office; **Friends of Dorothy** (021 465 1871, www. friendsofdorothytours.co.za) specialise in the campest and most exclusive gay tours in the Mother City; and **Sea More Express Tours & Guest House** also offers excellent tours and accommodation (021 554 3321, www.seamore-express.com).

Websites to browse through whether looking for info and ideas or friendship and fun (or both) include, for boys, www.gay dar.co.za, www.mambaonline.co.za, www. exit.co.za and www.gaypagessa.co.za; while for the girls www.gaydargirls.com, www. mambagirl.com and www.lushcapetown. co.za are excellent.

Also be sure to check out the local press, including the *Pink Tongue* and *Exit* newspapers, for details of clubs, parties and gigs, and other information about events and resources.

Dancing Queens

Don your party shoes and shake it up at these events.

Cape Town Pride.

Honk on, horn
you like
at the
Cape Town
festival.

Cape Town Pride (021 425 6463, www.capetownpride.co.za) celebrates everything 'pink' in Cape Town. Festivities take place each year across ten days somewhere from mid to late February. The festival celebrates the city and the country's diversity – the title of 'Rainbow Nation' really rings true during the festivities. Expect beauty pageants (love your hair, hope you win), champagne hikes (athletic bubbled-up queens hiking up mountains), seminars and workshops (helpful and embracing), and much more. The festival culminates with the Pride Carnival Parade and Closing Party. Don't expect the spectacle of Sydney's Mardi Gras but it's a great party nonetheless. But it's by no means the only action around. Many would now claim that **Pink Loerie Mardi Gras** (www.pinkloerie.com) is the pinkest of all festivals in the Western Cape. It takes place in Knysna on the last weekend of April and it's very much worth driving four hours from Cape Town along the gorgeous Garden Route for it. The festival has grown significantly over the last few years and features all types of gay and gay-friendly participants, usually sporting the colour pink.

For the cinephile, **Out in Africa: South African Gay & Lesbian Film Festival** (021 461 4027/www.oia.co.za) at the Nu Metro cinema (*see p166*) in September, is not to

be missed. This long-running annual film festival is hailed as the best-dressed, best-attended and longest-running human rights-themed film festival on the African continent.

If Out in Africa can seem a bit earnest, then **MCQP: Mother City Queer Project Party** (www.mcqp.co.za) is the solution. Unless you want to be sent home in shame, don't bother showing up unless you're in costume. Better yet, create a themed uniform your entire entourage can sport. Every queen, prince and princess goes to town – and often beyond – to exhibit their interpretation of the year's theme. From 'shopping trolleys' and 'weddings' to 'comic strips', no expense is spared to make this the most decadent themed event on the gay calendar.

And if that hasn't quenched your party ardour, then try the **GAT Party** (Theo Marais Park, Koeberg Road, Milnerton, 082 821 9185), a sort of gay tea dance or hoedown. At this slightly out-of-town sports hall you can expect a divine mixture of gay Afrikaans suburban men, lipstick lesbians, dykes with bikes and a handful of *Strictly Come Dancing* wannabes. The music is probably the most varied on earth, ranging from *boeremusiek* to rave and *kwaito* (with everything in between thrown in for good measure). The party takes place on the first, second and last Saturday of every month… all year round.

CLUBS & BARS

Bar Code
18 Cobern Street, off Somerset Road, Green Point (021 421 5305/www.leatherbar.co.za). **Open** 9pm-late Mon; 10pm-late Tue-Sun. **Admission** R40 Tue, Thur; R50 Mon, Wed, Fri-Sun and themed nights. **No credit cards.** **Map** p276 G2.
A maze of darkrooms, slings and more await the leather, rubber, uniformed or denim-clad visitor (make sure you know what night it is as the dress code is strictly enforced – check online or phone for details). You can also expect secure lockers for your gear, videos and an outdoor deck for those balmy summer nights.

★ Beaulah Bar
Cnr Somerset & Cobern streets, Green Point (021 421 6798/082 565 6174/www.beaulah bar.co.za). **Open** 5pm-2am Tue-Thur; 5pm-4am Fri, Sat. **Admission** free. **Credit** AmEx, MC, V. **Map** p276 G2.
The word 'beaulah' means beautiful in the local gay-speak and describes perfectly many of the customers at this quaint bar/club. Girl-power abounds, although often with boys in tow. Locals mainly go here as a warm-up to a more serious night on the town, but that means getting drinks at the bar can take some time when the place is full. The dancefloor is small and set back but the DJs dish up healthy servings of commercial hits and floor-fillers.

★ Bronx Action Bar
22 Somerset Road, cnr Napier Street, Green Point (021 419 9216/www.bronx.co.za). **Open** 8pm-late daily. **Admission** varies, but usually free. **No credit cards.** **Map** p276 G3.
Cape Town's longest-running gay and lesbian bar and dance club, Bronx's recent relocation across the road has in no way detracted from its popularity. Wall-to-wall all-sorts mean the Bronx definitely has something for everyone. The commercial pop and dance music of the downstairs bar is within keeping of the original Bronx experience while the new upstairs dance club, called Navigaytion (021 419 9216, www.navigaytion.co.za), is open Wednesdays, Fridays and Saturdays serving up a more serious dose of music for the more discerning clubber.
► *Bronx is straight-friendly, although you may find yourself being treated as eye candy.*

Friendly Society & Salsa Lounge
125A Waterkant Street, De Waterkant (021 421 6969). **Open** 4pm-2am Mon-Thur; 9am-4am Fri, Sat. **Admission** varies. **Credit** MC, V. **Map** p276 G3.
The upstairs lounge bar – the Salsa Lounge – is ideal for a chilled cocktail or refreshing beer after a hot day. Sexy sounds drift from the sound system or are performed live on the venue's resident

baby grand. The downstairs bar/club Friendly Society springs into life from around 9pm until the small hours.

Loft Lounge
24 Napier Street, De Waterkant (021 425 2647/www.loftlounge.co.za). **Open** 5pm-2am Tue-Sun. **Admission** free. **Credit** MC, V. **Map** p276 G2.
At this pre-clubbing favourite, you'd be forgiven for thinking you were entering someone's plush loft apartment (hence the name we suppose). The decor is a mixture of retro-esque 1980s and ultra modern, while the local artwork on the walls is for sale and as such is always changing. A more than decent place to drink and meet people. *Photo p181.*

RESTAURANTS & CAFES

★ Café Manhattan
74 Waterkant Street, De Waterkant (021 421 6666/www.manhattan.co.za). **Open** 10am-2am daily. **Credit** AmEx, DC, MC, V. **Map** p276 G3.
Affectionately known as the 'Gay Spur' (ask a local to explain), this is one of the longest-running eateries and bars in Cape Town. Always friendly and always busy, this favoured hangout is renowned for its tasty pieces of meat (the type you throw on a grill, people). Its popularity recently led to a second branch opening at 247 Main Road, Sea Point (021 439 9666).

Evita se Perron
Old Darling Railway Station, Arcadia Street, Darling, about 50min out of Cape Town on the R27 (022 492 2851/022 492 2831/www.evita.co.za). **Open** 10am-4pm Tue-Sun & for evening shows. **Credit** DC, MC, V.
Take a trip up the West Coast and discover South Africa's most famous political satirist, Pieter-Dirk Uys, sending up everything 'rainbow nation' through the eyes (but mostly tongue) of his alter-ego Evita Bezuidenhout. A traditionally South African menu is served in colourfully kitsch and eye-catchingly patriotic surroundings in an old railway station. Like the name of the town, the Evita experience is just 'darling', so make sure you book in advance.
► *For more on Darling, see p243.*

INSIDE TRACK
CAPE TOWN'S GAY VILLAGE

Head over to **Green Point** for a slice of the city's gay culture – a wealth of gay- and lesbian-friendly guesthouses, clubs, restaurants, cafés and tour companies can be found in the area.

ARTS & ENTERTAINMENT

ARTS & ENTERTAINMENT

Lazari Food Gallery

Cnr Upper Maynard Street & Vredehoek Avenue, Vredehoek (021 461 9865). **Open** 7.30am-5pm Mon-Fri; 8am-3.30pm Sat; 8.30am-2.30pm Sun. **Credit** AmEx, MC, V.

Lazari Food Gallery is a retro chic café and patisserie featuring gastro delights ranging from the city's best eggs Benedict to delicious award-winning cupcakes. Owner Chris Lazari's hospitality is as famous as the family recipes that inspire the café's menu.

▶ *See also p101.*

★ Lola's

228 Long Street, City Centre (021 423 0885). **Open** 8am-midnight daily. **Credit** AmEx, DC, MC, V. **Map** p276 G4.

Become part of the city's bohemian subculture and enjoy a lazy breakfast, lunch or dinner at one of Cape Town's most eccentric cafés. Fifties charm abounds, with a strictly veggie menu and a unique offering of drinks. If the kitsch interior doesn't entice you then the off-the-wall patrons lazing on the sidewalk certainly will.

On Broadway

88 Shortmarket Street, City Centre (021 424 1194/www.onbroadway.co.za). **Open** 6.30pm-late Tue-Sun. **Shows** 8.30pm Tue-Sun. **Credit** AmEx, DC, MC, V. **Map** p276 G3.

Dinner and a show! Basic yet wholesome meals (the baked cheesecake is delicious) are outshone by the fabulous talent on stage. Entertainment ranges from South Africa's most outrageous comedians to the campest-lip-synching-feather-plumed-high-kicking drag queens south of the equator (although sometimes the distinction is not always obvious).

▶ *See also p205.*

Soho Restaurant

49 Napier Street, De Waterkant (021 421 9898/www.thevillagelodge.com). **Open** 7.30am-10.30pm daily. **Credit** AmEx, MC, V. **Map** p276 G2-3.

Reminiscent of the Asian-inspired restaurants of London's Soho, this chic restaurant, which combines designer charm with delicious Thai food, is located in the heart of the gay village. The bijou outside terrace is ideal for watching the street's frivolities, while inside the fireplace is ideal for cosy winter evenings.

SPAS & SAUNAS

Hot House

18 Jarvis Street, De Waterkant (021 418 3888/www.hothouse.co.za). **Open** noon-2am Mon-Thur; 24hrs Fri-Sun. **Credit** AmEx, DC, MC, V. **Map** p276 G3.

Almost 1,000sq m of 'sauna'! Let your adventurous side loose in the city's most renowned maze of steam

rooms, jacuzzis, saunas and private cubicles. Top up your tan on the roof's sun deck or work up some 'courage' while watching a video in three TV lounges. The staff are friendly and the environment is clean and comfortable.

WHERE TO STAY

Amsterdam Guest House

19 Forest Road, Oranjezicht (021 461 8236/www.amsterdam.co.za). **Rates** R525-R1 450. **Credit** MC, V.

The Amsterdam, a stylish, men-only guesthouse, is award-winning, centrally located and has breathtaking views to boot. A heated pool, jacuzzi and sauna make it an ideal location for summer and winter. The in-house video library includes cult favourites like *I Love Lucy* and a few riskier choices for naughty nights in.

Business lounge. Concierge. Internet. Parking (free). Pool (1 solar heated). Spa (jacuzzi, sauna). TV: DStv, DVD, Video.

L'Avenir Country Lodge

L'Avenir Wine Estate, off the R44 Klapmuts Road, Stellenbosch, outside Cape Town (021 889 5001/www.lavenir-lodge.com). **Rates** R415-R1 000. **Credit** AmEx, DC, MC, V.

This gorgeous country lodge is situated on a working wine farm. The manager and staff's hospitality is legendary, the decor sublime, the setting breathtaking and the boutique-style wine absolutely delicious.

Business centre. Disabled-adapted rooms. Internet (free wireless). Parking (free). Pool (1 outdoor). TV: DStv, DVD in honeymoon suite.

Blackheath Lodge

6 Blackheath Road, Sea Point (021 439 2541/ 076 130 6888/www.blackheathlodge.co.za). **Rates** from R1 450. **Credit** AmEx, DC, MC, V. **Map** p274 E2.

This picturesque Victorian oasis comes complete with breakfast and pool and very, very good prices. Book a room if you can get it, as the picture perfect rooms are few, very stylish, sweetly decadent and a sin to miss.

Bar. Business centre. Concierge. Internet (free shared terminals, free wireless). Parking (free). Pool (1 outdoor, heated, salt water). TV: DStv, DVD.

INSIDE TRACK
BEST BEACH

Cape Town's unofficial gay beach is **Clifton Third** – great for swimming, sunning and ogling eye candy (Victoria Road, Clifton).

Loft Lounge. *See p179.*

Glen Boutique Hotel

3 The Glen, Sea Point (021 439 0086/ www.glenhotel.co.za). **Rates** R1 450-R3 950. **Credit** AmEx, MC, V. **Map** p272 C3.

The Glen is a discreet four-star refuge for the discerning gay traveller, infamous for its pool parties and hunky international guests. Strut your stuff round the sparkling pool or choose from an array of spa facilities ranging from traditional Swedish sauna to Moroccan steam room. A choice of individually styled rooms and suites are trendy and comfortable. Stylish self-catering apartments in nearby Bantry Bay are available too.

Bar. Business centre. Internet (free shared terminals, free wireless). Parking (free). Pool (1 outdoor). Restaurant (breakfast, lunch). Room service. Spa. TV: DStv, DVD depends on room.

Pink Palace Backpackers

136 Main Road, Kalk Bay (021 788 2760). **Rates** *Twin* R150pp. *Double* R175pp. **No credit cards**.

A women-only boutique backpackers' hotel situated in this picturesque False Bay seaside suburb. Besides delightfully pretty (Biggie Best meets Ikea) accommodation it also boasts meeting rooms and therapeutic massages.

Romney Park All Suite Hotel & Spa

Cnr Hill & Romney roads, Green Point (021 439 4555/www.romneypark.co.za). **Rates** R1 490-R3 000. **Credit** AmEx, DC, MC, V. **Map** p274 E2.

Recently redecorated by interior designer Christo Koegelenberg, this self-catering hotel is a firm favourite. The hotel's sexy-meets-colonial-styled bar is set to become a gracious favourite hideaway among locals, while the spa offers everything you need to relax and revive the spirits.

Bar. Business centre. Concierge. Disabled-adapted room. Internet (free shared terminal, free wireless). Parking (R55). Pool (1 outdoor). Restaurant. Room service. Spa. TV: DStv, DVD.

Village Lodge

49 Napier Street, De Waterkant (021 421 1106/ www.thevillagelodge.com). **Rates** R880-R1 900. **Credit** AmEx, DC, MC, V. **Map** p276 G3.

Located on a steep cobbled street in a quaint part of the village, this chic boutique hotel is a convenient and luxurious option from the Village Lodge group. Eleven luxury rooms sport all the trimmings – including air-con – while its four standard rooms offer ceiling fans for those balmy summer evenings. The gorgeous rooftop pool and bar have panoramic views.

Bar. Internet (free wireless). Pool (1 outdoor, rooftop). Restaurant. TV: DStv.

Music

Diversity is the name of the tune in Cape Town.

Music in Cape Town is as diverse as it is vibrant. The inner-city streets buzz with live electronic artists and indie rock scenesters. If you're after classical music, you'll find an abundance of talent and venues, with frequent performances by the reputable Philharmonic Orchestra and big opera productions. African jazz is a Cape Town trademark – some say it's the easygoing lifestyle and attitude of the Capetonians that creates the perfect climate for foot-tapping music – and you'll find live performances in the city every day of the week.

The city is a musical melting pot of Western and African influences, a place where genres get lost, run into one another and cross over at free will. Don't be surprised to find a mixed bag of artists all sharing a stage in the city.

Classical & Opera

Cape Town's opera and classical productions are continually raising the bar, despite a lack of key resources and with no help from the government. For more information, visit www.cpo.org.za and www.capetownopera.co.za.

Tickets & information

For ticket agencies, *see p156*. Check the local weekly newspaper, *Cape Times*, as well as free paper *Next 48hours* to find out what's on.

VENUES

City Bowl

Artscape Theatre Centre
DF Malan Street, Foreshore (021 410 9800/www. artscape.co.za). **Open** *Box office* 9am-5pm Mon-Fri; 9am-12.30pm Sat. *Bookings* Computicket, Dial-a-Seat. **Credit** AmEx, DC, MC, V. **Map** p275 I3.
Staging operas, ballets and other dramas as well as orchestral performance Artscape is one of the best venues for performing arts in South Africa. The fully equipped opera house is the largest in the

About the author
Stefan de Witt *is an entertainment journalist, a musician and a rock 'n' roll aficionado. He persistently lurks in the city's best and worst venues in search of the best live music on offer.*

Western Cape and seats 1,187 people. The lighting, sound and production work is impressive, and considered world class even by most virtuosos. (There's plenty of parking, but it might take you a while to get to your seat. Try to arrive 30mins early.)
► *There's more about Artscape in the Theatre chapter; see p203.*

★ **City Hall**
Darling Street, Grand Parade. **Bookings** Computicket, Dial-a-Seat.
In the east side of the city, and part of an urban renewal development, City Hall has undergone some recent renovations. The Edwardian building, originally built out of sandstone in 1905, is also home to the famous and acclaimed Cape Town Philharmonic Orchestra and hosts various concerts by other regulars. The organ, which was specially designed by Norman Beard, has 3,165 pipes and is second to none in the country. The clarity of the acoustics is particularly impressive (and no amplification is used). The Cape Town Philharmonic Orchestra can be contacted on 021 410 9809 or at www.cpo.org.za.
► *A sight in its own right, City Hall is also covered in the Sightseeing section; see p45.*

St George's Cathedral
5 Wale Street, City Centre (021 424 7360/ www.stgeorgescathedral.com). **Admission** *Mass* free; *Concerts* varies. **Bookings** Computicket or an hour before performance at venue. **No credit cards** at venue. **Map** p274 G4.

This beautiful, richly historic Victorian cathedral opened its doors in 1848 and became known for keeping those doors open to people of all races during apartheid. It boasts a Hill organ that raises the roof at every ceremony, and whether it's a mass or a choral concert, expect crisp, clear pitch.
▶ *To learn more about the cathedral and its work, see p54.*

Southern Suburbs

Baxter Theatre Complex
Main Road, Rondebosch (021 685 7880/021 680 3989/www.baxter.co.za). **Open** *Box office* 9am-start of performance Mon-Sat; or Computicket. **Credit** AmEx, DC, MC, V.
On the University of Cape Town's grounds, the Theatre Complex presents performing arts from diverse cultures, with international classics as well as works by local composers. The three-venue complex has great acoustics. The popular UCT big band also fills in regular slots. If you'd like to know more about an artist currently performing at the Baxter, go to the bookstall in the foyer.
▶ *For more on the Baxter, see p203.*

Outside Cape Town

Endler Hall
Cnr Neethling and Victoria streets, Stellenbosch (021 808 2335/www.sun.ac.za). **Bookings** Computicket or an hour before concert at venue. **Credit** AmEx, DC, MC, V.
Endler Hall is where musical purists gather to enjoy, discuss and ponder a wide variety of classical music, although more and more pop and alternative concerts are slipping in. The annual International

Chamber Music Festival is a highlight during the winter months, and the venue is also known for its world-class Marcussen organ. The University of Stellenbosch's Symphony Orchestra is in residence, but others like the CTPO and the scholastic Hugo Lambrechts orchestra can often be heard as well.

OUTDOOR VENUES

There's something special about seeing and hearing live music without a roof overhead. It's worth driving a few extra kilometres to experience two of the most soothing things in the world – music and the great outdoors – simultaneously.

Kirstenbosch National Botanical Gardens
Rhodes Avenue, Newlands (021 761 2866/ www.sanbi.org). **Bookings** Normal concerts no advance bookings; varies for big concerts. **Credit** AmEx, DC, MC, V.
All kinds of music, from local rock gigs to big-band jazz. Bring a picnic and enjoy the spectacular setting.
▶ *For more about the botanical gardens at Kirstenbosch, see p64.*

Oude Libertas Amphitheatre
Oude Libertas Centre, Adam Tas Road, Stellenbosch, outside Cape Town (021 809 7473/www.oudelibertas.co.za). **Bookings** Computicket or 021 809 7380. **Open** *Box office* 9am-5pm Mon-Fri; 9am-1pm Sat; 1 hour prior to performance. **Credit** MC, V.
This venue hosts an array of performances, from rock and classical music to theatre and ballet.
▶ *For the venue's theatrical activities, see p206.*

City Hall.

Jazz

Cape Town's jazz scene is a crucial part of its heritage. The city's rich jazz tradition stems from artists finding inspiration in their struggles during the apartheid years. Since then, the music has evolved into its own genre, Cape Jazz, a style with a distinct African spice. It's a way of life in the Cape – and you'll find it from the heart of the townships to the most lavish cigar lounge. The number of jazz festivals and venues speaks for itself, and events like the Cape Town International Jazz Festival (*see p186*) and the Jazzathon (*see p186*) draw enthusiasts from all over the world.

Tickets & information

For ticket agencies, *see p156*. Local weekly newspapers *Cape Times* and *Next 48hours* have information on jazz events.

VENUES

City Bowl

Asoka Son of Dharma
68 Kloof Street, Tamboerskloof (021 422 0909/ www.asokabar.co.za). **Open** 5pm-2am daily. **Admission** free. **Credit** AmEx, DC, MC, V.
A warm little lounge, crawling with cool cats and sophisticated types. On Tuesdays, the groups are known to bounce through upbeat sets of '50s and '60s-style jazz with lengthy solos, improvisations on a grab-bag of different instruments and dizzying build-ups.
▶ *It's a good place for a drink too; see p123.*

Marco's African Place
15 Rose Street, Bo-Kaap (021 423 5412/www. marcosafricanplace.co.za). **Open** noon-late Tue-Sat; 3pm-late Sun. **Admission** R15. **Credit** AmEx, DC, MC, V. **Map** p276 G3.

Indie Rock Revival

Our lowdown on the local music scene.

The word on the street is that there is an indie rock 'revival' coursing through Cape Town's blustery veins – but a revival of what, precisely? It's not as if indie rock is a particularly old genre that disappeared and is resurfacing after a long and dusty hiatus out of the limelight. It seems that as long as rock 'n' roll has been mainstream music, so has there also been independent rock that shuns the light of the mass-marketed radio world.

But indie rock in Cape Town has become a genre that is embraced by almost every subculture variant – a brand of music that attracts everyone from the emo girls with asymmetrical hair and impossibly tight jeans to the jock types more typically taken with Jagerbombs and rugby. So what is it that makes it so remarkable?

From the guitar-heavy indie pop sounds of **Eat This, Horse!** – who can be heard at venues like Evol (*see p187*) and Zula Sound Bar (*see p188*) – to the grooving synthesizers of **Unit R**, Capetonian bands span the genre. There doesn't seem to be a specific sound that can be labelled our inimitable sound of Cape Town indie rock.

True, the most popular bands seem to rely heavily upon a beat that their desperately fashion-conscious fans can wriggle and shake to – take the wildly popular **Dirty Skirts** (who headline nearly every rock festival in the region) for example.

All this is a refreshing change from the long years when locals referred exclusively to British and American music as the standard bearers for indie rock. Now, with bands such as **Dirty Skirts**, **Ashtray Electric** (*pictured*), the **Beams** and **New Loud Rockets** frequenting the stage at venues including Obz Café (*see p189*) and Klein Libertas Theatre (*see p189*), Capetonians have their own home-grown representatives from the house of hip making music that is comparable to the hype coming out of the northern hemisphere.

To sample some of Cape Town's finest music, visit the MySpace pages of the bands mentioned above.

The theme and live music are strictly African and thus Marco's is perfect for tourists looking for local kicks. There are shows nearly every night, with popular jazz musicians like Jimmy Dludlu and Sibongile Khumalo. Artists like to get the crowd involved.

▶ *For the food, see p96* **Hello Africa**.

Marimba Restaurant

CTICC, Heerengracht, Foreshore (021 418 3366/www.marimbasa.com). **Open** 6.30pm-late daily. **Admission** free. **Credit** AmEx, DC, MC, V. **Map** p275 I3.

If it's a dose of world music, something more sophisticated or just ambient jazz you need, hop down to this sultry African venue. There's a cool terrace, a good menu, a cigar lounge and, of course, intense marimba playing.

Atlantic Seaboard & V&A Waterfront

Green Dolphin

Victoria & Alfred Arcade, V&A Waterfront (021 421 7471/www.greendolphin.co.za). **Open** 8.15pm-midnight. **Admission** R30-R35. **Credit** AmEx, DC, MC, V. **Map** p275 H1.

Green Dolphin is pledged to the preservation of jazz and thus has arguably the highest jazz standards in the city. It's a fine place to see the big guns from all around the country as well as international stars, as it embodies the purism of the Cape jazz scene.

Winchester Mansions Hotel

221 Beach Road, Sea Point (021 434 2351/ www.winchester.co.za). **Open** 11am-2pm Sun. **Admission** R195. **Credit** AmEx, DC, MC, V. **Map** p273 B2.

Sunday jazz at the Mansions is undoubtedly the perfect way to slow things down after a busy weekend. With the serene courtyard wrapped around the stage, you get front row seats while enjoying a buffet brunch and a glass of champers. The band only adds to the breezy mood – expect a selection of trios, vocalists and even international jazz stars. Locals tend to laze about religiously at the Mansions on Sundays, so be sure to book.

Southern Suburbs

Baxter Theatre

Main Road, Rondebosch (021 685 7880/021 680 3989/www.baxter.co.za). **Open** Box office 9am-start of performances. **Admission** varies. **Credit** AmEx, DC, MC, V.

This institution features University of Cape Town jazz ensembles going all out on stage and playing in an array of styles. It's a major live venue with good acoustics and it plays host to the South African College of Jazz festival around October. Arrive early to find parking.

▶ *For information on its theatre, see p203.*

Swingers

1 Wetton Road, Lansdowne (021 762 2443). **Open** 12.30pm-3am Mon-Fri; noon-4am Sat; 8.30pm-3am Sun. **Admission** R30.
Credit DC, MC, V.

If you're not inclined to nod along with fellow jazz sophisticates but rather are in the mood for a down-and-dirty booty shake-a-thon on the dancefloor, then try Swingers. An electrically energetic venue, its Monday nights are famous for untamed, experimental jazz sessions – as well as 'experimental' behaviour on the dancefloor. This is not a venue for the inhibited.

Festivals

Cape Town International Jazz Fest

CTICC, Heerengracht, Foreshore (021 422 5651/ www.capetownjazzfest.com). **Dates** March/April. **Bookings** Computicket.

This hugely successful annual festival, ranked number four in the world, showcases more than 40 jazz greats, local and international. There are multiple stages catering for different tastes, including a series of community concerts staged free to the public.

Jazzathon

Amphitheatre, V&A Waterfront (021 696 6961/082 450 0079/www.jazzathon.co.za). **Dates** Jan. **Admission** free amphitheatre; varies other venues. **Credit** AmEx, DC, MC, V.

Masses of supporters frequent the various stages to soak up the all-African jazz talents on display here. When you need a break from the crowds, grab a bite to eat at the stalls or walk to one of the exhibitions.

Kirstenbosch Sundowner Concerts

Kirstenbosch Botanical Gardens, Rhodes Avenue, Newlands (021 799 8783/021 761 2866/www.sanbi.org). **Concerts** Summer 5.30pm Sun. **Admission** R50-R70.
Credit AmEx, DC, MC, V.

Whether you're a tourist or not, the Sunday summer concerts are as good as it gets. Pack your picnic and blanket and enjoy the live pop, rock or jazz in the most tranquil of atmospheres. *See also p158.*

Rock

'Rock 'n' roll is dead.' This, unfortunately, is the popular opinion on the once thriving musical genre that set the world on fire. With even iconic clubs like New York's CBGBs closing down, few cities seem able to withstand the trend, although Cape Town is making a better fist of it than most. The locals provide a lively variety of progressive indie rock, with everything from rockabilly to dance-rock

ARTS & ENTERTAINMENT

INSIDE TRACK
SWEET SOUNDS AND SUNSETS

Finding parking for the Kirstenbosch National Botanical Gardens' popular Summer Sunset Concerts (*see p186*) can be a nightmare. One way to enjoy the concerts hassle-free is to pay your entry fee at the gardens around noon, have lunch, walk about and, come dusk, find a spot near the concert lawn where you can listen to the concert at no extra charge.

and, occasionally, the heavier sounds of slash metal beasts. The scene is often very style-focused, which can be a good or a bad thing.

Tickets & information

For ticket agencies, *see p156*. Local weekly newspapers *Cape Times* and *Next 48hours* have information on music events.

VENUES
City Bowl & City Centre

Assembly
61 Harrington Street, District Six (021 465 7286/www.theassembly.co.za). **Open** 9pm-2am Fri, Sat. Check press for events during the week. **Bookings** www.webtickets.co.za/assembly. **Admission** varies. **Credit** MC, V. **Map** p275 I5.
Noise complaints from residents in the area have caused the Assembly to enhance its soundproofing but, to the delight of both musos and their fans, the sound inside the club has also been perked up. This old furniture assembly factory has a spacious hall with a big and a small stage, on which edgy electronica, rock, indie, pop and jazz acts play, among them the country's most popular acts. All in all, one of Cape Town's coolest new vibes.
▶ *For its club, see p189.*

Evol
Hectic on Hope, 69 Hope Street, Gardens (021 465 4918). **Open** 10pm-late Fri. **Admission** R15-R40. **Credit** MC, V. **Map** p276 G5.
If you're looking for a late-night underground party, step inside. The edgiest electronic, indie and punk bands torch the stage every Friday night, usually followed by a dance party of whatever's trendiest with the cool kids. If the crowded dance area gets too much, play a few games of table football in the more relaxed backroom. It's dark inside and not very hygienic. We recommend using the toilets in the bar downstairs.

Jo'burg
218 Long Street, City Centre (021 422 0142/ www.joburgbar.com). **Open** 10am-late Mon-Sat; 6pm-late Sun. **Admission** After 11pm R10 women; R20 men. **Credit** AmEx, DC, MC, V. **Map** p274 G4.
When you're exploring the nightlife on Long Street, be sure to see what's on at this established bar. Expect anything from placid rock to rockabilly at their snug Sunday shows. Most other nights there are DJs playing everything from electro to rock. Be wary of the lurkers and dodgy folk who frequent this area, especially when walking back to your car.
▶ *It's a good bar too; see p124.*

★ Mercury Live & Lounge
43 De Villiers Street, Zonnebloem (021 465 2106/www.mercuryl.co.za). **Open** 8pm-4am Mon, Wed, Fri, Sat. **Admission** R10-R40. **Credit** MC, V. **Map** p275 H5.
The Lounge section downstairs plays host to smaller, more intimate performances; upstairs, Mercury Live stages the biggest rock 'n' roll, indie and punk acts that you'll find in the country. Look out for special events like album and music video launches, battle of the bands and the Super Six Gun Sessions, which serve as a platform for up and coming talent. There are long queues on popular nights, so try to get there early.

Rafiki's
13B Kloof Nek Road, Tamboerskloof (021 426 4731/www.rafikis.co.za). **Open** 8am-late daily. **Admission** Free. **Credit** AmEx, DC, MC, V. **Map** p274 F5.
This hippie bar has been around since 2000 and attracts laid-back twentysomethings as well as visitors from the nearby backpackers' hostel. With acoustic musos doing their thing on a regular basis, Rafiki's (Rafiki means 'friend' in Swahili) is a good place to meet up with your amigos for a chilled vibe.
▶ *For more about Rafiki's, see p125.*

Zula Sound Bar
194 Long Street, City Centre (021 424 2442/ www.zulabar.co.za). **Open** 10am-late daily. **Admission** Varies. **Credit** DC, MC, V. **Map** p274 G4.
This cool inner-city hideout takes you off the buzzing Long Street and into an atmospheric music bar one storey up. Acts range from obscure progressive rock and reggae, to commercial pop and rock. The in-house PA system can crank up enough sound to grab your attention even if you're standing on the balcony, watching what's going on down below. But inside, in the red, dimly lit room, is the best place to soak up the performance. Leave your pretentions at the door, for this is the sort of place where band members mingle with gushy fans and the service ambassadors (aka the waiting staff) are welcoming.

Southern Suburbs

Fogey's Railway House
177 Main Road, Muizenberg (021 788 3252/
www.fogeys.co.za). **Open** 6pm-late Fri; noon-late
Sat, Sun. **Admission** varies. **Credit** AmEx,
DC, MC, V.
The fishing town's carefree attitude is reflected in
the type of live music that's performed here: acoustic
rock and blues. It's a wonderful venue if you're
looking for a combination of seaside ambience
with something a bit downbeat. There's jazz on
Saturday afternoons.

Obz Café
Lower Main Road, Observatory (021 448 5555/
www.obzcafe.co.za). **Open** 7am-late daily.
Admission varies. **Credit** DC, MC, V.
The Obz Café, appropriately set in the heart of the
Observatory, is equipped to put on a show, be it
theatrical or musical, although the stage is tiny. The
crowd consists of students and creatives looking for
something a bit more sophisticated than pub music.

Roar
299 Lower Main Road, Observatory (083 330
0700). **Open** 9pm-4am Tue-Sat. **Admission**
Free Mon-Thur; R20-R40 Fri, Sat (depending on
band). **No credit cards.**
A long set of stairs takes you into a dark and dingy
rock 'n' roll bar that caters to disciples of metal, hard-
core, punk and thrash. Be aware that black is the
official colour to wear – which might come in handy
as it doesn't show dirt and this not the cleanest
venue around. Most artists who play here prefer
substance over style when it comes to their music,
a refreshing change from many of the city's venues.

Roots
Lower Main Road, Observatory (021 448
7656/www.rootsclub.co.za). **Open** noon-4am
Mon-Sat; noon-midnight Sun. **Admission**
Varies. **Credit** MC, V.
This beach bar has the appearance of a tropical
island, making it quite obvious what type of patron
it intends to lure in. Foot-tapping ska, reggae and
rock bands take to the stage on Saturday and
Sunday nights and if it's more of a local flavour
you're after, there's live traditional African music on
Thursdays. Roots is best suited for people leaning
towards the hippie side of laid-back.
► *For more on Roots as a club, see p194.*

Northern Suburbs

Bellville Velodrome
Carl Cronjé Drive, Bellville. **Bookings**
Computicket. **Credit** AmEx, DC, MC, V.
This sports arena opens its doors for international
chart-topping stars who play to thousands of
screaming fans.

Obz Café. See p189.

Corner Bar
Cnr Queens Road and New Street, Durbanville
(021 975 6412/www.cornerbar.co.za).
Admission varies. **Credit** MC, V.
Carrying the torch of the local music industry, this
welcoming venue deep in the suburbs gives up-and-
coming bands across the rock genres a chance to
reach fans hoping to discover something new. The
set-up is intimate, with a good PA and in-house
sound engineer making it worth the drive. There's
an open mic night on Thursdays.

GrandWest Casino
1 Vanguard Drive, Goodwood (021 505 7777/
www.grandwest.co.za). **Open** Times vary.
Admission varies. **Bookings** Computicket.
Since the GrandWest Arena was erected in 2008,
there's been no shortage of huge international acts
wowing audiences here. The Roxy Revue Bar,
while taking a back seat to its younger brother,
has a host of fun theatrical musicals and live concerts on its busy schedule. Make sure you're not
sitting too far back; and if a camp, casino-esque
environment puts you off, this might not be ideal.

Outside Cape Town

Klein Libertas Theatre
Bergzicht Plein, Du Toit Street, Stellenbosch
(021 883 8164/www.kleinlibertasteater.co.za).
Open 7pm until show ends, Mon-Sat.
Admission varies. **No credit cards.**

This community theatre has been around since 1960 and is synonymous with Stellenbosch. The shows are of a high quality and it is the best place to see live music in the student town. Book your meals and tickets beforehand.

Rocking the Daisies
Cloof Wine Estate, Darling (www.rockingthe daisies.com). **Dates** 9-11 Oct. **Admission** R400 full weekend; R330 Sat & Sun. R120 Sun. **No credit cards**.
A young, annual festival, where some of the country's biggest rock, blues, pop and folk bands play alongside lesser-known artists. It has gone from strength to strength with better line-ups every year.

Make sure your camping gear is sorted, pack warm clothes and avoid blow-up mattresses and open shoes as the devil thorns in the area are from hell.

Up the Creek
Near Swellendam on the Breede River (021 510 0547/www.upthecreek.co.za). **Open** February. **Bookings** check website for details.
This festival has come a long way since it started in 1990. But the ethos has remained the same – good music on the riverbank with an eclectic group of people. Big names from all over the country come to rock out at one of the country's best popular music gatherings. Look out for a few Afrikaans rockers on the bill.

Local Beats

Get your groove on with the newest local music talent.

Don't look for penny whistles and bongo drums if you're seeking authentic local sounds. South Africa's unique sounds cover hip hop to jazz and pretty well everything in between. For local-flavour infused hip hop, look no further than **Hip Hop Pantsula** (HHP), who has been taking the country by storm with *motswako*, a genre that involves rapping in English and seTswana over a steady beat. Merging hip hop and African sounds has turned out to be an exceptionally good idea for artists like HHP, Tumi & the Volume and Zeus – they're being flown all over the world and are gaining a massive following at home.

For an interesting twist on hip hop, Waddy Jones's latest outfit, **Die Antwoord** (Afrikaans for 'The Answer'), are ones to watch. Waddy – who made his mark with Max Normal – is one of SA's quirkiest talents, with a seemingly bottomless creative well.

Afro-soul also has a slew of new artists. **Chad Saaiman**, **Lloyd Jansen** and **Byron Clarke** perform under the Stereotype Records banner. Jansen's debut single, 'Call Off the Search' and Clarke's 'In the Grey' spent time on local charts. And Saaiman, an *Idol* alumni, has performed as supporting act for international reggae star Eddie Grant.

In that vein, take a listen to Khayelitsha's **Nomfusi Gotyana**, who fuses traditional African jazz, gospel, R&B and a '60s Motown sound. She has performed at some high-profile events but also does the rounds at more intimate gigs around the city.

Cape jazz, whose iconic representatives include **Abdullah Ibrahim** and **Mac**

McKenzie, is home-grown and hot – *goema* influences (which can be traced back to Cape Malay rhythms and instruments) interact in jovial harmony with American jazz and bebop.

There are two excellent music shops, specialising in rare and second-hand records: the **African Music Store** (134 Long Street, 021 426 0857) or **Mabu Vinyl** (2 Ede Street, Gardens, 021 423 7635).

Nightlife

Get your groove on at these killer clubs.

The Mother City is a fickle woman, and her children are notorious for spreading their favours widely. Having said that, there are plenty of established clubs that have earned their stripes and their popularity. They'll be supplemented by plenty more opening in time to take advantage of the summer season.

Music styles and geography still divide Cape Town clubs more or less down racial lines, but unless you're heading down to the dodgy end of Loop Street towards the harbour (don't), skin colour isn't going to make a bit of difference.

TIMES & PLACES

Capetonians love their nightlife and boogie until 4am, but no later, as the law says bars have to close then, and switch off their music. But before the big switch off, you'll have the chance to hear R&B and hip hop, all kinds of house, rock, pop, commercial, alternative, drum 'n' bass and more. The best way to find out what is going on is to go Mr Pickwick's at no.158 Long Street, where you can suck down a decadent milkshake and pick up the latest party flyers.

There's a thriving psychedelic trance scene and in summer outdoor parties are held every weekend. The biggest and best are the New Year's Eve and Easter Vortex parties (www.vortexsa.co.za), but there's also Alien Safari (www.aliensafari.net) and the global Earthdance (www.earthdance.org.za) in September, which always signals the beginning of summer for trance bunnies. Most parties happen at beautiful venues within two hours' drive of the city centre but there are also regular trance nights at clubs in town.

Besides normal club nights, there are lots of special events, especially during summer when you can expect to find big-name DJs playing alongside Cape Town's finest on the decks. Again, Long Street is a good place to trawl for

About the author
Bianca Coleman was nightclub and dance music columnist at the Cape Argus *for six years, and now writes lifestyle features and DJ profiles on a freelance basis.*

information via the all-important word of mouth. Alternatively, check out the internet for Facebook groups.

Best tip: always, always take sunglasses. The sun comes up early in December and you'll be the envy of all your buddies if you have a big pair of shades to hide behind.

CITY BOWL

★ Assembly
61 Harrington Street, District Six (021 465 7286/ www.theassembly.co.za). **Open** 9pm-2am Fri, Sat. Check press for events. **Bookings** www.webtickets.co.za/assembly. **Admission** Varies. **Credit** MC, V. **Map** p276 H4.
A huge warehouse-style venue, the Assembly is the product of a bunch of young guys' passion for music and dedication to putting the best local and international musicians (live bands and DJs) under one roof. Eclectic is the key word – indie, punk, rock, jazz, ska, blues, electronica and even comedy have made their way across the stage. The bar is massive and there's a very convenient in-house tab/card system to allow ease of drinking.
► *See also p187.*

INSIDE TRACK
MIDNIGHT MUNCHIES

Long Street's late-night **falafel and schwarma stall** (outside Miam Miam) is famous among clubbers for satisfying those 2am cravings.

Assembly. See p189.

Bang Bang Club

70 Loop Street, City Centre (021 426 2011/ www.thebangbangclub.co.za). **Open** 10pm-4am Wed-Sat. **Admission** R40 women; R60 men; Wed R30 all. **Credit** AmEx, DC, MC, V. **Map** p276 G4.

One of the most popular clubs in the city centre, BBC regularly hosts international DJs as well as the polished South African deck veterans who play accessible deep, sexy house for an up-for-it crowd. The place gets absolutely rammed on weekends; you'll fit in if you wear white pointy shoes with no laces and gel your hair (guys) or minuscule skirts and impossibly high heels (girls). It's hot and it's cool, all at the same time. In the middle of all this sleek chic comes PsynOpticz, a rocking trance night on the first and third Thursdays of the month.

Chrome

6 Pepper Street, City Centre (083 700 6078/9/ www.chromect.com). **Open** 9pm-4am Wed; 10pm-4am Thur-Sun in season. **Admission** R50 Wed, Thur; R60 Fri, Sat. **Credit** MC, V. **Map** p276 G4.

Chrome has a big main dancefloor and club area, moodily lit in red with lots of mirrors, and a separate VIP area. Most Wanted on Friday nights is hosted by the founders of one of the longest-running and most popular club nights, Deep Heet (look out for one happening around town), with DJs playing strictly house music – the good kind. Elsewhere in the club you'll hear lots of R&B and hip hop, while on Saturdays they play a different genre every hour.

► *There's an ATM located inside the club.*

DecoDance Underground

Old Biscuit Mill, 375 Albert Road, Salt River (084 330 1162/www.decodance.co.za). **Open** 8.30pm-2am Wed; 8.30pm-4am Fri, Sat. **Admission** R30 before 10pm. **No credit cards**.

Head here for the music you forgot to remember, from The Cure and The Clash to Metallica, Nine Inch Nails and Nirvana. The black and white checked dancefloor is a classic and on it you'll dance the night away to the best of 1980s and '90s alternative rock. Resident DJ Rokka is happy to take requests over weekends. Wednesday nights are currently classic movie nights followed by guest DJs playing alternative, metal and goth.

► *There are two bars, clean toilets, an ATM right outside the front door and plenty of secure parking.*

Deluxe

Cnr Long & Longmarket streets, City Centre (021 422 4832). **Open** 10pm-4am Fri, Sat. **Admission** R50. **Credit** DC, MC, V. **Map** p276 G4.

The last true bastion of deep house, with a smattering of funk and soul, Deluxe is comfortable, intimate and unpretentious – but that doesn't mean it isn't chic. The decor is minimalist but a row of bass bins means the sound isn't. Friendly bar staff, the absolute finest in deep, progressive, tech or minimal house, and a separate lounge area off the dancefloor make this a firm favourite, delivering everything you need for a good night out.

Fashion TV Café

114 Hout Street, City Centre (021 426 6000). **Open** 8pm-4am Wed, Fri, Sat. **Admission** R50-R100. **Credit** DC, MC, V. **Map** p276 G3.

The name should tell you everything you need to know. It's about the bodies beautiful and the clothes draped strategically over them. See and be seen while sipping champagne or cocktails, and venture on to the dancefloor for the ubiquitous R&B and hip hop mixed with commercial house.

► *The hair straightening iron in the ladies' loo is fabulous.*

Fiction DJ Bar & Lounge

226 Long Street, City Centre (021 424 5709/ www.fictionbar.com). **Open** 9pm-4am Tue-Sat. **Admission** Varies. **Credit** MC, V. **Map** p276 G4.

Totally funky and cool, this place has a large wraparound balcony from which you can watch the insanity and mayhem in Long Street below. Fiction has something different every night, beginning with Untamed Youth on Tuesdays (indie, rock, pop, and electro). Wednesdays are 3000AD, a collaboration with African Dope, with DJ sets and live electronic acts spanning the genres, while Thursday takes it down a few BPM for It Came From the Jungle drum 'n' bass. Killer Robot on Fridays is an absolute must for fans of the minimal electro sound that is incredibly dancefloor-friendly. Saturdays are open to anything. Get your drinks from one of two bars, but expect long queues at the unisex toilets.

★ Hemisphere

31st Floor, Absa Building, 2 Riebeek Street, City Centre (021 421 0581/www.hemisphere.org.za). **Open** 9pm-late Thur; 4.30pm-late Fri; 10pm-late Sat. **Admission** R50 women; R70 men. **Credit** AmEx, DC, MC, V. **Map** p275 H3.

There is something incredibly special about partying the night away so high in the sky. Hand over the car keys to the valet parking attendants and be whisked up 31 floors in the elevator to the most magnificent 180 degree view in the city centre. Go early for sundowners and sip a cocktail as the sun slips behind Lion's Head and the city begins to sparkle. The music is mainstream, with a blend of '70s to '90s retro, a big dose of R&B and commercial house. Glam it up and don't wear T-shirts or trainers, and the party line is no under-25s.

Liquid

84 Sir Lowry Road, Woodstock (021 461 9649/ www.liquidonline.co.za). **Open** 9pm-4am Fri, Sat. **Admission** R40-R60. **No credit cards**. **Map** p275 J4.

This is another one of those legends, albeit under a new name. Hard dance fans will fondly recall the Gallery back in those days before the 4am liquor licence laws curbed our partying. Now it's called Liquid but the music remains the same – hard, harder, hardest, and it attracts names like Lisa Lashes, Anne Savage, Cosmic Gate, Armin van Buren and more. The place is massive, with four bars and three dancefloors over two levels. Killer sound, intelligent lighting and big-screen projections add to the experience.

INSIDE TRACK
SEXY SALSA

Que Pasa, Cape Town's only salsa club, has reopened its doors below Diaz Tavern in Caledon Street (15 Caledon Street, City Centre, 083 556 7466, www.quepasa.co.za).

Vertigo

96 Long Street, City Centre (072 323 7621/ www.clubtonic.co.za). **Open** 10pm-4am Fri, Sat & Wed-Sat in season. **Admission** R40-R50. **No credit cards**. **Map** p276 G4.

It's all about the young, sexy, stylish crowd here. The dress code is 'to the nines' and it's strictly observed. Don't bother trying your luck at the door if you're not wearing a shirt with a collar. It's a big venue with huge mirrors to admire your moves on the dancefloor as you shake what mamma gave you to music that is predominantly R&B and hip hop, with a bit of house.

ATLANTIC SEABOARD

Bambu

21B Somerset Road, Green Point (021 421 4660/ www.bambu.co.za). **Open** 10pm-4am Wed-Sat. **Admission** R60. **Credit** AmEx, DC, MC, V. **Map** p275 F2.

Green Point and De Waterkant are predominantly pink but there are plenty of clubs and bars that are straight-friendly, and this is one of them. There are two bars, one for VIPs where there are comfy upholstered booths for private conversations, and the other for the mere mortals. There's lots of dark

ARTS & ENTERTAINMENT

Fiction DJ Bar & Lounge.

wood evoking the oriental feeling that is intended, complemented with opulent fabrics and textures like silk and leather. With model parties and clothing label launches you can pin the crowd down as young and fashionable with a taste for the good things in life.

Karma Lounge

3rd Floor Penthouse Suite, Victoria Road, Camps Bay (021 438 7773/www.karmalounge.co.za). **Open** 9pm-2am Wed-Sun. **Admission** R50 women; R100 men. **Credit** AmEx, DC, MC, V. **Map** p273 A8.

Camps Bay and Clifton beaches are indisputably the places to head to during the day, and by night you can take that sun-kissed feeling with you to one of the newer additions to Cape Town's nightlife scene and the only place of its kind in Camps Bay. It's stylish and upmarket and glitzy and will take you from early sundowners and sushi through till stronger tipples in the wee hours, with DJs playing sexy soulful dirty beats. Lounge in the beach bar or get intimate in the Moët & Chandon champagne bar. There's officially a 21 for men/23 for women age restriction, but whether it's strictly enforced or not is another story.

SOUTHERN SUBURBS

@mospheer

Cnr Castor & Pollux roads, Lansdowne (021 797 3108/www.atmospheer.com). **Open** 9.30pm-4am Fri, Sat. **Admission** R10 Fri; R25 Sat. **Credit** AmEx, DC, MC, V.

Clubbing in the 'burbs is somewhat different. It's all about bigger, better, brighter with all the bells and whistles and drinks specials you can handle. This place hosts some of the biggest names in the business on the decks, like Paul van Dyk for example, and it's been the after-party venue of choice for Snoop Dogg and Kanye West. This is about dressing up, making an effort and putting everything you have into the party.

Barmooda

Cnr Lower Main & Station roads, Observatory (021 447 6752/www.barmooda.co.za). **Open** 9pm-4am Fri, Sat. **Admission** R20-R40. **Credit** AmEx, DC, MC, V.

The restaurant is open in the day for pizzas and what-not but things kick up a gear or five after the dinner crowd have done their thing. There's a relaxed loungey feel that can seem a bit out of sorts with the high-energy beats from the DJs. Weekends are party-harder but look out for live bands on Thursdays and famous – and infamous – street parties.

Galaxy/West End

College Road, Rylands (021 637 9132/www.superclubs.co.za). **Open** 9pm-late Thur, Fri; 4pm-late Sat. **Admission** R50. **Credit** AmEx, DC, MC, V.

This is the longest-running club in the greater Cape Town area. A dual venue combining contemporary fusion club West End and the mainstream Galaxy, they have been going strong for 15 and 30 years respectively. The bigger and better rule applies with no less than four dancefloors and – count 'em – nine speed bars. Make it an entire night out with a meal followed by cigars and champagne in the VIP section. Thursday nights are off the wall, and there are regular sundowner sessions on a Friday.

Gandalf's

299 Lower Main Road, Observatory (083 330 0700/www.gandalfs.co.za). **Open** 9pm-4am Tue-Sat. **Admission** R10 women, R40 men Thur. R10 all Sat. Free Tue, Wed, Fri. **No credit cards**.

This medieval fantasy/*Lord of the Rings*-themed venue is the portal to neighbouring Gotham and ROAR live music venue upstairs. Gotham is where the coffin kids hang out – those gorgeous creatures of the night with the luminously pale skin, black-rimmed eyes and tight, studded PVC and leather gear. Every Friday Reanimator plays alternative indie-rock, with other nights dedicated to EBM and/or industrial goth complete with smoke machines and strobe lights. Gandalf's itself is slightly tamer and more middle of the road.

Mojo

96 Station Road, Observatory (021 424 0408/072 147 1224). **Open** 5pm-4am daily. **Admission** free-R30. **Credit** MC, V.

Mojo is a cute little bar/lounge where you can sit inside or on the deck with a cocktail and enjoy everything from Cardigan Buzz – a band that is kind of a mix between Jack Johnson and Michael Bublé with covers and original jazz and swing – to old-school '80s, hip hop, R&B and house every Friday. Organica, on the first Saturday of every month, is progressive trance for the discerning clubber who gags at the sound of commercial dance music.

Take a Trance on Me

Get back to Mother Nature just outside the Mother City.

In an ever-moving and constantly changing city that revolves around leisure and entertainment, a club that manages two years is considered to be lasting well. You'll be hard pressed to find a Capetonian who still frequents the same haunts they did a few years ago, either because they no longer exist or they've fallen out of favour. But one scene that has not only remained fairly constant but has actually grown and thrived for more than a decade is trance, emerging from the warehouse rave scene in the mid-1990s.

Once firmly rooted in the underground, trance parties have blossomed into the mainstream, with the events getting bigger and better. While there are clubs in the city centre and in the suburbs that provide regular weeknight trance events, followers live for the outdoor summer season. One or two brave organisers might put on a party in early September when the weather starts to warm up, but the party that always unofficially heralds the start of summer is **Earthdance** (www.earthdance.org.za).

Just one of a series of global events uniting more than 50 countries at well over 300 locations, Earthdance is a highlight on the trance calendar. What follows is at least seven months of regular outdoor events – virtually every weekend – at some of the most beautiful farms, orchards, valleys, rivers and dams in the Western Cape.

Some are closer to the centre of town than others, but they're usually no more than two or three hours' drive away. There are two ends of the spectrum when approaching how you attend a trance party: you could be lucky enough to be part of a group that takes its camping seriously and end up in a campsite with all the comforts of home, or you can take off with just the clothes on your back. Either way, make sure you take enough money to keep yourself fed and watered throughout the weekend; there are always bars and food stalls. Also, make sure you keep back a few rand for the tollgate if your party is on the other side of the Huguenot Tunnel on the N1.

For the better organised trance bunny, the checklist will include sunglasses (an absolute essential for those legendary stomping sunrise sets on a Sunday morning…), sunblock, and – especially for girls – toilet paper. If there's one downside to an outdoor trance party, it has to be the porta-loos, which are notoriously grim. Having your own toilet paper makes it that much more bearable.

Whether it's for the full weekend or just a day trip, it's also wise to pack ice, ice and more ice, a cooler box, bubbly, hat, cigarettes, lighter, folding chairs, comfortable slip-off shoes, a raincoat, money and a friend.

Alien Safari (www.aliensafari.net) and **Vortex** (www.vortexsa.co.za) are the two best-known and established trance organisers, but there are many more. Some punters prefer the smaller, less commercial events. Whatever your choice, you can expect mind-bending decor and lighting, and top-notch sound systems.

South African trance and trance DJs are ranked among the best in the world. Look out for names like Protoculture, Slug, Twisted System, and Lost & Found, or log on to some of these websites for more information: www.3am.co.za, www.bomelakiesie.co.za, www.bpmmag.co.za and www.callapizza.co.za.

ARTS & ENTERTAINMENT

Roots

Lower Main Road, Observatory (021 448 7656/
www.rootsclub.co.za). **Open** noon-4am daily.
Admission R20-R40 Wed, Fri, Sat. Free Mon,
Tue, Thur, Sun. **Credit** MC, V.
The Caribbean-style venue has its own beach where
you can bring and *braai* (barbecue) on Sunday afternoons. Mondays are student nights, so you have been
warned. Organik (not to be confused with Organica
at Mojo) is the wildly popular Wednesday trance
night; how anyone manages to dance in that crowd
is a mystery. Thursdays are given over to reggae and
dancehall, while live bands play on Friday.
▶ *Get in early for daily happy hours and delicious*
pizza specials.

Tiger Tiger

Stadium on Main, 103 Main Road, Claremont
(021 683 2220/www.tigertiger.co.za). **Open**
8pm-4am Tue, Thur; 8.30pm-4am Fri, Sat.
Admission R20-R40 Tue, Thur; R40-R50
Fri, Sat. **Credit** MC, V.
The heart of the southern suburbs makes this the
destination of choice for students, who are well
catered for on week nights with masses of drinks
specials. These continue into the weekend with two-
for-one cocktail specials and selected drinks on
Fridays and Saturdays respectively. This one has
six bars to keep the punters watered, and the spacious dancefloor has seen the likes of Graeme Smith
and Robbie Fleck. The sports stars also like the
southern suburbs, which may or may not have anything to do with the proximity of Newlands rugby
and cricket grounds.

Wadda

14 Stegman Road, Claremont (021 683 7700/
084 505 1524/www.wadda.co.za).

Tiger Tiger

Open 9pm-4am Mon, Wed, Fri, Sat.
Admission free-R40. **Credit** MC, V.
Another suburban superclub with three bars, huge
dancefloor and a top-notch VIP room all spread over
two floors. The DJ line-up is diverse and impressive,
with the likes of Dino Moran, Roger Goode, Dean
FUEL, Lady Lea and 5FM's Gareth Cliff all making
appearances here. There are always, but always,
plenty of drinks specials to ensure you get completely plastered for as little as possible. Don't leave
home without the telephone numbers of at least two
or three reliable taxi companies.

NORTHERN SUBURBS

Ku De Ta

1st Floor, 112 Bloemhof Building, Edward
Street, Tyger Valley (021 910 2002/www.ku-
de-ta.co.za). **Open** 8pm-2am Wed; 8pm-4am
Thur; 9pm-4am Fri, Sat. **Admission** R30.
Credit DC, MC, V.
Put your bluffing skills to the test on poker nights
on Wednesdays, or prepare for a raucous all-nighter
on Thursdays with live music and battles of the
bands events which are enormously popular with
fans of home-grown musical talent. Over the weekends the music is R&B, hip hop and commercial
house till midnight, before the electro and dirty
house takes over. It's a smart club with comfy couches
to take a load off, a bit on the yuppie side but the VIP
area is funky. The club attracts all ages and sizes,
although there is a strict no under-23 policy.

Vacca Matta

100 Manhattan Piazza, Edward Street, Tyger
Valley (021 910 1855/www.vacca-matta.co.za).
Open 7pm-4am Thur-Sat. **Admission** R30 after
10pm. **Credit** MC, V.
Like Somerset Road in Green Point, and Long Street
in the City Bowl, the deep north has its own strip
and Edward Street is it. Vacca Matta has four
lounges, two dancefloors and amazing bar ladies
strutting their stuff on the bar counter à la *Coyote*
Ugly, suggestively sexy silhouette dancers, and host-
esses to make your every dream a reality. The music
is R&B, hip hop and electro house, with DJs like
Theo, Snake and Kingsize on the decks from 10pm
to help you bring sexy back.

Sport & Fitness

Dramatic mountains, miles of coastline and sports-mad locals.

With those long, hot summers, and mild, warm springs and autumns, combined with mountains, seas, forests, rivers and waterways, Cape Town seems purpose-built for people with healthy, active lifestyles. Most locals are (or want to be) active in some kind of sport – whether that be a semi-regular game of Ultimate Frisbee, a regular jog around the block, or an entirely irregular date with a mountain-biking trail. And while Cape Town's range of spectator sports is pretty limited, its field of active sports is much, much broader.

Before you hit the waves or gear up for the mountains, here's a slice of local knowledge: the prevailing south-easterly wind (locals call it the 'Cape Doctor') can make conditions on the eastern side of the Table Mountain chain quite unpleasant in the summer, but it works the other way round in winter. So if you're planning a wind-free run or cycle in summer, stick to the Atlantic Seaboard; in winter, keep to the False Bay side.

SPECTATOR SPORTS

South African spectator sport – and its accompanying water-cooler conversation – is all about the Big Three: football (called 'soccer'), rugby union (called 'rugby') and cricket (called 'cricket'). Some sports, like athletics and motor racing, do have a minor following, but disciplines like cycling and road running are – despite Cape Town's hosting of the annual Cycle Tour and Two Oceans Marathon (*see p196* **Sports Events**) – primarily considered participation sports. Boxing and tennis are virtually non-events in the Cape.

What this means for the visiting or neutral supporter is that rugby union – historically an 'Afrikaner sport' – still attracts mainly white and/or Afrikaans-speaking fans; cricket –

historically an 'Englishman's sport' – still pulls in predominantly white and/or English-speaking crowds; and soccer is… well, don't expect to see too many white faces at a local soccer match.

Don't let any of this put you off, though: as South African society becomes more and more multiracial, so does its sport – and the demographics described above are becoming increasingly integrated.

Tickets for all major games are available through Computicket (083 915 8000, www.computicket.com). But be warned: Cape sports fans (and don't tell them we told you this!) are notoriously fickle, so if the home team's losing, expect the stadium to empty out before the final whistle as 'fans' try to avoid the post-match traffic.

Athletics

South African track and field athletes are always there or thereabouts at big events like the All-Africa or Commonwealth Games, and local events – though not as well attended as those involving the Big Three – showcase the best of the local talent. Meets happen either at Coetzenburg in Stellenbosch or at the Belleville Velodrome's athletics track. **Athletics South Africa** (011 880 5800, www.athletics.org.za)

**INSIDE TRACK
KITE BEACH**

'Kite beach' (as locals call it) in Blouberg (*see p76*) is world famous among kite surfers, and each year the world's bests flock to the tiny beach to practise during the European winter (Otto du Plessis Drive, Blouberg).

Sports Events

Get in on the action with these Cape Town calendar staples.

Cape Town is seventh heaven for sports addicts, offering an array of outdoorsy activities such as hikes, marathons and cycle races to get the adrenaline pumping. Sluggish souls intent on avoiding elevated heart rates needn't be excluded from the sporty fun, and can get in on the action at the wide variety of spectator events.

SPRING
Crazy Store Table Mountain Challenge

Table Mountain, Tafelberg Road (021 424 4760/www.crazystore.co.za). **Date** Mid Sept. Yes, the zany store that sells everything from plastic roses to hula-hoops and nail clippers also sponsors a 35km run around Table Mountain. You can run the fynbos-bedazzled circuit on your own or split up the slog between your mates into somewhat more manageable 17km snatches.

Discovery Cape Times Big Walk

Various locations in Cape Peninsula (021 685 3333/www.bigwalk.co.za). **Date** 9 Nov. Put on your walking shoes and work those calves for charity (all proceeds are donated to a selected organisation). The Big Walk is made up of eight different routes starting at Mowbray. Timorous trundlers can opt for

the 5km or 10km walks, while the fighting fit will get their lion's share of cardio from the double-digit routes.

SUMMER
L'Ormarins Queen's Plate

Kenilworth Race Course, Rosmead Avenue (021 700 1600/www.lqp.co.za). **Date** Early Jan. Horsing around takes on a distinctly classy air at this annual racing event. Already in its 148th year, the Queen's Plate (in honour of Her Royal Majesty, Queen Elizabeth II, naturally) will see Kenilworth racecourse transformed into an arena of haute couture, vintage cars, fine wine and gleaming thoroughbred fillies ready to tear up the track.

J&B Metropolitan Handicap

Kenilworth Race Course, Rosmead Avenue (021 426 5775/www.jbmet.co.za). **Date** End Jan/Beginning Feb. Fancy takes on a whole new meaning at this swish equestrian extravaganza. Primped and preened lads and ladies get kitted out in their theme-appropriate best, sip champagne, pose for the social pages, and of course watch the feisty fillies kick up clumps of grass all along the ten furlongs of the Kenilworth Racecourse.

organise the competitions, so consult its website to see when the next event's happening.

Cricket

Sahara Park Newlands sees plenty of cricket through the year. The Cape Cobras compete in the domestic Pro20 Series (usually Mar-Apr), the 45-over MTN Domestic Championship (usually Feb-Mar) and the first-class (four-day) SuperSport Series (usually Oct-Jan). Contact the Western Province Cricket Association (146 Camp Ground Road, Newlands; 021 657 2003/www.capecobras.co.za) for information.

Sahara Park Newlands Cricket Ground

146 Campground Road, Newlands (021 657 2003/www.capecobras.co.za).

Football

With the new Green Point Stadium still under construction, Cape Town did not host any games in the 2009 FIFA Confederations Cup

(a World Cup dress rehearsal), but there are games involving local sides Santos FC (www.santosfc.co.za) and Ajax Cape Town (www.ajaxct.com) virtually all year round at **Athlone Stadium**.

South Africa will be the focus of world attention when it hosts the 2010 World Cup. For more on the competition and Green Point Stadium, where matches will be played, *see p60* **Fever Pitch**.

Athlone Stadium

Cross Boulevard, Athlone (021 637 6607/www.athlonestadium.co.za).

Motor racing

There's a universal appeal to watching racing cars compete (and occasionally crash) at high speeds, and while Cape Town's motor racing scene isn't hugely well supported, there are still a range of races – from karts to stock cars – at the **Killarney Motor Racing Complex** (021 557 1639, www.killarney.co.za).

Old Mutual Two Oceans Marathon

ARTS & ENTERTAINMENT

AUTUMN

Cape Argus Cycle Tour

Cape Peninsula (www.cycletour.co.za).
Date Early March.
Each year over 40,000 keen cyclists from hither and thither converge to partake in this epic 109km pedal. The scenic circular route starts in the City Centre, and snakes its way through the Southern Peninsula and past the Atlantic Coast before coming to an end in Green Point.

Old Mutual Two Oceans Marathon

Newlands (021 671 9407/www.twooceans marathon.co.za).
Date Sat, Easter weekend.
Every Easter Weekend dedicated joggers slog it out in the 56km ultra marathon, which starts in Newlands and winds its way along the bends of the picturesque Chapman's Peak Drive before ending at the UCT campus. The more timid athletes trot the equally popular 21km half marathon route following the length of Southern Cross Drive.

WINTER

Knysna Marathon

Knysna Forest, N2, Knysna, outside Cape Town (www.knysnamarathon.org.za).
Date Mid July.
Mollusc maniacs can work off their over-indulgence during this beautiful marathon which is part of the Knysna Oyster Festival. The trail winds its way through the majestic Knysna Forest, and there is a 21km half and 42km full marathon, so both the fiddling fit and leisurely lopers will be able to see the woods for the trees.

Rugby Union

Rugby Union is avidly supported in South Africa. Cape Town heroes Western Province and the Stormers play their home games at the historic Newlands Rugby Stadium, with the main local rugby union competitions being the Super 14 (the Stormers against regional franchises from South Africa, New Zealand and Australia) and the Absa Currie Cup (Western Province and the Wellington-based Boland Kavaliers against other South African provincial sides).

If Test match ticket prices (more than R300, depending on the opponents) scare you off, that doesn't mean you've missed your chance to watch some good rugby Union. Cape Town's fine rugby schools – including Bishops, Rondebosch, Wynberg, Paarl Gym, Paarl Boys, Paul Roos – take each other on in the very well-attended schoolboy clashes, or see if you can catch an Ikeys vs Maties (University of Cape Town vs University of Stellenbosch) game.

Newlands Rugby Stadium

8 Boundary Road, Newlands (021 659 4600/ www.iamastormer.com).
▶ *See p65 for for Newlands Rugby Stadium and the South African Rugby Museum.*

PARTICIPATION SPORTS

Abseiling

If you fancy following a rope 112 metres down Table Mountain (and we'd recommend it as the world's highest commercial abseil even without views), then **Abseil Africa** (297 Long Street, 1 Vredenburg Lane; 021 424 4760, www.abseilafrica.co.za) is your best bet. There's regular abseiling or – for the brave – face-first rap-jumping.

Airborne

If you didn't get a window seat on your flight into Cape Town (or if you just fancy a different view), there are few better ways of

Sahara Park Newlands Cricket Ground. *See p196.*

seeing the Fairest Cape than by dangling from a parachute a few hundred feet above the ground. Skydiving options (either 45 minutes out of town up the West Coast, or four hours out of town in Ceres) range from full courses (from zero to Static Line or Accelerated Freefall) to quickie tandem jumps with a qualified expert. Paragliding, meanwhile, tends to take place from the upper slopes of Lion's Head, with dramatic views over the Atlantic Seaboard before you land, breathlessly, at Camps Bay. There are a number of companies offering paragliding courses, including **Birdmen Paragliding** (36 Champagne Way, Table View, 082 658 6710, www.birdmen.co.za), **Skydive Cape Town** (R27 West Coast Road, Melkbosstrand, 082 800 6290, www.skydivecapetown.za.net), **Skydive Robertson/Ceres** (Robertson Flying Club, Robertson, 083 462 5666, www.skydive.co.za) and **Wallend-Air School of Paragliding** (368 Main Road, Wynberg, 021 762 2441, www.wallendair.com).

Angling

Cape Town is, at heart, one big fishing village: many locals do (or used to) make their living from fishing, and many are amateur catch-and-releasers or catch-and-call-your-friends-around-for-a-fish-*braai*-ers. If you're not planning on hiring a boat and hauling in some big 'uns, try casting a line off the Kalk Bay harbour wall. Remember, though, that some of the beaches and rocky shores around the city fall within the Table Mountain National Park, so you'll not be allowed to fish in some areas, and you'll need a permit to fish in others. Permits are available from most local post offices. Remember, too, that if you're an out-of-towner you'll have to learn the names of the local fishes – so while you're out there waiting for tight lines, practise getting your tongue around *snoek*, *galjoen*, *kreef* (crayfish) and the like. If you want to try some serious sea fishing, contact **Hooked on Africa** (Hout Bay Harbour, 021 790 5332, www.hookedonafrica.co.za).

Climbing

While the mountains outside Montagu and Oudtshoorn in the Klein-Karoo deservedly get all the hype, there is (you may have noticed) a pretty decent mountain in Cape Town itself as well. You'll find climbing bolts in various spots around the mountain – some even as far south as the mountains above Noordhoek. Beginners and out-of-towners should be warned that the temperature at the top of Table Mountain is sometimes several degrees colder than at the bottom, and the mountain's

INSIDE TRACK
RUNNING AGAINST GRAVITY

CRAG (Cape Runners Against Gravity) is a fraternity of runners who prefer mountain, beach and forest paths to tarred roads. They host 90-minute runs every Wednesday at 5.30pm and longer runs on weekends. Anyone can join in the fun; route descriptions can be found on their website (021 507 6327, www.crag.org.za).

famous 'tablecloth' cloud cover has been known to make hikers and climbers lose their way.

To help you get into climbing shape, there's **CityROCK Indoor Climbing Centre** (21 Anson Road, Observatory, 021 447 1326, www.cityrock.co.za), and the **Mountain Club of South Africa** (97 Hatfield Street, Gardens; 021 465 3412/www.mcsa.org.za) has more information on local climbs.

▶ *The Cederberg in the West Coast and Montagu in the Winelands are favourite climbing haunts.*

Cycling

The Cape hosts three major international cycling events – the **Giro del Capo** (March, www.girodelcapo.co.za), **Cape Epic** (March, www.cape-epic.com) and **Cape Argus Cycle Tour** (*see p197* **Sports Events**) – and the city's roads are perpetually punctuated with amateurs in between. Many locals practise on weekend mornings on Main Road between Muizenberg and Simon's Town, raising the ire of motorists (the road is narrow and potholed at the best of times) as they weave between the roadworks. Other popular routes include the tarred back roads outside Durbanville (try Vissershok Road for some calf-burning climbing), while Chapmans Peak Drive has the advantage of being a toll road for motorists and a very scenic route for cyclists. For information on other cycling events in and around Cape Town, consult www.bicycling.co.za.

Golf

Between the fine weather, the open spaces and the proud heritage of top PGA Tour pros (Player, Els, Goosen, Immelman), South Africa in general,

Abseil Africa. *See p197*.

and Cape Town in particular, has a wealth of golf courses. The best of those include **Clovelly Country Club** (Clovelly Road, Clovelly, 021 784 2111, www.clovelly.co.za); **Mowbray Golf Club** (Raapenberg Road, Mowbray, 021 685 3018, www.mowbraygolfclub.co.za); and the **Royal Cape GC** (174 Ottery Road, Wynberg, 021 761 6551, www.royalcapegolf.co.za). Further afield you'll find **Pearl Valley Signature Golf Estate** (Wemmershoek R301, between Franschhoek and Paarl, 021 867 8000, www.pearlvalley.co.za); **Arabella GC** (R44, Kleinmond, 028 284 0105, www.arabella.co.za); **Fancourt** (044 804 0030, www.fancourt.co.za); and **George GC** (044 873 6116, www.georgegolfclub.co.za). Green fees can be pricey, but caddies are fairly cheap. If you're just looking to swing a few clubs around, then hit the driving range at the **River Club** (cnr Liesbeeck Parkway and Observatory Road, Observatory, 021 448 6117, www.riverclub.co.za).

Fitness centres

When the weather turns sour, keep-fit Capetonians head indoors to any number of local gyms – the **Virgin Active** (021 684 3000, www.virginactive.co.za) and **Planet Fitness** (www.planetfitness.co.za) chains being the most popular. South Africa's **Sports Science Institute** (021 659 5600,

www.ssisa.com; *see also p66*), based next to the Newlands rugby stadium, also has gym facilities.

Ice skating

What with this being sunny Africa and all, beach or field sports take precedence while ice-bound activities like figure skating and ice hockey are left out in the cold. But the city does boast an ice rink – the Ice Station (021 535 2260, www.icerink.co.za; *see also p165* GrandWest Casino & Entertainment World) is located at the GrandWest Casino complex.

Motor racing

Motor racing as a participation sport? Well it is in Cape Town. **Fantastic Racing**

Sports Science Institute.

(2 Roeland Street, 021 461 1414, www.fantastic racing.com) has two former Jordan F1 Grand Prix-winning cars that you can race around Killarney Race Track as part of the Formula 1 experience. Other race cars include the classic Birkin S3 and the super-fast Ashley APV347is. With all that horsepower, you're likely to miss the track's incredible view of Table Mountain.

Mountain biking

In the city and surrounds, mountain biking enthusiasts tend to stick to Tokai Forest, where the MTB trails and the hiking trails are kept apart, much to everybody's joy. Deer Park (on the front slopes of Table Mountain) is another popular choice, as are Silvermine (on the South Peninsula – you'll need to get a Wild Card from the Table Mountain National Park office at the foot of Ou Kaapse Weg) and Majik Forest (in the northern suburbs near Durbanville). About half an hour north of the city is the **Dirtopia Trail Centre** (Delvera Farm, R44, Klapmuts, 021 884 4752, www.dirtopia.co.za), which has several trails of varying degrees of difficulty (beginners will want to try the Farm Trail first).

Road running

On weekday evenings and weekend mornings the city's streets are peppered with runners, ranging from get-fit joggers to stay-fit runners. For seriously active runners, Cape Town also hosts the Two Oceans Marathon (*see p197* **Sports Events**) and the traditional Gun Run (September). Local race events and updates can be found at www.runnersworld.co.za.

Sand boarding

On the surface it all sounds pretty pointless: you trudge up a sand dune, hop on a board, slide down, and then do it all over again. But anybody who's ever been skiing will understand the principle, and anybody who's gone skidding down a sand heap (either toboggan- or snowboard-style) will swear by it. Head down the peninsula and sign up at **Sunscene Outdoor Adventures** (7 Rubbi Road, Kommetjie, 021 783 0203, www.sunscene.co.za).

Scuba diving

While the waves tend to be too choppy for snorkelling, Cape Town's waters – with their kelp forests and shipwrecks – are great for scuba diving. The Cape Peninsula gives divers two oceans to choose from so, if conditions in one ocean aren't great, you're

free to head to any one of the dive sites in the other. Scuba lessons here are also relatively cheap, with some courses taking you all the way from absolute beginner to Aquarium Shark Tank diver.

There are plenty of local clubs and dive centres, including **Pisces Divers** (12 Glen Road, Glencairn, 021 782 7205, www.pisces divers.co.za), **Pro Divers** (Shop 88B, Main Road, Sea Point, 021 433 0472, www.prodivers.co.za) and **Scuba Shack Dive Centre** (289 Long Street, 021 424 9368, www.scubashack.co.za).

Shark diving

Though it's not a competitive sport, shark diving is pretty extreme and now that the industry is being strictly regulated, cage diving with the Great Whites isn't as disturbing to the sharks as it once was. Shark diving excursions cost about R1,200 on average, and the best season is in the early winter (April to June).

Shark-tour operators include: **African Shark Eco-Charters** (021 785 1947, www.ultimate-animals.com), **Apex Shark Expeditions** (021 786 3038, www.apex predators.com), **Unreal Dive Expeditions** (021 553 0748, www.unrealdive.com) and **White Shark Ecoventures** (021 532 0470, www.white-shark-diving.com). For more on shark diving, *see p72* **Shark Tactics**.

Surfing

Even if you're not quite ready to take on the monster waves at Dungeons (leave that to the Red Bull Big Wave Africa pros!), Cape Town's beaches still have plenty of good surf. By some counts, there are at least 50 surf spots within an hour's drive of Cape Town – although about half of those, being on the Atlantic side, probably require a wetsuit before you try braving the icy waters. Muizenberg's famous Surfers Corner is always a popular spot (no surprises – the Indian Ocean is marginally less chilly), and there are plenty of good spots up the West Coast. Though neither you nor we wish to get involved in local surfing politics, do be warned that the surfers at some beaches can try to enforce a nasty 'locals only' policy – you'll know those beaches by the bad spelling in the 'no kooks' graffiti. Consult Wavescape (www.wavescape.co.za) or *ZigZag* magazine's website (www.zigzag.co.za) for updates on the best swells.

Tenpin bowling

While the city does have its own bowling leagues, most players tend to be casual competitors who're just looking for a night out. League play is hosted by **Let's Go Bowling** (www.letsgobowling.co.za) in its shopping mall venues at Stadium On Main (Claremont), N1 City (Goodwood) and Tyger Valley Shopping Centre (Bellville), with the lanes in between open to amateurs.
▶ *GrandWest Casino & Entertainment World, see p164, has bowling facilities.*

Trail running

Hiking is for sightseers, and running is for athletes. But you want the best of both worlds? The mountains around Cape Town (especially some of the lower Table Mountain trails) offer excellent trail running opportunities, and the sport has enough momentum going locally that races (www.trailrunning.co.za) are organised regularly.

Ultimate Frisbee

Though the sport's name may not sound like much, Ultimate Frisbee is far tougher and far more energetic than just tossing a plastic disc around. Formal league and informal pick-up games are held throughout the week at Wynberg Sports Club (Rosmead Avenue, Kenilworth) and UCT Rugby Club – but contact the **South African Flying Disc Association** (www.safda.org.za) for updates.

Watersports

With its two oceans, its numerous bays, its several *vleis* and its many rivers, Cape Town can't help but be a centre for paddling, canoeing, rafting, kayaking and surfskiing. But don't get your hopes up too much about the rivers: Cape Town's rainfall is seasonal, so it doesn't rain (in summer), but it pours (in winter, usually causing flash floods). No, the oceans and *vleis* (Flamingo Vlei near Table View and Zeekoevlei near Muizenberg especially) are a better bet.

The waters around Three Anchor Bay and Mouille Point are sheltered from the infamous southeaster, and are great for sea kayaking. Surf kayakers, meanwhile, might prefer Muizenburg, Hout Bay or Witsand (near Misty Cliffs on the South Peninsula), and beginners – surfskiers especially – tend to head for Simon's Town on the False Bay coast. But do be careful of sharks, especially in False Bay's deeper waters.

There are numerous clubs and shops specialising in watersports around Cape Town, including: the **African Paddling Association** (21 Selous Road, Claremont, 021 674 1645, www.apa.org.za), **Brian's Kayaks & Sports** (Unit 8, Northgate Estate, Highway Park, Section Street, Paarden Eiland, 021 511 9695, www.kayaks.co.za), **Paddlers Kayak Shop** (62 St George's Street, Simon's Town, 021 786 2626, www.kayakcapetown.co.za), **Real Cape Adventures** (Hout Bay, Simon's Town, Plettenberg Bay, 021 790 5611, www.seakayak.co.za) and the **Surfski School** (Fish Hoek Beach Sailing Club, Fish Hoek, 021 782 4311, www.surfskischool.com).

Yoga

Cape Town is gloriously (or notoriously – try doing business to any kind of schedule here!) laid-back, so it makes sense that there are dozens of yoga studios around the city, with students practising meditation and perfecting their physical and mental balance. The various studios employ different yoga styles, including the Cape Town favourite Bikram, where the room is heated to 40.5°C with 40 per cent humidity. Some of the best studios are **Satyananda Yoga Centre** (11 Marine House, St Johns Road, Sea Point, 021 434 3694, www.satyanandayoga.co.za), **Yogazone Cape Town** (10th floor, Picbel Arcade, 58 Strand Street, 021 421 8136, www.yogazone.co.za) and the **Centre: Yoga Meditation** (2nd floor, Heritage House, 55 Somerset Road, Green Point, 082 377 1994, www.thecentre.co.za).

Theatre & Dance

Everything from big-name musicals to fringe theatre.

Eyelash-curling queer cabaret, contortion acts or monster puppets: the Mother City has them all, in addition to its fair share of Shakespeare and serious local drama. In post-apartheid South Africa, the range of cultural expression pretty much matches the diversity of the country. Indeed, one of the city's most captivating and unusual treats is the annual Out the Box festival of puppetry, with puppetry theatre productions, workshops, conferences and street parades as well as a 3D animation and puppetry film festival.

Playwrights and directors are unafraid to tackle topical issues of the day, from AIDS to racism and homophobia.

So what are you waiting for? There are a lot of thought-provoking and entertaining productions. Get out there and enjoy them.

INFORMATION

For an insight into the diverse city theatre scene visit the website of the annual Fleur du Cap Theatre Awards – given to professional productions in the Cape (www.fdcawards.co.za).

Bookings for shows at most of the larger venues can be made through Computicket or Dial-a-Seat (*see p156*).

Theatre

MAJOR VENUES

★ Artscape Theatre Centre
DF Malan Street, Foreshore (021 410 9800/ www.artscape.co.za). **Open** *Box office* 9am-5pm Mon-Fri; 9am-12.30pm Sat. **Credit** AmEx, DC, MC, V. **Map** p275 I3.
The city's premier theatre venue oozes an old-world majesty. Come here for a serious cultural fix – the Artscape is the home base of such major players as the Cape Town City Ballet, Cape Town Opera, Cape Town Philharmonic Orchestra and the Jazzart contemporary dance company. Award-winning theatre is also regularly performed.

★ Baxter Theatre
Main Road, Rondebosch (021 685 7880/021 680 3989/www.baxter.co.za). **Open** *Box office* 9am-start of performance Mon-Sat. **Credit** AmEx, DC, MC, V.

There's a certain retro appeal to the huge orange lampshades dangling from the ceiling of the Baxter. But apart from the lighting, the theatre provides a wide range of entertainment options, from cutting-edge and major theatre from Africa and beyond to comedy, dance and children's plays. Its Monday-night special – R50 for a meal and a selected show – is a deal clincher.

Grand Arena
Grand West Casino & Entertainment World, 1 Vanguard Drive, Goodwood (021 505 7777/ www.grandwest.co.za). **Open** Showtimes vary. **Tickets** vary. **Credit** AmEx, DC, MC, V.
The city's biggest entertainment venue can seat a whopping 5,000 punters. It focuses mainly on international headline acts like funny man Chris Rock, R&B diva Mary J Blige and Irish foot-stomping sensation *Lord of the Dance*.

Theatre on the Bay
1 Link Street, Camps Bay (021 438 3300/ www.theatreonthebay.co.za). **Open** *Box office* 9.30am-5pm Mon-Sat. **Credit** AmEx, DC, MC, V. **Map** p273 A8.
Behind a concrete curtained façade – a stone's throw from Camps Bay's palm-fringed beach front – you'll find Pieter Toerien's Theatre on the Bay. Toerien is a legend in South African theatrical circles, best known for importing big-budget international shows to Africa. Here the focus is on adapting Broadway and West End productions, like *Chess* and *Hair*, for the local stage with SA actors. *Photo p204.*

Theatre on the Bay. *See p203.*

ARTS & ENTERTAINMENT

OTHER VENUES

Barnyard Theatre

Shop F09, 1st Floor, Willowbridge Lifestyle Centre, 39 Carl Cronjé Drive, Tyger Valley (021 914 8898/083 913 3434/www.barnyard theatre.co.za). **Shows** *Summer* 8.30pm Tue-Sat. *Winter* 8pm Tue-Sat; 2pm Sun. **Tickets** R95; buy one get one free every Tue, Sun. **Credit** AmEx, DC, MC, V.

The Barnyard Theatre chain has its roots in a barn on a dairy farm outside Plettenberg Bay. The focus is on rollicking tribute shows and musical theatre.

Dorp Street Theatre Café

59 Dorp Street, Stellenbosch, outside Cape Town (021 886 6107/www.dorpstraat.co.za). **Open** 3pm-late Tue-Sat when there are shows. **Credit** DC, MC, V.

You only need to look at the autographed show posters vying for space on the walls of this little theatre café to know that it's achieved almost mythical status. Everyone from emerging cabaret acts to one-woman shows and elusive musical mavericks like Rodriguez has appeared on its stage.

HB Thom

Cnr Victoria & Andringa streets, Stellenbosch, outside Cape Town (021 808 3216/bookings 021 808 3084/http://academic.sun.ac.za/drama). **No credit cards.**

The drama department of the University of Stellenbosch plays host to one of the oldest theatres in the Cape – its foundations were laid way back in 1965. The old girl still carries herself well, though, her stately foyer evoking an old-world grandeur.

Productions range from student fare to professional offerings by South Africa's top performers.

Die Hoenderhok

Langverwagt Farm, Lanchverwagt Road, Kuilsriver (021 906 4636/www.hoenderhok. co.za). **No credit cards.**

A historic chicken coop on Langverwagt Farm has found a new purpose as an atmospheric theatre venue. Due to the small stage area, the wee henhouse tends to draw mostly one- and two-person plays, live music, cabaret and the occasional poetry reading. Audiences are treated to light farm-style meals as part of the ticket price; after the meal, recorded clucking noises signal the audience to take their seats.

Kalk Bay Theatre

52 Main Road, Kalk Bay (021 788 7257/ 073 220 5430/bookings 073 220 5430/ www.kbt.co.za). **Credit** DC, MC, V.

A historic Dutch Reformed Church in the colourful fishing village of Kalk Bay now houses one of the city's favourite independent theatres. The venue only has room for 78 punters and the ensuing sense of intimacy is an enormous part of its appeal. Top theatre personalities have graced this tiny stage in productions ranging from one- and two-man plays to magic shows, comedy acts and children's theatre. Tuesday nights are reserved for the improv antics of Cape Town's favourite Theatre Sports troupe.

Little Theatre Complex

Hiddingh Campus, 37 Orange Street, Gardens (021 480 7129/www.drama.uct.ac.za/www. intimatetheatre.net). **Open** *Box office* 9am-4.30pm; or at the door. **No credit cards.** **Map** p276 G5.

The Little Theatre Complex on Orange Street is home to the University of Cape Town's drama and fine arts departments. It's also where you'll find this theatre trio. Ironically, the Little Theatre is the biggest of the three, with seats for 240 people, with the Intimate and Arena offering space for about 70-80 folks. The threesome showcases a tombola of delights, from cutting-edge plays by critically acclaimed playwrights to work by emerging performers and students. There's also a poster-plastered bar for pre-show socialising.

Masque Theatre

37 Main Road, Muizenberg (021 788 6999/ bookings 021 788 1898/www.muizenberg.info). **Open** *Box office* 9am-4pm Mon-Fri; 9am-noon Sat. **No credit cards**.

Think you can act? Now's your chance to prove it. This community seaside theatre, next to the Muizenberg train station, has been around since the 1950s. It's run by the Muizenberg Dramatical Society and everyone stands a chance to tread its boards (provided they've auditioned for a part, of course).

★ NewSpace

44 Long Street, City Centre (www.newspace theatre.co.za). **Open** 11am-late daily. **Credit** AmEx, DC, MC, V. **Map** p276 H3.

Twenty-four years after closing its doors, the grande dame of South African theatre, the Space, has been reincarnated into a brand-spanking new playhouse. Apart from the state-of-the-art 180-seater main theatre, there's an additional 80-seater

---

---

multi-purpose stage dedicated to stand-up comedy, film and experimental works. There's an Italian restaurant and tea emporium on the premises. *See also p207* **Profile**.

Obz Café

Lower Main Road, Observatory (021 448 5555/ www.obzcafe.co.za). **Open** 7am-late. **Admission** varies. **Credit** DC, MC, V.

This legendary local hangout in the heart of bohemian Observatory boasts a speck-sized stage – complete with red velvet Coca-Cola curtains – that regularly plays host to live bands, intimate plays and stand-up acts. Come early for a hearty meal or a snack from its deli.

★ On Broadway

88 Shortmarket Street, City Centre (021 424 1194/www.onbroadway.co.za). **Open** 6.30pm for dinner; shows begin 8.30pm Tue-Sun. **Credit** AmEx, DC, MC, V. **Map** p276 G3.

ARTS & ENTERTAINMENT

Baxter Theatre. *See p203.*

Saunter through a narrow chandelier-lit corridor and up the stairs for a dinner theatre experience that's sure to be loads of fun. The fare here is pure escapism, dominated by musical tribute shows, queer cabaret, magicians and the city's hottest comedic acts. Meals are hearty and reasonably priced, with the baked cheesecake a must.

Rainbow Puppet Theatre
Constantia Waldorf School, Spaanchemat River Road, Constantia (021 783 2063). **Shows** 10am, 11.15am Sat. **Tickets** R15. **No credit cards.**
The Constantia Waldorf School plays host to the country's only dedicated puppet theatre and its merry troupe of wee performers has been delighting the over-fours since 1992.

Roxy Revue Bar
GrandWest Casino & Entertainment World, 1 Vanguard Drive, Goodwood (021 505 7777/ www.grandwest.co.za). **Open** 8pm until after show. **Tickets** vary. **Credit** AmEx, DC, MC, V.
As the name suggests, productions on offer are mostly thigh-slapping, booty-shaking musical variety shows where patrons get the opportunity to travel through time and swivel crotches with Elvis or clap hands in time with Queen.

Theatre in the District
106 Chapel Street, Woodstock (021 686 2150/ bookings 079 770 4686/www.theatrein thedistrict.co.za). **No credit cards.**
An old stone church – one of the last surviving remnants of the historic suburb, District Six – provides the atmospheric setting for Cape Town's newest theatre experience. Andrew Russel and Brian Notcutt started the theatre as a base for their unique Cape cultural dinner theatre experience, Woza Cape Town, a community theatre production that acts as a showcase for young aspiring performers from diverse backgrounds. Your ticket includes a traditional Cape Malay dinner. The theatre also plays host to live jazz and acoustic sessions, work by emerging playwrights and internationally acclaimed productions like *Moj of the Antarctic.*

THEATRE COMPANIES

Handspring Puppet Company
15A Clairvaux Road, Kalk Bay (021 788 8233/ www.handspringpuppet.co.za).
This puppetry company is hot property. Renowned around the world for its boundary-breaking work, Handspring has been revolutionising adult puppet theatre since the early 1980s. The company has collaborated with acclaimed names like art superstar William Kentridge, toured the world with its mesmerising productions and recently won a string of international awards, including the London Critics' Theatre Award for its new show, *Warhorse.*
▶ *For Out the Box puppetry festival, see p208.*

Magnet Theatre Company
UCT Hiddingh campus, 37 Orange Street, Gardens (021 480 7173/082 469 2560/ www.magnettheatre.co.za). **Map** p276 G5.
A pioneering physical theatre company that's been whipping up cutting-edge contemporary movement performances since 1987. Started by theatre heavyweights Jennie Reznek and Mark Fleishman, the company has been reaping awards left, right and centre for its innovative, politically conscious productions since inception. It's collaborated extensively with the Jazzart contemporary dance company and this marriage has given birth to some bewitchingly arresting productions.

OUTDOOR THEATRES

★ Maynardville Open-Air Theatre
Cnr Wolfe & Church streets, Wynberg (021 421 7695/www.maynardville.co.za). **Shows** Jan-Feb. **Credit** AmEx, DC, MC, V.
The bard's legacy is celebrated every summer when hundreds of Shakespeare enthusiasts, lovers (and schoolchildren struggling to get to grips with their English coursework) congregate to enjoy his plays under a blanket of stars. Well-known directors vie for a chance to interpret the plays, often lending them their own twist.

Oude Libertas Amphitheatre
Oude Libertas Centre, Adam Tas Road, Stellenbosch, outside Cape Town (021 809 7473/www.oudelibertas.co.za). **Open** Box office 9am-5pm Mon-Fri; 9am-1pm Sat; 1hr before performance. **Shows** Nov-March. **Credit** MC, V.
For years now Capetonians have been packing a picnic and making the annual summer pilgrimage to the Oude Libertas Amphitheatre in Stellenbosch to indulge in a selection of top dance, drama, comedy and music under a star-studded sky. These days, the scales are tipping more towards live music, but theatre acts are still on the menu; past productions have included work by acclaimed local heavyweights.

CIRCUS

South African National Circus School
2 Willow Road, Hartleyvale, Observatory (021 692 4287/073 273 3538). **Show times** Vary. **Tickets** Vary. **No credit cards.**
Aerial acrobatics, helicopter neck spins, human pyramids, unicyclists, stilt-walkers and a one of a kind contortionist act. These are just some of the fantastical antics the performers of the South African National Circus School regularly get up to. Their youngest performer, the daughter of school-founders Nicky and Dimitri Slaverse, was a toddler at the time of writing and can already wow you with her comedic prowess. Dad Dimitri is the World Single Trapeze champion and his pupils, who hail from all walks of life, are following in his soaring footsteps.

Profile NewSpace

Independent artists take to the stage.

Stepping in to the beautifully renovated NewSpace Theatre is akin to stepping back in time. It's all still there, from the balustraded stairwell lined with posters from the People's Space heyday to the undisputed *pièce de resistance*, the main theatre arena – all red velvet curtains and upholstered antique seats.

The social context within which the theatre now exists is, however, a far cry from the politically turbulent period of 1972, when theatre photographer Brian Astbury and his actress wife Yvonne Bryceland opened the original theatre, then called the Space Theatre – the first to proudly define itself as a non-racial venue.

The premiere of playwright Athol Fugard's *Statements After an Arrest Under the Immorality Act* set the scene for the host of progressive and thought-provoking productions, and the theatre became a hub of forward-thinking artists like John Kani, Pieter-Dirk Uys and David Kramer. Jon Caviggia, thespian and academic, who was involved from its inception, remembers the Space as much for its subversive ethos as for its hospitable, all-inclusive sense of community.

He refers to the time in 1976 when the Space moved from its original Bloem Street venue to Long Street. The actors, directors and members of the audience all ceremonially picked up the theatre's wooden chairs during its last show and relocated en masse to Long Street. Shortly after this move, the name was aptly changed to the People's Space.

'The whole of Long Street was involved with the People's Space in one way or another,' Caviggia continues. 'The meter maids would come and watch us rehearse over their lunch breaks, and in turn never ticketed us, while the ladies from the brothel opposite would bring us food on their nights off.'

By 1983, the tumultuous political climate saw a significant diaspora of city slickers to the suburbs, sadly leading to the city council withdrawing its funding of the People's Space, which was then forced to close down.

When the dilapidated building was put on the market again almost two decades later, Long Street real-estate mogul Nick Ferguson jumped at the chance to restore the grand old dame to her former glory.

Even though she's been given a new lease of life, she hasn't forgotten her rebel roots and still proffers her planks to cutting-edge creatives.

▶ For listings, *see p205*.

MORE TO SEE

Tsotsi
Athol Fugard's novel was made into an Academy-Award winning film in 2005.

On Broadway. *See p205.*

★ Zip-Zap Circus School
Founders Garden, Jan Smuts Street, City Centre (021 421 8622/www.zip-zap.co.za). **Show times** Vary. **Tickets** Vary. **No credit cards**. **Map** p275 I3.
At Zip-Zap children of all backgrounds, from those born in mansions to those living on the street, are taught the ways of the circus – for free. The troupe has wowed audiences around the world, performing at festivals in Denmark, Australia and France. Apart from classes at its home base in Jan Smuts Street, the school also holds regular outreach workshops in an attempt to bring the magic of the big top to disadvantaged communities.
▶ *See also p165* **Running Away to the Circus**.

COMEDY

★ Cape Town International Comedy Festival
Baxter Theatre, Main Road, Rondebosch (021 685 7880/021 680 3989/www.comedy festival.co.za). **Date** Sept.
Laugh till it hurts at Cape Town's International Comedy Festival. The event has been going for 13 years now and has no intention of bowing out any time soon. It draws leading stand-up acts from across the globe.

Jou Ma Se Comedy Club
Albert Hall, 208 Albert Road, Woodstock (021 447 7237/www.joumasecomedy.com). **Shows** 8.30pm Thur (doors open 7.30pm). **Tickets** R70; students R35. **No credit cards**.

Rubber-faced comedian Kurt Schoonraad's new comedy venture is proving a hit with the locals. The idea behind this cheekily titled club is that talented young guns get to strut their stuff alongside side-splitting heavyweights like Marc Lottering and Ndumiso Lindi.

FESTIVALS

Out the Box
Various locations in City Bowl (www2.unima.za. org/festival.html). **Date** Early Sept.
Far superseding the humble Punch and Judy sockpuppet show, this week-long puppetry and visual performance festival organised by UNIMA SA (the International Association of Puppetry, South Africa) is the largest of its kind to take place in Africa. Indulge in a little suspension of disbelief as you watch puppets from around the world – from France and the Czech Republic to Burkina Faso – become magically animated, some even interacting with audience members. Apart from the live puppet shows, the festival also screens an inspiring array of documentaries and films, and hosts puppetry workshops for aspiring Geppettos.

Shakespeare at the Maynardville Open-Air Theatre
20 Piers Street, Maynardville (www.maynardville. co.za). **Date** Early Jan-late Feb.
The annual Shakespeare-in-Maynardville experience is an essential experience, as is the preceding picnic in the park. Each year sees a different Bard production brought to life on the tree-shrouded

stage. Be sure to bring a blanket or two, as the open-air theatre gets quite chilly in the evenings.

Vodacom Funny Festival

Baxter Theatre, Main Road, Rondebosch (021 685 7880/021 680 3989/www.baxter.co.za). **Date** June-July.

Although this comedy festival is on the small side, it still elicits big laughs.

Dance

The annual Danscape event (021 410 9848, www.jazzart.co.za) at the Artscape is the best place to gauge the city's hot young talent.

Bookings for shows at most of the larger venues can be made through Computicket or Dial-a-Seat (*see p156*).

VENUES & CLASSES

Cape Town City Ballet

Artscape Theatre Complex, DF Malan Street, Foreshore. Based at UCT School of Dance, Woolsack Drive, Rosebank (021 650 2400/ www.capetowncityballet.org.za). **Credit** AmEx, DC, MC, V. **Map** p275 I3.

Dating from 1934, South Africa's leading ballet company is still going strong and consistently putting on productions of an international standard. The focus is on reinterpreting classics like *Giselle* and *Carmen*, but from time to time contemporary pieces like rock ballets or tributes to James Bond and the tango are stirred into the mix. It's also involved in various outreach programmes.

Dance for All Youth Company

10 Aden Avenue, Athlone (021 697 5509/ www.danceforall.co.za). **Classes** Mon-Wed, Fri, Sat. **Rates** R100 per mth (1 class per wk); R140 per mth (2 of same class per wk); R250 per mth (unlimited). **No credit cards.**

In 1991 Philip Boyd, former principal dancer with CAPAB (now Cape Town City Ballet), started teaching ballet to historically disadvantaged children in the township of Gugulethu. Since then this non-profit social upliftment organisation has blossomed into a highly esteemed dance school, producing top-notch professional dancers. The Dance for All Youth Company, boasting its own signature style with a neoclassical/Afro-contemporary repertoire, was launched in 2005.

Jazzart Dance Theatre

Artscape Theatre Complex, DF Malan Street, Foreshore (021 410 9848/www.jazzart.co.za). **Classes** Mon-Fri adults; Sat children. **Rates** from R40 per class adults; from R35 students; R220 per term children. **No credit cards.** **Map** p275 I3.

The country's top contemporary dance company employs an amalgamation of Western and African dance styles in its productions. It's renowned for coming up with groundbreaking, pioneering work and for its involvement in outreach initiatives, including Namjive – a project that teaches dance and the arts to impoverished communities in Namaqualand. It also trains bright young guns and is responsible for hosting the annual Danscape showcase for emerging talents.

Jikeleza

Sentinel Primary School, Hout Bay Harbour (021 434 3100/www.jikeleza.co.za). **Open** Mon-Fri afternoons. **Rates** free.

At Jikeleza, children from marginalised communities and rehabilitated street children are initiated into the secrets of dancing. Dance genres taught range from African and Spanish to contemporary and ballet. The project's learners have graced stages across the city, and put on a big show at On Broadway (*see p205*) every year. Past students have gone on to have bright futures as professional dancers and dance teachers. Spirited founding member Edmund Thwaites is as proud of his pupils as if they were his own children and would be more than happy to show you around.

Remix Dance Company

Oppenheimer Institute Building, Centre for African Studies, UCT, Engineering Mall, Upper Campus, Rondebosch (021 650 2538/ www.remixdanceproject.co.za). **Studio** *Hodgens Hall, Rosebank Methodist Church, cnr Main & Chapel roads, Rosebank.* **Open** check website.

This is contemporary dance as you've probably never seen it before. Dancers with a range of physical disabilities work together with able-bodied performers to subvert preconceived ideas about the body and its boundaries, culminating in innovative, groundbreaking dance theatre. The Remix Dance Company regularly collaborates with theatre practitioners from a range of backgrounds, bringing genres such as mime and puppetry into its own work. Open classes are held at its studios in Rosebank.

La Rosa Spanish Dance Theatre

4th Floor, Loop Street Studios, City Centre (021 421 6437/www.larosa.co.za). **Classes** 6-7pm Mon, Thur adults; 5-6pm Mon children. **Rates** R55. **No credit cards.** **Map** p276 G4.

Artistic director Carolyn Holden and her team regularly wow audiences with their foot-stomping prowess at venues across SA. Apart from performing, La Rosa also teaches the tricks of its trade to children in hard-up communities like Elsies River, Gugulethu and Hout Bay, as well as to other interested parties across the city.

ARTS & ENTERTAINMENT

Escapes & Excursions

Winelands. *See p213.*

Winelands

Good food, great wines and amazing scenery.

It's only an hour's drive from Cape Town – though it's a very scenic hour – but the famous Cape Winelands feel like a different world. There are rolling vineyards, towering mountains, historic wine estates and more than enough wine to keep even the thirstiest old soak satisfied.

Cape wine enjoys an impressive reputation, and the Winelands are home to most of South Africa's premier wine estates. The good news is that nearly every farm and estate in the area offers wine-tasting: you'll need a designated driver, though.

Paarl, **Franschhoek** and **Stellenbosch** are the largest, nearest and most famous towns in the region, but the further you go the more you'll discover. The Winelands, and their rustic, rural gems such as **Robertson** and **Montagu**, offer more than just wine presses and vineyards.

INFORMATION

If you need some more assistance in planning your tour of the winelands, contact the Wine Desk at the Waterfront (V&A Waterfront, 021 405 4550, 082 822 6127, www.winedesk waterfront.co.za), which can tailor-make a winelands experience that's slightly off the beaten track.

Information for this chapter is taken from *Time Out Cape Town Weekend Breaks*, available from www.timeout.com.

BONNIEVALE, McGREGOR & MONTAGU

At the heart of the Breede River Valley lie three drowsy hamlets, each with their own unique personality. While pretty in a rough-around-the-edges sort of way, the wine-and-cheese valley around **Bonnievale** lacks tourist infrastructure. This unaffectedness is exactly its selling point, though, making it perfect for those keen on playing hermit for a weekend, with nothing more to look forward to than long walks and good wine.

At the end of a road between Robertson and nowhere you'll find another peaceful haven, **McGregor**, which oozes old-fashioned charm. One of the best-preserved examples of 19th-century townscapes in the Cape, the village is flanked by two nature reserves, making it a haven for hippie types.

On the doorstep of the Klein Karoo lies **Montagu**. Bar the quaint architecture and tree-lined streets, the first thing you notice is the large number of hotels per square metre. It's hardly surprising – the place is a picture. Apart from its dashing looks, the town is most famous for two things: the quality of its muscadel and its top-notch status among adventure junkies.

Sightseeing

Avalon Springs
Uitvlucht Street, Montagu (023 614 1150/ www.avalonsprings.co.za). **Open** 8am-11pm daily. **Rates** R40; R20 children. *School holidays & long weekends* R60; R40 children. **Credit** AmEx, DC, MC, V.
On the surface, Avalon Springs is just another family resort and hotel, but the impressive rock formations surrounding its curvy swimming pools are the real deal. The little ones can practise their putt-putt swings or squeal down the water slide, while their parents get pampered at the spa or dine at one of the restaurants.

Breede River Goose
Eureka Farm, Gelukshoop Road, Bonnievale (082 759 5727). **Open** *Tours* daily, weather permitting; booking essential. **Rates** R60; R30 reductions. **No credit cards**.
Drift downstream aboard the *River Goose*. Ogle the view, go for a dip, watch the birds or fish for bass. Wine-tasting trips can also be arranged.

De Bos Rock Climbing

8 Brown Street, Montagu (023 614 2532/ www.debos.co.za). **Rates** R350-R900. **No credit cards.**

If you're keen for a scramble, contact Stuart Brown, a certified Swiss rock-climbing instructor who knows the nooks and crannies of Montagu's mountains like the back of his hand.

▶ *Adrenalin-hungry readers are also directed to our Sports section; see p195.*

Where to eat & drink

Jessica's

47 Bath Street, Montagu (023 614 1805/www. jessicasrestaurant.co.za). **Open** *Summer* 6-10pm daily. *Winter* 6-10pm Mon, Wed-Sun. **Credit** MC, V.

A favourite with the locals, the restaurant at this stately brown Victorian building serves modern food – anything from chargrilled fillet of beef drizzled in cabernet sauce to crispy roast duck.

Mimosa Lodge

Church Street, Montagu (023 614 2351/ www.mimosa.co.za). **Open** *Winter* 6.30pm-late daily. *Summer* 7pm-late daily. **Credit** AmEx, DC, MC, V.

A historic Edwardian house plays host to an award-winning four-course fine-dining experience. Swiss-trained chef Bernard Hess heads up the kitchen, combining French cuisine with modern trends. His wife, Fida, runs the adjoining guesthouse. Herbs and veg are picked fresh from their garden and dishes are paired with wines from the area.

Tebaldi's

Cnr Bree & Voortrekker Streets, McGregor (023 625 1115/www.temenos.org.za). **Open** 8am-4pm Tue, Wed; 8am-4pm, from 7pm Thur-Sat; 8am-3pm Sun. **Credit** MC, V.

This ode to Italian soprano Renata Tebaldi is great for vegetarians, with dishes ranging from aubergine, butternut and caramelised onion steak to Welsh rarebit. The home-made lemon ice-cream is dreamy, while the Italian evenings on Thursdays win praise from the locals.

Where to stay

Montagu Country Hotel

27 Bath Street, Montagu (023 614 3125/www. montagucountryhotel.co.za). **Rates** R480-R770. **Credit** AmEx, DC, MC, V.

Put on your flapper dress and light up a cigarillo as you live it up at the historic Montagu Country Hotel. This art deco hotel is the oldest in town, and its apricot-coloured walls ooze retro charm. Step back in time at the restaurant, with its brass candlesticks and chandeliers, and resident piano player tapping out crooning tunes.

Temenos Country Retreat

Cnr Bree & Voortrekker Streets, McGregor (023 625 1871/www.temenos.org.za). **Rates** R460-R715. **Credit** MC, V.

Escape the rat race at this non-denominational spiritual retreat. Guests stay in thatched cottages, the walls adorned with blooming creepers. Apart from meditation and yoga sessions, there's a library packed with spiritual classics and therapists administering everything from massages to reiki.

Vic 1906 Hotel

35 Bath Street, Montagu (023 614 2440/ www.thevictorian.co.za). **Rates** R650-R850. **Credit** MC, V.

Indulge in a dose of retro glam at this new kid on the accommodation block. Expect opulent Victorian pop – rooms all sport sparkly see-through chandeliers, Persian carpets and handmade neo-Victorian furniture.

Tourist information

Bonnievale Tourism Bureau *023 616 3563/ www.bonnievale.co.za.*
McGregor Tourism Bureau *023 625 1954/ www.tourismmcgregor.co.za.*
Montagu Tourism Bureau *023 614 2471/ www.montagu.org.za.*

Getting there

Bonnievale and McGregor are both around 180 kilometres (111 miles) from Cape Town; Montagu lies 20 kilometres (12 miles) further along the road. To get to Montagu, take the Worcester turn-off on the N1 and follow the R60 through Robertson and Ashton into the town.

To get to McGregor, turn right at the McGregor sign opposite the Roodezandt winery in Robertson, and follow the road for another 18 kilometres (11 miles). To get to Bonnievale, take the N2 towards Caledon and Riviersonderend, turn left at Stormsvlei and continue for 10 kilometres; alternatively, follow the route from the N1 as if you were heading for McGregor, but take the Bonnievale turn-off instead.

INSIDE TRACK SAY CHEESE

Discover Cape cheese gems with Frenchman **Didier Bertrand**. On his tour, you get the chance to nibble on handmade cheeses, meet boutique cheese-makers, and taste some of the finest wines that the Cape has to offer (073 613 2561, www.cheeseandwine.co.za).

Franschhoek.

Founded by the wealthy Rupert family, the museum houses over 220 classic cars covering a century of driving history. Eighty cars are on display at any one time, ranging from the country's first Model T Ford to the super-rare Ferrari Enzo.

Horse trails

Combine horse-riding with wine-tasting for a fresh view of these two favourite activities. Rayanne Schafer at **Mont Rochelle Equestrian Centre** (083 300 4368) and Pieter Hugo at **Paradise Stables** on the Robertsvlei Road (021 876 2160, www.paradisestables.co.za) will provide a horse to suit your abilities, and an unforgettable experience to boot.

Where to eat & drink

★ Bread & Wine

Môreson Wine Farm (021 876 3692/ www.moreson.co.za). **Open** noon-3pm daily. **Credit** AmEx, DC, MC, V

Chef Neil Jewell is justifiably famous for his delicious cured meats, and the antipasti platter is a must at this lunchtime-only venue. Elegant yet hearty dishes are the name of the game – the pork belly is worth a special mention. The laid-back courtyard setting makes this a perfect place to bring the whole family; reasonably priced wine from the estate won't leave too large a dent in your wallet.

Dieu Donné Restaurant

Dieu Donné Vineyard, top of Uitkyk Street (021 876 3384/www.dieudonnevineyards.com). **Open** 10am-3.30pm, 6-10pm Mon-Sat; 11am-4pm Sun. **Credit** AmEx, DC, MC, V.

Wine-maker Stephan du Toit is pulling some admirable pints from his underground micro-brewery, with a lager, ale and stout on tap to be enjoyed with delicious eats from the extensive menu in this cellar-style restaurant with stupendous views.

Genot Restaurant

Green Valley Road (021 876 2729/www.klein genot.com). **Open** noon-3m, 7-11pm Tue-Sat; noon-3pm Sunday. **Credit** MC, V.

The name of this chic Winelands stop means 'pleasure' and it is certainly a pleasant stop. The rather cavernous dining area is prettied up with splashes of cerise and sparkling chandeliers, while the open kitchen creates a sense of intimacy. The menu features contemporary flavour marriages, many of them with a distinctive South African twist – the likes of smoked snoek, *bobotie* and *koeksusters* given a tasty shake-up. Local star offerings and estate wines make for a balanced wine list.

Haute Cabrière

Cabrière Estate, Franschhoek Pass (021 876 3688/www.hautecabriere.com). **Open** *Summer* noon-3pm, 7-9pm daily. *Winter* noon-3pm

FRANSCHHOEK

great drive – a bit twee

If only the Franschhoek valley weren't so darn gorgeous. If only it didn't lay claim to some of South Africa's top restaurants. If only somewhere else produced such excellent wines. If it had none of these things, locals would have an excuse to scoff at the faux-French names and crowds of daytrippers and find somewhere else to indulge in all things gourmet.

However, Franschhoek has all of these things and more, so look past the crowded cafés, Sunday bikers and the red, white and blue fluttering outside every La-this or Le-that. Franschhoek may have been first settled by Huguenots fleeing religious persecution in France in the late 1600s, but today you're likely to find another sort of migrant here – thousands of tourists that flock to what is the most popular destination in the Cape Winelands.

Sightseeing

lots of fussy restaurants.

Franschhoek Motor Museum

L'Ormarins Wine Estate, R45 (021 874 9020/ www.fmm.co.za). **Open** 10am-4pm Tue-Fri; 10am-3pm Sat, Sun. **Admission** R60. **Credit** AmEx, DC, MC, V.

ESCAPES & EXCURSIONS

Experience

the lifestyle .

wine

The taste of innovation ...

cheese

handcrafted goodness ...

Goatshed

a coming together ...

The finest winelands fare awaits you at Fairview estate in Paarl.

Award winning wines, gourmet cheeses and freshly prepared farm favourite
will tempt your tastebuds and welcome you to our Fairview family.
Let our resident goats entertain you whilst enjoying a chilled glass of Viogn
at the Goatshed or let our tasting room hosts
guide you through our range of fine wines and gourmet cheeses.

Tel. +27 21 8632450   tasting@fairview.co.za   goatshed@fairview.co.za

Mon-Thur, Sun; noon-3pm, 7-9pm Fri, Sat.
Credit AmEx, DC, MC, V
Wine-maker Achim von Arnim is famous for his Saturday morning cellar tours and his sabrage: the art of opening a bottle of champagne with a sword – there's nothing like a bit of sword-play to get you in the mood for food. Wander next door to the cellar restaurant, where most of the delectable dishes can be ordered as half or full portions.

Mont Rochelle Country Kitchen

Mont Rochelle Hotel & Mountain Vineyards, Dassenberg Road (021 876 2770/www.mon trochelle.co.za). **Open** 10am-4pm, 7-9.30pm daily. **Credit** AmEx, DC, MC, V

A country kitchen in the true sense of the word, rustic charm abounds here. Start off with a selection of fresh, seasonal tapas and then dig into heartier dishes of veal or *porcini* risotto. The perfect place for a relaxed and cosy afternoon.
▶ *For the hotel part of the Mont Rochelle operation, see right.*

Restaurant in the Vines

Rickety Bridge, R45 (021 876 3650/www.rickety bridge.com). **Open** *Summer* noon-4pm daily, 5pm-8pm (tapas) daily. *Winter* 9am-5pm daily. **Credit** MC, V

Situated smack-bang in the middle of a vineyard with breathtaking views of the valley, the Restaurant in the Vines is presided over by chef Rob Hahn. His menus of seasonal fare change often: the winter menu features hearty warmers such as curries and soups, while summer food is lighter. The restaurant also puts together great picnic baskets, crammed with smoked salmon baguettes and syrupy *koeksisters*.

★ Reuben's

19 Huguenot Road (021 876 3772/www.reubens. co.za). **Open** noon-3pm, 7-9pm daily. **Credit** AmEx, DC, MC, V

Reuben Riffel has picked up a cutlery drawer of awards, but it's not just the silverware that keeps bringing in the crowds. Asian influences dovetail nicely with the local specialities, and dishes are easily paired with the good selection of local wines served by the glass.

★ Tasting Room at Le Quartier Français

16 Huguenot Road (021 876 2151/www.le quartier.co.za). **Open** 7-9pm daily. **Credit** AmEx, DC, MC, V

Margot Janse's artistry in the kitchen made the Tasting Room at Le Quartier Français South Africa's top restaurant in 2007, collecting a host of international awards along the way. For your money, you'll get your pick of the clouds, foams and kitchen wizardry that Janse conjures up using fresh, local ingredients.

Where to stay

Akademie Street Guesthouses

5 Akademie Street (021 876 3027/www.aka. co.za). **Rates** R2,400-R3,500 per guesthouse. **Credit** AmEx, DC, MC, V.

The Akademie Street Guesthouses offer visitors a deliciously peaceful escape from the crowds. The poetically named Oortuiging, Vreugde and Gelatenheid cottages each have a private pool and shady garden; Twyfeling and Uitsig share a garden and pool. However, the double-storey Gelatenheid is definitely the pick of the bunch, with its own outdoor bath on the upstairs balcony.

Le Franschhoek Hotel & Spa

Excelsior Road (021 876 8900/www.le franschhoek.co.za). **Rates** R1370-R2210. **Credit** AmEx, DC, MC, V.

Le Franschhoek is tucked away on the picturesque Excelsior Road and the rooms are nicely spread out, so you'll rarely bump into the other guests who are staying at the 63-room property (40 standard rooms, 21 suites and a pair of villas). The hotel's fine-dining Relais Gourmand restaurant is worth a visit in its own right.

★ Klein Genot

3 Green Valley Road (021 876 2738/www.klein genot.com). **Rates** R1,194. **Credit** AmEx, DC, MC, V.

Luxury meets tranquillity at Klein Genot. The stunning guest suites on this working wine farm have owner Angie Diamond's individual stamp of style, with excellent personalised service. Get pampered at the spa, stroll in the vineyards or contemplate love, life and everything else in the hotel's gardens and lounges.

★ Mont Rochelle

Dassenberg Road (021 876 2770/www.mont rochelle.co.za). **Rates** R2,950-R6,500. **Credit** AmEx, DC, MC, V.

Spread across three separate wings, Mont Rochelle is more rambling country house than anonymous hotel, but with all the five-star trappings you'd expect. Splash out on one of the deluxe suites with a private splash pool.
▶ *For more, see p215 Horse trails.*

Tourist information

Franschhoek Wine Valley & Tourist Association
70 Huguenot Road (021 876 3603/ www.franschhoek.org.za).

Getting there

Franschhoek is 78 kilometres (50 miles) from Cape Town. Turn right at exit 47 off the N1 and follow the signs.

Paarl.

PAARL

The Afrikaners are a serious bunch. Well, that's if you take to heart the inscribed plaque at the foot of the **Afrikaans Language Monument**, reading, '*Dit is ons erns*' ('This is our resolve'). But if you look at the slightly silly shape of the monument, you can't help but wonder whether the *stoere boere* (serious boers) didn't have a mischievous sense of humour after all. This bastion of Afrikaans was designed by architect Jan van Wijk and completed in 1975.

Meander along the 12-kilometre-long Main Street (the longest in the country) to get a feel for the town. Apart from the historical landmarks, food-lovers will have their fill of flavour at a host of Main Street hotspots, and bargain hunters will be ecstatic at the sight of the ridiculous number of antique shops. Tipplers wanting to restock their dwindling cellars will have to move slightly further afield than Main Street to explore the best of Paarl's wine estates.

The nearby landmark of **Paarl Rock** is a huge granite rock comprised of three rounded outcrops. It's so named because when it rains, the rounds glisten like pearls; the word 'paarl' is derived from *parel*, which is Dutch for pearl.

Sightseeing

Afrikaans Language Monument
Gabbema Doordrift Road (021 863 4809/ www.taalmonument.co.za). **Open** *Winter* 8am-5pm daily. *Summer* 8am-8pm daily. **Admission** R12; R2-R5 reductions. **No credit cards.**
Whether it elicits a few giggles or stunned gasps of awe, the Taal Monument is worth seeing, even if simply to marvel at the panoramic views it affords of the Paarl landscape.

Drakenstein Lion Park
R101 between Klapmuts and Paarl (021 863 3290/www.lionrescue.org.za). **Open** 9.30am-5pm daily. **Admission** R40; R20 children. **Credit** MC, V.
This lion park with a conscience offers a haven to 15 magnificent, albeit downtrodden, beasts that were rescued from captive environments such as circuses and zoos. Enjoy these jungle kings from a respectful distance, either from one of the raised platforms or with a self-guided tour through the cages.

★ Fairview Wine Estate
Suid-Agter-Paarl Road, Southern Paarl (021 863 2450/www.fairview.co.za). **Open** *Tastings* 8.30am-5pm Mon-Fri; 8.30am-4pm Sat; 9.30am-4pm Sun. *Goatshed Restaurant* 9am-5pm daily. **Rates** R20 standard; R60 master. **Credit** AmEx, DC, MC, V.
The cheeky goats in front of the Goatshed Restaurant love kidding around for the cameras. They have completely stolen the limelight from all that this lovely wine estate has to offer: three wineries producing well-loved wines; a cheeserie producing a range of creamylicious cheeses, and a range of top-notch olive oils.

Where to eat & drink

Marc's Mediterranean Cuisine
129 Main Street (021 863 3980/www.marcs restaurant.co.za). **Open** 10am-late daily. **Credit** AmEx, DC, MC, V.
This restaurant offers Mediterranean cuisine with a sophisticated flair and culinary influences reaching as far afield as Lebanon. The undisputed favourite remains the traditional meze platter brimful of baba ganoush, tsatsiki, houmous and spanakopita.

Terra Mare
90A Main Street (021 863 4805). **Open** 10am-10pm Tue-Sat. **Credit** AmEx, MC, V.
The classic black-and-beige interior perfectly showcases an unblemished view of Paarl Rock, and the terrace has become quite the hot spot among locals. The menu features simple but flavourful wonders such as the lamb osso bucco and seared tuna steak.

Afrikaans Language Monument.

Where to stay

Goedemoed Country Inn

Cecilia Street (021 863 1102/www.goedemoed. com). **Rates** R495-R750. **Credit** AmEx, DC, MC, V.
The spacious en-suite rooms of this manor house have an appropriately old-world charm without being stuffy or intimidating. Those looking for something a bit more private can opt for the garden cottages overlooking the vineyards.

Grande Roche

Plantasie Street (021 863 5100/www.grande roche.co.za). **Rates** R2,800-R4,300. **Credit** AmEx, DC, MC, V.
This 18th-century Cape Dutch manor house offers luxury accommodation with all the creature com-forts. There's fine dining at the award-winning Bosman's, or more relaxed eating at Bistro Allegro.

Tourist information

Paarl Tourism Bureau *216 Main Road (021 872 0860/www.paarlonline.com).*

Getting there

Paarl is 60 kilometres (37 miles) from Cape Town; take the N1 north. After around 60 kilometres, turn left on to the R45 into Paarl.

WORCESTER & ROBERTSON

While historic Church Street in **Worcester** is a fine sight, the main road won't elicit any oohs or aahs. But that doesn't mean you should follow suit. In additions to the attractions listed below, the **Karoo Botanical Gardens** (Roux Road, Van Riebeeck Park, off N1, 023 347 0785, www. sanbi.org) is beautiful; the **Kleinplasie Open Air Museum** (R60, outside Worcester, 023 342 2225, www.kleinplasie.co.za) gives a window into daily life in days past. Firewater fans may enjoy **KWV** (cnr Smith & Church Streets, 023 342 0255, www.kwvhouseofbrandy.com), the largest brandy distilling cellar on the globe.

Further along Route 62, you'll find yourself in **Robertson**, renowned for its jacaranda-lined streets and beautiful gardens. It's also famous for its wine. The surrounding countryside has a host of quirky attractions, many on the banks of the lush Breede River.

Sightseeing

Klipdrift Brandy Distillery

4 Voortrekker Road, Robertson (023 626 3027/ www.klipdrift.co.za). **Open** 8am-5pm Mon-Fri; 9am-4pm Sat. **Tours** 10am, noon, 2.30pm Mon-Fri; 10am, noon, 2pm Sat. **Rates** *Tours* R30. *Tastings* R20 full; R10 single. **Credit** DC, MC, V.

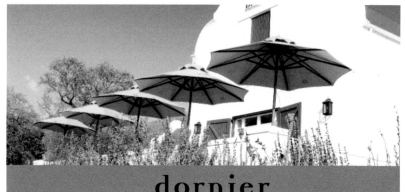

dornier
BODEGA

STELLENBOSCH

Food from the Heart

Welcome to the Home of Farm Cuisine, inspired by fresh ingredients and fine wines.
Lunch daily from 12:00 - 17:00/Dinner Thursday to Saturday from 18:00 - 21:30
Tel: 021 880 0557 / www.bodega.co.za / GPS: 33°59'31 S; 18°52'15 E

The Hout Street Gallery specialises in South African Fine Art. The Gallery also offers a range of Ceramics, Creative Jewellery, Glass, Crafts and Functional Art. Enjoy the homely atmosphere and personalised service. The Gallery is open seven days a week at 270 Main Street, Paarl.

est. 1975 Gail & David Zetler

HOUT STREET GALLERY - PAARL

Tel: + 27 (0)21 872 5030 Fax: + 27 (0)21 872 7133 zetler@icon.co.za www.houtstreetgallery.co.za

You don't have to be a brandy fan to consider a pit stop: a sense of humour and an appreciation for great branding will do. The tour takes you through the distillery and ends with a tasting.

Soekershof Walkabout – Mazes & Botanical Gardens

Klaas Voogds West, Robertson (023 626 4134/ www.soekershof.com). **Tours** 11am Wed-Sun (and at other times by arrangement). **Rates** R60; R40 under-12s; free toddlers. **No credit cards**.

Soekershof is magical: it's the largest hedge maze in the southern hemisphere. The noises from whispering pine trees accompany you and hares may dart past as you struggle through leafy corridors, attempting to solve the mystery of Klaas Voogds.

Where to eat & drink

Fraai Uitzicht 1798

Klaas Voogds East, Robertson (023 626 6156/ www.fraaiuitzicht.com). **Open** noon-3pm, 6pm-close Wed-Sun. Closed June-Aug. **Credit** AmEx, DC, MC, V.

Climb the white steps from the middle-of-nowhere dirt road to the restaurant, where a spectacular view awaits. If you're in the mood for something indulgent, try the seven-course *dégustation* menu.

★ Viljoensdrift Wines & River Cruises

12km from Robertson on R317 (023 615 1901/ www.viljoensdrift.co.za). **Open** *Riverboat Deli* 9am-5pm Mon-Fri; 10am-4pm Sat, 1st Sun of mth. *Boat trips* by appointment. **Cost** (boat trips) R35; R15 reductions. **Credit** MC, V.

Viljoensdrift offers wine-tasting boat trips down the Breede River. If all the tasting leaves you peckish, make up your own picnic basket with scrumptious goodies like smoked salmon trout, vine-wrapped figs and chocolate salami from the deli.

Where to stay

Excelsior Manor

Turn right to Bonnievale 10km past the circle outside Robertson, then continue for a further 3km (023 615 2050/www.excelsior.co.za). **Rates** R600-R900. **Credit** MC, V.

Built in the ostrich feather boom years, the historic house radiates old-world grandeur. Taste the estate's wines in front of the elaborately carved fireplace, or explore the vineyards in an off-road golf cart adventure.

Rosendal Spa & Wellness Retreat

Klaas Voogds West, Robertson (023 626 1570/ 072 686 2031/www.rosendalwinery.co.za). **Rates** R595-R655. **Credit** MC, V.

This intimate weekend hideaway lies along a quiet dirt road amid rolling vineyards. Rooms have private entrances with vine-covered porches and look out on to a rim-flow pool. Treat yourself to a massage at the spa, then tuck into fine Belgian-French cuisine.

Tourist information

Robertson Tourism Bureau *Voortrekker Street (023 626 4437/www.robertsontourism. co.za)*.
Worcester Tourism Bureau *23 Baring Street (023 348 2795/www.worcestertourism.co.za)*.

Getting there

Worcester is approximately 100 kilometres (62 miles) from Cape Town, and Robertson around 160 kilometres (99 miles). To get to Worcester, follow the N1 north and take the Worcester turn-off after the tunnel. Robertson is on the R60 following Worcester.

ESCAPES & EXCURSIONS

Fairview Wine Estate. *See p218.*

Stellenbosch.

ESCAPES & EXCURSIONS

STELLENBOSCH

Despite the fact that it's the second oldest town in South Africa, Stellenbosch has an intoxicating cosmopolitan and youthful atmosphere, thanks to the proliferation of students – or Maties – who call the university town home for most of the year.

Named in 1679 by the governor of the Cape, Simon van der Stel, Stellenbosch is steeped in history, from the centuries-old oak trees that line the streets to the beautifully maintained buildings that date back to its earliest days. Come harvest time, the heady smell of grape must envelopes the town, offering the promise that a new vintage of wine will bring, and with over 300 estates included in the regional wine route, there's more than enough to go round.

If you enjoy more energetic activities than tasting the local wine, there are walking and mountain-biking trails in the **Jonkershoek Nature Reserve** (Jonkershoek Valley, 021 866 1560, www.capenature.org.za). Hikers should visit **Delvera Farm** (cnr R44 & Muldersvlei Road between Stellenbosch & Paarl, 021 884 4752), a collection of enterprises, including wine walks, a wine shop, dirt biking and a nature conservancy with walking trail.

Sightseeing

Brandy Route
021 887 3157/www.brandyroutes.co.za. **Rates** Up to 15 distilleries, charging R20-R65 for tasting.
Visit a number of historic distilleries in the area, getting to grips with the process of distillation and the nuances of different brandies.

Stellenbosch American Express Wine Route
Wine Route Office, 36 Market Street (021 886 4310/www.wineroute.co.za). **Open** 8.30am-5pm Mon-Fri. **Rates** R150 unguided; R380-R500 guided tours.
At this dedicated wine route office, staff are on hand to help you tailor-make your own tour to suit your priorities: big, classic wines or new, unusual tastes; restaurants, or child-friendly activities.

Where to eat & drink

Big Easy
95 Dorp Street (021 887 3462). **Open** noon-10pm Mon-Fri; 9-11.30am, noon-10pm Sat, Sun. **Credit** AmEx, DC, MC, V.
Housed in one of the largest houses on historic Dorp Street, this restaurant's name is in reference to one of its major shareholders, South African golfing great Ernie Els. The premises houses various places to eat, from the colourful Karoo bar to the elegant dining rooms for dinner, dressed in starched linen and sumptuous fabrics. Fabulous wines are key.

Cuvée
Kromme Rhee Road, Koelenhof (021 888 4932/www.cuveeatsimonsig.co.za). **Open** 11am-3pm Tue-Thur; 11am-3pm, 7-10pm Fri, Sat; 11am-2pm Sun. **Credit** AmEx, MC, V.
▶ *See p113* **Wine and Dine**.

De Volkskombuis Restaurant
Aan-de-Wagen Road (021 887 2121/www.volkskombuis.co.za). **Open** noon-3pm, 6.30pm-10pm daily. **Credit** AmEx, DC, MC, V.
If it's old-school traditional South African cuisine you're after, then this decades-old dining room is the

place to visit, offering everything from biltong salad and *bobotie* to *waterblommetjiebredie* and perfectly seared ostrich fillet.

★ Moyo at Spier

Spier Estate, Lynedoch Road/R310 (021 809 1100/www.moyo.co.za). **Open** noon-4pm; 6-11pm daily. **Credit** AmEx, DC, MC, V.

An alphabet of locally flavoured food awaits, from seafood to slow-cooked *potjies*, spice-rubbed lamb cutlets straight off the braai. Private treehouses are a novel way to enjoy dinner *à deux*. *Photo p224.*

96 Winery Road

Zandberg Farm, Winery Road; off R44 between Somerset West & Stellenbosch (021 842 2020). **Open** noon-3pm, 6.30pm-late Mon-Sat; noon-3pm Sun. **Credit** AmEx, DC, MC, V.
▶ *See p113* **Wine and Dine.**

★ Overture

Hidden Valley Wine Estate, Annandale Road, Stellenbosch (021 880 2721/www.dineat overture.co.za). **Open** noon-3pm Tue, Wed, Sat, Sun; noon-3pm, 7-10pm Thur, Fri. **Main courses** R195. **Credit** AmEx, DC, MC, V.
▶ *See p113* **Wine and Dine.**

★ Rust en Vrede Restaurant

Rust en Vrede Estate, Annandale Road (021 881 3881/www.rustenvrede.com). **Open** noon-3pm for 1-course winemaker's lunch (weather

INSIDE TRACK VINE NOT?

Taste the fruits of the Winelands while someone else does the driving. The **Vine Hopper** is a unique hop-on-hop-off wine-tasting taxi service. You choose between two routes, each with six wine estates, and hop on and off as you please (Vine Hopper at the Stellenbosch Adventure Centre, 36 Market Street, Stellenbosch, 021 882 8112, www.vinehopper.co.za).

permitting), 7pm-close Tue-Sat. **Credit** AmEx, DC, MC, V.

Revel in chef David Higgs's immaculate, delicate menu inspired by the classical French tradition, but with a light, modern touch. Set tasting menus ensure you experience his entire repertoire, and the somme-lier's wine pairings are innovative and exciting.

★ Terroir

Kleine Zalze Estate, R44 (021 880 8167/www. kleinezalze.com). **Open** noon-2.30pm, 6.45-9.30pm Mon-Sat; noon-2.30pm Sun. **Credit** AmEx, DC, MC, V.

Book a table under the oak trees in the summer months and savour dishes from chef Michael Broughton's inspired chalkboard menu – featuring the likes of his now-famous risotto, perfectly poached fish with the lightest slick of a sauce and

Jonkershoek Nature Reserve.

ESCAPES & EXCURSIONS

decadent chocolate pudding with pistachio crème anglaise. A delightfully laid-back environment, considering the excellent food.

▶ *See also p113* **Wine and Dine**.

Tokara Restaurant

Tokara, Helshoogte Pass (021 808 5959/ www.tokararestaurant.co.za). **Open** 12.30-3pm, 7.30-9pm Tue-Sat. **Credit** AmEx, DC, MC, V.

Master chef Etienne Bonthuys's beautifully prepared and elegantly presented seasonal offerings are evidence of a classically trained talent, with his feather-light sauces and thoughtful flavour combinations almost always given a locally inspired bent. The contemporary surrounds and exquisite views complete this excellent eating experience.

▶ *See also p113* **Wine and Dine**.

Where to stay

Batavia Boutique Hotel

12 Louw Street (021 887 2914/www.batavia house.co.za). **Rates** R385-R1,485. **Credit** AmEx, DC, MC, V.

In the heart of the town, this multi award-winning boutique hotel is a private and elegant escape. Sophisticated old-world decor combined with all the mod cons ensure a comfortable stay.

★ Lanzerac Hotel & Spa

Lanzerac Street (021 887 1132/www.lanzerac. co.za). **Rates** R1,345-R3,250. **Credit** AmEx, DC, MC, V.

With views of Table Mountain, beautiful manicured gardens, a wellness centre and top-notch dining facilities, this one's a favourite with well-heeled travellers. Each of the 48 suites is individually decorated, with a private patio and vineyard or garden views.

★ Majeka House

26-32 Houtkapper Street, Paradyskloof (021 880 1549/www.majekahouse.co.za). **Rates** R800. **Credit** AmEx, DC, MC, V.

With a library and bar as well as a gym, steam room, sauna and huge indoor pool, newly opened Majeka House pushes all the right buttons. There are 15 rooms and a self-catering villa if you prefer to do your own thing.

Tourist information

Stellenbosch Tourism Bureau *021 883 3584/ www.tourismstellenbosch.co.za.*

Getting there

Stellenbosch is 45 kilometres (28 miles) from Cape Town. Take the N2 highway past Cape Town International towards Somerset West, take exit 43, and then follow the R44 all the way into Stellenbosch.

Moyo at Spier. *See p223.*

TULBAGH

Tulbagh is fast becoming the wedding capital of the Winelands, with wine estates such as Montpellier and Manley Private Cellar building wedding chapels. It doesn't take a leap of the imagination to see why it has become so popular with the love struck: the valley is surrounded by the picturesque Obiqua, Winterhoek and Witzenberg mountains, and during spring it's abloom with wildflowers and orchard blossoms.

Today, most of the historic buildings in the town's bustling Church Street are used as guesthouses and restaurants, which is very convenient for the hordes of strolling tourists that come here at weekends. If you're staying in town and keen for a day trip, head out to the nearby game reserves **Inverdoorn** (021 434 4639, www.inverdoorn.com) and **Aquila** (021 431 8400, www.aquilasafari.com) for a walk on the wild side.

Sightseeing

Silwerfontein Hiking Trail

R44 towards Tulbagh (023 232 0531/ www.silwerfontein.co.za). **Rates** R120. **No credit cards**.
This two-day hiking trail goes through the Voëlvlei Nature Conservancy. Starting at base camp, hikers trundle through pine and eucalyptus forests and scramble over rocks to spend the first night at the Ontongs cave. From there, head up the gully to the Ontongskop and descend back through the protected Mountain Flora Reserve; keep your eyes peeled for some great views of Tulbagh and Voëlvlei along the way.

Where to eat & drink

Pielow's

De Oude Herberg Restaurant, Church Street (023 230 0432/www.pielows.co.za). **Open** 7pm-late Tue-Sat. **Credit** MC, V.
Colin and Theresa Pielow left the green grass of Ireland and two successful restaurants behind to open this chic gourmet gem in the stately De Oude Herberg. Ingredients are locally sourced and signature dishes like the roast springbok loin in port sauce are what keep the foodies coming back for more.

Readers

12 Church Street (023 230 0087). **Open** 9am-late Mon, Wed-Sun. **Credit** DC, MC, V.
Silwood-trained chef Carol Collins describes her menu as global with a local flavour, one of the firm favourites being the rack of lamb with Pernod, asparagus and feta. Equally bold in flavours are her home-made ice-creams, with flavours such as curry and garlic.

Where to stay

Montpellier

Twee Jonge Gezellen Road (023 230 0723/ www.montpellier.co.za). **Rates** R350-R400. **Credit** AmEx, DC, MC, V.
Book yourself into this grandiose old Cape Dutch manor house, and live out the aristocratic fantasy further with a spot of horse-riding. There are also three self-catering cottages on the periphery.

Vin Doux Luxury Treehouses

Vindoux Guest Farm, Van der Stel Street (023 230 0635/www.vindoux.com). **Rates** R500-R1,000. **Credit** MC, V.
Each romantic tree house boasts its own corner spa bath, perfect for soaking in with a glass of bubbly and some good company while looking out over the vista of vineyards and the Saronsberg Mountains.

Tourist information

Tulbagh Tourism Bureau *023 230 1348/ www.tulbaghtourism.org.za.*

Getting there

Tulbagh is approx 120 kilometres (75 miles) from Cape Town. Take the N1 northbound and turn left at the Wellington/Klapmuts off-ramp. Follow the R44 towards Ceres through the Nuwekloof Pass; look out for signs to Tulbagh.

Lanzerac Hotel & Spa.

Whale Route

Beautiful beaches, lovely countryside and those wonderful whales.

Each spring sees the elusive southern right whales coming to mate in the warmer waters of this southern area of the Cape; especially near to **Hermanus**, which has dedicated an annual festival to the blubbery beasts. Just around the bend, **Gansbaai** is Shark Valley and has a booming shark-diving industry to show for it.

Heading east, you'll reach **Agulhas** (the southernmost tip of Africa) and the neighbouring towns of **Struisbaai** and **Arniston**. All three are popular with local holidaymakers, with temperate waters and beautiful hiking trails. Distinctly more inland but by no means less beautiful, nestled against the Riviersonderend mountains, is the quaint, sleepy villiage of **Greyton**, a favoured retreat for city slickers in the mood for a classy countryside break.

ARNISTON, AGULHAS & STRUISBAAI

The tiny village of **Arniston** is a popular stop on the tourist trail for the region of Overberg and a plum spot to swim, surf, paddle and simply relax. You'll hear Arniston called **Waen-huiskrans**, the town's official Afrikaans name, after a huge **cave** around two kilometres south of the village. You can walk to the cave, but don't forget to check the tide tables before you set out, as the cave can only be accessed at low tide.

Most visitors to **Agulhas** zip down to the **lighthouse** (028 435 6078; 9am-5pm daily, R15, R7.50 reductions), take a few photos, gaze at the two oceans meeting and then head north to greener pastures. But the southernmost tip of Africa certainly has more to offer, like fantastic bird-watching at places like **Soetendalsvlei**, the largest natural freshwater lake in South Africa, and the **Cape Agulhas National Park** (www.sanparks.org). Towards Bredasdorp, the town of **Struisbaai** draws holidaymakers to its enormous white-sand beach: at 14 kilometres, it's the longest in the southern hemisphere.

If you're spending a few days in the Agulhas area it's worth taking a tour to get under the skin of the region. **Derick Burger** (028 435 6903, www.agulhassouthafrica.co.za, rates R300) runs fantastic tours that'll bring the fauna, flora, geology and history of the area to life. **Coastal Tours** (082 774 4448, www.coastaltours.co.za, rates R300) offers three to five-hour tours of the area.

There are two well-marked **walking trails** in and around Agulhas. The Spookdraai Hiking Trail takes you through the village and into the hills above town, and can be completed in under two hours. The circular Rasperpunt trail starts and ends at the Meisho Maru wreck and takes around three hours. Dual-language maps for both trails are available at the lighthouse information office.

Boat trips

Cape Agulhas Adventures *082 372 3354/ www.capeagulhasbackpackers.com.* **Rates** R180 for 1.5hrs. **Awesome Charters** *082 870 2783/ www.awesomecharters.co.za.* **Rates** R700; booking essential.

What's a trip to the southern tip of Africa without seeing it from the sea? Cape Agulhas Adventures run sightseeing trips from Struisbaai harbour into the bay, while Awesome Charters can take you fishing for yellowtail, garrick and Cape salmon.

Whale Trail

De Hoop Nature Reserve (021 659 3500/www. capenature.org.za). **Price** R950, plus R300 for optional luggage porterage. **Credit** MC, V. The good news is that the Western Cape's most popular slackpacking trail is a short drive from Arniston. The bad news is that you need to book months in advance to secure a spot. Nonetheless, get organised and make a booking for this wonderful combination of rolling *fynbos* hills, rare birdlife, whale-watching and outstanding accommodation.

Where to eat & drink

L'Agulhas Seafoods
Main Road, Agulhas (028 435 7207). **Open** 9am-7pm Mon-Sat; 9am-3pm Sun. **Credit** MC, V.
The best snoek and chips in the Overberg, guaranteed. If you don't want to snack on snoek there's also a choice of hake, calamari and the day's line fish. Ignore the tables on the roadside out front and take your box of fish down to the water's edge to enjoy the sea view.

Arniston Spa Hotel
Beach Road, Arniston Bay (028 445 9000/www. arnistonhotel.com). **Open** 7am-10am, noon-3pm, 6.30pm-9pm daily. **Credit** AmEx, DC, MC, V.
The Arniston Spa Hotel is the smartest place to stay in the village, and the same goes when it comes to dining, where the day's catch dictates the menu. This is also the best place in town to sample wines from the Cape, and private dinners in the wine cellar can be arranged on request.
▶ *For the hotel, see right.*

Cave Fish 'n Chips
Arniston Harbour (no phone). **Open** 10am-6pm daily. **No credit cards**.
Pack the extra napkins and settle in for a slap-up fish and chips lunch at this no-frills caravan right on the harbour. The tables are rustic, fingers are your cutlery and everything's deep-fried, but you won't find fresher fish in Arniston.

Agulhas.

Where to stay

Arniston Lodge
23 Main Road, Arniston (028 445 9175/ www.arnistonlodge.co.za). **Rates** R295-R395. **Credit** MC, V.
This two-storey thatched cottage is a stone's throw from the beach and blends in well with the traditional cottages of Kassiesbaai. With just four en-suite rooms on offer it's a homely spot to base yourself in the village.

★ Arniston Spa Hotel
See left. **Rates** R1,100-R1,800.
The grand Arniston Spa Hotel is unmistakable as you pull into town, occupying pride of place above the harbour. Most of the 40 rooms have fireplaces for when the notorious wintry cold fronts roll into town, but during summer the private balconies on the sea-facing rooms offer fantastic ocean views. There's also a Ginkgo spa.

Southermost B&B
Cnr Lighthouse & Van Breda streets, Agulhas (028 435 6565/www.southermost.co.za). **Rates** R275-R300. Closed winter. **No credit cards**.
The southernmost home on the continent sits with its shoulders hunched against the salty spray, much as it has done for the last 80-odd years. However, it also has a friendly face as the most southerly B&B in Africa. There are only three rooms; the honeymoon room adjoining the main house is the best.

Tip of Africa Guesthouse
Main Road, Agulhas (028 435 6903/ www.agulhassouthafrica.co.za). **Rates** R350-R550. **Credit** MC, V.
'Where Africa meets the sea,' is how Derick and Petro Burger bill their guesthouse, located on the road to the lighthouse. Hunting trophies and shipwreck portraits compete for space on the walls of the building. Guests staying in the seven en-suite rooms have the run of the house, from a comfortable upstairs lounge with a view to the cosy fireplace and indoor braai downstairs.

Tourist information

Bredasdorp Tourism *028 424 2584/ www.tourismcapeagulhas.co.za*.
Cape Agulhas Tourism Bureau *028 435 7185/ www.tourismcapeagulhas.co.za*.

Getting there

Arniston is approximately 220 kilometres (137 miles) from Cape Town. To get there, take the N2 to Caledon, turn off onto the R316 and follow the signs to Bredasdorp. From there, head towards Agulhas and Struisbaai by following the R319 for about 38 kilometres (24 miles).

ESCAPES & EXCURSIONS

Shark diving.

GANSBAAI

Along the coast between Cape Agulhas and Cape Point a once-snoring fishing village has swelled into a booming adventure hub, thanks to the hundreds of great whites patrolling its shores. This is shark city, or Big-2-Town to those in the know, and the sharks and whales run the show.

At first sight, the town itself seems five shades of grey. If you came for the scenery, you'd be forgiven for considering making an immediate U-turn and heading home. Don't be so hasty: the surrounding area – **De Kelders** on the one side and **Danger Point**, **Franskraal** and **Kleinbaai** on the other – has spectacular views.

De Kelders' cliffs boast some of the best land-based whale-watching in the world, with numerous caves dotting its rugged shoreline, while the Danger Point Peninsula is a shipwreck graveyard with a lighthouse from the top of which visitors can ogle the magnificent view.

Sea Kayak Cave Tours

Eco Adventures, 1 Main Road, De Kelders (028 384 3846/072 190 3800/www.eco-adventures. co.za). **Open** Oct-Dec. **Rates** *Cave tour* R80; R50 reductions. *Sea kayaking & cave tour* R450. **Credit** MC, V.

Paddle away on a sea kayak to the famous Drip Kelders caves. Mosey along the De Kelders coastline past a seal colony and, if you're lucky, you'll see a whale or two. Arriving at the caves you'll go on a tour and enjoy a dip in the mineral water that filters through the rock. If your sea legs aren't that sturdy, skip the kayaking and just do the tour.

★ White Shark Diving

Gansbaai isn't called the white shark capital of the world for laughs – shark cage diving is big business and the tourism bureau endorses a whopping eight companies. Most charge around R1,100 for a session, but offer different packages (refreshments, shuttle service to and from Cape Town and so on) so phone around to find one that suits your needs.

Great White Shark Tours *028 384 1418/ 083 300 2138/www.sharkcagediving.net.*
Marine Dynamics *028 384 1005/082 380 3405/www.sharkwatchsouthafrica.com.*
Shark Diving Unlimited *028 384 2787/082 441 4555/www.sharkdivingunlimited.com.*
Shark Lady *028 312 3287/083 746 8985/ www.sharklady.co.za.*
UnrealDive *021 553 0748/083 273 4920/ www.unrealdive.com.*
White Shark Ecoventures *021 532 0470/ 083 412 3733/www.white-shark-diving.com.*
White Shark Projects *028 384 1774/076 245 5880/www.whitesharkprojects.co.za.*
▶ *For more info on these ocean dwellers, see p72* **Shark Tactics**.

Where to eat & drink

Thyme & Rosemary

13 Main Road, Gansbaai (028 384 2076/072 884 4936). **Open** 9am-4.30pm, 6.30pm-late daily. **Credit** MC, V.

During the daytime, food is served in the garden, where herbs sprout from old boots and Victorian bath tubs. A silver bell on each table is for beckoning your waiter. Dig into hearty stews, soups, salads and seedloaf sandwiches, all served on a mismatched selection of antique crockery.

Where to stay

Great White House

5 Geelbek Street, Kleinbaai (028 384 3273/ www.white-house.co.za). **Rates** R250 per person. **Credit** AmEx, DC, MC, V.

Spend the night in a thatched fisherman's cottage, complete with whitewashed walls and fireplace. The Great White House is a stone's throw from Kleinbaai harbour, from where the shark-diving and whale-watching boats launch.

Misty Waves Cottage

Danger Point (021 449 2400). **Rates** R995 for cottage (1-4 people), plus R150 per person. **Credit** AmEx, DC, MC, V.

City slickers seeking to join with nature can spend the night in a stylish self-catering cottage next to the Danger Point Lighthouse. Barring the lighthouse, all you'll see for miles is *fynbos* and big blue sea.

Tourist information

Gansbaai Tourism Bureau *Gateway Centre, Kapokblom street (028 384 1439/www.gansbaai info.com/www.agulhassouthafrica.co.za)*.

Getting there

Gansbaai is 175 kilometres (110 miles) from Cape Town. Take the Hermanus turn-off from the N2 near Bot River and follow the R43 for 85 kilometres (53 miles) through Hermanus, Stanford and De Kelders into Gansbaai.

GREYTON

There's not a lot to do in Greyton, but that's exactly what locals and visitors love about this quaint village set against the Riviersonderend mountains. With church steeples peeking out from the morning mist (it's always misty until 11am, the locals say) and rose gardens lining the road, you could almost imagine yourself in Oxfordshire, not a quiet corner of the Overberg.

Attesting to the growing numbers of tourists, there's a restaurant on almost every corner, art galleries and interesting shops aplenty, and the region is even starting to produce its own wine with the likes of Lismore Estate Vineyards and Oewerzicht Cellars becoming popular.

There are a number of pretty walks from the village that can take anywhere from one to three hours. Maps are available from the tourism information office (*see p230*).

Where to eat & drink

★ Oak & Vigne Café

DS Botha Street (028 254 9037/www.oakand vigne.co.za). **Open** 8am-5pm daily. **Credit** DC, MC, V.

The veranda outside this café is a great spot for lunches, with substantial sandwiches and decadent cakes, but it's especially popular for the mean breakfasts. The adjoining deli is chock-full of fresh farm produce, home bakes and local wines – the ideal place to stock up for your weekend.

Pepper Tree

14 Main Road (028 254 9164. **Open** 4.30-9pm Tue; 10am-2pm, 4.30-9pm Wed-Fri; 10am-9pm Sat, Sun. **Credit** MC, V.

The first restaurant as you pull into Greyton should also be your first stop. This quaint little spot is famous for its lamb shank, but vegetarians will also have plenty of choice, with a good range of non-meaty meals. Unpretentious dining and friendly service have made this a popular place, so it's best to book in advance.

Where to stay

Acorns on Oak

2-4 Oak Street (028 254 9567/www.acorns-on-oak.co.za). **Rates** R395. **Credit** MC, V.

These charming suites have everything to make your stay as comfy as possible – including heated towel rails. Breakfasts are legendary. Spend some time roaming around the beautiful gardens.

Barnards

16 Main Road (028 254 9394/www.barnards hotel.co.za). **Rates** R325-R475. **Credit** AmEx, DC, MC, V.

From farmhouse to boutique hotel – this attractive building on Main Road has been both in its 170 years, but its latest chic incarnation offers city sophistication in a mix of rooms and cottages.

Lord Pickleby

58 Main Road (028 254 9839/www.thelord picklebly.co.za). **Rates** R300-R380. **Credit** MC, V.

A funky and eclectic addition to the Greyton accommodation scene, Lord Pickleby is perfect for townies who are here in search of a rural getaway with high-design touches.

Post House

Cnr Main and DS Botha Streets (028 254 9995/ www.theposthouse.co.za). **Rates** R425-R525 per person. **Credit** MC, V.

The Post House, which dates back to 1860, is brimming with character. Rooms are all clustered around a pretty country garden, and all boast fireplaces for those chilly winter nights. Make sure you sample the local Von Geusau chocolates at Le Petit Chocolat.

ESCAPES & EXCURSIONS

Tourist information

Greyton Tourism Bureau *29 Main Road (028 254 9564/www.greyton.net).*

Getting there

Greyton is 145 kilometres (90 miles) from Cape Town. By car, turn off the N2 about 20 kilometres (12 miles) past Bot River and follow the R406 to Greyton.

HERMANUS

Visitors flock to Hermanus every summer for some much-needed R&R. And to spy on the southern right whales, of course, who migrate here each spring to mate and calve. The town has been hailed as one of the best places for land-based whale-watching on the planet. The quaint Old Harbour has colourful fishing boats parked on its concrete shores, and is home to the **Harbour Museum** (028 312 1475), which sheds light on the town's fishing and whaling history. The **De Wet's Huis Photo Museum** (028 313 0418) in the market square depicts life in Hermanus way back in the day, while the **Whale House** (028 313 0418) next door is a new addition and boasts stylishly designed touch-screen displays, as well as a southern right whale skeleton.

▌FREE▐ Hermanus Cliff Path

New Harbour to Klein River along the coast (028 313 8100/www.fernkloof.com).
The best location in town for spotting whales, this 10km (six-mile) trail winds all along the shoreline from the New Harbour to the mouth of the Klein River, passing *fynbos*, tidal pools, fishing spots and lookout benches.

▶ *For whale-spotting locations in and around Cape Town, see p69* **Inside Track***.*

Horse Trail Safaris

17th Avenue, Lakeview Chalet Grounds (021 703 4396/www.horsetrailsafaris.co.za). **Rates** R200-R1,800. **No credit cards**.
Go for guided trots along Grotto Beach and all the way to De Kelders, exploring silvery sands and *fynbos*-clad mountains along the way.

Southern Right Charters

The Whale Shack, New Harbour (082 353 0550/www.southernrightcharters.co.za). **Cost** R550 June-Dec; R150 sundowners Jan-May. **Trips** *Sundowner trips* 6pm. *Whale-watching* 9am, noon, 3pm daily. **Credit** MC, V.
Watch the whales from a swanky white catamaran. Trips take around two hours and sightings are guaranteed in season. There's even a bar on board.

Walker Bay Adventures

Old Harbour (082 739 0159/www.walkerbay adventures.co.za). **Open** Sunrise-sunset daily. **Rates** R300. *Kayak wine tour* R400 per person, minimum 6. **No credit cards**.
Get up close and personal with whales, in kayaks or boats out in the big blue. Walker Bay Adventures is the only business with a permit to enter the Walker Bay Whale Sanctuary and get as close as 300m (985ft) to the whales. There are also longer trips with bird spotting and picnicking along the way.

Where to eat & drink

Bientang's Cave

Below Marine Drive, between Old Harbour & Marine Hotel (028 312 3454/www.bientangs cave.com). **Open** 11.30am-4pm daily; dinner by appointment. **Credit** DC, MC, V.

Hermanus.

Marine.

Dine inside a real cave. Try the set menu, which includes a range of oceanic delights. The restaurant is a prime whale-watching spot; the menu doles out useful information on whale behaviours, such as spy-hopping, lob-tailing, blowing and grunting.

Harbour Rock Seagrill & Sushi Bar

Site 24A, New Harbour (028 312 2920/www. harbourrock.co.za). **Open** 9am-10pm daily. **Credit** AmEx, DC, MC, V.

Perched on a cliff above the new harbour, Harbour Rock dishes up buffet breakfasts, grills and seafood – from sherried mussels to lemon-grilled sole. Decor is simple yet stylish, with wooden floors, bent pitchfork lampshades and enormous windows overlooking the big blue ocean. Outside, fishing boats and whales entertain you in season. Harbour Rock is also the only haven for sushi addicts in this part of the world – and a pretty lip-licking one at that.

★ Quayside Cabin

Lower Slipway, New Harbour (028 313 0752). **Open** noon-4pm, 7-10pm daily. **Credit** MC, V.

An orange shipping container on the edge of the new harbour has been transformed into a comfy seafood shack, complete with wooden tables and benches and a ceiling dripping with shells, signal lights and buoys. With such an enormous menu, it's tough to make up your mind; best just to close your eyes and point. The Malay-inspired dishes are great: try the snoek samosas or seafood hotpot in a Cape Malay masala sauce, served with rice and poppadoms.

La Vierge Restaurant & Champagne Verandah

R36, Hemel-en-Aarde Valley (028 313 2007/ www.lavierge.co.za). **Open** 9am-10pm daily. **Credit** AmEx, DC, MC, V.

La Vierge is the latest fine-dining hotspot on the lips of the locals. On the wine estate in the stunning Hemel-en-Aarde Valley, it boasts a French-inspired menu, swish decor and sweeping views over vineyards and farmland.

Where to stay

Auberge Burgundy

16 Harbour Road (028 313 1201/www.auberge. co.za). **Rates** R520-R690. **Credit** AmEx, DC, MC, V.

A stone's throw from the harbour, this Provençal-style guesthouse, with baby-blue shutters and terracotta walls, oozes Euro-charm. Lounge in the leafy garden, take a dip in the rooftop pool or step outside to explore the town. Breakfast is served at the seafront Burgundy restaurant, across the street.

★ Marine

Marine Drive (028 313 1000/www.marine-hermanus.co.za). **Rates** R1,750-R3,250. **Credit** AmEx, DC, MC, V.

This swanky hotel drips with swish touches, from executive housekeeper David de Vries's Zen *fynbos* flower arrangements to the posh seaside cocktail bar and lounge, with its lily-white whalebone wall pieces. The individually decorated rooms all have sea or mountain views and luxury amenities. The Pavilion and Seafood at the Marine restaurants serve exceptional food.

Tourist information

Hermanus Tourism Bureau *Old Station, Michell Street (028 312 2629/www.hermanus accommodation.co.za).*

Getting there

Hermanus is 125 kilometres (78 miles) from Cape Town. By car, take the Hermanus off-ramp off the N2 near Bot River and follow the R43 for 35 kilometres (22 miles) to Hermanus.

Garden Route

Spectacular forest scenery, endless beaches and a laid-back attitude.

Encompassing the towns of **George**, **Knysna** and **Plettenberg Bay**, among others, the lush and scenic stretch of coastline known as the Garden Route is a popular summer destination, largely thanks to its scenic and family-friendly beaches. It's a far cry from the low-key, remote coastal villages of the West Coast, however, and come December you'll be hard-pressed to find a secluded spot. A positive result of the tourist boom is that there's no shortage of good restaurants, hotels, accommodation and activities to make for a great visit.

GEORGE

This little city is ideally situated for exploring the Klein Karoo and the surrounding region. All you can see from the highway is its industrial sprawl; you need to drive nearly all the way through town before George starts showing itself in a prettier light – backlit by the dramatic **Outeniqua Mountains**, with forests, rolling farmland and golf courses. At the imposing steeple of Courtenay Street's Moederkerk, take a turn up Caledon Street, lined with stately historic residences, to the delightful **Botanical Gardens** (044 874 1558, www.botanicalgarden.co.za), and you'll see why this is such a popular destination among families and retirees.

The **Outeniqua Transport Museum** (2 Mission Street, 044 801 8243) showcases steam locomotives and model trains. A ride on the **Outeniqua Choo-Tjoe passenger train** (044 801 8202), departing from the station next door, is a lovely way of seeing the beautiful countryside between George and Mossel Bay.

Be sure to have your picture taken at the old oak tree on York Street, also known as the slave tree. This famous landmark was planted in 1811 and has an old metal chain and padlock embedded in it.

Fancourt Hotel & Country Club Golf Estate

Montagu Street, Blanco (044 804 0000/ www.fancourt.co.za). **Open** 10am-5pm daily. **Rates** R300-R690. **Credit** AmEx, DC, MC, V.

One of the reasons George has grown in popularitty is because of its proximity to this famous hotel and its surrounding golf courses. In fact, Fancourt is one of the Garden Route's pioneering luxury golf estates. Play the top-notch course at Bramble Hill or indulge at its five-star spa (044 804 0013) and no less than four excellent restaurants.

Where to eat & drink

Kafe Serefé

60 Courtenay Street (044 884 1012). **Open** 10am-4.30pm, 7pm-late Mon-Fri; 7pm-late Sat. **Credit** AmEx, DC, MC, V.
Kafe Serefé combines Turkish and Mediterranean flavours with hearty portions and Boere-kitsch decor. The meze are delicious; on Wednesday and Friday nights, a local belly-dancer entertains.

Old Townhouse

Cnr York & Market Streets (044 874 3663). **Open** noon-3pm, 6pm-late Mon-Fri; 6pm-late Sat. **Credit** AmEx, DC, MC, V.
George's oldest restaurant remains a hit among the locals. The muscadel-roasted lamb shank and kudu fillet are particularly popular.

Where to stay

See also left **Fancourt Hotel & Country Club Golf Estate**.

Fairview Historical Homestead

36 Stander Street (044 874 7781/www.fairview homestead.com). **Rates** R380-R450. **Credit** AmEx, DC, MC, V.

Garden of Eden.

ESCAPES & EXCURSIONS

This gracious 150-year-old house has been restored and now offers three comfortable and homely bedrooms. Dinner is served on request.

Tourist information

George Tourism Office *044 801 9295/ www.visitgeorge.co.za.*

Getting there

George is 440 kilometres (273 miles) from Cape Town. Take the N2.

KNYSNA

Knysna lies on the shores of a picturesque lagoon, its mouth flanked by two bluffs known as the Knysna Heads. Ships have come to a sticky end here – most notably the *Paquita* in 1903. Once a sleepy hamlet, popular with hippies, the town has grown dramatically over the past decade and more. Its town centre reflects Knysna's roots as a forestry station that boomed in the 1800s. Many of the original Victorian buildings survive and have been sensitively restored, helping to maintain the town's charm despite its growth. New Englandstyle **Thesen Island** is a development of exclusive boutiques and apartments on the site of an old sawmill. The **Knysna Quays** hum with activity every day and are a good place to browse for gifts and enjoy a waterside meal. Oysters are synonymous with the town and the crowds pour in for the annual oyster festival in July (www.oysterfestival.co.za). Visitors should consider a stop at Mitchell's Knysna Brewery (044 382 4685, www.mitchells knysnabrewery.com) for a tour and a tasting.

The Knysna forest and surrounding Outeniqua Mountains are good for hiking and bird-watching, and for spotting the elusive Knysna elephant.

Featherbed Company
Featherbed Ferry Terminus, Remembrance Avenue off Waterfront Drive (044 382 1693/7/ www.featherbed.co.za). **Open** 8am-5pm daily. **Rates** R85-R490. **Credit** AmEx, DC, MC, V.

**INSIDE TRACK
COAST TO COAST**

Free **Coast to Coast** backpacking guides are available at hostels across the country. Pick one up for a lowdown on South Africa's cheapest sleeps (www.coastingafrica.com).

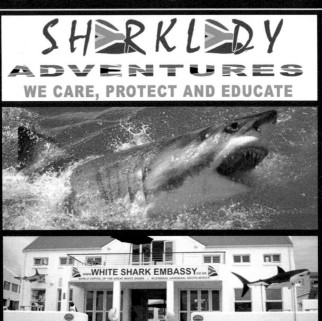

Choose from a variety of cruise options – from a quick trip to the Heads to a four-hour trek to the spectacular Featherbed Nature Reserve.

Knysna Elephant Park

N2, 22km outside Knysna (044 532 7732/ www.knysnaelephantpark.co.za). **Rates** R145; R75-R122 reductions. **Credit** AmEx, DC, MC, V.

Get up close and personal with these gentle giants with walks and rides on orphaned elephants from around the country. It's an inspirational experience.

Where to eat & drink

★ Firefly

152A Old Cape Road (044 382 1490/www. fireflyeatinghouse.co.za). **Open** 6.30-10pm Tue-Sat. **No credit cards**.

This tiny gem, complete with its fairy lights and cosy fireplace, is almost too good to share, but impossible not to tell the world about. Start with the renowned *bobotie* spring rolls and move on to one of the aromatic curries.

★ Ile de Pain

Boatshed, Thesen Island (044 302 5707). **Open** 8am-3pm Tue-Sat; 9am-1.30pm Sun. **Credit** AmEx, MC, V.

Once there, you'll understand why Ile de Pain has so many regulars. Pop in to grab the freshest breads hot from the wood-burning oven or stay in for a hearty breakfast or indulgent lunch from around the globe.
▶ *Master baker Markus Farbinger taught Jason Lilley of Jardine Bakery the art of breadmaking; see p103 Well Bread.*

★ Zachary's

Pezula Resort Hotel & Spa, Lagoonview Drive (044 302 3333/www.pezula.com). **Open** 7am-10pm daily. **Credit** AmEx, DC, MC, V.

Chef Geoffrey Murray's intense passion and respect for all things organic come to the fore at this swanky hotel restaurant, where he wows diners with the likes of roast butternut and lime soup with smoked crocodile or pork belly with citrus.
▶ *For more on the hotel in which it's housed, see right.*

Where to stay

Belvidere Manor Hotel

169 Duthie Drive, Belvidere Estate (044 387 1055/www.belvidere.co.za). **Rates** R600-R1,310. **Credit** AmEx, DC, MC, V.

Belvidere Estate is a hidden jewel oozing English countryside charm, and the Belvidere Manor Hotel fits in perfectly. The cosy cottages are equipped with kitchens if you don't feel like dining at the in-house pub or restaurant.

Lightley's Holiday Houseboats

Pick-up/berth Phantom Pass Road (044 386 0007/www.houseboats.co.za). **Rates** R1,295-R1,975. **Credit** MC, V.

The Knysna lagoon is your playground, and you can while away the day puttering about, catching some fish, and some sun. There are four- and six-berth options with fully equipped galleys.
▶ *You can also rent a houseboat on the Langebaan lagoon on the West Coast; for details, see p246.*

★ Pezula Resort Hotel & Spa

Lagoon View Drive, East Head (044 302 3333/ www.pezularesorthotel.com). **Rates** R5,350-R5,510. **Credit** AmEx, DC, MC, V.

The multi-award-winning Pezula Resort Hotel & Spa is one of the Garden Route's premier destinations. The 76 suites are modern and exceptionally comfortable and there are activities galore to keep you occupied – from a round of golf on the magnificent greens and fine dining at Zachary's (*see left*) to pamper sessions at the spa.

★ Phantom Forest

Phantom Pass Road (044 386 0046/www. phantomforest.com). **Rates** R1,450-R1,775. **Credit** AmEx, DC, MC, V.

A unique and magical place, Phantom Forest is a private nature reserve perched high in the forest. Accommodation consists of luxury tree suites or Moroccan-inspired havens. Explore the lodge through its suspended forest walkways, taking care not to disturb the naughty vervet monkeys.

Tourist information

Tourism Knysna *044 382 5510/www.tourism knysna.co.za.*

Getting there

Knysna is 500 kilometres (310 miles) from Cape Town. Take the N2.

PLETTENBERG BAY

Despite its rapid growth and enormous popularity, this former whaling station is still one of the most attractive destinations on the Garden Route. Unless you're prepared to brave the crowds, it's best to avoid the town during summer holidays when families descend en masse. It's fairly quiet out of season, though.

Plettenberg Bay, or Plett as it's colloquially known, is one of those towns that really does have something for everyone: gourmet restaurants, farm stalls and local markets for foodies; boutiques and decor shops for the fashion-conscious, and for nature lovers there are awe-inspiring hikes in one of the most lush

ESCAPES & EXCURSIONS

and beautiful spots in the country, as well as encounters with animals. **Robberg Marine & Nature Reserve** (permits at the entrance, about ten kilometres from town off Robberg Road) has great hikes for walkers of all levels in surroundings of jaw-dropping natural beauty. Plet is also blessed with some lovely beaches in the surrounding area – **Robberg Beach**, **Keurboomstrand** and **Nature's Valley**.

Just outside town, the area known as the **Crags** (www.cruisethecrags.co.za), named for its steep cliffs, is a great daytime destination with a range of venues to explore.

★ Bloukrans Bungy

Bloukrans River Bridge (042 281 1458/www. faceadrenalin.com). **Open** 8.30am-5pm daily. **Rates** R620. **Credit** AmEx, MC, V.
Yes, at 216m (709ft), this is the world's highest bungee jump, from the spectacular Bloukrans River Bridge east of Plett. If you're not quite up to handling so much adrenalin, you can opt for the cable slide or do the bridge walk – but a surprisingly large number of people do take the plunge.

Elephant Sanctuary

The Crags (044 534 8145/www.elephant sanctuary.co.za). **Tours** 8am-3.30pm daily. **Rates** R275; R150 reductions. **Credit** DC, MC, V.
Deepen your understanding of these magnificent creatures with trunk-in-hand walks, rides, brush-downs and sunrise and sunset tours. A marvellous way to spend a few hours, it'll leave you enlightened and inspired.

Keurbooms River Ferries

N2, Keurbooms River (083 254 3551/www.ferry. co.za). **Open** *Trips* 11am & 2pm (also 5pm in summer) daily. **Rates** R110; R55 reductions. **No credit cards**.
Take a magical journey up the Keurbooms River Estuary with your guide sharing interesting facts about the Keurbooms River Nature Reserve on the two-and-a-half-hour journey. Stop halfway for a river beach picnic and return rejuvenated.

★ Monkeyland & Birds of Eden

The Crags (044 534 8906/www.monkeyland. co.za/www.birdsofeden.co.za). **Open** 8am-5pm daily. **Admission** *One park* R115; R57.50 reductions. *Both parks* R184; R92 reductions. **Credit** AmEx, DC, MC, V.
These two animal sanctuaries are situated next to each other in the centre of the Crags. See lemurs, monkeys and apes on a one-hour guided walk and learn more about them, too; alternatively, walk through Birds of Eden's indigenous forest on elevated walkways and admire the array of colourful birds from around the world.

Plettenberg Bay Game Reserve

R340 (044 535 0000/www.plettenbergbay gamereserve.co.za). **Drives** *Summer* 8.30am, 10am, 11am, 12.30pm, 3pm, 4pm daily. *Winter* 10am, 11am, 12.30pm, 3pm daily. **Rates** R295. **Credit** MC, V.
Just outside Plett you can see over 30 species of game from the comfort of a Land Rover. If you're feeling particularly brave and active, try spotting some wild animals from horseback.

★ Tenikwa Wildlife Awareness Centre

The Crags (044 534 8170/www.tenikwa.co.za). **Tours** 9am-4.30pm daily. **Rates** R130; R60 reductions. **Credit** MC, V.
The latest wildlife addition to the Crags, Tenikwa introduces the visitor first-hand to all the lesser cats of Southern Africa, from lynx to serval, living in semi-natural surroundings. An informative guide will take you through the various enclosures in a one-hour tour to meet the bigger pussy cats, culminating in visiting a pair of cheetahs.

Tenikwa Wildlife Awareness Centre.

Where to eat & drink

★ Bramon Wine Estate

*N2, The Crags, 18km from Plettenberg Bay
(044 534 8007/www.bramonwines.co.za).* **Open**
11am-sunset daily. **Credit** AmEx, DC, MC, V.
Sit outside and chill among the vines at this, the
most eastern wine estate in South Africa. Make-
your-own meze platters, oysters, cheeses, pâtés and
heavenly bread are nicely accompanied with its
own-label Cap Classique.

Cornuti al Mare Restaurant & Bar

1 Perestrella Street (044 533 1277). **Open** noon-
11pm daily. **Credit** DC, MC, V.
You know you'll get a satisfying Italian meal at
Cornuti, a Plett stalwart. Dig into generous pastas
(the vongole is excellent), fishy specials or unusual
pizzas with unbelievably thin bases.

fu.shi & Boma

*Upperdeck Building, 3 Strand Street (044 533
6489/www.fushi.co.za).* **Open** *Boma* noon-10pm
daily (terrace menu). *fu.shi* 6-10pm daily (fine-
dining menu). **Credit** AmEx, DC, MC, V.
This zen-inspired multiple-venue establishment will
manage to please most of the people most of the
time. Start off with pre-dinner drinks and Asian-
style snacks at Boma, then move on to the main
restaurant, fu.shi, where you can dig into anything
from sushi and mild aromatic curries to chilli fests.

Ristorante Enrico

*Main Beach, Keurboomstrand (044 535 9818/
9585).* **Open** 11.30am-10pm daily (closed 4-6pm
in season). **Credit** AmEx, DC, MC, V.
Come home to Italy – slap bang on the beach at
Keurbooms, from where you can take in the endless
ocean views on a balmy day and dig into fabulous
pizzas and hearty pastas. Inside things are a bit
more formal, with an array of dishes from seafood
to veal and interesting salads. Don't leave without a
grappa shot.

Where to stay

Emily Moon River Lodge

*Rietvlei Road, off N2 (044 533 2982/www.emily
moon.co.za).* **Rates** R1,070. **Credit** AmEx, DC,
MC, V.
Eclectic African artefacts and studded doorways
welcome you to this lodge perched above the Bitou
River. Each of the eight suites has its own balcony
and outdoor shower. The rooms are airy and comfortable, with modern, clean lines and all the amenities you need.

★ Grand

*27 Main Road (044 533 3301/www.thegrand.
co.za).* **Rates** R950-R1,350. **Credit** AmEx, DC,
MC, V.

INSIDE TRACK
BACKPACKERS BUS

The **Baz Bus** is a hop-on, hop-off bus
service aimed at independent travellers.
The idea is that you buy one ticket to your
final destination, and then get on and off
as often as you like along the way. Buses
pick you up and drop you off at your hostel
door (cnr 275 Main & Frere Roads, Sea
Point, 021 439 2323, www.bazbus.com).

A bastion of over-the-top fabulousness, the Grand
is all about dark, moody walls, massive king-size
beds (they're so high you have to first climb on to a
footstool), vast open showers and fabulous views
over the ocean. *Photo p240.*

Kurland

*Kurland Estate, The Crags, 21km on N2 towards
Port Elizabeth (044 534 8082/www.kurland.
co.za).* **Rates** R1,300-R3,630. **Credit** AmEx, DC,
MC, V.
Home to the polo set during the summer months, this
hotel has 12 exclusive suites (some with their own
plunge pools) and has a huge focus on families – kids
have their own attic bedrooms, games room and
entertainment area.

Plettenberg

*40 Church Street, Lookout Rocks (044 533 2030/
www.plettenberg.com).* **Rates** R3,600-R7,150.
Credit AmEx, DC, MC, V.
The Plettenberg has the most stupendous views in
town. You can lounge away the day and drink in the
gorgeous views from a choice of two pools. The
Carchele Spa next door can give you whatever treatment you desire; finish the day with a meal at in-
house restaurant the Sand. *Photo p241.*

Tourist information

Plettenberg Bay Tourism Centre *044 533
4065/www.plettenbergbay.co.za.*

Getting there

Plettenberg Bay is 550 kilometres (340 miles)
from Cape Town. Take the N2.

OUDTSHOORN

Although not strictly part of the Garden Route,
Oudtshoorn is a popular destination within the
general area. It's the business centre of the
Klein Karoo and unapologetically cashes in
on the original Big Bird to whom it owes its
existence, with more ostrich memorabilia than
you'd think good taste would allow.

Grand. *See p239.*

To get a sense of Oudtshoorn, head to one of the hilly suburban streets on either side of the town, from where you'll be able to appreciate just how green the setting for the town is against the dry, rocky semi-desert stretching out around it. The surroundings are worth exploring by hiking, biking, quad-biking or kloofing (an adventure sport involving descending into ravines and watercourses) in the Swartberg or Outeniqua mountains.

You can also visit the town's famous **Cango Caves** for a spot of caving. And try to check out the annual **Klein Karoo National Arts Festival** (www.kknk.co.za), South Africa's largest arts festival, for a taste of the country's idiosyncratic Afrikaans culture.

★ Cango Caves

Off the R328, 30km from Oudtshoorn (044 272 7410/www.cangocaves.co.za). **Open** 9am-4pm daily. **Rates** *Standard tour* R55; R30 children. *Adventure tour* R70; R45 children. **Credit** AmEx, DC, MC, V.

The caves are an other-worldly experience. Take the standard guided tour that departs on the hour and sticks to the larger, airier chambers, like Fairy Queen's Palace and the Drum Room, or take the adventure tour, going deeper and further through

the narrow Devil's Chimney and Devil's Postbox, where wriggling through very narrow spaces on your belly is compulsory.

Cango Wildlife Ranch

On the R29 towards the Cango Caves (044 272 5593/www.cango.co.za). **Open** 8am-4.30pm daily. **Rates** R95; R60 children. **Credit** AmEx, DC, MC, V.

Get up close and personal with some of the wildest animals the planet has to offer. The hand-reared cheetahs are a premier draw, though residents are by no means restricted to African origins, and also include the white tiger and wallaby.

Oudtshoorn Ballooning

Launch from rugby field, middle of town (082 784 8539/www.oudtshoornballooning.co.za). **Rates** R2,100. **Credit** DC, MC, V.

In many ways, there's nothing quite as magnificent as seeing the surrounding landscape from a hot-air balloon. The hour-long flight can be both adrenalin-fuelled and romantic.

Safari Ostrich Show Farm

Off the R328 towards Mossel Bay, 6km from Oudtshoorn (044 272 7311/2/www.safari ostrich.co.za). **Open** 8am-5pm daily.

Admission R56 adults; R28 reductions.
Credit AmEx, DC, MC, V.

The Safari Ostrich Show Farm has been one of Oudtshoorn's most popular tourist attractions for more than 40 years. Take full advantage of the opportunity to stand on an ostrich egg (just to say you have), see chicks hatching and even ride one of these strange creatures. The Welgeluk Homestead is a national monument and gives a good glimpse into what life was like during the feather boom, especially in the showroom crammed with ostrich-related paraphernalia.

Where to eat & drink

Colony Restaurant

Queen's Hotel, Baron van Reede Street (044 272 2101/www.queenshotel.co.za). **Open** 6-10pm daily. **Credit** AmEx, DC, MC, V.

While the menu is similar to others in the area – solid fare heavy on the meat (and the haunches) – it's done with a fine-dining flair at the Colony, located in the gracious Queen's Hotel.

Jemima's

94 Baron van Reede Street (044 272 0808/www.jemimas.com). **Open** 11am-3pm, 6pm-late Mon-Fri; 6pm-late Sat, Sun. **Credit** AmEx, DC, MC, V.

Jemima's, on a historic stretch of the main road, is the most popular restaurant in town. It's easy to see why with its warm and convivial atmosphere, and meaty menu.

Where to stay

Oakdene Bed & Breakfast

99 Baron van Reede Street (044 272 3018/www. oakdene.co.za). **Rates** R375-R395. **Credit** MC, V.

A lovely traditional choice for bed and breakfast in one of the original historic houses in town, declared a national monument in 1998. The six three-star en-suite rooms are furnished with warm wood and cottage-like touches.

Queen's Hotel

5 Baron van Reede Street (044 272 2101/www.queenshotel.co.za). **Rates** R525. **Credit** AmEx, DC, MC, V.

The Queen's is a classic old hotel that's still at the hub of town life (just like it was when Queen Elizabeth visited in 1947). It's been completely refurbished with every mod con, and while the result is sometimes a little sterile, the lovely gardens and professional service make up for it.

Tourist information

Oudtshoorn Tourism Bureau *044 279 2532/www.oudtshoorn.com.*

Getting there

Oudtshoorn is 420 kilometres (261 miles) from Cape Town. To get there, take the N1, turning off at Worcester and following Route 62 into Oudtshoorn.

ESCAPES & EXCURSIONS

Plettenberg. *See p239.*

West Coast

Fields of flowers and a rugged coastline.

The natural splendour and laid-back ethos of the tranquil West Coast lend a distinct flavour to the area. Perhaps its most characteristic inland feature are the fields that burst into bloom with flowers of every colour each spring, bringing with them throngs of tourists. In coastal towns such as **Paternoster** and **Langebaan**, you'll find ubiquitous tubs of salty, dried fish known as *bokkoms*, a true West Coast delicacy. As you'd expect, there are plenty of fresh fish and crustaceans to be found too; expect to see them, in their battered and bouillabaissed form, on the

menus of the area's many seafood restaurants. A word of warning: the sea from which they are pulled is very cold. But for many there's no better way to refresh body and soul than to dip into its icy waters.

ESCAPES & EXCURSIONS

CITRUSDAL & CLANWILLIAM

Apart from the pristine natural surrounds of the fertile Olifants River Valley, this area offers watersports at Clanwilliam dam, plenty of hiking, and San Bushman rock-art sites in the ochre mountains of the Cederberg towards the east. Produce is another characteristic of the area, for sale at farm stalls dotted along the roads.

You can get a feel for the area's history by strolling down the main road of **Clanwilliam** and visiting the beautiful Cape Dutch **Blomkerk**, which now houses the local museum. The village is perhaps most famous for its dam, and summer holidays see it come alive with boaters and waterskiers.

During winter the lush citrus orchards of **Citrusdal** are highlighted with bright oranges, tangerines, satsumas, *naartjies* and clementines, earning its nickname of Golden Valley.

INSIDE TRACK
BOKKOMS

One of the West Coast's most prized local delicacies, *bokkoms* are small fish (called harders) that are salted, sewn together into bunches and then strung up and left in the sun to dry. Try them with bread, jam and a generous glass of white wine.

★ Cederberg Wilderness Reserve
From N7, turn off at sign to Algeria & drive 17km (021 659 3500/www.capenature.org.za). **Open** 7.30am-4.30pm daily. **Rates** R35 day hike; R55 overnight hike. **Credit** MC, V.
Time has carved spectacular rock formations from the ochre stone of the Cederberg Wilderness; in particular, look out for those called the Maltese Cross and Wolfberg Arch. A variety of hiking routes of varying intensity are available in the reserve; if you hardy enough to tackle them, it's advisable to contact Cape Nature Conservation at the Algeria station for permits, detailed hiking maps and accommodation options.
▶ *Avid climbers should also explore the mountains surrounding Montagu in the Winelands; see p213.*

Where to stay & eat

★ Bushman's Kloof
On Clanwilliam–Wupperthal road, 43km from Clanwilliam (021 685 2598/www.bushmans kloof.co.za). **Rate** R2,600. **Credit** AmEx, DC, MC, V.
Bushman's Kloof Wilderness Reserve has luxury rooms with private patios and top-notch dining options that can cater to every possible whim. Alternatively, book in with a group of friends at the Koro Lodge, where you'll have a villa to yourself, and your own chef and guide too. Either way, there's nothing quite like unwinding at the spa while staring at the spectacular rocky scenery.

Clanwilliam Lodge

*Graafwater Road, Clanwilliam (027 482 1777/
www.clanwilliamlodge.co.za)*. **Rates** R450-R1,500.
Credit AmEx, MC, V.
This elegantly refurbished former girls' hostel, dating from 1916, offers contemporary accommodation in large, air-conditioned rooms (a necessity, as thermometers often push close to 40°C in summer). The poolside restaurant serves light meals during the day; dinner is a more refined affair, with choices such as walnut-crumbed kingklip.

Mount Ceder

*From R303, turn right at Op-die-Berg at the
Cederberg/Ceres Karoo turn-off and follow signs
for a further 51km (023 317 0848/www.mount
ceder.co.za)*. **Rates** R585-R2,470. **Credit** MC, V.
If the deafening silence of the Koue Bokkeveld doesn't get you in the holiday mood, relaxing in the jacuzzi of one of these self-catering cottages surely will. It's hard to tire of the uninterrupted views of the Cederberg and the soothing sound of nearby babbling brooks.

Tourist information

Citrusdal Tourism Bureau *022 921 3210/
www.citrusdal.info*.
Clanwilliam Tourism Bureau *027 482 2024/
www.clanwilliam.info*.

Getting there

For both, head north out of Cape Town on the N7. Citrusdal is about 170 kilometres (106 miles) from Cape Town, Clanwilliam is around 240 kilometres (149 miles) away.

DARLING

Surrounded by farmlands, Darling is something of an artists' colony. It's also home to one of South Africa's most famous satirists, Evita Bezuidenhout, who holds court at the original station with her act *Evita se Perron* (*see p244*). But despite its sense of rural remoteness, Darling is less than an hour from Cape Town. It's also home to a good selection of restaurants, a wine route and a handful of antiques shops.

Darling Museum

Cnr Pastorie & Hill Streets (022 492 3361).
Open 9am-1pm, 2-4pm Mon-Thur; 9am-1pm, 2-3.30pm Fri; 10am-3pm Sat, Sun. **Admission** R5; R2 children. **No credit cards**.
A well-curated and fascinating exhibition of items collected from long-standing families and homesteads in the area, including farm implements, machinery and household essentials. It's also home to the Butter Museum – Darling was a centre of the butter industry in its heyday.

Cederberg Wilderness Reserve, including the **Maltese Cross** (*above*) and the **Wolfberg Arch** (*below right*).

Citrusdal. *See p242.*

★ Darling Wine & Art Experience

*Cloof Wine Estate (022 492 2839/www.cloof.
co.za); Groote Post (022 492 3430/www.groote
post.com); Darling Cellars (022 492 2276/
www.darlingcellars.co.za); Ormonde Vineyards
(022 492 3540/www.ormonde.co.za); Oudepost
Estate Wines (022 492 3553).*

This country wine route is one that gets visitors up close and personal with the winemakers and has made massive inroads in showcasing the excellent wines produced in the region. The route now encompasses some art and culture happenings around town.

★ Evita se Perron

*Old Darling Railway Station, Arcadia Street
(022 492 2831/2851/www.evita.co.za).* **Open**
10am-4pm Tue-Sun, and for evening shows.
Credit DC, MC, V.

Not only does the town's most famous citizen have a street named after her – she's also credited with helping to put what was once a one-horse West Coast town on the cultural map. Look out for the pink building that used to house the Darling Railway Station, and book a spot at a weekend show where theatre personality Pieter Dirk Uys dons his Evita personality and raises the rafters.

ᴿᴿᴱᴱ !Khwa ttu

*R27, 4km before Yzerfontein/Darling turn-off
(022 492 2998/www.khwattu.org).* **Open** 9am-
5pm Tue-Sun. **Credit** DC, MC, V. **Rates** free;
R175 guided tour.

At the !Khwa ttu project, San Bushmen share their nomadic culture with visitors. Aside from a community benefit craft shop, there's an on-site restaurant where San Bushman kitchen and restaurant trainees serve locally grown and produced fare. Enjoy homemade breads and mouth-watering cakes from a locally inspired menu.

Rondeberg Nature Reserve

*R27, 29km S of Darling (022 492 3435/
www.rondeberg.co.za).* **Open** Aug, Sept only.

Admission R90 for 2hr guided tour.
No credit cards.

You don't have to be a flower obsessive to appreciate the beauty of this pristine private nature reserve. Guided tours showcasing some of the 900 flower species are a highlight.

Where to eat & drink

Cloof Wine Estate

*From R315, turn off at Darling Cellars (022 492
2839/www.cloof.co.za).* **Open** *Restaurant* noon-
2pm daily. *Tastings* 10am-4pm daily. **Credit**
AmEx, DC, MC, V.

Lunch on Sunday at Cloof Gourmet BBQ is perfect after a wine-tasting morning. Expect a seasonal, often Asian-inspired menu and, of course, Cloof wines to accompany the meal. Huge lawns, tables under the trees and a sparkling pool make it an ideal lunch stop for families.

Hilda's Kitchen at Groote Post

*Groote Post Wine Farm, Darling Hills Road (022
492 2825/022 492 3430/www.grootepost.com).*
Open noon-2.30pm Wed-Sun. Closed July.
Credit MC, V.

This excellent eaterie has plenty of city fans, and it's easy to see why. The menu brims with locally sourced produce and is designed to complement the farm's range of wines. Expect the likes of springbok carpaccio with plum relish or a down-to-earth Old Man steak roll, served with hand-cut potato fries. Booking essential.

Where to stay

Darling Lodge

*22 Pastorie Street (022 492 3062/www.darling
lodge.co.za).* **Rates** R400-R450. **Credit** AmEx,
DC, MC, V.

Victorian details abound at this quality guesthouse, located in the heart of the village, where each of the six en-suite rooms is named after a local artist.

Trinity Guest Lodge & Restaurant

19 Long Street (022 492 3430/www.trinity lodge.co.za). **Rates** From R350. **Credit** AmEx, DC, MC, V.

New life has been breathed into this charming country stop. You can book the whole place if you're travelling with a group: it now sleeps 12, and there's a family suite. It also hosts expert-led culinary weekends that include wine and olive tastings at local estates. There's a lovely garden, and a pool too.

Tourist information

Darling Tourism Bureau *022 492 3361/ www.darlingtourism.co.za.*

Getting there

Darling is 72 kilometres (44 miles) from Cape Town. Take the R27 north, then turn right on to the R307. At the T-junction turn left to Darling.

LANGEBAAN

The town of Langebaan is a well-known holiday destination, much loved for its lagoon. This warm body of water is a life-giver to some 70,000 birds that migrate here for the summer each year. In similar vein, sun seekers from far and wide descend upon the lagoon during the summer holidays, transforming the otherwise quiet town into a rather rowdy mix of fishermen, watersports fanatics and sunbathers. It might not be one of the most picturesque towns on the West Coast, but it's certainly the closest you'll get to a small-town seaside getaway this close to the Mother City.

Bugaloo Boat Trips

Berth No.1, Club Mykonos Marina (022 772 0277/www.bugalooadventures.co.za). **Open** 9am-5pm Sat, Sun; by appointment Mon-Fri. **Rates** from R200. **Credit** MC, V.

Sheltered from the open seas, the Langebaan lagoon is ideal for boating trips in most weather conditions. These boats seat up to ten, so take the whole family and opt for the three-hour Three Island trip, which includes Jutten, Vondeling and Schaapen Islands.

Cape Sports Centre

98 Main Road (022 772 1114/www.capesport. co.za). **Open** *Summer* 9am-5pm daily. *Winter* 10am-4pm daily. **Rates** R60-R545 to hire equipment for 2hrs; R995-R2,185 for lessons. **Credit** AmEx, DC, MC, V.

On the Langebaan lagoon, the Cape Sports Centre offers watersports enthusiasts all the wind-fuelled activities their hearts could desire – from kite-boarding to wind-surfing. Expertly trained staff are on hand if you're a less experienced adventurer or brave first-timer.

Where to eat & drink

Geelbek

West Coast National Park, Langebaan Lagoon (022 772 2134/www.geelbek.co.za). **Open** 9am-5pm daily. **Credit** DC, MC, V.

Situated right in the National Park, Geelbek offers Cape Malay cuisine in the historic homestead of the Geelbeksfontein farm. Expect generously sized portions of home-made chicken pie, slow-cooked lamb stew and Cape Malay lamb curry with all the traditional trimmings of stewed fruit, sambals and roti.

Die Strandloper Restaurant & Beach Bar

On the beach, off the road to Club Mykonos (022 772 2490/083 227 7195/www.strandloper. com). **Open** *Summer* from noon (lunch); from 6pm (dinner) daily. *Winter* phone to check. **No credit cards**.

Die Strandloper follows in the footsteps of the equally popular Muisbosskerm open-air restaurant at Lambert's Bay, not so very far from here. It's quite refined: think grilled harders with sweet potato, mussels in garlic, smoked angelfish or grilled white stumpnose.

Where to stay

Farmhouse Hotel

5 Egret Street (022 772 2062/www.the farmhousehotel.com). **Rates** R560-R800. **Credit** AmEx, DC, MC, V.

Just far enough from the hustle and bustle of the beach-going holiday crowds, the Farmhouse offers elegant, luxury accommodation in a Cape Dutch-styled homestead. The cosy Superior rooms are perfectly equipped for winter, each with a fireplace; they also have beautiful views of Saldanha bay. If you're on a tighter budget, the smaller Traveller's room makes for a fine deal.

Friday Island

92 Main Road (022 772 2506/www.friday island.co.za). **Rates** R300-R380. **Credit** DC, MC, V.

The comfortable and whitewashed rooms of the upmarket, backpacker-type lodging at Friday Island will have you in holiday mode, pronto. Near to the popular Cape Sports Centre, this haunt is frequented by young, fit and fabulously tanned surfers. The lovely restaurant offers a bit of everything, with a view of the lagoon to boot.

★ Larus & Nirvana Houseboats

Kraalbaai, West Coast National Park, Langebaan Lagoon (021 689 9718/021 689 5639/www.houseboating.co.za). **Rates** *Larus* R1,200 (for 4 people). *Nirvana* R6,000 (for 10 people minimum). **No credit cards**.

These two luxurious houseboats float in the quiet waters of Kraalbaai. *Nirvana* sleeps up to 24 people. You can dine alfresco on the foredeck, while the spacious lounge is equipped with sleeper couches and a fireplace, perfect for cosying up on chilly evenings. Not quite as sleek, the smaller *Larus* accommodates up to six guests for a more intimate break.

▶ *For more houseboats, try Lightleys Holiday Houseboats on the Knysna lagoon; see p235.*

Tourist information

Langebaan Tourism Bureau *022 772 1515/ www.langebaaninfo.com.*

Getting there

Langebaan is 124 kilometres (77 miles) from Cape Town. Take the R27 north.

PATERNOSTER

There is no scenery more typical of the West Coast than what you'll see at the fishing village of Paternoster. As you reach the coast the rather harsh Swartland landscape suddenly gives way to the welcome sight of white beaches, often littered with brightly coloured *kreefbakkies* (crayfish traps) – testimony to the fact that life on the West Coast is pretty much concentrated on fishing. Apart from the freezing cold water, you'd be forgiven for thinking you'd been teleported to the Mediterranean.

★ Cape Columbine Nature Reserve
5km from Paternoster (022 752 2718).
Open daily. **Admission** R10; R7 reductions.
No credit cards.
As with the rest of the West Coast, the veld here comes alive with flowers in late winter and early spring, although it does not become as densely carpeted with daisies as surrounding areas. The reserve consists mainly of *strandveld* – a thriving combination of coastal *fynbos* and peculiarly shaped succulents that bear unusually colourful blossoms in spring. Two self-catering cottages are located adjacent to the Cape Columbine lighthouse, each with accommodation for eight people (021 449 2400).

Where to eat & drink

★ Noisy Oyster
62 St Augustine Road (022 752 2196/079 491 5765/www.noisyoysterseafood.com). **Open** noon-3pm, 6-9pm Wed-Sat; noon-3pm Sun. **Credit** DC, MC, V.
This cosy restaurant easily rivals trendy city establishments. In summer, there's alfresco dining in the colourful back garden, while on colder days the outside fireplace roars away and warm blankets are handed out. Expect seasonal creations

such as yellowtail with fresh mango and papaya salsa drenched in beurre blanc, or delicious Asian-inspired fish cakes.

Voorstrandt
Strandloper Street (022 752 2038). **Open** 11am-9pm Mon-Fri; 11am-9.30pm Sat, Sun. **Credit** MC, V.
Right on the beach, Voorstrandt has one of the most spectacular views of pristine West Coast beach. Seafood is available in abundance, with a few regional catches. If you're hungry, try the generous fish plate with three kinds of fish and three different sauces.

Where to stay

★ Oystercatcher's Haven
48 Sonkwas Road, Bekbaai (022 752 2193/ www.oystercatchershaven.com). **Rates** R685. **Credit** MC, V.
Perched on the rocks in the most spectacular location in Bekbaai, this colonial-style guesthouse offers luxury sea-facing accommodation. Enjoy a hearty breakfast or sundowners on the veranda, or have a romantic picnic among the secluded boulders of Bekbaai's unspoiled beach, which is but a couple of steps away.

Paternoster Seaside Cottages
St Augustine Road (073 844 7722/www. seasidecottage.co.za). **Rates** R1,600 (sleeps 4). **Credit** MC, V.
The stars of this self-catering portfolio are two quaint houses boasting some of the best views of Paternoster bay. All the luxuries are here – including infinity pools that overlook the azure waters.

Salt Coast Fine Foods & Inn
Mosselbank Street (022 752 2063/www.saltcoast. co.za). **Rates** R600. *Cooking courses* from R1,500 per day. **No credit cards.**
Two cosy, en suite double rooms are available here, but the cooking classes are just as much of a draw. They span three to four days, and guests join owner and cook extraordinaire Suzi Holzhausen in everything from gathering ingredients to cooking and wine pairing; and, of course, eating the results.

Tourist information

Paternoster Tourism Bureau *c/o Vredenburg Tourism (022 752 2323/www.paternosterinfo. co.za).*

Getting there

Paternoster is 145 kilometres (90 miles) from Cape Town. Take the R27 north until you get to the junction with the R45. Turn left and follow the signs to Vredenburg and then Paternoster.

Long Street. *See p43.*

Getting Around

DIRECTORY

ARRIVING & LEAVING

By air

An estimated R1 billion has been spent on a long-overdue rehauling of **Cape Town International Airport** (011 921 6262, www.acsa.co.za) in time for the 2010 FIFA Soccer World Cup. This includes the addition of a huge car park, a shopping mall and, most importantly, a brand spanking new terminal building.

The airport is about 22km (14 miles) from Cape Town's city centre and the N2 highway is the fastest and most direct route between the two. Excluding any unexpected delays, it should take you about 30 minutes to drive into the centre outside peak hours (7-9am and 4.30-6pm); otherwise it can easily take up to an hour. Reputable airport car rental companies include **Avis** (www.avis.co.za), **Hertz** (www.hertz.co.za) and **Budget** (www.budget.co.za).

If you are not driving, you can make your way to the city with one of the airport's shuttle services like **Way2Go** (0861 929 246), **Magic Bus** (021 505 6300) and **City Hopper** (021 934 4440) or organise a **Rikkis** shuttle (0861 745547/ www.rikkis.co.za). Hail a cab from the airport-authorised **Touch Down Taxis** (021 919 4659). Depending on which company you use the journey to the centre should cost R180-R280.

Major airlines

Besides the national carrier, **South African Airways** (www.flysaa. com), other international airlines with daily direct flights to Cape Town include **Air Malaysia** (www.malaysiaairlines.co.za), **KLM** (www.klm.com), **Air Namibia** (www.airnamibia.com), **Qatar** (www.qatarairways.com) and **Air Mauritius** (www.airmauritius.com).

Domestic carriers are **SAA** (www.flysaa.co.za), **SA Airlink** (www.saairlink.co.za) and **British Airways** (www.ba.co.za). There are always flight specials on offer at the various airline carriers, so it's a good idea to keep checking their websites. The Airports Company of South Africa (021 937 1200/086 727 7888/ www.airports.co.za) has three budget domestic airlines, namely **Kulula.com** (www.kulula.com), **1Time** (www.1time.co.za) and **Mango Air** (www.flymango.com).

PUBLIC TRANSPORT

Cape Town's public transport isn't exactly the embodiment of efficiency, and if you're travelling on a tight schedule, you should organise your own car. Failing that, you can organise a taxi service or even brave the local minibus taxis.

Buses

Golden Arrow Buses (0800 656 463/www.gabs.co.za) are omnipresent within the city limits and the suburbs. The 'Bus for Us' isn't a touristy mode of transport and won't take you to remote sightseeing destinations, but it will get you from A to B in the city for a relatively humble amount. Tickets cost around R10 to R15 for a one-way journey.

The **City Sightseeing Bus** (021 511 6000/www.citysight seeing.co.za) caters to foreigners, touring the expanses of the Southern Peninsula on the Blue Route and exploring the City Bowl sights on the Red Route. The first bus leaves from the Aquarium at the V&A Waterfront at around 9am (and every 20 minutes thereafter until 5pm). Day tickets (where you can hop on and off to your heart's content) will set you back about R120.

Minibus taxis

In South Africa the term 'taxi' can refer either to a meter-running sedan vehicle (see below) or to a gung-ho, packed-to-the-rafters minibus. The latter is one of the country's most popular modes of transport because they're cheap (about R5 for an inner-city trip), super-speedy and generally reliable. If you're up for a thrilling ride through the city, stick out your hand to the side and a taxi will materialise from the ether. Be sure to find out the end destination beforehand and have your fare ready for the taxi guard.

Taxis

Sedan taxis are also an ever-present fixture in the city, but are more expensive, charging around R12 a kilometre. The Cape Town Tourism Visitor Information Centre (021 426 4260/021 405 4500) will gladly point you in the right direction with a list of their recommended taxi companies. **Unicab** (021 486 1600) and **Excite** (021 418 4444) are generally reliable options.

You'd be forgiven for doing a double take when seeing cars looking suspiciously akin to England's black cabs driving around town. These **Rikkis taxis** (0861 745547/www.rikkis.co.za) are very much local, however, and fast becoming one of the city's preferred modes of transport. An added bonus is that if you've left your mobile phone at home, you can make a free call to them from one of the many canary-yellow Rikki phones scattered about the city. Fares are fixed-rate rather than metered so work out better value than ordinary taxis if you are taking a long journey or sharing the ride with others.

Trains

The Cape Town railway service, **Metrorail** (0800 656 463/www. capemetrorail.co.za), isn't exactly predictable, with local trains being bang on time one day and hopelessly delayed the next, so relying on this mode of transport if you want to be punctual isn't a good idea. The **Cape Town Railway Station** (021 449 2991) in Adderley Street is the centre of all train networks in the Western Cape. The safest time to travel is between 7am-9am and 4pm-6pm. Minimise unnecessary risks by travelling first class and keeping all your valuables close at hand and out of sight.

Most long-distance trains have dining cars and catering trolleys, and it's definitely worth opting for a first-class cabin. Ticket prices and timetables are available from **Shosholoza Meyl** (086 000 8888/ www.spoornet.co.za).

If you really want to splash out, there's also the option of travelling up-country with one of South Africa's two luxury train services.

The **Blue Train** (021 449 2672/www.bluetrain.co.za) or **Rovos Rail** (021 421 4020/www.rovos.co.za).

CYCLING

There are several options if you have a penchant for getting about on two wheels rather than four. You can hire a bicycle from the adventure travel experts, **Downhill Adventures** (021 422 0388/www.downhilladventures.com), or you can rent a Harley from urban specialists **Harley-Davidson Cape Town** (021 446 2980/www.harley-davidson-capetown.com). Other motorbike rental companies include **The Bike Business** (33 Buitengracht, between Castle and Strand streets, 072 250 1691/www.thebikebusiness.co.za) and **La Dolce Vita Biking Rentals** 13D Kloof Nek Road, Gardens, (021 423 5000/www.ldvbiking.co.za).

DRIVING

Driving is on the left. Maybe it's the fresh mountain air or the sunshine and sea breezes, but Capetonians seem pretty casual in their approach to driving: they aren't particularly bothered about trivialities like indicating before changing lanes or checking their blind spots and minibus taxis are no exception.

Road safety statistics aren't much to shout about either – drink driving and speeding are the biggest culprits for accidents, especially at Christmas. Don't take unnecessary (and pricey) risks by speeding or driving under the influence; it's just not worth it.

Vehicle hire

If you're over 25 and have an international driver's license, hiring a car in the Mother City is easy. There's a list of rental agencies as long as your arm, but the most reputable of these remain **Avis** (021 424 1177/086 102 1111) and **Hertz** (021 935 4800). The rates are generally worked out according to the amount of kilometres travelled. It's worth doing comparative price check beforehand – some agencies offer specials like free mileage. 'No frills' rental companies include **Value Car Hire** (021 386 7699/www.valuecarhire.co.za) and **Budget** (021 418 5232).

Petrol stations

There's no shortage of petrol (gas) stations in the city, particularly along main roads such as Buitengracht, Orange and Somerset Roads.

The majority of these stations are open 24 hours a day, and most have convenience stores offering midnight snacks, but it's never advisable to drive around in the sticks if you are low on petrol. At the time of going to print, petrol cost R7 per litre, but it fluctuates as much as the local weather. It's customary to tip your pump attendant or 'petrol jockey' R5-R10 after filling up, if you've had good service and a friendly smile.

Insurance

Make sure to establish whether or not your car insurance covers road damage to the car – driving around on gravel roads tends to be tricky, and even dangerous. When renting a car, check your agreement for all details pertaining to damage and liability insurance, as levels of cover vary. If you don't have a home policy that covers you for every eventuality, it's best to pre-book via a multinational car hire company while still in your home country.

Parking

Finding a parking space in the city centre can be a bit of a nightmare, especially during peak hours. The ubiquitous neon-bibbed traffic wardens, or car guards, as they're known here, are another factor to contend with when deciding on where to park. Some are official, donning orange vests and carrying around meters, and some are chancers, appearing from out of nowhere and expecting alms when the time comes for you to leave. If you aren't keen to contend with this, drive around a bit longer and find an underground parking garage or parking lot, which are generally safer and involve less unwanted hassle.

When parking on the street during the day, don't under any circumstances leave your car on a yellow or red line, because your vehicle will be clamped, or worse towed, resulting in a painfully tedious and pricey (up to R1,000) recovery process. If your car has been towed, contact the traffic department's **towing section** (021 406 8861). Remember to park in a well-lit, populated area if you can't find an official parking lot when going out at night.

WALKING

Apart from the City Bowl, which is easily navigable afoot, the rest of Cape Town is really more of a driver's town, predominantly because of the distances involved, but also because it's the safest way to get around. The city centre, V&A Waterfront and beachside promenades lend themselves to leisurely strolling and are quite safe thanks to efforts made through local initiatives and authorities. Walking around the periphery of the City Bowl on your own isn't advisable if you're unfamiliar with the area though – tourists unfortunately make the softest targets. Here are some general safety tips worth bearing in mind:

● Avoid dark, isolated areas.
● Don't walk alone.
● When lost, try to find a police or traffic officer, or go to the nearest shop or petrol station to ask for directions.
● Wearing a flashy camera around your neck is tantamount to carrying a neon sign flashing, 'Tourist!'. If you're packing valuables, keep them in a backpack or shoulder bag and carry it close to your body.
● Never carry large sums of cash with you. Keep small change in your wallet or purse and bank notes and credit cards in an inside pocket.
● Steer clear of anyone claiming to have a stash of Calvin Klein perfume at a special discount or offering you the opportunity to get rich quickly. Sadly, there are also con artists who'll play on your sympathies to make a quick buck.
● When in doubt, call a cab. Always carry the number of a reliable company (see p248).

Walking tours

Tours are a great way to explore the city's bustling, ever-changing streets, squares and hotspots – and get clued up on the preparations for 2010. There are also many specialist tours that delve a little deeper into various aspects of the Cape's history. The following are recommended walking tour operators. See p255 for further information on other tours in the City.
Central City Walking Tours (021 419 1881/www.capetownpartnership.co.za). **Cape Town on Foot** (021 462 4252/www.wanderlust.co.za). **Footsteps to Freedom** (021 671 6878/083 452 1112/www.footstepsto freedom.co.za).

DIRECTORY

Resources A-Z

DIRECTORY

AGE RESTRICTIONS

The legal age for both driving and buying (and drinking) alcohol is 18. The age of consent is 16. Smoking and purchasing tobacco is legal for people over 16.

ATTITUDE & ETIQUETTE

Much like in Australia, a generally friendly, informal atmosphere reigns in South Africa and people usually introduce themselves by their first name, even in business relationships.

As a rule of thumb, Capetonians are more relaxed and laid back than their Gauteng brethren – much to the disdain of many people from Gauteng. Most organised events start on time, but a true Capetonian will always manage to be at least half an hour late for informal gatherings.

BUSINESS

Business organisations

Cape Chamber House *19 Louis Gradner Street, City Bowl (021 402 4300/www.caperegional chamber.co.za).* **Open** 8.30am-4.15pm Mon-Fri. **Map** p275 I3.
The Cape Regional Chamber is the principal source for business information and services. Cape Town is regarded as the hub of South African commerce.
Wesgro *021 487 8600/ www.wesgro.org.za.*
Wesgro is the official Trade and Investment Promotion Agency for the Western Cape and is the first point of contact for local exporters, foreign importers and investors wishing to take advantage of Cape investment opportunities.

Conventions & conferences

Cape Town International Convention Centre *021 410 5000/ www.capetownconvention.com.* **Map** p275 H3. *See also p45.*
This conference centre offers a strong array of facilities, including a dedicated exhibition space and generous facilities for both meetings and banquets.
Other spacious venues include the **Good Hope Centre** (021 465 4688) and the **Civic Centre** (021 400 1111), but they are decidedly more retro and less glamorous.

Couriers

DHL Worldwide Express *086 034 5000/www.dhl.co.za.*
Fedex *080 003 3339/ www.fedex.com/za.*
TNT *086 012 2441/www.tnt.com.*
XPS *021 380 2400/http://xps.co.za.*
UPS *021 555 2745/www.ups.co.za.*

Shipping

Britannia *021 556 9448/ www.britannia.co.za.*
Island View Shipping *021 425 2285/www.ivs.co.za.*

Translators & interpreters

Folio Translation Consultants *021 426 2727/www.folio-online. co.za.*
SATI – South African Translators' Institute *021 976 9563/011 803 2681/ www.translators.org.za.*

Consumer affairs

Call these companies with any consumer-related problems, enquiries and complaints:

Consumer Affairs Office *021 483 5133.*
Consumer Complaint Line *0800 007 081.*

CUSTOMS

There is a huge list of prohibited goods. If in doubt, visit www. sars.gov.za, and follow the Customs link, or call 0860 121218.
Used personal effects are duty free, as are new personal effects up to the value of R3,000. For additional goods up to the value of R12,000, a flat rate of 20% duty will be charged. Other allowances for visitors to South Africa are as follows (per adult):

1 litre of spirits
2 litres of wine
400 cigarettes
50 cigars
50ml perfume
250ml eau de toilette

People who are under 18 years old are not allowed to bring any tobacco or alcohol products into the country, and adults need a permit for firearms (available at entry points, valid for 180 days).

DISABLED

Since Cape Town is such a major international tourist destination, most of its hotels, attractions and malls have some form of disabled access and are usually graded according to how disabled-friendly they are. If you're disabled you can usually arrange with your airline for someone to come and meet you on arrival and they will also make the necessary arrangements for you while on board the plane. Most reputable car-hire companies provide vehicles with hand control. For any further enquiries phone the **Association for the Physically Disabled** (011 646 8331, www.apd.org.za), based in Johannesburg or, if you are blind, the **SA National Council for the Blind** (021 979 2451, www.sancb.org.za).

DRUGS

Cannabis, or dagga as it's locally known, is available around most street corners in Cape Town, but it remains illegal, and its possession is a punishable offence. Harder drugs are also available, but once again, prohibited and could land you in prison if you are caught with them in your possession. Among locals, the rave generation still favours the likes of ecstasy and cocaine, while hallucinagenics like LSD and magic mushrooms are popular at trance parties. Cape Town also has a huge problem with the drugs mandrax (or buttons), heroin, crack cocaine and especially crystal meth (or tik).

ELECTRICITY

The power supply in South Africa is 220/230 volts AC. The standard plug in South Africa is the 15-amp round-pin, three-prong plug. Euro- and US-style two-pin plugs, and UK-style three-pin plugs, can be used with an adaptor, available at supermarkets; bring transformers along for larger appliances where necessary. Most hotels have 110-volt outlets for electric shavers.

EMBASSIES & CONSULATES

Check the local phone book or *Yellow Pages* for a complete list of foreign consulates and embassies in Cape Town, or call directory enquiries on 1023.

British Consulate General
Southern Life Centre, 8 Riebeek Street, City Centre (021 405 2400). **Map** p275 H3.
Canadian Consulate General
19th Floor, Reserve Bank Building, 60 St George's Mall, City Centre (021 423 5240). **Map** p275 H4.
French Consulate *78 Queen Victoria Street, Gardens (021 423 1575).* **Map** p274 G4.
German Consulate General & Embassy *19th Floor, Safmarine House, 22 Riebeek Street, City Centre (021 405 3000).* **Map** p275 H3.

Netherlands Consulate General *100 Strand Street, corner Buitengracht, City Centre (021 421 5660).* **Map** p275 H3.
US Consulate *2 Reddam Avenue, Westlake, Tokai (021 702 7300).*

EMERGENCIES

Ambulance *10177.*
Police *10111.*
Fire *021 480 7700.*
General emergencies *107 from a landline/021 480 7700 or 112 from a mobile phone.*
Mountain Rescue Service *021 948 9900.*
Poison Crisis Centre *021 689 5227.*
Red Cross Children's Hospital *021 658 5111.*
National Sea Rescue Institute *021 449 3500.*

GAY & LESBIAN

For more on gay and lesbian Cape Town, *see pp177-181.*

Triangle Project *021 448 3812/ helpline 021 712 6699/ www.triangle.org.za.* Counselling, medical services, confidential HIV testing. For more on HIV/AIDS, *see below.*

HEALTH

Cape Town has a number of private and public hospitals. Even though there is no difference (in terms of medical expertise) between them, tourists are recommended to use the private ones for treatment, as the doctor-to-patient ratio is much better – and any costs should be paid for by your travel and medical insurance cover. Cape Town's hospitals are considered to be world-class and have a high standard of both medical facilities and expertise as well as competitive costs. No wonder 'health-care tourism' is booming here.

Contraception & abortion

Government hospitals and clinics offer free services like family planning counselling, pregnancy tests and abortions to both South Africans and tourists. Free contraceptive pills are handed out at most family planning clinics, and condoms are readily available at clinics and most public toilets in Cape Town. Over-the-counter pregnancy tests are available from most Clicks (a health, beauty

and pharmacy chain store) outlets and can be bought for around R30, while the morning-after pill can cost anywhere from R40 to R90.

Doctors & dentists

Both the **Talking Yellow Pages** (10118) and **Cape Town Tourism Bureau** (021 426 5639, www.tourismcapetown.co.za) should be able to supply you with a list of registered medical practitioners and dentists in or near the area where you are staying. However, if you're a tourist wanting to visit a doctor or dentist, you'll probably be expected to pay your bill upfront.

SAA-Netcare Travel Clinic *58 Strand Street, City Bowl (021 419 3172/www.travelclinic.co.za).* **Map** p275 H4. A national network of specialised mobile medical centres offering services to locals and tourists. Services include immunisations, pre- and post-travel examinations, malaria pills and first-aid travel kits.

Helplines

All helplines run 24 hours a day, seven days a week.

Alcoholics Anonymous *021 510 2288.*
Childline *0800 055 555.*
Gender Violence Helpline *0800 150 150/www.stopwomen abusehelpline.org.za.*
Lifeline *0861 322 322/ www.lifeline.org.za.*
Narcotics Anonymous *088 130 0327/www.na.org.za.*
National AIDS Helpline *0800 012 322/www.aidshelpline.org.za.*
Rape Crisis Centre *021 447 9762/www.rapecrisis.org.za.*

HIV & AIDS

South Africa's AIDS and HIV statistics are among the highest in the world, resulting in millions of rand having been invested in HIV/AIDS research and educational programmes, that are now of a first-world standard. If you suspect that you might have contracted the virus call the **National AIDS Helpline** (0800 012 322, www.aidshelpline. org.za) immediately for assistance and anti-retroviral treatment.

Other clinics providing support and assistance to HIV/AIDS sufferers include the following:

DIRECTORY

Cape Town Station Reproductive Health Clinic *Cape Town Railway Station (021 425 2004)*. **Map** p275 H4.
Chapel Street Clinic *corner Chapel & Balfour Streets, Woodstock (021 465 2793)*.
Dorp Street Reproductive Health Clinic *3 Dorp Street, City Centre (021 483 4662)*.
Marie Stopes Clinic *91 Bree Street, City Centre (021 422 4660)*. **Map** p274 G4.

Hospitals

Cape Town Medi Clinic *21 Hof Street, Oranjezicht, City Bowl (021 464 5555/www.capetownmc.co.za)*.
Groote Schuur Hospital *Main Road, Observatory, Southern Suburbs (021 404 9111/ www.gsh.co.za)*.
Somerset Hospital *Beach Road, Sea Point (021 402 6911)*.

Pharmacies

These pharmacies are all open late:

Clicks Glengariff Pharmacy *2 Main Road, Sea Point (021 434 8622)*. **Open** 8am-10pm Mon, Tue, Thur-Sat; 9am-10pm Wed; 9am-9pm Sun. **Credit** AmEx, DC, MC, V. **Map** p272 C2.
Lite-Kem *24 Darling Street, City Centre (021 461 8040)*. **Open** 8am-11pm Mon-Fri; 9am-11pm Sat, Sun. **Credit** AmEx, DC, MC, V. **Map** p275 C2.
M-Kem Medicine City *corner Durban & Raglan Roads, Bellville (021 948 5707)*. **Open** 24hrs daily. **Credit** AmEx, DC, MC, V.

ID

Since it's the legal age for drinking alcohol, you have to be 18 years or older to get into a club. However, bouncers rarely ask for ID unless you look like a teenager. Don't carry your passport with you when sightseeing for the day. Instead, leave it in your hotel safe.

INSURANCE

As is the case in all countries, you are strongly advised to take out travel insurance that also covers repatriation to your home country in the event of serious medical problems or accidents.

INTERNET

Most top hotels in Cape Town have Wi-Fi. In the unlikely event that your hotel doesn't have internet access, they'll definitely be able to point you in the direction of an internet café. That said, these cafés are becoming increasingly passé due to the availability of Wi-Fi at coffee shops like **Vida e Caffè** (www.caffe.co.za) and **Mugg and Bean** (www.themugg. com). But there are still a few around town such as the **Info Café** (021 426 4424, www.infocafe.co.za) at the tourism bureau in the city centre. If you plan on sticking around for a bit, open an account with a local internet service provider such as **Polka.co.za** (0860 00 4455, www.polka.co.za), **M-Web** (0860 032 000, www.mweb.co.za) or **iBurst** (www.iburst.co.za).

LANGUAGE

South Africa has no fewer than 11 official languages: Afrikaans, English, Ndebele, Sepedi, Sesotho, Setswana, siSwati, Tsonga, Venda, Xhosa and Zulu. In the Western Cape, English, Afrikaans and Xhosa are the most commonly spoken. Since there is such a large international community based in Cape Town, staff at some establishments and attractions speak German, French or Italian.

LEFT LUGGAGE

Left Luggage *Cape Town Airport domestic terminal (021 935 3187). Cape Town Airport international terminal (021 936 2494)*.

LEGAL HELP

Law Society of the Cape of Good Hope *29th & 30th Floors, ABSA Centre, 2 Riebeeck Street, City Bowl (021 443 6700)*. **Map** p275 H3.
Legalwise Leza Legal Insurance *Shop 4, Fountain Place, 1 Heerengracht, Adderley Street, City Bowl (021 419 6905)*. **Map** p275 H3.
Legal Resources Centre *54 Shortmarket Street, City Bowl (021 423 8285)*. **Map** p274 G3.

LIBRARIES

You can register as a temporary member at any Cape Town City Library branch (see the telephone directory under Municipality of Cape Town for local branch details). **City Library Head Office** (021 467 1500) can also help.

LOST PROPERTY

If you're missing luggage following a flight, phone Cape Town International Airport (021 937 1200), who'll put you in contact with the police.

If you've lost something in the city, report it to the police (*see p253*) or you could try placing an advert in the classifieds section of a local newspaper such as the *Cape Times* (www.capetimes.co.za), the *Cape Argus* (www.capeargus. co.za) or the free city newspaper the *Capetowner* (021 488 4911).

For lost and stolen credit card helplines, *see p253*.

MEDIA

Magazines

The magazine stands are positively groaning under the weight of local publications, and most good bookshops stock a variety of international (and super-pricey) magazines. **Cosmopolitan**, **Elle**, **Marie Claire** and **Glamour** all have local editions. If you're in the mood for a bit of celebrity gossip, look out for **TvPlus**, **People**, **Heat** and **You**.

Newspapers

The Western Cape's newspapers focus mainly on local news, covering everything from sensationalist murder trials of high-profile musicians to the price of crude oil. If you're curious about the city's happenings, there's also a good selection of local community weekly newspapers available, such as the **Atlantic Sun** and the **Capetowner**. Appearing every Friday, *The Next 48hOURS* has an excellent and up-to-date entertainment guide.

Daily morning newspapers include **Cape Times** & **Business Day** (English), **Die Burger** (Afrikaans). The **Cape Argus** (English) is an afternoon newspaper. On Sundays there's the **Sunday Argus** (English), **Sunday Times** (English), and **Rapport** (Afrikaans).

Radio

Cape Talk (567 AM) broadcasts news, traffic reports, detailed weather information, and arts and entertainment updates – a great local resource for any tourist.

Other local, largely music-oriented FM radio stations such as **5FM** (89.9 FM), **KFM** (94.5 FM), **Heart** (104.9 FM) and **Good Hope FM** (94-97 FM) give South African bands their fare share of air time and also supply information on upcoming live performances. **Fine Music Radio** (101.3 FM) has a more classical line-up.

Television

SABC (South African Broadcasting Commission) owns SABC 1, 2 and 3. **SABC 1** caters almost exclusively to South Africa's black audience and has local shows, international sitcoms, news and soaps. **SABC 2** also has multilingual programmes, including in Afrikaans. **SABC 3** is an exclusively English channel and tries to cater for a higher income bracket, with much US and some British programmes.

e.tv is a privately owned station that tries to push the limits, but also has some not-so-great local shows alongside its big US series. Unfortunately, all these channels are renowned for their constant reruns of old films and TV series. **M-net** is a subscriber channel, big on sport, series and movies. **DStv** is South Africa's own digital satellite TV provider and offers local, American, British and European channels.

MONEY

Banks

ABSA Bank LTD *136 Adderley Street, City Bowl (021 480 1911).* **Map** p275 H4.
First National Bank *82 Adderley Street, City Bowl (021 487 6000).* **Map** p275 H4.
Nedbank *85 St George's Mall, City Bowl (021 469 9500).* **Map** p275 H4.
Standard Bank *10th Floor, Standard Bank Towers, Standard Bank Building, Heerengracht, City Bowl (021 401 3396).* **Map** p275 I3.

Bureaux de change

Foreign exchange facilities are found at large commercial banks, as well as at Cape Town Tourism Visitor Information centres (*see p255*), the airport and bureaux de change such as Rennies Travel and American Express.
American Express *V&A Waterfront, Atlantic Seaboard*

(021 419 3917); Thibault House, Thibault Square, City Bowl (021 425 7991/www.american express.co.za). **Map** p275 H1.
Rennies Travel *2nd Floor, The Terraces, Black River Office Park, Fir Road, Observatory (021 486 3600/www.renniestravel.co.za).* **Map** p275 H3.

Credit cards & ATMs

Most shops and hotels in Cape Town accept credit cards, including international cards such as Visa and MasterCard (and to a lesser extent American Express and Diners Club). In far-flung towns the use of cards might be restricted. 'Skimming' of cards has recently become a problem, so ask always keep your card in your sight or walk over to the machine at a restaurant. Note that petrol (gas) stations in South Africa do not accept credit cards; you will have to pay with cash. Automatic Teller Machines (ATMs) are widespread (and also often conveniently located in petrol stations) and accept most international cards. Most ATMs also offer the option to top up mobile phone credit.

Lost or stolen cards

American Express *0800 991 021* (note: for both credit cards and traveller's cheques).
Diners Club *011 358 8406.*
MasterCard *0800 990 418.*
Visa *0800 990 475.*

Currency

The local currency is the South African rand. It's quite weak on international currency markets, which makes Cape Town a great destination for bargain luxury. (At the time of print one US dollar was worth around R11, one British pound R15 and one euro R13.)

There are 100 South African cents in a rand. Coins in circulation are: 5c, 10c, 20c, 50c, R1, R2, and R5; and banknotes in circulation are R10, R20, R50, R100 and R200.

Tax

South Africa's VAT (Value Added Tax) is 14 per cent on purchases and services, and can be claimed back for purchases of R250 or more upon departure. You can't, however, reclaim on services.

If you want to reclaim tax, go to the VAT office in the international departure hall at the airport,

making sure to leave yourself plenty of time before your plane departs. You'll need to take along your passport and original tax-invoiced receipts together with the purchased goods. Once you've filled in the necessary paperwork and had your application processed, you can pick up a refund in your home currency from one of the banks in the departure lounge. You can also do the paperwork at the VAT Refund Offices at the Tourism Visitor Information Centres (*see p255*).

NATURAL HAZARDS

Local tap water is safe to drink. Visitors unaccustomed to South Africa's strong sun should cover up with factor 30 (or more) sunscreen and wear a hat, especially between noon and 3pm. Although reasonably rare in these parts, venomous snakes and spiders do sometimes make an appearance. If bitten, try to get a look at the culprit and then call the poison hotline (021 689 5227) for assistance.

OPENING HOURS

Most city shops (bar a few popular touristy hotspots in Kloof and Long Street) operate between 9am and 5pm during weekdays and until 1pm on Saturdays. Some shops also open on Sundays. Larger malls open daily from 9am to 9pm. On Sundays and public holidays things start up a bit later, usually from 10am. Banks are open from 9am to 3.30pm on weekdays and 8.30am to 11.30pm on Saturdays. Muslim-owned businesses are closed for prayers between noon and 1pm on Fridays.

POLICE STATIONS

The police's national emergency number is 10111. If you've been the victim of a crime, tell them what happened, where you're phoning from and what your contact details are. Always ask for the officer's name, rank and a case number.

When reporting a crime after the event, phone your nearest police station; they're listed in the blue section at the back of the telephone directory, or you can call directory enquiries at 1023.

Other useful contacts include: **Cape Town Charge Office** (021 467 8000); **Cape Town International Airport Police**

DIRECTORY

Station (021 934 0707); **Consumer Protector** (0800 007 081); **Metro Protection Service** (021 449 4336).

POSTAL SERVICES

The **South African Post Office** (0860 111 502, www.sapo.co.za) can't always guarantee safe and timely delivery with standard mail but, for a little bit extra, you could opt for the much more reliable registered mail and even add a tracking option for extra peace of mind.

Sending a postcard overseas costs a very reasonable R5. The post office offers a 24-hour door-to-door service between the major centres in South Africa. Post offices are open 8.30am-4.30pm during the week and 8am-noon on Saturdays. Smaller offices sometimes tend to vary their hours on certain days. Postage stamps are available from post offices, newsagents and some retail outlets.

Never send money or important documents with standard mail. Send them with registered post, or use a courier or shipping company (see p250).

RELIGION

St George's Cathedral (Anglican) Corner of Queen Victoria & Wale Streets, City Bowl (021 424 7360/www.st georgescathedral.com). **Map** p274 G4. See also p54.

Buddhist Information 6 Morgenrood Road, Kenilworth, Southern Suburbs (021 761 2978/ www.kagyu.org.za).

Central Methodist Mission Corner Longmarket & Burg Streets, Greenmarket Square, City Bowl (021 422 2744). **Map** p275 H4. See also p44.

Dutch Reformed Church Groote Kerk, 39 Adderley Street, City Bowl (021 422 0569). **Map** p275 H4.

Greek Orthodox Church 24 Bay Road, Mouille Point (021 433 2374).

Hindu Temple Siva Aalayam 41 Ruth Road, Rylands, Southern Suburbs (083 794 2542/021 638 2542).

Jewish Cape Town Hebrew Congregation 88 Hatfield Street, City Bowl (021 465 1405). **Map** 274 G5.

Nurul Islam Mosque 134 Buitengracht Street, City Bowl (021 423 4202/www.nurulislam mosque.org.za). **Map** p274 G5.

Salvation Army Corner Vrede & Plein Streets, City Bowl (021 423 4613). **Map** p274 G5.

St Mary's Roman Catholic Cathedral Roeland Street, opposite Parliament, City Bowl (021 461 1167). **Map** p274 G4.

Uniting Presbyterian Church St Stephens Road, Southern Suburbs (021 531 8408).

SAFETY & SECURITY

It's a sad fact that South Africa has a terrible reputation as far as crime is concerned. Luckily, since Cape Town has been made a host city for the 2010 FIFA World Cup, the provincial safety and security team has gone to great lengths in an attempt to make the Mother City a safer place.

The inner city has effective crime deterrents, such as closed-circuit security cameras as well as mounted and vehicular police patrols, but petty crimes like pickpocketing, as well as more serious muggings, do unfortunately still occur.

The best advice for tourists is not to act like tourists. The fanny-pack is a dead giveaway, as are travellers' cheques and flashy cameras. Always park in well-lit, busy areas and avoid driving around in the early hours of the morning; especially if you don't know your way around. Remotely situated ATMs are also no-nos. Since debit and credit cards are accepted almost everywhere in the city, it isn't really necessary to draw out huge amounts of cash.

Muggings have been known to occur on Table Mountain's hiking routes, and even though the mountain security has been considerably improved over recent years, you should never hike on your own. Always hike in large groups, tell a friend when to expect you back and leave any unnecessary electronics at home. Apart from pepper spray, an old-fashioned whistle is a trusted method for alerting other hikers when you're in a scary situation.

For information on what to do if you get bitten by a poisonous animal, see p253 **Natural Hazards**.

SMOKING

Smoking in enclosed public spaces in Cape Town is strictly prohibited. Some restaurants and bars do provide specially demarcated smoking sections for customers, however.

STUDY

Being such a cosmopolitan hub, there's a good selection of language schools dotted around the city where you can learn local or foreign languages. For more information contact the **International School of Languages** (021 674 4117).

TELEPHONES

Making a call

To make a phone call within South Africa, dial the area code followed by the phone number. To make an international call, dial 00 before the International Direct Dialling code, the area code and then the phone number. Cape Town's area code is 021, Jo'Burg is 011, Pretoria is 012 and Durban is 031. Phone **Directory Enquiries** (1023) if you're looking for a specific number that isn't listed in the phone book. Otherwise call the **Talking Yellow Pages** (10118) or try **iFind** (www.ifind.co.za/34600), a mobile directory service that you can call or SMS (text message) to find the required numbers of local shops and services.

Public phones

Green and blue public phone booths can be found all over the city. The blue phones are coin-operated, and the green ones work with a telephone card that can be bought at post offices, newsagents and Telkom offices, as well as selected grocery stores.

Mobile phones

All new mobile phones should operate in South Africa and SIM cards for all of the four national networks – **Cell C** (www.cellc.co.za), **Vodacom** (www.vodacom.co.za), **MTN** (www.mtn.co.za) and **Virgin Mobile** (www.virgin mobile.co.za) – can be puchased at their respective outlets, at supermarkets like Pick n Pay and Spar, and also at newsagent chains such as CNA and PNA.

TIME

South Africa is two hours ahead of GMT, seven ahead of Eastern

Standard Winter Time and ten ahead of Pacific Standard Time. There is no daylight saving time in summer.

TIPPING

The general guideline for tipping in restaurants is between 10% and 20% of your total bill. Taxi drivers are usually tipped about 10% of the total fare, porters up to R10 a bag and petrol pump attendants R5 to R10. Car guards settle for about R2-R5.

TOILETS

Public toilets in shopping malls and restaurants are generally clean and are preferable to the city centre's public facilities.

TOURIST INFORMATION

The **Cape Town Tourism Visitor Centre** is on the corner of Castle and Burg streets in the city centre (021 426 4260). If you're having trouble deciding what to include on your itinerary, they'll help you make up your mind with a selection of maps, brochures, tour outings and other essential information on what's happening in the Mother City. Bookings and reservations can be made at the help desks. The V&A Waterfront also has a visitor centre, the **Cape Town Tourism Office** (021 405 4500/www.tourismcapetown.co.za), located in the Clock Tower.

Township tours

If you'd like to check out the townships fringing the city, but find the thought of hitching a ride with one of the minibus taxis daunting, then opt for a guided tour instead. Try these reputable companies:
Camissa Tours 021 462 6199/083 452 1112/www.gocamissa.co.za.
Inkululeko Freedom Tours 021 425 5642/www.inkululeko tours.co.za.
Nthuseng Tours 021 559 6753/ 083 453 2544/www.nthuseng tours.co.za.
Zibonele Tours and Transfers 021 511 4263/072 740 1604/ www.ziboneletours.com.

VISAS & IMMIGRATION

Visa requirements

Citizens from the UK, the Republic of Ireland, most European countries and Australia do not need visas,

as long as they have a national passport valid for 30 days beyond the length of their trip, a return ticket, proof of accommodation and, if travelling for business, a letter from the inviting organisation. If they stay for longer than 90 days (up to a year is allowed without a visa), they also need a letter from a chartered accountant offering proof of funds.

The requirements for trips of up to 90 days are the same for US travellers, but a visa will be required for longer trips.

Entry requirements can change at any time, so check carefully before you travel. For more information, visit www.home-affairs.gov.za/ visa_schedule.asp.

WEIGHTS & MEASUREMENTS

South Africa uses the metric system. Useful conversions are given below.
1 kilometre = 0.62 miles
1 metre = 1.094 yards
1 centimetre = 0.39 inches
1 kilogram = 2.2 pounds
1 gram = 0.035 ounces
1 litre = 1.75 pints
0°C = 32°F

WHEN TO GO

Cape Town's climate is Mediterranean, with warm, dry summers and mild, moist winters. During summer (November to February) the temperature on the coast generally ranges between 15°C and 35°C (while inland it increases by approximately 3-5°C), although recent summers have seen temperatures in the City Bowl soaring to over 40°C. In winter (May to August) it ranges between 7°C and 18°C.

Cape Town's summer months are crammed with festivals, fun runs, concerts and carnivals, with the weeks around Christmas and New Year being especially hectic. The summer sun is no laughing matter, however, so make sure that you slap on plenty of strong sunscreen. The south-easterly wind known as the Cape Doctor also makes its appearance in summer, wreaking havoc on hairstyles and beach parties, but performing a vital service to the city by clearing it of smog.

The season starts getting slightly chillier around April. The lovely autumn colours draw people out of town to forests in Newlands and Constantia, as well as the Winelands, while winter is synonymous with rain showers and the odd thunderstorm.

PUBLIC HOLIDAYS

New Year's Day (1 Jan); **Human Rights Day** (21 Mar); **Good Friday** (varies); **Easter Monday and Family Day** (Monday after Easter Sunday); **Freedom Day** (27 Apr); **Workers Day** (1 May); Youth Day (16 June); **National Women's Day** (9 Aug); **Heritage Day** (24 Sept); **Day of Reconciliation** (16 Dec); **Christmas Day** (25 Dec); **Day of Goodwill** (26 Dec).

WORKING

Find information from your nearest **Department of Home Affairs** office (Private Bag X114, Pretoria 0001, 0800 601 190/www.home-affairs.gov.za) if you're in South Africa. If you're abroad, do so on the websites given under the Visa section (*see above*).

DIRECTORY

THE LOCAL CLIMATE

Average temperatures and monthly rainfall in Cape Town.

	High (˚C/˚F)	Low (˚C/˚F)	Rainfall (mm/in)
Jan	26 / 79	16 / 61	15 / 0.6
Feb	27 / 81	16 / 61	17 / 0.7
Mar	25 / 77	14 / 57	20 / 0.8
Apr	23 / 73	12 / 54	41 / 1.6
May	20 / 68	9 / 48	68 / 2.7
June	18 / 64	8 / 46	93 / 3.7
July	18 / 64	7 / 45	82 / 3.2
Aug	18 / 64	8 / 46	77 / 3.0
Sept	19 / 66	9 / 48	40 / 1.6
Oct	21 / 70	11 / 52	30 / 1.2
Nov	24 / 75	13 / 55	14 / 0.5
Dec	25 / 77	15 / 59	17 / 0.7

Further Reference

BOOKS

Fiction & literature

Badal, Sean *Fall of the Black-Eyed Night*
A young Muslim man returns to Cape Town after the 7/7 bombings in London.

Beukes, Lauren *Moxyland*
A gritty cyber-punk novel depicting a dystopian, corporation-run Cape Town of the future.

Brink, André *Rumours of Rain, A Dry White Season* and *Praying Mantis*
Intriguing politicised novels by one of South Africa's most acclaimed writers.

Brown, Andrew *Coldsleep Lullaby*
Winner of the *Sunday Times* Fiction Award in 2006, this novel combines crime thriller and historical drama.

Coetzee, JM *Disgrace, Waiting for the Barbarians, The Life and Times of Michael K* and *Dusklands*
Winner of the Nobel prize for literature in 2003, Coetzee goes to the heart of the South African psyche and questions the country's political and social landscape.

Duiker, K Sello *The Quiet Violence of Dreams* and *Thirteen Cents*
Duiker convincingly depicted the harsh realities of Cape Town's underbelly, exploring issues such as homelessness, mental illness, drug abuse, prostitution and the overwhelming sense of isolation to be found in any city. He committed suicide in 2005.

Fugard, Athol *Blood Knot, Boesman and Lena* and *A Lesson from Aloes*
One of South Africa's most esteemed playwrights, most famous as a campaigning dramatist, tackling issues of apartheid.

Galgut, Damon *The Good Doctor*
Short-listed for the 2003 Man Booker prize, Galgut's novel explores post-apartheid South Africa, where deep-rooted social and political tensions threaten shared dreams for the future.

Gordimer, Nadine *July's People, Burger's Daughter* and *Sport of Nature*
Nobel prize-winning novelist dealing with the tensions of her racially divided country.

Khumalo, Sihle *Dark Continent My Black Arse*
A humorous account of a womaniser's journey from the Cape to Cairo.

Matlwa, Kopano *Coconut*
A novel about two young black women growing up in white, privileged suburbs and the social ostracism and identity struggles they experience.

Matthee, Dalene *Circles in a Forest* and *Fiela's Child*
Historical novels with the lush Knysna Forest as a backdrop.

Mda, Jakes *Heart of Redness* and *Ways of Dying*
Magic realism gets a contemporary African twist.

Paton, Alan *Cry the Beloved Country*
A South African classic, about families, racism, reconciliation and forgiveness.

Schreiner, Olive *The Story of an African Farm*
An early South African classic, exploring themes around women and society.

Sleigh, Dan *Islands*
The first years of the settlement of the Dutch colony in the Cape are documented through the accounts of seven historically based characters.

Van Niekerk, Marlene *Triomf* and *Agaat*
Two multi-award winning books giving glimpses into the dark side of Afrikaner identity.

Non-fiction

Breytenbach, Breyten *The True Confessions of an Albino Terrorist*
A memoir of the well-known poet's seven-year imprisonment in South Africa.

Cameron, Edwin *A Witness to AIDS*
Constitutional Court Justice Edwin Cameron's extremely frank account of contracting and living with HIV/AIDS.

De Vries, Fred *The Fred de Vries Interviews: From Abdullah to Zille*
A collection of insightful interviews by the renowned Dutch South African travel writer and journalist.

Dommisse, Ebbe *Anton Rupert: A Biography*
The remarkable life story of one of the richest businessmen in the

world, whose group of Rembrandt companies owns brands such as Cartier, Mont Blanc and Dunhill.

Du Preez, Max *Pale Native*
Not known for mincing words, this roving reporter writes of his times in a troubled South Africa.

Gevisser, Mark *Thabo Mbeki: The Dream Deferred*
A glimpse into the political and personal life of the man who followed in Nelson Mandela's footsteps as president.

Gilliomee, Herman *The Afrikaners*
Traces the history of the Afrikaner from Dutch settler to constructor of apartheid.

Gordin, Jeremy *Zuma: A Biography*
Sheds some light on South Africa's president.

Kanfer, Stefan *The Last Empire: De Beers, Diamonds and the World*
A story of cutthroat capitalism as well as the economic and racial development of South Africa.

Krog, Antjie *Country of My Skull, A Change of Tongue* and *Down to My Last Skin*
Krog analyses the country and its people in an erudite manner.

Mandela, Nelson *Long Walk to Freedom*
A truly inspiring and humbling autobiographical account of his life.

Nicol, Mike *Mandela: The Authorised Biography*
A comprehensive biography encompassing 60 interviews with world leaders and friends, as well as previously unpublished photos and letters.

Pakenham, Thomas *The Scramble for Africa*
A disturbing look at the colonisation of the African continent.

Tutu, Desmond *No Future Without Forgiveness*
Essential reading to gain a sense of empathy.

Food & wine

Engelbrecht, Stan and De Beer, Tamsen *African Salad: A Portrait of South Africans at Home*
Acclaimed photographer Stan Engelbrecht documents 120 authentic South African families and their favourite recipes.

Platter, John and Erica
Africa Uncorked
The Platters explore the continent in search of weird wine.
Riffel, Reuben *Reuben Cooks!*
A colourful cookbook from renowned chef Reuben Riffel, featuring delicious dishes served in his award-winning restaurant.
Goffe-Wood, Pete *Kitchen Cowboys*
Known as the food alchemist, Goffe-Wood wows with a compilation of stalwart recipes.
Snyman, Lannice *Tortoises and Tumbleweeds*
South Africa's undisputed food doyenne takes readers on a journey through the history and cuisine of her homeland.

FILM

Amandla! – A revolution in four-part harmony
(Lee Hirsch 2002)
Stunning documentary tracking the history of South Africa protest music and the role it played in the struggle against apartheid.
Bunny Chow (John Barker 2006)
A classic road trip movie about three stand-up comedians travelling to the annual music festival, Oppikoppi.
Confessions of a Gambler
(Amanda Lane 2007)
Based on the novel by Rayda Jacobs, this gives a rare glimpse into Cape Town's Muslim society, telling the story of a woman's addiction to gambling.
Cry, the Beloved Country
(Darrell James Roodt 1995)
A film adaptation of Alan Paton's novel, telling the heart-wrenching story of a father's love for his son.
Cry Freedom (Richard Attenborough 1987)
True story of an inspiring friendship in a politically turbulent time.
Gandhi (Richard Attenborough 1982)
Insight into Gandhi's experiences as a young lawyer in South Africa.
Country of My Skull
(John Boorman 2004)
Adapted from Antjie Krog's book about her time as a foreign journalist at the Truth and Reconciliation trials.
Promised Land (Jason Xenopoulos 2002)
Adapted from the Afrikaans novel by Karel Schoeman, and winner of the best screenplay award at the Tokyo International Film Festival, it tells a story of hidden truths and near impossible quests.

Sarafina! (Darrell James Roodt 1992)
In this film adaptation of Mbongeni Ngema's stage musical, Whoopi Goldberg plays an idealistic teacher who helps a sensitive teenage girl throw off the shackles of apartheid.
Son of Man (Mark Donford-May 2005)
The story of Jesus re-told in a modern-day African fable.
Triomf (Michael Raeburn 2008)
Based on Marlene van Niekerk's acclaimed novel, this disturbing movie follows the lives of one family living in the backwater suburb of Triomf at the dawn of the 1994 elections.
Stander (Bronwen Hughes 2003)
Based on true events, this movie tells the tale of South African police officer Captain André Stander, who became a notorious bank robber.
Tsotsi (Gavin Hood 2005)
A ruthless gang leader undergoes an existential crisis after finding a baby on the back seat of a car that he has hijacked. Winner of the Academy Award for best foreign-language film in 2005.
U-Carmen eKhayelitsha
(Dimpho Di Kopan 2005)
George Bizet's 1875 opera is given a dramatic new guise in this Xhosa film adaptation set in Cape Town's densely populated township, Khayelitsha.

MUSIC

Brenda Fassie *Memeza, Mina Nawe*
The late Fassie was hailed by many as Africa's queen of pop and had a string of hits to her name, including the infectious 'Weekend Special'.
Freshlyground *Jika Jika, Nomvula, Ma Cherie*
Winner of the MTV Europe award for best African act 2006, this ensemble cast of talented musos will have you on your feet in no time.
Johnny Clegg *Third World Child, Shadowman* and *Cruel, Crazy Beautiful World*
Known as the 'white Zulu', Clegg's been performing with the groups Juluka and Suvuka since the apartheid years, combining Zulu and English lyrics with Celtic influences.
Ladysmith Black Mambazo
The Ultimate Collection
The Grammy-award winning male choral group that performed on Paul Simon's *Graceland* album.
Lucky Dube *Soul Taker*
South Africa's greatest reggae star was murdered in 2007 but the optimism of his music lives on.

Mafikizolo *Sibongile, Kwela* and *Six Mabone*
Award-winning kwaito-pop with retro Sophiatown influences.
Nomfusi *Kwazibani*
This pint-sized Afro-soul singer certainly knows how to belt out some powerful tunes.
Soweto String Quartet *Zebra Crossing, Renaissance*
SSQ make their instruments sing, incorporating kwela and jazz rhythms.
Yvonne Chaka Chaka *The Best of Yvonne Chaka Chaka*
A leading figure in South African popular music.
Zola *Undiwembe, Khokuvula*
The undisputed king of kwaito.
Goldfish *Caught in the Loop, Perceptions of Pacha*
A talented Cape Town duo mixing their own distinctive brand of electro-jazz.
The Dirty Skirts *Daddy Don't Disco*
A quirky indie-pop act now with several hits to their name – think catchy hooks and vocals uncannily reminiscent of the Cure.

WEBSITES

www.capetownkids.co.za
Jam-packed with fun family-friendly ideas.
www.capetowndailyphoto.com
A blog featuring myriad photos of the Mother City and its inhabitants.
www.capetownmagazine.co.za
Keep a finger on the pulse of Cape Town's goings-on.
www.capetowntoday.co.za
Featuring everything from the weather to festivals.
www.cape-town.org
The city's resources at your fingertips.
www.eatout.co.za
A comprehensive directory of restaurants and reviews.
www.hikecapetown.co.za
The go-to site for those keen to break a sweat.
www.letsgocapetown.co.za
A gamut of entertainment and outdoor activities in the city.
www.weathersa.co.za
Cape Town weather is ridiculously unpredictable, so best keep an eye on the forecasts.
www.tablemountain.net
Check out all there is to know about the Cape's iconic mountain.
www.capetourism.org
Official tourist board site, with plenty of practical detail.
www.winelands.co.za
Essential resource of regions and estates for avid tipplers.

DIRECTORY

Index A-Z

INDEX

INDEX

INDEX

Advertisers' Index

Please refer to the relevant pages for contact details

INDEX

Maps

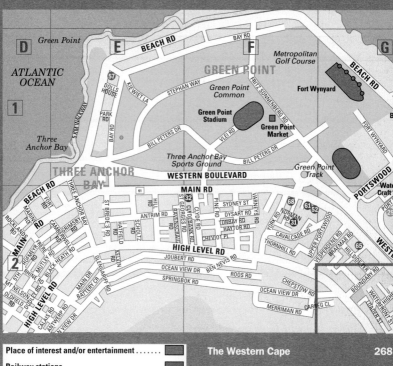

Place of interest and/or entertainment . . . .

Railway stations . . . .

Parks . . . .

Hospitals . . . .

Area name . . . . **CLIFTON**

Hotel . . . . **❶**

Restaurants & Cafés . . . . **❶**

Pubs & Bars . . . . **❶**

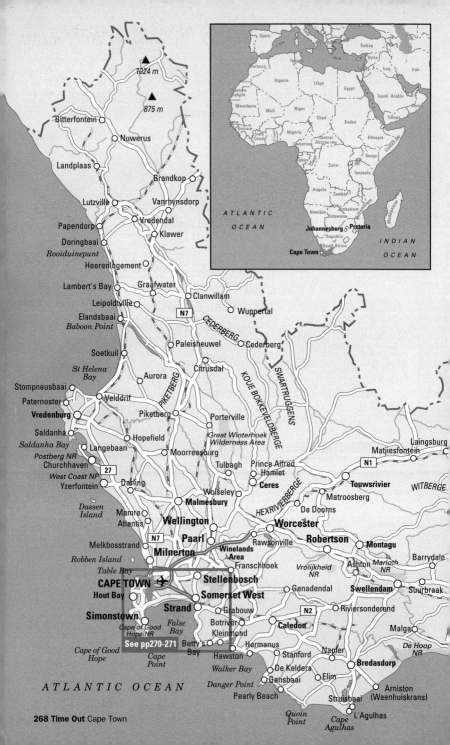

The Western Cape

0 _____ 100 km

0 _____ 50 miles

© Copyright Time Out Guides 2009

Sneeukraal

Murraysburg

Nelspoort

Karoo
National Park

NUWEVELDBERGE
1913 m

Beaufort West

N1

KOMSBERG

Merweville

Wiegnaarspoort

Leeu-Gamka
Kruidfontein

N12

Seekoegat

Prince
Albert

Klaarstroom

GROOT-SWARTBERGE

Matjiesrivier

De Rust

KLEIN-SWARTBERGE

Ladismith

Calitzdorp

Oudtshoorn

Dysselsdorp

KAMMANASSIE MTNS

Uniondale

Volmoed

62

Van Wyksdorp

N12

N9

Haarlem

OUTENIQUA MTNS

George

Barrington

LANGEBERG

Herbertsdale

Blanco

Wilderness

Knysna National
Lake Area

Tsitsikamma
NP

Heidelberg

Riversdale

Groot-
Brakrivier

Wilderness
National Park

Knysna

Plettenberg
Bay

Slangrivier

N2

Albertinia

Mossel Bay

Witsand

Still Bay

Vleesbaai

Infanta

Gouritsmond

Cape
Infanta

St Sebastian
Bay

INDIAN OCEAN

Robben
Island

ATLANTIC OCEAN

Table Bay

Bloubergstrand

West Beach

Table View

NORTHERN SUBURBS

Durbanville

Milnerton

Milnerton Beach

Montague
Gardens

N1

Century City

Mouille Point

V & A
Waterfront

Ysterplaat

Goodwood

Bellville

See p272

Green Point

Three Anchor Bay

Cape Town

Paarden Eiland

Parow

See pp274-275

Sea Point

Fresnaye

Tamboerskloof

N7

Bantry Bay

Woodstock

Salt River

Clifton Bay

Zonnebloem

Observatory

Pinelands

Clifton

Vredehoek

Gardens

Camps Bay

Oranjezicht

Mowbray

TABLE MOUNTAIN

Groote Schuur
Estate

Rondebosch

SOUTHERN
SUBURBS

Cape Town
International

See p273

Newlands

Claremont

Llandudno

Bishopscourt

Kenilworth

CAPE FLATS

Sandy Bay

Alphen

Wynberg

Rust-en-Vrede

Plumstead

Mitchell's Plain

KARBONKELBERG

Hout Bay

Constantia

Parkwood

High Constantia

Diep River

Zeekoevlei

M3

Noordhoek

Muizenberg

Sunnydale

Kalk Bay

St James

Kommetjie

Fish Hoek

Sweetwater
(Soetwater)

Glencairn

False Bay

Simonstown

Schusterskraal

SWARTKOPBERGE

Smitswinkel Bay

Cape of Good
Hope Nature
Reserve

0   5 km

0   3 miles

© Copyright Time Out Guides 2009

*Cape of
Good Hope*

Cape Point

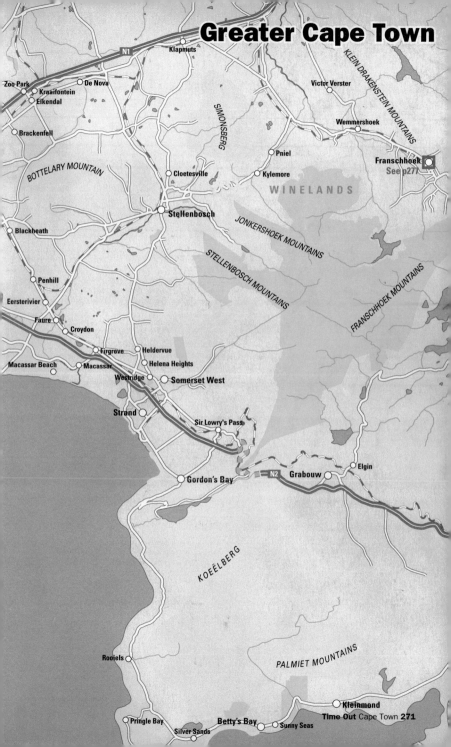

Greater Cape Town

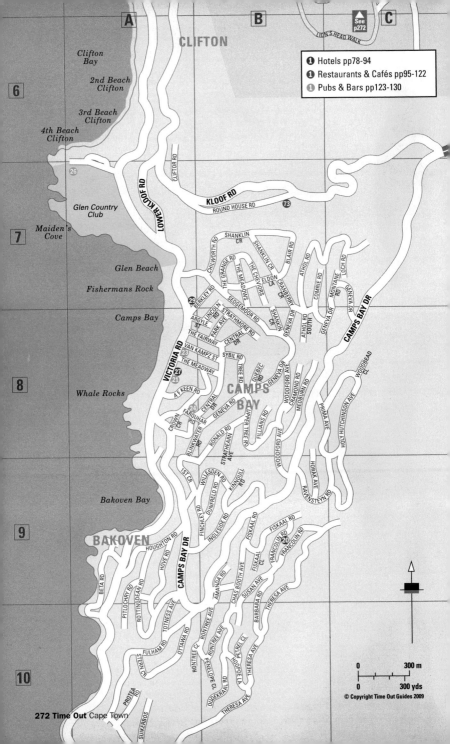

CLIFTON

A B C

Clifton
Bay

2nd Beach
Clifton

3rd Beach
Clifton

4th Beach
Clifton

See p272

LION'S HEAD WALK

❶ Hotels pp78-94
❶ Restaurants & Cafés pp95-122
❶ Pubs & Bars pp123-130

6

26

LOWER KLOOF RD

CLIFTON RD

KLOOF RD

ROUND HOUSE RD

73

Glen Country
Club

7

Maiden's
Cove

SHANKLIN
CR

CHILWORTH RD

SHANKLIN CR

BLAIR RD

ELDON
LA

CRANBERRY

ATHOL RD

COMRIE RD

LOCH RD

MONTANE
RD

GENEVA DR

Glen Beach

THE GRANGE RD

THE MEADOWS

THE CHEVIORS

Fishermans Rock

BERKLEY RD

LINCOLN RD

SEDGEMOOR RD

SHANKLIN
CR

GENEVA DR

ATHOL RD
SOUTH

GENEVA DR

CAMPS BAY DR

Camps Bay

29

ARGYLE
ST

STRATHMORE RD

PARK AVE

CENTRAL
DR

8

VICTORIA RD

THE FAIRWAY

VAN KAMPZ ST

CENTRAL
DR

SYBIL RD

QUEBEC

GENEVA DR

WOODFORD AVE

CRAMOND RD

MEDBURN RD

WOODHEAD
CL

23

THE MEADWAY

21

TREE RD

PRIMA AVE

HOLY HUTCHINSON AVE

Whale Rocks

A F KEEN RD

CAMPS
BAY

CENTRAL
DR

UPPER TREE RD

FILLIANS RD

20

FARQUHAR
RD

GENEVA RD

WOODFORD AVE

HORAK AVE

CROWN
CR·T

BLINKWATER

RONALD RD

STRATHEARN
AVE

RAVENSTEYN RD

WILLESDEN RD

KINNOULL
RD

1ST CR

DUINFIELD RD

FINCHLEY RD

INGLESIDE RD

FISKAAL RD

FISKAAL RD

FRANCOLIN
CL

FRANCOLIN RD

Bakoven Bay

9

BAKOVEN

HOUGHTON RD

CAMPS BAY DR

HOVE RD

AMANDA RD

FISKAAL
CL

20

BETA RD

PITLOCHRY RD

ROTTINGDEAN RD

TOTNESS AVE

OTTAWA RD

CHAS BOOTH AVE

SUSAN AVE

BARBARA RD

THERESA AVE

FULHAM RD

RONTREE CR

RONTREE AVE

PENTRICH RD

OUDEKRAAL RD

PETREL CL

THERESA AVE

STEILS CR

PROTEA
RD

SUIKERBOS

OUDEKRAAL RD

THERESA AVE

10

272 Time Out Cape Town

0 ──── 300 m

0 ──── 300 yds

© Copyright Time Out Guides 2009

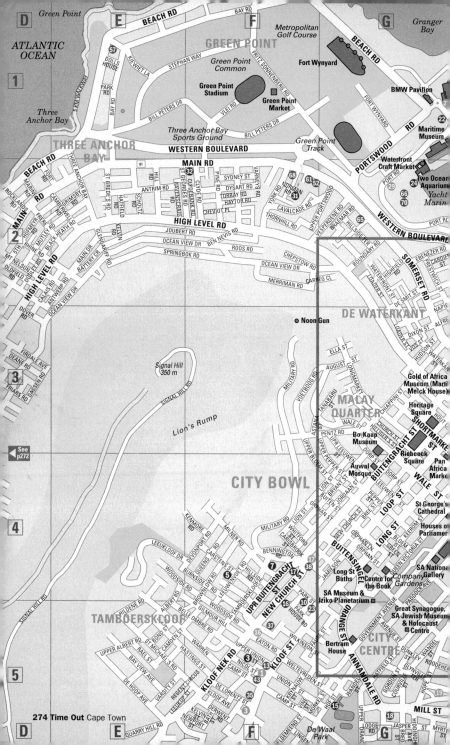

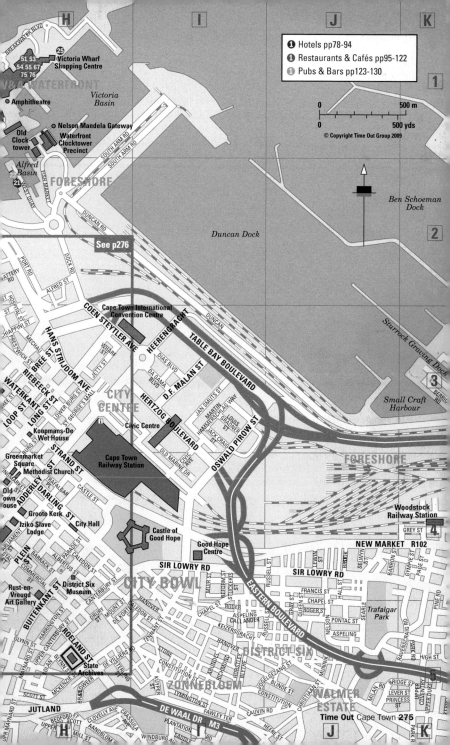

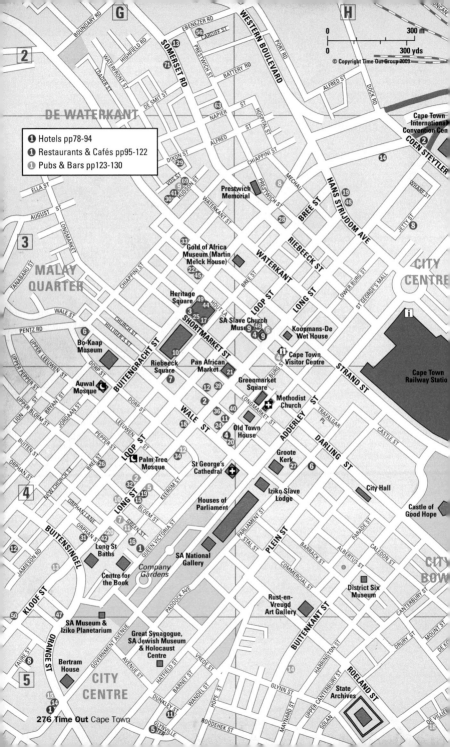

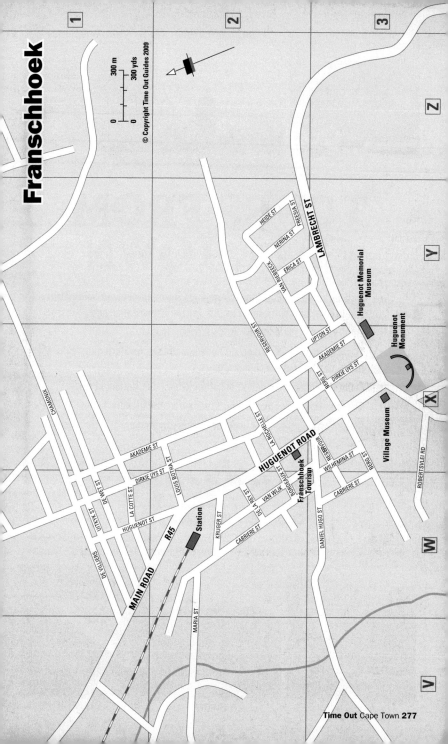

Franschhoek

0 300 m
0 300 yds

© Copyright Time Out Guides 2009

1

2

3

Z

Y

X

W

V

HEIDE ST

NERINA ST

FREESIA ST

ERICA ST

VAN RIEBECK ST

LAMBRECHT ST

Huguenot Memorial Museum

RESSOURCE ST

UPTON ST

AKADEMIE ST

BERG ST

DIRKIE UYS ST

Huguenot Monument

Village Museum

CHAMONIX

AKADEMIE ST

LA ROCHELLE ST

HUGUENOT ROAD

RESSOURCE ST

WILHEMINA ST

BERG ST

ROBERTSVLEI RD

UITKYK ST

DE WET ST

DIRKIE UYS ST

LOUIS BOTHA ST

BORDEAUX ST

Franschhoek Tourism

CABRIERE ST

DE VILLIERS

LA COTTE ST

HUGUENOT ST

DE LA REY ST

VAN WIJK ST

DANIEL HUGO ST

R45

Station

KRUGER ST

CABRIERE ST

MAIN ROAD

MARIA ST

Street Index